SENSATION AND PERCEPTION
FOURTH EDITION

E. BRUCE GOLDSTEIN
University of Pittsburgh

Brooks/Cole Publishing Company

I(T)P™ An International Thomson Publishing Company

Pacific Grove • Albany • Bonn • Boston • Cincinnati • Detroit • London • Madrid • Melbourne
Mexico City • New York • Paris • San Francisco • Singapore • Tokyo • Toronto • Washington

Psychology Editor: *Marianne Taflinger*
Developmental Editor: *Rebecca Johnson*
Marketing Team: *Carolyn Crocket and Jean Thompson*
Marketing Representative: *Ann Salas*
Editorial Assistant: *Laura Donahue*
Production Editor: *Kirk Bomont*
Manuscript Editor: *Margaret Ritchie*
Permissions Editor: *Linda Rill*

Cover and Interior Design: *Cloyce Wall*
Interior Illustration: *Lotus Art, Wayne Clark, MacArt Design, Cyndie C. H. Wooley, John Foster, and Elizabeth Clark*
Cover Image: *Lia Cook, "Landforms West," detail*
Art Editor: *Lisa Torri*
Photo Researcher: *Kathleen Olson*
Typesetting: *Weimer Graphics*
Printing and Binding: *Quebecor/Fairfield*

About the cover: *See page 671.*

For more information, contact:

BROOKS/COLE PUBLISHING COMPANY
511 Forest Lodge Road
Pacific Grove, CA 93950
USA

International Thomson Publishing Europe
Berkshire House 168-173
High Holborn
London WC1V 7AA
England

Thomas Nelson Australia
102 Dodds Street
South Melbourne, 3205
Victoria, Australia

Nelson Canada
1120 Birchmount Road
Scarborough, Ontario
Canada M1K 5G4

International Thomson Editores
Campos Eliseos 385, Piso 7
Col. Polanco
11560 México D. F. México

International Thomson Publishing GmbH
Königswinterer Strasse 418
53227 Bonn
Germany

International Thomson Publishing Asia
221 Henderson Road
#05-10 Henderson Building
Singapore 0315

International Thomson Publishing Japan
Hirakawacho Kyowa Building, 3F
2-2-1 Hirakawacho
Chiyoda-ku, Tokyo 102
Japan

Printed in the United States of America

10   9   8   7   6   5   4   3

Library of Congress Cataloging-in-Publication Data
Goldstein, E. Bruce, [date]
    Sensation and perception/E. Bruce Goldstein.—4th ed.
      p.   cm.
    Includes bibliographical references and index.
    ISBN 0-534-26622-3 (alk. paper)
    1. Senses and sensation.   2. Perception.
QP431.G64   1996
152.1—dc20

95-34884
CIP

ABOUT THE AUTHOR

E. Bruce Goldstein is Associate Professor of Psychology at the University of Pittsburgh. He received his bachelor's degree in chemical engineering from Tufts University, his Ph.D. in experimental psychology from Brown University, and was a post-doctoral fellow in the biology department at Harvard University. Bruce is the author of *Psychology* (also published by Brooks/Cole) and has published numerous papers on visual physiology and visual perception. He teaches sensation and perception, introductory psychology as a natural science, the psychology of gender, and the psychology of art.

BRIEF CONTENTS

Contents

1

Introduction to Perception

2

Introduction to Vision: Receptors and Neural Processing

❸

INTRODUCTION TO VISION: CENTRAL PROCESSING

❹

PERCEIVING COLOR

5

PERCEIVING OBJECTS

6

PERCEIVING DEPTH AND SIZE

❼

PERCEIVING MOVEMENT

❽

AUDITION I: AUDITORY
PHYSIOLOGY

(9)

AUDITION II: HEARING

(10)

SPEECH PERCEPTION

⑫

THE CHEMICAL SENSES

⑬

CLINICAL ASPECTS OF VISION AND HEARING

Demonstrations

PREFACE

My first research projects as a graduate student at Brown University asked the following questions about early events in the process of visual perception: How do visual pigments in the receptors react to light, and what is the nature of the electrical signals generated by these pigments? In my youthful enthusiasm I thought I would be able to understand perception by answering questions such as these about events in the receptors. I was not totally wrong, because the receptors do play a crucial role in the perceptual process. However, as I took my first graduate vision seminar with Lorrin Riggs, I soon realized that the perceptual process extends far beyond the receptors, stretching into the visual cortex and—as research was just beginning to suggest in the late 1960s—even into cortical areas beyond the visual cortex. I also became aware that perception cannot be understood by studying physiology alone. I learned that psychophysics—the study of the relationships between stimuli and perception—is central to our understanding of perception.

My appreciation for both the psychophysical and physiological underpinnings of perception has been reflected in each of the editions of *Sensation and Perception*, beginning with the first edition, which I began writing in 1977 and which was published in 1980. As I wrote the first edition and the revisions that followed, I have been motivated by a desire to tell both the psychophysical and physiological parts of the story of perception in a way that students will find interesting and easy to follow and which transmits the excitement I feel about this fascinating topic. As I have

pursued this goal in each edition I have made changes to update the story to reflect new developments in the field and to improve its telling to make it clearer and more accessible. In this, the fourth edition, I have made numerous changes in both content and presentation, while keeping the characteristics that so many people have appreciated in the previous editions. The following summarizes some of the features and changes in this edition of *Sensation and Perception*.

Telling the Story of Perception More Clearly

The story of perception is a fascinating one that includes one of the most profound questions posed by nature: "How are electrical signals processed and interpreted by the nervous system to create perceptions?" The story of the search for the answer to this question is a theme that runs through this book. This story begins with a completely rewritten Chapter 1, which introduces the basic principles behind the physiological, psychophysical, and cognitive approaches to perception. Those familiar with the third edition will notice that the psychophysical methods, which previously were described in an appendix at the end of the book, have been moved to a more prominent place in this opening chapter.

Chapters 2 and 3 have also been reorganized to create a more logical unfolding of the story as we follow the visual process from the receptors (Chapter 2) to the lateral geniculate nucleus and cortex (Chapter 3). The first three chapters are designed to provide the basic tools that the student needs to understand the rest of the book. As the story of perception continues past these introductory chapters we consider the specific visual qualities of color, form, depth, and motion. The third edition's chapter on brightness and contrast has been eliminated to make space for new developments in perception. However, much of the material from this chapter has been moved to Chapters 2 and 4. The chapters on hearing have also been reorganized, moving the physiological story to the front, followed by psychophysics and then speech perception. The result is a clearer, more logical treatment of the sense of hearing.

This edition's organization has also been streamlined by eliminating the Boxes that appeared in the third edition. Although many readers appreciated the interesting material contained in the boxes, others felt that they broke up the flow of the text. My solution was to eliminate the boxes, but to integrate most of the previously boxed material into the text.

New Research and Expanded Coverage

One of the most rewarding aspects of preparing this revision was the opportunity it afforded to explore the new research in perception that has appeared in the seven years since I completed the third edition. There are far too many new additions to list them all here, but some examples are research on the binding problem in vision, parallel processing in the visual system, the newly proposed timing code for auditory localization, the phenomenon of duplex perception in speech perception, psychophysical channels for tactile perception, and new information on the role of genetics in determining taste experience. In addition, I have updated or expanded many topics, including neural coding, biologically based motion, the computational and spatial frequency approaches to visual perception, Fourier analysis

in hearing, auditory masking, and the perception of flavor.

Principles That Cut Across Senses

An important theme of this text is that although each of the senses has its own unique qualities, there are basic principles that cut across all of the senses. This idea of basic principles is mentioned a number of times in the text but is especially highlighted in a few places. The chapter on color vision (Chapter 4), ends with a table showing how principles introduced in Chapters 2 and 3, such as convergence, excitation and inhibition, columnar organization, and parallel pathways, apply to the processing of information for color perception. The chapter on auditory physiology (Chapter 8) ends with a section called "Comparing the Senses," which points out parallels between audition and vision. Finally, the chapters on the somatic senses (Chapter 11) and chemical senses (Chapter 12) draw numerous parallels with the other senses.

Demonstrations

The *Demonstrations*, a popular feature of previous editions, have been continued in this one. The purpose of these demonstrations is to provide perceptual experiences to illustrate some of the principles discussed in the text. The philosophy behind the demonstrations is to make them simple so that students will do them, and to integrate them into the flow of the text so that they become part of the ongoing story. This edition contains 52 demonstrations, a dozen of which are new.

The Medical Side of Perception

Although material on the treatment of medical problems connected with the senses has not traditionally been included in books such as this one, I decided to add material on clinical aspects of vision to the second edition because of my own curiosity about what was going on when I had my eyes examined. I have found that students think this material is as interesting as I do, and for this edition I have therefore expanded this chapter (Chapter 13) to include clinical aspects of hearing. It is particularly fitting that the book ends with a description of the cochlear implant operation, which was made possible by research on basic principles of auditory physiology described in Chapter 8.

The Illustration Program and Color Essays

The extensive illustration program for which this text is known has been continued in this edition. There are over 600 diagrams, anatomical drawings, graphs, and photographs, about a dozen more than the number in the third edition; however, over 200 of these illustrations are new to this edition! Old illustrations were pruned and new ones added to reflect advances in research since the last edition. In addition, I have taken a new approach to color illustrations. Rather than presenting a group of color plates that are referred to at various places in the text but seem unrelated to each other, I have written three short "color essays," which stand on their own but which also illustrate phenomena that are described elsewhere in the text.

Developmental Dimensions

Perhaps the most obvious change in this edition are two new end-of-chapter features, *Developmental Dimensions* and *Other Worlds of Perception*. The Developmental Dimension feature expands the treatment of perceptual development to include all of the senses by presenting material on perceptual development in a special section at the end of each chapter. Each of the Developmental Dimensions can be considered separately along with the chapter to which it relates, or a number of them can be combined to create customized units on perceptual development (see Appendixes A and B).

Other Worlds of Perception

Other Worlds of Perception answers students' questions about what nonhuman animals perceive. However, the purpose of this feature goes beyond simply answering students' questions about what their dog or cat sees and hears. Its broader purpose is to introduce the idea that other species experience different perceptual realities than humans (such as the bat's perception of sonar pulses and the honeybee's perception of ultraviolet light) and that these different perceptual realities are interesting not only because they make us think about the nature of other animal's experiences, but also because they emphasize the fact that the nature of perceptual reality is determined by the functioning of an organism's sensory systems. Thus, Other Worlds of Perception reinforces one of the central themes of this book: Perceptual abilities can be traced to the way sensory systems are constructed. They also make the additional point that an animal's sensory systems are often adapted to fit the animal's needs and environment.

Other Learning Aids

Another new feature is the end-of-chapter *Review*, with a general outline of the chapter in the left column and questions related to this outline in the right column. The data behind this new approach, which combines what used to be separate sections titled "summary" and "study questions," is to provide a more meaningful and effective way to review the chapters. The outline provides a context for the study questions, which the students can answer by returning to the keyed pages in the text. Another change is the placing of all of the definitions of bold-faced terms in a single glossary at the end of the book.

Help for the Instructor

Two teaching aids, available to instructors, are a set of transparencies of some of the text's illustrations and a test bank, which I have written. The test bank, which is available both as a book and, for the first time, in computerized form, includes over 600 questions, many of which I have "class tested" in my own classes.

Exploring Perception CD-ROM

Exploring Perception, a CD-ROM for Macintosh and IBM Windows is an exciting new ancillary available from Brooks/Cole. This interactive CD-ROM, which has been developed by Colin Ryan of James Cook University, North Queensland, Australia, gives students an opportunity to actively explore many of the concepts described in the text, including psychophysics, physiological principles, and perceiving color, form, motion, and depth. For further information about *Exploring Perception*, instructors can contact their local Brooks/Cole representative or inquire via email to *info@brookscole.com*.

A Message to the Student

Although most of this preface has been directed to instructors, I want to close by addressing a few words to the students who will be using this book. As you read this book you will see that it is a story about experiences that may initially seem simple, such as seeing a face or smelling a rose, but that turn out to be extremely complex. I hope that reading this book helps you appreciate both the complexity and the beauty of the mechanisms responsible for these experiences. I hope that as you gain an appreciation for the impressive advances that researchers have made toward understanding perception, you will also appreciate how much is still left to be discovered. But most important of all, I hope that reading this book will make you more aware of how perception affects you personally. After all, perception is something you experience all the time, and the study of perception can enhance this experience. I've found that studying perception has made me more observant of my environment, more aware of my perceptions, and more appreciative of the miraculous process that transforms energy falling on receptors into the richness of experience. I hope reading this book has the same effect on you. If you have questions, comments or other feedback about this book, I invite you to communicate with me via email at bruceg+@pitt.edu.

E. Bruce Goldstein

ACKNOWLEDGMENTS

Although I have been writing textbooks for almost two decades, I am still impressed by the extent to which creating a textbook is a group effort. Among those who have played indispensable roles in the creation of this book are Marianne Taflinger, my editor, who I thank for pushing me to finish it much sooner than I had planned and who provided valuable support in the form of reviews and the many behind-the-scenes things that editors do unbeknownst to authors. I also thank her assistant Laura Donahue, who took care of obtaining reviews and handling my various queries in such an efficient and cheerful way.

My special thanks go to Kirk Bomont, my production editor, who once again has made the process of producing a book almost fun. I especially appreciate his amazing attention to detail and his commitment to high standards of both production values and pedagogy. I am also indebted to Ellen Brownstein who was kind enough to assign Kirk to my book.

I also wish to thank Lisa Torri who has again demonstrated grace under difficult conditions as director of the art program, Vernon Boes, for his support as head of the design department at Brooks/Cole, Cloyce Wall, who contributed elegant designs for the text and cover, and Lia Cook, who allowed me to use a photograph of one of her wonderful weavings for the cover illustration. In addition I thank two people who supported me during some difficult times during the writing of this book, Vicki Knight at Brooks/Cole, and especially my wife, Barbara, who has persevered with love and understanding through numerous book projects.

I thank the following people who kindly provided new photographs for this edition: Linda Bartoshuk, Stephen Dear, David Hubel, Inglis Miller, Edward Morrison, Patricia Kuhl, David Knill, Maggie Shiffrar, Harvey Sussman, and Ian Witten. Finally, I thank the following reviewers and colleagues who provided such valuable feedback about the third edition and the manuscript for this edition.

Israel Abramov
    City University of New York, Brooklyn College

Richard A. Abrams
    Washington University in St. Louis

Frank M. Bagrash
    California State University, Fullerton

Suzanne Baker
    James Madison University

Lou Banderet
    Northeastern University, University College

Linda M. Bartoshuk
    Yale University School of Medicine

Bennett Bertenthal
    University of Virginia

Bruce Bridgeman
    University of California, Santa Cruz

Charles Collyer
    University of Rhode Island

Cynthia Connine
SUNY-Binghamton

Peter Eimas
Brown University

Rhea Eskew
Northeastern University

Marion Frank
University of Connecticut Health Center

George Gescheider
Hamilton College

Kerry Green
University of Arizona

Donald Greenfield
Eye Institute of New Jersey

W. Lawrence Gulick
University of Delaware

Kathleen Kowal
University of North Carolina at Wilmington

Thomas Mauger
Ohio State University

Alan Musicant
Middle Tennessee State University

Lynne Nygaard
Indiana University

Catherine Palmer
University of Pittsburgh

Theodore Parks
University of California, Davis

Bob Patterson
Washington State University

Mary A. Peterson
University of Arizona

Sheila R. Pratt
University of Pittsburgh

Wayne Quirk
Wayne State University

David Robbins
Ohio Wesleyan University

Helena Saldaña
Indiana University

Pamela Sample
University of California, San Diego

Alan Searleman
St. Lawrence University

George A. Sharp
Kutztown University

Mike Sloan
University of Alabama at Birmingham

Steven Specht
Lebanon Valley College

Charles E. Sternheim
University of Maryland

Harvey Sussman
University of Texas

William Tedford Jr.
Southern Methodist University

Christopher Tyler
Smith-Kettlewell Institute, San Francisco

Ronald Verrillo
Syracuse University

Jeremy Wolfe
Brigham & Woman's Hospital, Boston

Steven Yantis
Johns Hopkins University

INTRODUCTION TO PERCEPTION

Perception Does Not Just "Happen"

The Physiological Approach to Perception

The Psychophysical Approach to Perception

The Cognitive Approach to Perception

The Approach in This Book

"You have been in Afghanistan, I perceive."
—SHERLOCK HOLMES—

Sherlock Holmes, the fictional detective created by Sir Arthur Conan Doyle, was famous for his ability to deduce startling conclusions from seemingly meager clues. One such example, in *A Study in Scarlet*, occurs when Holmes is introduced to his future sidekick, Dr. Watson, in London. Without prompting, Holmes immediately observes that Watson has just come from Afghanistan. Amazed that Holmes knows this fact about him, Watson naturally assumes that someone must have told Holmes that he had been an army doctor serving in Afghanistan. "Nothing of the sort," Holmes protests. He goes on to explain:

> "I *knew* you came from Afghanistan. From long habit the train of thoughts ran so swiftly through my mind that I arrived at the conclusion without being conscious of intermediate steps. There were such steps, however. The train of reasoning ran, 'Here is a gentleman of the medical type, but with the air of a military man. Certainly an army doctor, then. He has just come from the tropics, for his face is dark, and that is not the natural tint of his skin, for his wrists are fair. He has undergone hardship and sickness, as his haggard face says clearly. His left arm has been injured. He holds it in a stiff and unnatural manner. Were in the tropics could an English army doctor have seen much hardship and got his arm wounded? Clearly in Afghanistan.'

> "The whole train of thought did not occupy a second. I then remarked that you came from Afghanistan, and you were astonished."

Doyle's readers are amused and entertained when Holmes claims that he performed such an elaborate chain of reasoning so instantaneously that he wasn't even "conscious of the intermediate steps." Only in fiction, we think, do detectives put theories together from fragmentary clues. Yet this is just what we do every time we open our eyes or listen with our ears: Every waking moment, you and I are engaged in perceptual exploits that involve performing complex, instantaneous feats of organizing and integrating information and making inferences from it. As you will see in this book, the processes involved in perceiving our environment are as remarkable as the exploits of the greatest fictional detectives.

Figure 1.1
Our perception of this scene depends on energy that reaches us from each of its components. Our visual perceptions are reactions to light energy (electromagnetic radiation); our auditory perceptions are reactions to sound energy (pressure changes in the air); and our perceptions of smell are reactions to the chemical energy in airborne molecules.

"But," you might say, "perception seems automatic to me. I don't really feel like I'm doing detective work. It feels as if my perceptions just happen." This common feeling is reflected in the kinds of questions my students ask when, on the first day of class, I tell them to write down questions about perception. They typically ask questions about situations that are out of the ordinary, such as the following: "Is it true that blind people have a sixth sense that enables them to detect obstacles before they hit them?" "Why does the eye still see the image of a spot of light after being exposed to a flashbulb?" "What does a person who is color-blind see?" Rarely, however, do they ask questions that refer to everyday experience, such as, "How do I perceive my friend's face?" or "Why doesn't the shape of my desk appear to change as I walk past it?" It doesn't occur to people to ask these questions because the situations they refer to occur so routinely and effortlessly that they appear to happen automatically.

Like most of my students, you probably take seeing your friend's face or the accurate shape of your desk for granted. However, seeing your friend's face involves a complex process in which numerous components—eyes, nose, mouth, and hair—are combined into a single organized per-

cept; and perceiving the shape of your desk involves its own complexities, since the image your desk creates inside your eye changes drastically as you look at it from different vantage points. Surely something must be happening to keep your perception of the desk from changing each time you observe it from a new angle. The purpose of this book is to describe the processes behind such common perceptions as seeing a friend or observing your desk from different angles, and to make you aware that much of what we take for granted in perception is really very complex and, in some cases, not well understood. You will see that perception does not just "happen."

PERCEPTION DOES NOT JUST "HAPPEN"

We can understand why we say perception does not just "happen" by looking at the process of perception. Let's begin by imagining that you are driving along a quiet country road. You are admiring the snow-covered landscape when a train

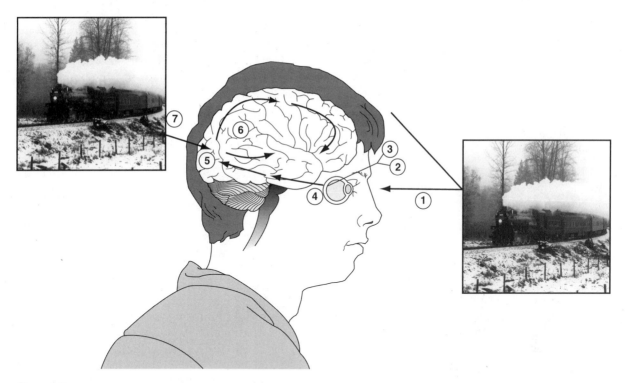

Figure 1.2

A very schematic picture of some of the steps in the perceptual process. Light bounces off of the train (1) and into the person's eye, where it forms an image on the retina (2) and generates electrical impulses in the receptors (3). Nerve impulses travel along nerve fibers (4), reach the brain (5) where they are "processed" (6), and the perceiver sees the train (7).

whistle breaks the silence. You pull over to the side of the road and get out of your car just in time to see a restored steam locomotive that you've heard about approaching with surprising speed (Figure 1.1). Even though you are some distance from the track, the sensory impact of the train hits you with surprising force—the wheels' clickity-clack, the windows passing by in a blur, and the deafening sound of the train whistle at close range. And in addition to these intense auditory and visual experiences you can actually feel the ground vibrating. Then, suddenly, the last car passes by and begins to vanish into the distance. The clickity-clack of the wheels becomes fainter and fainter, until all that remains is your memory of the train, a few wisps of smoke, and a slight sulfurous smell in the air.

What process allowed you to experience the powerful sensory effects of the train? The answer to this question is "energy." You heard the train's whistle and clacking of its wheels because *sound energy* traveled from the train into your ears. You saw the train's form, color, and movement because the train reflected patterns of *light energy* into your eyes. You felt vibrations because *mechanical energy* was transmitted through the ground to your feet. And you smelled the train's smoke because *chemical energy* was released when chemical components of the smoke reached your nose.

We can begin to appreciate how these various forms of energy result in perceptions by breaking the process of perception into the following steps (also see Figure 1.2), using seeing the train as an example:

Introduction to Perception

1. Light energy hits the train and is reflected into your eyes. This light transmits properties of the train into your eyes because the light is *structured* by the train's shape and by the properties of its surfaces.

2. An image of the train is formed on your retina, a network of cells that lines the back of your eye.

3. Electrical signals are generated by cells in the retina called *receptors*, which change the light energy into electrical energy.

4. These electrical signals are transmitted through the retina in a network of cells called *neurons*, which transmit electrical nerve impulses in the nervous system.

5. These electrical signals are transmitted out of the eye along neurons and eventually reach the visual receiving area of the brain.

6. These electrical signals are "processed" or "analyzed" by neurons in the visual receiving area, and in other areas of the brain.

7. You perceive the train.

These steps are a good starting point, but they don't do justice to the complexity of the perceptual process. First of all, perceiving a complex object such as a train involves the simultaneous activity of tens or hundreds of thousands of neurons. The perceptual process is also made more complex by the fact that the train is moving. In fact, movement is associated with most objects in the environment, since either objects are moving relative to the observer, the observer is moving relative to objects, or the observer is looking at various parts of the object by moving his or her eyes.

The almost continual presence of movement means that it is more accurate to think of perception as an active, continuous process rather than as the series of discrete, individual steps implied by our list above. Thus, at the very moment that

electrical signals are reaching the brain to create one moment's perception of the train, new signals are being generated at the receptors and are beginning their journey toward the brain to create the next moment's perception. The end result is a smooth, continuous perception of the train as it moves across your field of view.

But perception is determined by more than a sequence of physiological steps. It is also determined by cognitive processes such as thinking and memory. For example, your prior knowledge of trains may influence your perception of the particular train you see, and your prior experience with seeing objects in the distance helps you judge the correct size and distance of the train. As we will see in this book, the process of perception involves an interaction between the information stimulating the receptors and information from our past experiences that is already within us.

How do researchers actually go about studying perception? In the remainder of this chapter, we will describe three different approaches to studying the perceptual process. One way to introduce these different approaches is to return to the idea, proposed at the beginning of the chapter, that our perceptual system acts like a detective as it sifts and combines many types of information to create our experience of perceiving. This way of describing perception—as a detective story—can be applied to many areas of psychology, but it is especially well suited to perception because of the perceptual system's task: The perceptual system must determine what is "out there" in the environment from clues contained in three types of information: (1) properties of the physical environment; (2) electrical activity in the nervous system; and (3) the prior experiences and knowledge of the perceiver.

Most detective stories begin with questions to be answered, and this one is no exception. In describing how researchers have studied the way these three types of clues contribute to the process of perception, we will consider the following three questions:

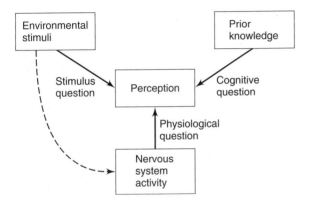

Figure 1.3

Solid lines indicate the relationships associated with each of the three questions about perception posed in the text. To fully understand perception, we need to study each of these relationships. The dashed line indicates another relationship, which is important for practical reasons because it is often difficult to directly study the relationship between nervous system activity and perception in either humans or animals. We can, however, often infer the relationship between nervous system activity and perception by determining both the relationships between stimuli and nervous system activity (dashed line), and stimuli and perception.

- *The physiological question:* How are properties of objects in the environment represented by activity in the nervous system?

- *The stimulus question:* How do we use information from the environment to create perceptions?

- *The cognitive question:* How do experiences and prior knowledge influence perceptions?

We will consider each of these questions by looking at the relationships diagrammed in Figure 1.3. As we describe how researchers have gone about determining each of these relationships, we will see that each one provides an important piece of the puzzle of perception, and that not until we have combined each of these

pieces can we say that we have completely described how perception operates. We will first look at the history of how each relationship has been studied and will then describe basic principles and methods associated with each approach to studying perception. We begin by considering the **physiological approach to perception** because, historically, perception was first studied scientifically by physiologists.

THE PHYSIOLOGICAL APPROACH TO PERCEPTION

What are the physiological mechanisms of perception? Modern research designed to answer this question has focused on the relationship between electrical signals called *nerve impulses* and specific perceptions. Before describing the nature of these nerve impulses, let's look at some of the early history that led to this approach.

The Physiological Approach: Historical Background

Our modern ideas about the physiological basis of perception are descended from a long line of speculation and research regarding the physiological workings of the mind. Early research and speculations in this area focused not on determining how we sense energy in the environment, but on determining the anatomical structures involved in the operation of the mind. In the fourth century B.C. the philosopher Aristotle (384–322 B.C.) stated that the heart, not the brain, was the seat of the mind and the soul. Most of those following Aristotle did not repeat his error and correctly identified the brain as the seat of the mind. But how does the brain work? Speculations about this question have reflected the technology of the day (Bloom, Lazerson, & Hofstadter, 1985; Nelson & Bower, 1990). Thus, Galen (ca. 130–200 A.D.) likened the

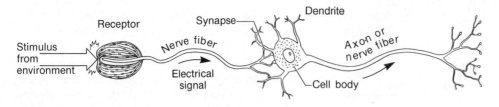

Figure 1.4

The neuron shown on the right consists of a cell body, dendrites, and an axon, or nerve fiber. A neuron that receives stimuli from the environment, shown on the left, has a receptor in place of the cell body.

functioning of the brain to the aqueducts and sewer systems of his time. Galen saw human health, thoughts, and emotions as being determined by four different fluids flowing from the cavities in the center of the brain. This idea of flowing fluids remained in force for 1,500 years.

Later ideas were also influenced by technology. Thus, the philosopher René Descartes (1596–1650), influenced by the mechanical devices of his day, pictured the human body as operating like a machine, and his contemporary, the "father of astronomy" Johannes Kepler (1571–1630), thought the eye operated like an ordinary optical instrument that projected images onto the sensory nerves of the retina. Kepler's idea contained an element of truth but did not explain how these sensory nerves work. Understanding how sensory nerves work had to await a better understanding of the nature of both electricity and the electrical signals that are conducted by these nerves.

During the 18th and 19th centuries many experiments were done that increased scientists' general knowledge about electricity and about how electricity occurs in the nervous system. By the end of the 19th century, researchers had shown that a wave of electricity was transmitted down the nerve. To explain how these electrical signals result in different perceptions, Johannes Müller (1842) proposed the **doctrine of specific nerve energies,** which states that our perceptions depend on "nerve energies" reaching the brain and that the specific quality we experience depends on which nerves are stimulated. Thus

stimulating the eye results in seeing, stimulating the ear results in hearing, and so on. By the end of the 1800s this idea had been expanded to include the idea that nerves from each of these senses reach different areas of the brain.

But exactly what do the nerves that carry signals from the sense organs to the brain look like? Most early research used nerves like the optic nerve, which conducts electrical signals from the eye toward the brain. **Nerves** are made up of tens or hundreds of thousands of smaller units called **neurons**, which, as it turns out, are the structures that tell us the most about the physiological basis of perception.

By the end of the 19th century it was known that neurons consist of (1) a **cell body**, which contains a nucleus and other metabolic mechanisms needed to keep the cell alive; (2) **dendrites**, which branch out from the cell body to receive electrical signals from other neurons; and (3) an **axon**, or **nerve fiber**, a fluid-filled tube that conducts electrical signals (Figure 1.4). There are variations on this basic neuron structure: Some neurons have long axons; others have short axons or none at all. In addition, some neurons are designed to receive signals from the environment through specialized structures called **receptors**, which are designed to receive environmental stimuli such as light or sound waves and to transform these stimuli into electrical signals.

By the beginning of the 20th century the following basic components of the physiological basis of perception had been established: Receptors transform environmental energy into electrical signals, which are transmitted along neurons to different areas of the brain for different senses. But an understanding of the nature of the electrical signals that are transmitted along these neurons had to await the development of electronic amplifiers powerful enough to make visible the extremely small electrical signals generated by the neuron. When this equipment became available in the 1920s, researchers began recording these electrical signals, called *nerve impulses*, and began to understand the chemical basis of nerve signals. Since nerve impulses form the centerpiece of our understanding of the physiology of perception, we will look at some basic facts about these signals.

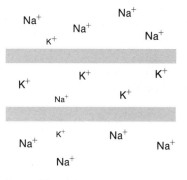

Figure 1.5

Cross section of a nerve fiber, showing the high concentration of sodium outside the fiber and potassium inside the fiber. Other ions, such as negatively charged chlorine, are not shown.

Recording Electrical Signals in Neurons

What kinds of electrical signals are transmitted by neurons? When most people think of electrical signals, they imagine signals conducted along electrical power lines or along the wires used for household appliances. Unlike the electrical wire of your television set, however, neurons are bathed in liquid. What kind of electrical signals can exist in this liquid environment?

The key to understanding the "wet" electrical signals transmitted by neurons is the makeup of the neuron's liquid environment. Neurons are immersed in a solution rich in **ions**, molecules that carry an electrical charge. Ions are created when molecules gain or lose electrons, as happens when compounds are dissolved in water. For example, adding table salt (sodium chloride = NaCl) to water creates positively charged sodium ions (Na^+) and negatively charged chlorine ions (Cl^-). The solution *outside* the axon of a neuron is rich in positively charged sodium (Na^+) ions, while the solution *inside* the axon is rich in positively charged potassium (K^+) ions (Figure 1.5).

How do these ions create electrical signals in the neuron? We can answer this question by means of a demonstration set up as shown in Figure 1.6. For this demonstration, we will push

on a pressure-sensitive receptor and record the resulting electrical signals with two **microelectrodes**, which are small shafts of glass or metal with tips small enough to record the electrical signals from a single neuron. In addition, we will also observe what happens to the sodium and potassium ions that are near one of the electrodes.

To begin our demonstration, we position one electrode, the **recording electrode**, inside the axon, and another electrode, the *null electrode*, outside the axon, as shown in Figure 1.6a. By placing a measuring device between the recording and the null electrodes, we can measure the difference in electrical charge between the inside and outside of the axon. When we do this, we find that the difference in charge is −70 millivolts (mV). That is, the inside of the neuron is 70 mV *negative* compared to the outside of the neuron. This negative charge inside the neuron is called the neuron's **resting potential**, because it is the neuron's charge when it is at rest.

Now that we have measured the resting potential, we are ready to begin our demonstration by recording what happens when a **nerve impulse** occurs in the fiber. The nerve impulse is caused by the flow of sodium into the fiber and of potassium out of the fiber. This flow is triggered by changes in the fiber's **permeability** to sodium

7

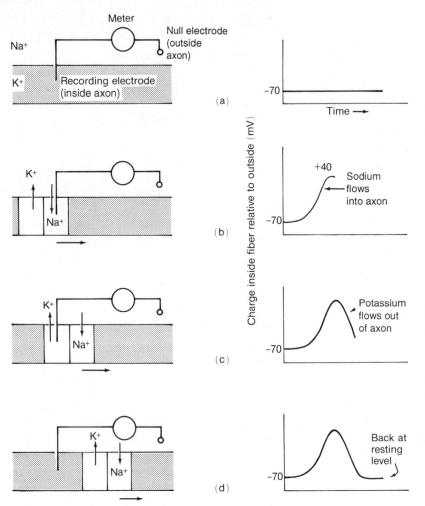

Figure 1.6

Effect of a nerve impulse as it travels down a nerve fiber. As long as the fiber is at rest, there is a difference in charge of −70 mV between the inside and the outside of the fiber, as shown in (a). Events that occur once a nerve impulse is generated are shown in (b), (c), and (d). The flow of sodium into the fiber and potassium out of the fiber is shown on the left, and the resulting change in the charge measured by the electrodes is shown on the right.

and potassium. Permeability, a property of the membrane that forms the wall of the nerve fiber, refers to the ease with which a molecule can pass through the membrane. Before the nerve impulse occurs, the membrane's permeability to sodium and potassium is low, so there is little flow of these molecules across the membrane, and the difference in the charge between the inside and outside of the nerve fiber remains at the level of the resting potential: −70 mV (Figure 1.6a).

The nerve impulse begins when the membrane suddenly becomes permeable to sodium, causing this positively charged ion to rush into the fiber. Since sodium has a positive charge, the recording electrode records an *increase* in positive charge inside the nerve fiber, as shown in Figure 1.6b. After sodium flows into the fiber for about 1/2,000 second, the membrane's permeability to sodium decreases, its permeability to potassium increases, and potassium flows out of the nerve fiber. Since potassium has a positive charge, the electrode records a decrease in positive charge inside the fiber until the charge returns to its original level, as shown in Figure 1.6c and d.

This process—sodium flowing in for 1/2,000 second, followed by potassium flowing out for

1/2,000 second—creates a positive charge inside the fiber that, from our vantage point at one place on the fiber, lasts only 1/1,000 second. However, this rapid change in the fiber's charge does not just occur at one place on the fiber but travels down the fiber to create our "wet" electrical signal, the nerve impulse. Nerve impulses, therefore, are traveling positive charges created by the flow of charged molecules called *ions* across the walls of the fiber.

After hearing this description of how Na^+ flows into the axon and K^+ flows out, students often ask whether there is a buildup of sodium inside the axon and of potassium outside the axon. No buildup occurs because a mechanism called the *sodium–potassium pump* in the axon continuously returns sodium to the outside of the axon and potassium to the inside, thereby maintaining sodium and potassium concentrations at their original levels so the fiber can continue to generate nerve impulses. Let's now consider some basic properties of nerve impulses.

Basic Properties of Nerve Impulses

One property of the nerve impulse is that it is a **propagated response**: Once it is triggered, it travels all the way down the axon. Another property of the nerve impulse is that it is an **all-or-none response**: Once it is triggered, it stays the same size, no matter how far it has traveled down the axon and no matter how intense the stimulus is. We can show that it stays the same size no matter what the stimulus intensity by returning to our demonstration and increasing the intensity of the stimulus generating the nerve impulse. The result of this demonstration is shown in the records of Figure 1.7. The most obvious thing about these records is that each nerve impulse appears as a sharp spike. This occurs because we have compressed the time scale, as compared to that of Figure 1.6, so that we can display a number of nerve impulses.

The three records in Figure 1.7 represent the fiber's response to three intensities of stimulation. Figure 1.7a shows how the fiber responds to

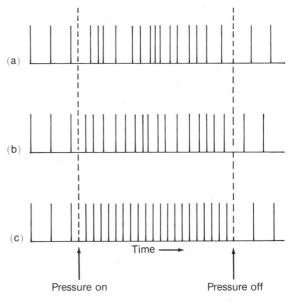

Figure 1.7

Response of a nerve fiber to (a) soft, (b) medium, and (c) strong stimulation. Increasing the stimulus strength increases both the rate and the regularity of nerve firing in this fiber.

gentle stimulation applied to the skin, while Figures 1.7b and 1.7c show how the response changes as the stimulation is increased. Comparing these three records leads to an important conclusion: Changing the stimulus intensity does not affect the *size* of the nerve impulses but does affect the *rate* of nerve firing.

It is important to realize, however, that, although increasing the stimulus intensity can increase the rate of nerve firing, there is an upper limit to the number of nerve impulses per second that can be conducted down a nerve fiber. This limit occurs because a neuron takes about 1 millisecond (1 msec = 1/1,000 sec) to recover from conducting a nerve impulse before it can conduct another one. This interval is called the **refractory period** of the fiber, and it sets the upper limit of the firing rate at about 500–800 impulses per second.

Another important property of nerve firing is illustrated by the beginning of each of the

Introduction to Perception

records in Figure 1.7. Notice that some nerve impulses occur even before the pressure stimulus is applied. In fact, many nerve fibers fire without any stimuli from the environment; this firing is called **spontaneous activity**. Although you may wonder why a nerve fiber would be designed to fire in the absence of outside stimulation, you will see later that this spontaneous activity plays an important role in determining our perceptions.

What do these properties of the nerve impulse mean in terms of their function for perceiving? The nerve impulse's function is to communicate information. We have seen that pushing harder on a pressure receptor increases the rate of nerve firing. Thus, these increased rates of nerve firing carry information about the intensity of the stimulus. But if this information remains within a single neuron, it has no meaning. In order to be meaningful to a person, this information must be transmitted to other neurons, and eventually to the brain or other organs that can react to this information.

This idea that the nerve impulse in one neuron must be transmitted to other neurons poses the following problem: Once the nerve impulses reach the end of the axon, how is the message that the impulses carry transmitted to other neurons? One idea, put forth by the Italian anatomist Camillo Golgi (1844–1926), was that neurons make direct contact with each other, so that a signal reaching the end of one neuron passes directly to the next neuron. But a Spanish anatomist, Santiago Ramón y Cajal (1852–1934) (Figure 1.8), showed that there is a microscopic space between the neurons, which is known as a **synapse** (Figure 1.9). Ramón y Cajal's discovery earned him the Nobel prize in 1906 (he shared the prize with Golgi, who was recognized for his research on the structure of the neuron).

The discovery of the synapse raised the question of how the electrical signals generated by one neuron are transmitted across the space separating this neuron from another one. As we will see, the answer lies in a remarkable chemical process that takes place at the synapse.

Figure 1.8
Santiago Ramón y Cajal, who received the Nobel prize in 1906 for his research on the nature of the synapse.

Chemical and Electrical Events at the Synapse

For neurons to communicate, the information carried by a nerve impulse in one neuron (the **presynaptic neuron**) must cross the synapse and generate a signal in another neuron (the **postsynaptic neuron**). If this does not occur, the message will stop at the end of the presynaptic neuron, like a messenger who comes to a large body of water and lacks a boat to get across. How does information get across the synapse?

Early in the 1900s, it was discovered that the nerve impulses themselves do not travel across the synapse. Instead, they trigger a *chemical* process that bridges the gap between neurons. What happens is this. When the nerve impulse reaches the end of the presynaptic neuron, it causes the release of a chemical called a **neurotransmitter** that is stored in *synaptic vesicles* in the presynaptic neuron. As the name implies, neurotransmitters transmit neural information. Let's look at how this transmission occurs.

When the nerve impulse reaches the synaptic vesicles at the end of the axon, the vesicles release a neurotransmitter. The neurotransmitter molecules flow across the synapse to receptor sites on the postsynaptic neuron, small areas that are sensitive to specific neurotransmitters. These receptor sites exist in a variety of shapes that match the shapes of particular neurotransmitter molecules. When a neurotransmitter makes contact with a receptor site matching its shape, it activates the

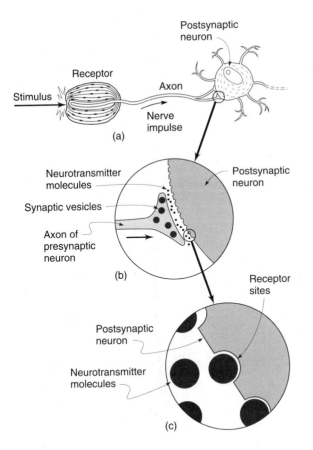

Figure 1.9

Synaptic transmission from one neuron to another. (a) A signal traveling down the axon of a neuron reaches the synapse at the end of the axon. (b) Close-up of the synapse showing the presynaptic neuron on the left and the postsynaptic neuron on the right. The nerve impulse reaching the synapse causes the release of neurotransmitter molecules from the synaptic vesicles of the presynaptic neuron. (c) The neurotransmitters fit into receptor sites and cause a voltage change in the postsynaptic neuron.

receptor site and triggers a voltage change in the postsynaptic neuron. Thus, a neurotransmitter is like a key that fits a specific lock. It has an effect on the postsynaptic neuron only if its shape matches that of the receptor site.

At the synapse, then, an electrical signal generates a chemical process that, in turn, triggers a change in voltage in the postsynaptic neuron. This is not to say, however, that the neurotransmitter's action at the receptor site automatically generates a new nerve impulse in the postsynaptic neuron. Instead, when a neurotransmitter molecule makes contact with a receptor site that matches its shape, it has one of two effects. The electrical response generated in the postsynaptic neuron can be either **excitatory** or **inhibitory**, depending on the type of transmitter and the nature of the cell body's membrane. **Excitation** increases the rate of nerve firing, whereas **inhibition** decreases the rate of nerve firing.

A neuron usually receives many excitatory and inhibitory inputs, and some neurons in the brain receive inputs from as many as a thousand other neurons. Figure 1.10 shows how the generation of nerve impulses depends on the interplay of the excitatory (E) and inhibitory (I) stimulation converging on the cell. When the neuron receives excitatory input, the rate of firing increases above the spontaneous level, as shown in Figure 1.10a, but as the amount of inhibition relative to excitation increases (Figure 1.10b through Figure 1.10e), the firing rate decreases. In Figure 1.10d and Figure 1.10e, the inhibition is so strong that the rate of nerve firing is decreased to below the level of spontaneous activity.

These facts about how neurons operate—especially the characteristics of their nerve impulses and the excitation and inhibition that occur at the synapse—provide the basis for much of the discussion of neurons and perception in the rest of this book. However, to complete our presentation of background information about the physiological approach to perception, we need to consider how these neurons work together in the brain.

The Brain and Perception

One of the major concerns of this book is the human brain, a structure that, with its 100 billion neurons, has been called "the most complex structure in the known universe" (Thompson,

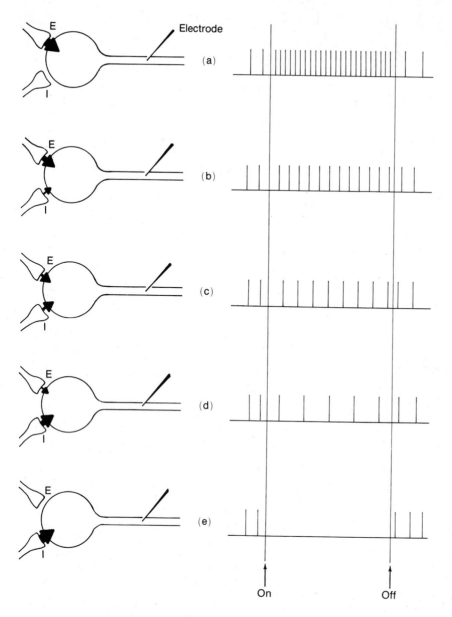

Figure 1.10

Effect of excitatory (E) and inhibitory (I) input on the firing rate of a neuron. The amount of excitatory and inhibitory input to the neuron is indicated by the size of the arrows at the synapse. The responses recorded by the electrode are indicated by the records on the right. The firing that occurs before the onset of the stimulus is spontaneous activity.

1985). This complexity comes not just from the number of neurons, but from the vast number of interconnections between them, numbering in the thousands for many neurons.

Although we are far from understanding the vast complexity of how the brain operates, we have learned a tremendous amount in the last few decades about the connection between the brain and our perceptions. Research on this connection has focused on two basic ideas:

1. *Localization of function:* Specific areas of the brain serve different functions.

2. *Sensory coding:* Nerve firing represents characteristics of the environment.

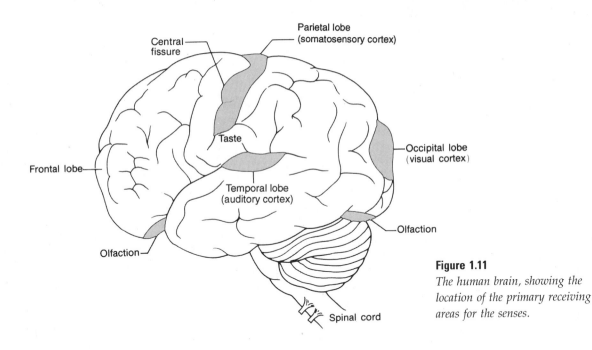

Central
fissure

Parietal lobe
(somatosensory cortex)

Taste

Occipital lobe
(visual cortex)

Frontal lobe

Temporal lobe
(auditory cortex)

Olfaction

Olfaction

Spinal cord

Figure 1.11

The human brain, showing the location of the primary receiving areas for the senses.

Let's briefly consider each of these ideas.

Localization of Function   Researchers studying the brain have found that specific areas serve different functions, a phenomenon called **localization of function**. This occurs for many brain functions, including memory, emotion, thinking, and the control of movement. Each sense has a primary receiving area in the **cerebral cortex**, the outer layer of the brain. The **primary receiving area** is the first area in the cerebral cortex to receive the signals initiated by that sense's receptors. The primary receiving area for vision is in the **occipital lobe**, for hearing it is in the **temporal lobe**, and for the skin senses—touch, temperature, and pain—it is in the **parietal lobe** (Figure 1.11). We will see that other areas in addition to the primary receiving areas are also associated with each sense.

Researchers have also found areas, called **nuclei**, in which there is a large concentration of synapses. For example, a structure near the center of the brain called the **thalamus** contains a number of nuclei where neurons from the vari-

ous senses synapse on their way to the brain. Throughout this book, we will be describing research that focuses on determining the roles that various nuclei and brain areas play in determining specific kinds of perceptions.

Sensory Coding   Brain researchers are also concerned with answering the question: How do nerve impulses represent characteristics of the environment? This question is the **problem of sensory coding**, and research on this problem seeks to determine the **sensory code**, the characteristics of nerve impulses that represent various characteristics of the environment. The following question, which was posed by one of my students, Bernita Rabinowitz, in response to my request for questions on the first day of class, is relevant to the problem of sensory coding:

A human perceives a stimulus (a sound, a taste, etc.). This is explained by the electrical impulses sent to the brain. This is so incomprehensible, so amazing. How can one electrical impulse be perceived as the taste of a sour lemon, another

Introduction to Perception

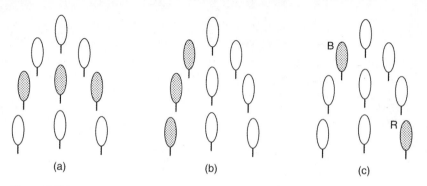

Figure 1.12

Possible solutions to the problem of sensory coding, using color perception as an example. Each symbol represents a neuron; activated neurons are shaded. (a) and (b) illustrate the idea that different colors could be signaled by different patterns of neural activity, the pattern of activity in (a) representing "blue" and the pattern in (b) representing "red." (c) illustrates the idea that different colors could be signaled by *activity in specific neurons,* activity in Neuron B representing blue and activity in Neuron R representing red.

impulse as a jumble of brilliant blues and greens and reds, and still another as bitter, cold wind? Can our whole complex range of sensations be explained by just the electrical impulses stimulating the brain? How can all of these varied and very concrete sensations—the ranges of perceptions of heat and cold, colors, sounds, fragrances and odors, tastes—be merely and so abstractly explained by differing electrical impulses?

We will be spending a great deal of effort in this text toward answering Bernita's question. We will do this both by asking what different brain areas do and by looking for relationships between electrical signals and perception. We can partially answer Bernita's question in terms of localization of function, by saying that she sees reds, blues, and greens because of electrical activity in one area of her cortex, and that she experiences a cold wind or the taste of lemon because of activity in other areas of her cortex. We can also answer it in terms of sensory coding by telling her that she perceives red because of a particular

pattern of firing in one group of neurons in the visual system, whereas her perception of blue is caused by a different pattern of firing in another group of neurons.

Let's look at sensory coding in a little more detail by introducing two proposals for the way the sensory code might work. One proposal, called **across-fiber pattern theory**, is that different perceptions are signaled by the *pattern of activity* in a group of neurons. According to this idea, the sensory code for blue might be the pattern of neural activity shown in Figure 1.12a, and the sensory code for red might be the pattern of neural activity in Figure 1.12b. Another proposal, called **specificity theory**, is that different perceptions are signaled by *activity in specific neurons*. According to this idea, shown in Figure 1.12c, when Neuron B fires, we perceive blue, and when Neuron R fires, we perceive red. When we discuss color vision in Chapter 4, we will see that the correct answer for color perception is closer to the across-fiber pattern theory. We will also see, in other chapters, examples of perceptions that are signaled by activity in specific neurons.

Describing sensory coding in this way may not, however, totally satisfy Bernita (since, as I found out during the term, she is a very inquisitive person), because she may inquire how it is that electrical impulses, which are, after all, actually just sodium and potassium ions flowing across membranes, can be *transformed* into the taste of a lemon or a jumble of blues and greens. When Bernita asks her question in this way, she is posing the **mind–body problem**. The mind–body problem asks how a physical event, such as molecules moving across membranes (the body part of the problem), can be transformed into the richness of perceptual experience (the mind part of the problem).

The mind–body problem is one of the great unsolved scientific and philosophical problems of our time. So it is here that we have to tell Bernita that one of the true signs of scientific wisdom is learning which questions we can potentially answer, and which questions are too difficult for our present state of knowledge. Luckily, even if scientists do not know how to go about studying the mind–body problem, we can still learn a tremendous amount about the more tractable problem of sensory coding. Sensory coding will therefore be one of our central concerns as we discuss the physiological approach to perception, and a great deal of this book will be concerned with looking for the ways in which the firing of nerve impulses signals specific qualities in the environment.

As we explore the physiological approach to perception, we will see that it offers a powerful way to understand how basic mechanisms that operate behind the scenes determine our experience. However, if we were to consider only physiological responses, we would have stopped short of learning about perception. Describing how neurons fire may tell us something about neurons, but it does not provide the full story of perception, because neurons don't perceive. Only people, or animals, can tell us about perception, because they are the ones who do the perceiving. It is therefore crucial that we study not only the

properties of neurons but perception as well. We do this by asking the stimulus question: How do we use information from the environment to create perceptions? Our primary tool for answering this question will be **psychophysics**, a number of methods for determining the relationship between stimuli and perception. We will therefore refer to research asking the stimulus question as the **psychophysical approach to perception**.

Taking a psychophysical approach enables us not only to provide perceptual data that we can use in conjunction with our physiological results, but also provides data that are important in their own right. As we will see in this book, there is much we can learn by focusing on the relationship between information in the environment and perception. To help us understand some of the methods by which this relationship is determined, we now consider the history and some of the basic principles behind the psychophysical approach to perception.

THE PSYCHOPHYSICAL APPROACH TO PERCEPTION

The psychophysical approach to perception is concerned with studying the relationship between stimuli from the environment, such as the locomotive and its surroundings, and people's perception of these stimuli. Today, the idea of measuring the relationship between stimuli and perception may seem reasonable. However, in the 18th and 19th centuries, many people were skeptical about the possibility of measuring experiences like perception. For example, the philosopher Immanuel Kant (1724–1804) stated that it wasn't possible to measure the products of the mind with any precision, and others stated that asking people to describe their experiences could drive them to madness (Hothersall, 1990).

Introduction to Perception

Nineteenth-Century Psychophysics

Amid the skepticism regarding the possibility of measuring experience, Gustav Fechner (1801–1887) (Figure 1.13), German physicist and philosopher, proposed that it would be possible to demonstrate a relationship between the functioning of the body and experience by having people report their experiences as a physical stimulus is systematically changed. In 1860 Fechner published his book *Elements of Psychophysics*, which explored the relationship between physical stimuli and experience by proposing a number of methods for measuring the **absolute threshold**, the smallest amount of stimulus energy necessary for an observer to detect a stimulus.

The idea of an absolute threshold dates back to the early 1800s, when German philosopher J. F. Herbart suggested that for a mental event to be experienced it had to be stronger than some critical amount (Gescheider, 1976). This idea forms the basis of what has come to be called *classical threshold theory*. The basic idea underlying this theory is that at the absolute threshold there is a sharp transition between a state in which an observer cannot detect the stimulus (i.e., if the intensity is below the threshold) and a state in which the observer can detect the stimulus (i.e., if the intensity is above the threshold). This situation is shown in Figure 1.14. According to this idea, an observer will never be able to detect a stimulus when the intensity is 10, 11, or just under 12 and will always be able to detect a stimulus when the intensity is 12 or higher; the absolute threshold would therefore be 12 in this case.

Results such as those plotted in Figure 1.14 rarely occur, however. A more usual result is shown in Figure 1.15. The transition between not detecting the stimulus and detecting it is usually gradual rather than abrupt. Classical threshold theory explains this result by saying that a sharp transition between nondetection and detection occurs only if all factors remain

Figure 1.13
Gustav Fechner, who introduced a number of psychophysical methods for measuring thresholds in his book Elements of Psychophysics.

constant during the experiment; in reality, however, everything does not remain constant. For example, the sensitivity of the receptors that respond to the stimulus, as well as the attention of the observer, may vary slightly with time. These variations cause slight shifts in the threshold so that the threshold is different at different points in time, and these variations cause the abrupt transition of Figure 1.14 to become the gradual transition of Figure 1.15.

In *Elements of Psychophysics*, Fechner described three methods of determining thresholds. These methods, which are known as the **classical psychophysical methods**, are important tools of the psychophysical approach to perception.

Method of Limits   To measure the threshold by using the **method of limits**, the experimenter presents different stimuli and asks the observer to indicate whether he or she can detect the stimulus. These stimuli are presented in either ascending or descending order, as shown in Figure 1.16, which also shows the results of an experiment that measures a person's threshold for seeing a light.

On the first series of trials, the experimenter presents a light above the threshold, and the observer indicates by a "yes" response that he sees the light. This response is indicated by a *Y* at an intensity of 105 on the table. The experimenter then decreases the intensity, and the observer

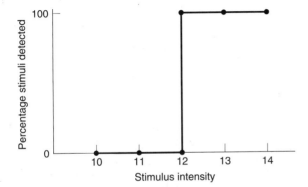

Figure 1.14
According to classical threshold theory, there is a sharp step between an intensity at which an observer can't detect a stimulus (slightly below 12, in this case) and the intensity at which an observer can detect a stimulus (slightly above 12).

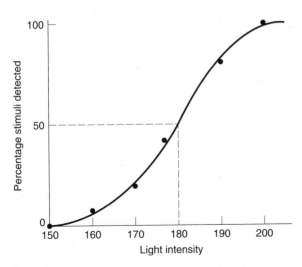

Figure 1.15
Results of a hypothetical experiment in which the threshold for seeing a light is measured by the method of constant stimuli. The threshold, the intensity at which the light is seen on half of its presentations (as indicated by the dashed line), is 180 in this experiment.

Intensity	1 ↓	2 ↑	3 ↓	4 ↑	5 ↓	6 ↑	7 ↓	8 ↑
105	Y						Y	
104	Y		Y		Y		Y	
103	Y		Y		Y		Y	
102	Y		Y		Y		Y	
101	Y		Y		Y		Y	Y
100	Y	Y	Y	Y	Y		Y	Y
99	Y	N	Y	N	Y	Y	Y	Y
98	N	N	Y	N	N	N	N	Y
97		N	N	N		N		N
96		N		N		N		N
95		N		N		N		N
Crossover values →	98.5	99.5	97.5	99.5	98.5	98.5	98.5	97.5

Threshold = mean of crossovers = 98.5

Figure 1.16
The results of an experiment to determine the threshold using the method of limits. There are eight series of trials in this experiment, the descending trials alternating with the ascending trials. See the text for details.

makes another judgment. This process continues until, at an intensity of 98, the observer indicates by an answer of "no" that he no longer sees the light. This change from "yes" at 99 to "no" at 98 is the *crossover point*, and the threshold value for this run is taken as the mean between 99 and 98, or 98.5. The procedure is then repeated in reverse, starting below the threshold and increasing the intensity until the subject says "yes." Both the descending and the ascending presentations are repeated a number of times, and the threshold is calculated as the mean of the crossover values for each run. The threshold is therefore 98.5 in this experiment.

Introduction to Perception

When using the method of limits, the experimenter presents the stimuli in both ascending and descending order to counteract the **error of perseveration**, which occurs if an observer persists in answering in the same way. For example, an observer might continue saying "yes" for one or two extra trials because she or he said "yes" on the previous trials. A similar bias may occur during the ascending series, as observers continue to say "no" for one or two additional trials because they said "no" on the previous trials. When both ascending and descending orders are used, these two biases cancel each other.

Method of Adjustment In the **method of adjustment**, the stimulus is slowly changed as either the observer or the experimenter adjusts the stimulus intensity until the observer says that he or she can just barely detect the stimulus. This just barely detectable intensity is then taken as the absolute threshold. This procedure can be repeated a few times and the threshold determined by taking the average setting. Having the observer adjust the stimuli has the advantage of giving the observer an active role in the proceedings, thus maximizing the probability that he or she will stay awake during the entire experiment!

Method of Constant Stimuli The **method of constant stimuli** is similar to the method of limits, since the experimenter presents a number of specific stimuli, but differs in that the stimuli are presented in random order. Five to nine stimuli are typically used, the most intense being clearly above the threshold so that an observer detects it without fail, and the least intense being clearly below the threshold so that an observer can never detect it. The stimuli between these two are of intermediate intensity, so that they are detected on some presentations and not on others. The experimenter presents each stimulus a number of times in random order. The results of a hypothetical determination of the threshold for seeing a light are shown in Figure 1.15. Each of the six light intensities is presented 10 times *in random order*, and the percentage of times that each intensity is detected is plotted on the vertical axis. The results indicate that the light with an intensity of 150 is never detected, the light with an intensity of 200 is always detected, and lights within intensities in between are sometimes detected and sometimes not detected. The threshold is usually taken as the intensity that results in detection on half the trials, so in this case the threshold is an intensity of 180.

Which of these methods is usually used to measure thresholds? The answer depends on both the accuracy that is needed and the amount of time available. The method of constant stimuli is the most accurate method but takes the longest time, whereas the method of adjustment is the least accurate but the fastest.

When Fechner published his *Elements of Psychophysics*, he not only described his methods for measuring the absolute threshold but also described the work of Ernst Weber (1795–1878), a physiologist, who, a few years before the publication of Fechner's book, measured another type of threshold, the difference threshold. The **difference threshold**, which is also called the **just noticeable difference (JND)**, is the smallest difference between two stimuli that a person can just detect.

Weber had subjects lift a small "standard" weight and then lift a slightly heavier "comparison" weight and judge which was heavier (Figure 1.17). When the difference between the standard and comparison weights was small, subjects found it difficult to tell the two weights apart, but they easily detected larger differences. That much is not surprising, but Weber went further. He found that the size of the JND depended on the size of the standard weight. For example, the JND for a 100-gram weight is 5 grams (a subject could tell the difference between a 100- and 105-gram weight, but smaller differences remained undetected), and the JND for a 200-gram weight is 10 grams. Thus, as the magnitude of the stimulus increases, so does the size of the JND.

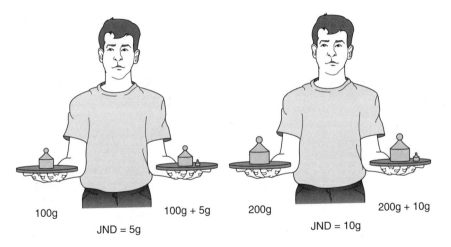

100g   100g + 5g   200g   200g + 10g
        JND = 5g   JND = 10g

Figure 1.17
The just noticeable difference (JND). The person can detect the difference between a 100-gram weight and a 105-gram comparison weight but cannot detect a smaller difference, so the JND is 5 grams. With a 200-gram weight, the comparison weight must be 210 grams before the person can detect the difference, so the JND is 10 grams. Note that for both the 100- and 200-gram weights, the ratio of JND to weight is the same. This ratio is the Weber fraction.

DEMONSTRATION
Measuring the JND

By doing a simple experiment with two boxes of wooden matches, you can demonstrate to yourself that the JND gets larger as the standard stimulus gets larger. Have a friend place 10 matches in one box (the standard) and 11 in the other (the comparison), and comparing the weights of the two boxes with your eyes closed, try to decide which box is heavier. After making this judgment, repeat this procedure; if you can't correctly judge which is heavier on three out of three trials, have your friend place another match in the comparison box, and try again. Continue this procedure until you can consistently judge which box is heavier. If, for example, you can consistently tell that the comparison box is heavier when it contains 12 matches, then the JND equals 2 matches. Now repeat the above procedures, but start with 20 matches in the standard box and 21 in the comparison. Since the JND gets larger as the weight of the standard gets larger, you should find that the JND for the 20-match standard is larger than the JND for the 10-match standard. ●

Research on a number of senses has shown that the JND is larger for larger standard stimuli, and that, over a fairly large range of intensities, the ratio of the JND to the standard stimulus is constant. This relationship, which is based on Weber's research, was stated mathematically by Fechner as $JND/S = K$ and was called **Weber's law**. K is a constant called the *Weber fraction*, and S is the value of the standard stimulus. Applying this equation to our example of lifted weights, we find that, for the 100-gram standard, $K = 5/100 = 0.05$, and that, for the 200-gram standard, $K = 10/200 = 0.05$. Thus, in this example, Weber's fraction (K) is constant.

Numerous investigators have tested Weber's law and found that it is true for most senses, as long as the stimulus intensity is not too close to the threshold. This principle is illustrated in Figure 1.18, which shows that the Weber fraction for lifted weights is fairly constant for two different observers, as long as the weight of the standard is

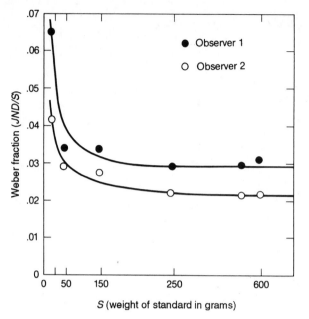

Figure 1.18

Relationship between the Weber fraction and the weight of the standard for two observers, showing that the Weber fraction is constant between about 150 and 600 grams.

greater than about 50 grams (Engen, 1972; Gescheider, 1976).

Fechner's statement of Weber's law for the difference threshold and his proposal of three psychophysical methods for measuring the absolute threshold were extremely important events in the history of scientific psychology because they demonstrated something that many people thought was impossible: the quantification of the mind. This was a notable achievement at the time, and the methods developed in the 1800s are still used today to measure absolute and difference thresholds. However, the psychophysical approach to perception goes beyond measuring thresholds. Since the vast majority of our experience takes place above threshold, where we can easily see a bright light or hear someone talking to us, it is important to ask what the relationship is between above-threshold stimuli and our perception of these stimuli. Specifically, we will ask what the relationship is between the *intensity* of a stimulus and our *perception of the magnitude* of the stimulus.

Measuring Magnitude above Threshold

If we double the intensity of a light, does it look twice as bright? If we double the intensity of a tone, does it sound twice as loud? Although a number of researchers, including Fechner, proposed equations that related perceived magnitude and stimulus intensity, it wasn't until 1957 that S. S. Stevens proposed an equation that is accepted today as accurately describing this relationship.

Stevens's equation grew from a technique, which he developed, called **magnitude estimation** (Stevens, 1957, 1961, 1962). This technique is very simple: The experimenter first presents a "standard" stimulus to the observer (let's say a light of moderate intensity) and assigns it a value of, say, 10; he or she then presents lights of different intensities, and the observer is asked to assign a number to each of these lights that is proportional to the brightness of the light. If the light appears twice as bright as the standard, it gets a 20; half as bright, a 5; and so on. Thus, each light intensity has a brightness assigned to it by the observer.

The results of a magnitude estimation experiment on brightness are plotted in Figure 1.19. This graph plots the means, for a number of observers, of the magnitude estimates of the brightness of a light versus the intensity of the light. You can see from this graph that doubling the intensity does not double the perceived brightness. Doubling the intensity causes only a small change in perceived brightness, particularly at higher intensities. This result is called **response compression**. As intensity is increased, the responses increase, but not as rapidly as the intensity. To double the brightness, it is necessary to multiply the intensity by about 9.

Figure 1.20 shows the results of magnitude estimation experiments for brightness, for the

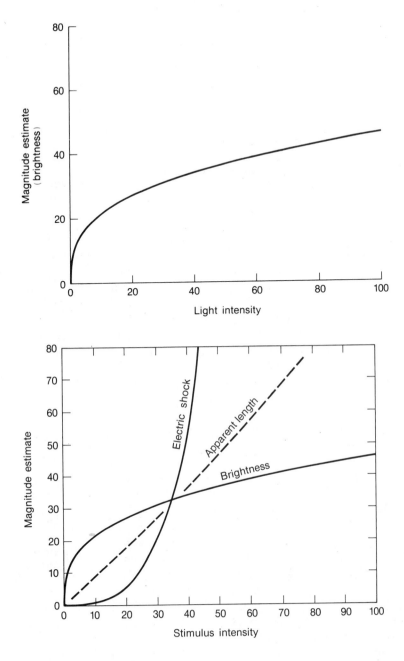

Figure 1.19
The magnitude estimates for the brightness of a light are plotted versus light intensity. (Adapted from Stevens, 1962.)

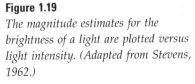

Figure 1.20
Curves showing the relationship between perceived magnitude and stimulus intensity for electric shock, line length, and brightness (adapted from Stevens 1962). The curve for brightness is the same one shown in Figure 1.19.

length of a line, and for the sensation caused by an electric shock presented to the finger. You can see that there are three different kinds of curves: (1) curves that bend down, such as the one for brightness; (2) curves that bend up, such as the one for electric shock; and (3) straight lines, such as the one for estimating line length. Curves that bend down show *response compression* (i.e., doubling the light intensity causes less than a doubling of the brightness). Curves that bend up

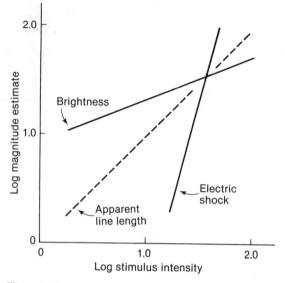

Figure 1.21

The three curves from Figure 1.20 plotted on log-log co-ordinates. Taking the logarithm of the magnitude estimates and the logarithm of the stimulus intensity turns the curves into straight lines. (Adapted from Stevens, 1962.)

Figure 1.22

If the length of line A equals 10, what is the length of line B? (No fair measuring.)

show **response expansion** (i.e., doubling the strength of a shock causes more than a doubling of the sensation of being shocked). Straight lines are *linear*, with a slope of close to 1.0, so the magnitude of the response almost exactly matches increases in the stimulus (i.e., doubling the line length doubles the observer's estimate of the length of the line).

The beauty of the relationships derived from magnitude estimation is that we can show that the relationship between the intensity of a stimulus and our perception of its magnitude follows the same general equation for each sense. We show this by replotting the curves as shown in Figure 1.21. When we plot the *logarithm* of the magnitude estimates versus the *logarithm* of the stimulus intensity, all three curves become straight lines. These functions are called **power functions** and are described by the equation $P = KS^n$. Perceived magnitude, P, equals a constant, K, times the stimulus intensity, S, raised to a power, n. This rela-

tionship is called **Stevens's power law**. The power n, the exponent of the power law, indicates the slope of the lines in Figure 1.21. Remembering our discussion of the three types of curves in Figure 1.20, we can see that the slope of the curve that shows response compression is less than 1.0, that the slope of the linear curve is about 1.0, and that the slope of the curve that shows response expansion is greater than 1.0. Thus the relationship between response magnitude and stimulus intensity is described by a power law for all senses, and the exponent of the power law indicates whether doubling the stimulus intensity causes more or less than a doubling of the response.

What do these exponents mean in terms of our experience? People other than photographers, artists, lighting engineers, and perceptual psychologists aren't really conscious of the actual values of the light intensities in their surroundings, so most people are surprised when you tell them that you have to multiply light intensity by 9 to double the brightness. But since we can be exposed to intensity ranges of 1 to 1,000 or more on a bright, sunny day, it makes sense that our perception of brightness should not span the same large range. If it did, we would probably be faced with such high contrasts and bright glare that looking at the scene would be difficult.

Estimating line lengths is something most people have had some experience with because of exposure to rulers and other measuring instruments, and most people are fairly good at it. The exponent for estimating line length is actually 1.1, but this is close enough to 1.0 so that the line in Figure 1.20 is very close to being straight. Try estimating the length of line B in Figure 1.22, assuming that the length of line A is 10. (See the answer at the bottom of page 29 after making your estimate.) You probably came fairly close or overestimated slightly, as would be predicted by the exponent of 1.1 for estimating line length.

Finally, the exponent of 3.5 for electric shock seems compatible with our need to avoid potentially damaging stimuli. The rapid increase in pain to small increases in shock intensity serves to warn us of impending danger, and we therefore tend to withdraw even from weak shocks.

We have seen that psychophysical methods have provided ways to measure the detectability and magnitudes of stimuli. Some psychologists reserve the term *psychophysics* to describe methods such as Fechner's, Weber's, and Stevens's that measure quantitative relationships between physical stimuli and perception. In this book, we use the term *psychophysics* in a broader sense to include not only quantitative methods of stimulus detection and magnitude estimation, but also the identification of information that we use to perceive perceptual qualities in the environment.

Identifying Perceptual Information in the Environment

We can illustrate this aspect of the psychophysical approach by showing how it has been applied to the perceptual quality of depth. Analysis of the environment pictured in Figure 1.23 reveals that a number of sources of information indicate the relative distances of various objects in the scene. The fact that the person in the foreground covers up, or overlaps, part of the car tells us that the person is between us and the car. Based on this observation, we can suggest that *overlap* is a source of information for depth. We also notice that the texture of the street is coarse in the foreground and becomes finer as the distance increases. This change in texture, which creates what perceptual psychologists call a *texture gradient*, is another source of information for depth.

We can also identify sources of information for other perceptual qualities. For example, pressure changes in the air provide information for

Figure 1.23

A scene with depth information. The fact that the person's body occludes the car indicates that she is in front of the car. The textured pattern of the bricks on the street provides another source of information for depth.

hearing the pitches of tones, and differences in the time at which sounds reach the left and right ears provides information for hearing where a sound is coming from.

As we end our description of the psychophysical approach to perception, let's return to the relationships in Figure 1.3. So far, we have described various ways researchers have dealt with the stimulus relationship and the physiological relationship, and it is these relationships that occupy most of our attention in this book.

Introduction to Perception

However, to complete our story we also need to consider the third relationship in Figure 1.3: the relationship between a person's cognitions (his or her prior knowledge and present thoughts) and the person's perceptions.

THE COGNITIVE APPROACH TO PERCEPTION

The **cognitive approach to perception** focuses on how perception is affected by the meaning of a stimulus, and by the subject's expectations. You can experience this approach by doing the following demonstration.

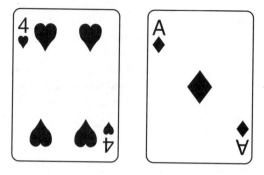

Figure 1.24

Two of the stimuli used in Bruner and Postman's (1949) experiment. They also used clubs and spades that were colored red.

DEMONSTRATION

Perceiving a Picture

After looking at the drawing in Figure 1.25, close your eyes, turn to the next page (the page just under page 25), and open and shut your eyes rapidly to briefly expose the picture in Figure 1.28. Decide what the picture is, and then open your eyes and read the explanation below it.   ●

Did you identify Figure 1.28 as a rat (or a mouse)? If you did, you were influenced by the clearly rat-like or mouselike figure you observed initially. But people who first observe Figure 1.31 on page 29 usually identify Figure 1.28 as a man. (Try this demonstration on some other people.) The **rat–man demonstration** shows how the stimulus's meaning and the subject's expectations can influence our perceptions.

The idea that people's cognitions can influence their perceptions is the central principle behind an approach called the *New Look in perception* that became popular in the late 1940s. One example of a New Look experiment involved the presentation of a stimulus such as the one in Figure 1.24. Presenting cards such as this that were the wrong color (since hearts and diamonds are red suits) caused subjects to take four times as long to identify the suit compared to cards that were the correct color (Bruner & Postman, 1949), a result that illustrates the role of prior knowledge in perception. When subjects in this experiment were provided with knowledge of the errors they were making, they became more aware of the types of stimuli that were being presented and made fewer errors, an interesting result that shows how people's immediate experience can affect their perception.

The New Look in perception was called *new* because it introduced a cognitive dimension to perception that was missing from the physiological and psychophysical approaches that had dominated perception until the 1950s. Beginning in the 1960s, another impetus for considering the cognitive dimension of perception was provided by the development of a new psychological specialty called **cognitive psychology** (Neisser, 1967). A major reason for the growth of cognitive psychology was the development of the digital computer, which provided a new model for

Figure 1.25
Look at this drawing first, then close your eyes and turn the page, so you are looking at the same place on the page directly under this one. Then open and shut your eyes rapidly. (Adapted from Bugelski & Alampay, 1961.)

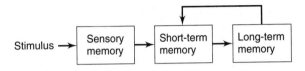

Figure 1.26
A flowchart developed by cognitive psychologists. This one illustrates interactions between the various stages of memory.

thinking about how the mind works. The original idea behind cognitive psychology was a relatively simple one: The mind, like the computer, was seen as a machine that processes information, and psychologists began constructing models of the mind that looked very much like the flowcharts used by computer programmers (Figure 1.26). Thus, information processing became a popular approach to the study of areas like memory, problem solving, and reasoning and, in addition, has influenced the study of perception.

An illustration of how the cognitive approach has influenced perception is the use of the terms *top-down processing* and *bottom-up processing.* **Top-down processing** is used to describe cognitive influences on perception. It occurs when perceptual processing is based on higher-level information (therefore, coming from the "top"), such as a person's prior knowledge, as in the rat–man demonstration, or the meaningful context in which a stimulus is seen.

An example of top-down processing based on meaningful context is illustrated by an experiment by Steven Palmer (1975), using the stimulus in Figure 1.27. Palmer first presented a context scene such as the one on the left and then briefly flashed one of the target pictures on the right. When Palmer asked subjects to identify the object in the target picture, they correctly identified an object like the loaf of bread (which is appropriate to the kitchen scene) 80 percent of the time but correctly identified the mailbox or the drum (two objects that don't fit into the scene) only 40 percent of the time. The subjects' ability to identify the object was affected by their expectation of what things are likely to be found in kitchens.

Bottom-up processing refers to processing based on properties of the stimulus, such as the distribution of light and dark areas or the arrangement of contours in a visual scene. Explaining perception of the scene in Figure 1.27 based solely on the way the lines are arranged, without any reference to the observer's knowledge of kitchens, would be an example of a perceptual explanation based on bottom-up processing. In

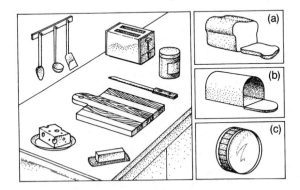

Figure 1.27
Stimuli used in Palmer's (1975) experiment. The scene at the left is presented first, and the observer is then asked to identify one of the objects on the right.

Introduction to Perception

this book, the majority of our explanations of perception will be based on the bottom-up approach, but we will also refer to top-down processing because of the importance of the link between perception and cognition.

THE APPROACH IN THIS BOOK

By looking in some detail at the processes that underlie our perceptions, this book celebrates the wonder of our ability to see, hear, taste, and smell and to feel qualities such as touch, temperature, and pain. Our basic philosophy is that to understand perception fully we need to study it by using all of the three approaches we have described: physiological, psychophysical, and cognitive. Each alone provides only part of the story; together they give us a much deeper understanding of the perceptual process.

You will see, as you read on, that although the physiological, psychophysical, and cognitive approaches have been described separately, they are closely interconnected. You will see that there is an especially strong link between the psychophysical and the physiological approaches, since psychophysics has been used as a tool to determine physiological mechanisms (McKee, 1993; Teller, 1990). We can use an analogy to explain this idea by considering an automobile engine in which one of the cylinders is defective. One way to diagnose this mechanical problem would be to look into the car's machinery and perhaps take the cylinder apart. This would be analogous to studying the physiology of perception directly by recording from neurons. But another way to diagnose the car's problem might be to notice a change in the sound of the engine. Just as we can diagnose a problem in the car's engine by noting the sound it makes, we can also draw conclusions

about the physiological workings of our sensory systems by noting how we perceive things. Later in the book, as we describe how we perceive various qualities, we will have a number of opportunities to show how researchers have used psychophysical results to guess at what is going on physiologically, "under the hood."

Another thing you will notice in this book is the repeating theme that perception is determined by how the perceptual system is constructed. Although it is a common conception that what we perceive is simply a reflection of the nature of the physical world, you will see that it is more accurate to see perception as the result of a filtering of the physical world through our perceptual system.

We will be exploring this interaction between the structure of our perceptual systems and our perceptions by looking at research on humans and closely related animals, such as monkeys. However, another approach to studying this interaction is to study how species very different from ourselves perceive. Thus, at the end of every chapter, in a section called "Other Worlds of Perception," we will consider how other species perceive the perceptual quality we are describing in that chapter. For example, in the chapter on color vision, we look at color vision in animals; in the chapter on hearing, we describe the range of stimuli that animals can hear. We will see that the perceptual world of other species may differ greatly from our own, and we will often be able to show how these differences in perception are related to differences in physiological functioning.

Another approach we will take to learning about perception is to ask how perception develops. Through an end-of-chapter section called "Developmental Dimension" we will look at research that focuses on this topic. We will describe psychophysical research about how human infants perceive and physiological research on how the neural mechanisms of perception develop. In a way similar to the Other Worlds of Perception sections, our discussion of development will match the material in that chapter. For example,

Figure 1.28
Did you see a "rat" or a "man"? Looking at the more ratlike picture in Figure 1.25 increased the chances that you would see this one as a rat. But if you had first seen the man version (Figure 1.31), you would have been more likely to perceive this figure as a man. (From Bugelski & Alampay, 1961.)

in the chapter on depth perception, we consider the development of infant depth perception; in the chapter on speech, we explore how infants perceive speech.

Finally, before forging ahead with the rest of the book, we can ask why we are interested in studying perception in the first place. Just from what you have read so far, you may be able to see that perception merits study simply because of the intellectual challenge it poses. As was mentioned in the chapter opening, our perceptual system acts like a "detective," sifting information that it receives in order to create perceptions. The intellectual challenge of figuring out how this "perceptual detective" works has motivated many thousands of researchers to spend their lives discovering the information we will be presenting in this book.

There are other reasons to study perception as well. Consider, for example, the importance of perception in our lives. To appreciate this, consider for a moment what life would be like without your senses. What would it be like to be without vision? Or without hearing? Or without touch? Most people who are missing just one of these senses learn to cope with their loss. But what if you were born lacking all three of these

senses *plus* lacking the ability to taste and smell? The effect would be shattering because you would be isolated from everything in your environment. Consider for a moment what this would mean. If you survived infancy, would you ever become conscious of your isolation? Would you ever be able to develop language or the capacity to think? We can only speculate on the answers to these questions, but one thing is certain: Your experience would be barren, and your very survival would depend on others.

While satisfying intellectual curiosity and recognizing perception's importance in our lives may be strong motives to study perception, we also study it for more practical reasons. The study of perception has enabled us to begin to design devices to help blind people see and deaf people hear. We have learned to make precise measurements of perceptual capacities so that we can describe normal perception and, more important, so that we can specify the perceptual losses that occur because of aging, disease, or injury. We have applied our knowledge of perception to the acoustical design of concert halls and to the analysis of perfume fragrances. And our knowledge of perception has been essential to understanding the perceptual demands encountered when driving cars, piloting airplanes, and making observations from inside space vehicles (Figure 1.29).

Understanding perception is also important in appreciating the perceptual experience called *art*. A person visiting an art museum has made a decision to spend some time "perceiving" art, but for most people this perceptual experience is not aided by any knowledge of perception. Students who take my course "The Psychology of Art," which relates our knowledge of perception to the process of perceiving pictures, see that an understanding of perception adds another dimension to their ability to "see" works of art (Figure 1.30). For example, one of the problems we consider in the course is how artists use perceptual principles to depict three-dimensional scenes on a two-dimensional canvas.

Figure 1.29
The ability of the driver of this car to negotiate the turn depends on a number of perceptual abilities, including the ability to perceive form, depth, motion, and forces acting on the body.

Figure 1.30
The painting Sunlight in a Cafeteria *(1958) by Edward Hopper illustrates a number of perceptual principles. It illustrates how perspective and other depth information can create the illusion that we are looking into a three-dimensional space even though this is a flat picture. It also illustrates the operation of cognition in perception, since most people would, based on their past experiences, interpret the two light areas on the walls to be light shining through the window rather than an interesting paint job. (Yale University Art Gallery, New Haven, Conn.)*

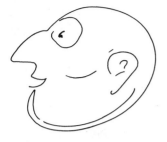

Figure 1.31
Man version of the rat–man stimulus. (Adapted from Bugelski & Alampay, 1961.)

So the reasons to study perception range from a need to satisfy our intellectual curiosity about how the body works, to a need to develop practical solutions to perceptual problems, to the desire to better appreciate the perceptual aspects of art. But even if these reasons didn't exist, there is another reason for studying perception that is relevant to everyone reading this book: *Perception is something you experience all the time*, and the study of perception can enhance this experience. Studying perception will make you more aware of the environment around you and the processes that transform this environment into the experiences we call *perception*.

The goal of this book is to help you to understand the entire process of perception, from the reception of the stimulus, to the physiological processes triggered by the stimulus, to perception of the stimulus. We introduce the basic principles of visual physiology in Chapters 2 and 3 and also illustrate how the physiological and psychophysical approaches work in concert with each other. These chapters focus on vision, but many of the principles that are introduced are also relevant to other senses. As you will see as you pursue the fascinating story of perception in the pages that follow, a true understanding of the process of perception is just as much about understanding broad principles that hold across all of the senses as it is about learning facts that are specific to just one of the senses.

Answer to line estimation problem (Figure 1.22): Length of B equals 25.

Introduction to Perception

WHAT DO OTHER SPECIES EXPERIENCE?

As you walk through your neighborhood, you see a variety of objects, colors, and textures. But what does the neighborhood cat or dog perceive when observing the same scene? There are surely some similarities between your perceptions and theirs because you all manage to negotiate your way through the environment without bumping into things. But the perceptual world of the cat or the dog differs from yours in a number of ways. And what about flies and bees? Do they perceive the world as you do, or do they miss certain things that stand out for you while sensing some things of which you are totally unaware? We will be answering such questions as we consider animal perception in our Other Worlds of Perception sections at the end of each chapter.

One of the goals of these sections is to identify connections between various organisms' perceptual abilities and the physiology of their sensory systems. Another goal is to look at the relationship of a particular animal's physiological mechanisms to its environment. We will see that sensory systems have evolved to provide animals with perceptual capacities that help them survive, usually by making it easier to detect prey or to avoid potential predators.

How can we know what animals that are very different from us see, hear, taste, or smell? Before answering that question, let's consider another one. You and a friend look at a ripe tomato and both say, "That looks red." Do you know for sure that both of your experiences of "redness" are exactly the same? The answer to this question is *no*, because each person's perceptual experience is essentially private to that person. Although we can guess that most people with intact sensory systems have similar experiences when looking at a red tomato, it is also possible that people's perceptions of the same stimuli differ— sometimes in subtle ways, sometimes perhaps in more major ways. If this is the case for you

and another person, then what about the difference between a person and a dog, a cat, or a fly? Large differences undoubtedly exist between human perception and the perception of animals,[1] but it is important to realize that, just as you have no way of really knowing what other humans are experiencing, you also have no way of knowing what animals are experiencing.

Even though we can't tell what animals are experiencing, we can determine whether they can tell the difference between two stimuli or whether a particular feature of the environment influences their behavior, and by doing this, we can uncover many facts about the capacities of other species. For our first example, let's consider a capacity similar to what we call hearing in humans. As we will see in Chapter 8, humans experience "sound" in response to pressure changes or "vibrations" in the air at frequencies ranging from about 20 vibrations per second (which sound very low-pitched to us) to 20,000 vibrations per second (which sound extremely high-pitched to us).

The animal kingdom abounds with examples of animals that can detect vibrations at frequencies either below or above humans' range of hearing. For example, elephants can detect frequencies below the range of human hearing, dogs can detect frequencies that are above the human range of hearing, and bats emit high-frequency sonar waves and sense their reflection in order to detect obstacles and locate prey.

An interesting example of an animal that can detect high-frequency vibrations is the preying mantis (Figure 1.32a). David Yager and Ronald Hoy (1986) discovered that the mantis has neurons that fire in response to a range of 25,000–45,000 vibrations per second. Once they recorded this

---

[1] Although humans are animals, we will adopt the convention in the rest of these sections of using the term *animal* to mean nonhuman animals.

Figure 1.32

Praying mantis. The drawing on the right shows the underside of the praying mantis; the square marks the location of the sound-sensing organ on the mantis's abdomen. (Adapted from Yager & Hoy, 1986.)

response, they began searching for the receptors for these vibrations. They found that coating most of the mantis's body with a heavy layer of Vaseline did not stop the responding of the neurons, but that placing a small drop of melted wax in a deep, narrow groove in the mantis's abdomen eliminated the response. Apparently the mantis has an "ear" on its abdomen. The purpose of this sound-sensing organ is not clear, but it could be to pick up bats' high-frequency sonar waves, thereby helping the mantis avoid becoming a bat's dinner.

Let's now look at some examples of the extraordinary powers of "vision" possessed by some animals. Many species of snakes can detect infrared radiation that is outside the range of human vision. Since infrared radiation is emitted as heat by warm-blooded animals, snakes can use their infrared receptors to detect possible prey, even in pitch blackness. Water moccasins, rattlesnakes, and copperheads accomplish this

detection by means of **pit organs**, small cavities in the head below and in front of the eye. Pythons have heat-sensitive pits on scales bordering their mouth (Figure 1.33). G. Kingsley Able and A. Schmidt discovered these heat-sensing pit organs in the 1930s by showing that as long as their pits are uncovered, snakes will strike warm light bulbs covered with an opaque cloth, but that they ignore the warm light bulbs if the pits are blocked. Later researchers discovered neurons in the snake that fire in response to infrared radiation (Newman & Hartline, 1982).

A large number of fish and amphibians can detect electrical fields. One of these animals is the duck-billed platypus (Figure 1.34). Scheich, Langner, Tidemann, Coles, and Guppy (1986) found that a platypus could detect a 1.5-volt battery placed at the bottom of the pool in which the platypus was swimming. When given a choice between a live battery, a piece of shrimp tail, or a

Figure 1.33
The python has heat-sensitive pits in the scales above and below its mouth.

Figure 1.34
The duck-billed platypus, which can detect electrical fields with receptors in its bill.

dead battery placed 10 cm apart from each other, the platypus preferred the live battery.

Detecting electrical fields would be useful to a platypus because animals generate electrical fields when they use their muscles. Thus, when a shrimp flicks its tail, it generates action potentials that the platypus can detect. The platypus accomplishes this detection by means of receptors in its large bill, which it sweeps back and forth as it swims, to pick up the electrical signals generated by the movement of potential victims.

Finally, let's consider birds' ability to detect magnetic fields. Research on this capacity has been motivated by a desire to understand how birds find their way over long migratory routes and how homing pigeons find their way home after being released far from their normal roosting place. One possible source of information that birds may use for navigation is the orientation of the earth's magnetic field. We know that the earth is a large magnet that has a magnetic north pole near Hudson Bay in Canada (Gould, 1984). Human navigators have long used compasses to help them find their way by orienting them to magnetic north. If birds have a way of sensing this magnetic field, then perhaps they use an "internal compass" to help guide them.

Many behavioral experiments support the idea that birds do, in fact, detect magnetic fields. When migratory birds are placed in a cage, they tend to orient themselves along a line close to magnetic north, and subjecting them to a magnetic field shifts their orientation to correspond to the direction of the new magnetic field (Figure 1.35) (Able & Able, 1993). Physiologically, it has been discovered that pigeons have small pieces

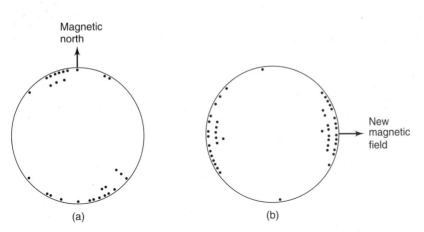

Magnetic
north

New
magnetic
field

(a)   (b)

Figure 1.35

Directions that birds face in a cage under the influence of two different magnetic fields. Each dot represents the direction one bird is facing. (a) When under the influence of the normal magnetic field, birds face either slightly left of magnetic north or in the opposite direction. (b) When the birds were subjected to a new magnetic field, they changed their orientation to match the new magnetic field. (Adapted from Able & Able, 1993.)

of a magnetic substance called *magnetite* in their heads (Walcott, Gould, & Kirschvink, 1979), and other behavioral studies support the idea that birds use magnetic fields as an aid to navigation (Keeton, Larkin, & Windson, 1974; Walcott & Green, 1974). However, research also shows that birds do not rely solely on their magnetic sense to navigate. They also use landmarks on the ground, as well as celestial cues such as the sun and the stars. Their magnetic sense is probably used as a backup mechanism to these other sources of information (Gould, 1993).

With these examples of some of the capacities of other species, we now have concrete evidence that other animals live in different perceptual worlds from humans. Our knowledge that other animals can sense many things that we are unaware of should help us realize that the world humans perceive is only one of many possible "realities."

But what do other animals actually *experience*? We have already acknowledged that we can't answer this question because the conscious experience of another organism is hidden from us. For example, it is said that flies "taste" with their feet since they react differently to substances we perceive as sweet or bitter when they step on them (Roeder, 1963). But does this mean that they expe-

rience the same kinds of taste sensations that we do? Not necessarily. In fact, for all we know they experience vibrations, or impressions that we call visual, in response to certain substances. Or consider the magnetic sense of birds. What is it like for a bird to experience a magnetic field? Again, there are a number of possibilities, one being that the field affects their behavior without their even being aware of the magnetism at all.

This book begins with these examples to emphasize the following points that we will be making throughout our discussion of both human and animal perception: An organism's perception is determined by its physiological makeup, and its experience is therefore created by these physiological mechanisms. Experience is not necessarily contained in the stimulus. A rock, a building, the vibrations of vocal cords, and heat from the sun are just physical stimuli. Nothing says that they must create a particular kind of experience in the organisms that are able to sense them. The important thing for the animal is that the information from physical objects helps them survive to "sense another day." As we continue our consideration of animal senses in other chapters, we will see that what animals are able to perceive is often closely connected to where they live, what eats them, and what they eat.

INFANT PSYCHOPHYSICS

In this chapter we have described a number of psychophysical techniques for measuring the relationship between stimuli and perception. The key to the success of these techniques is that the subject can respond to instructions such as "Tell me when you hear the tone" or "Press that button when you see the light." Applying psychophysics to infants, who can't understand our instructions or respond verbally, is more difficult and requires the use of special techniques.

Techniques do exist that enable us to make psychophysical measurements on infants. These techniques are based on monitoring aspects of an infant's behavior that inform us that the infant can tell the difference between two stimuli. One of these behaviors is looking: Infants tend to look longer at stimuli that interest them. Two techniques based on this fact have been developed: preferential looking and habituation.

Preferential Looking

In the **preferential looking technique**, two stimuli are presented, and the experimenter watches the infant's eyes to see whether the infant looks at one of the stimuli more than at the other. If so, the experimenter concludes that the infant can tell the difference between the stimuli.

The reason preferential looking works is that infants have **spontaneous looking preferences**; that is, they prefer to look at certain types of stimuli. For example, to measure visual acuity (the ability to detect small details), we can use the fact that infants choose to look at objects with contours, such as the "grating" stimulus at the left in Figure 1.36 over one that is homogeneous, such as the one at the right in the figure (Fantz, Ordy, & Udelf, 1962). To measure acuity, we present the two stimuli in Figure 1.36 to an infant, making sure the homogeneous stimulus has the same average intensity as the grating. (Just think of the homogeneous stimulus as one in which the black bars have been smeared out to cover the whole field evenly, the result being a shade of gray.)

Figure 1.37 shows an infant being tested, as the mother holds her infant in front of the display. An experimenter, who does not know the location of the grating on any given trial, looks through a peephole (barely visible between the grating and the gray field) and judges whether the infant is looking to the left or to the right. If we start out using a grating with very wide bars that the infant can see, he or she will look at the grating more than at the gray field. If we decrease the size of the bars, it becomes more difficult for the infant to tell the difference between the grating and the gray field, until, when the bars are very narrow, the grating looks gray to the infant, and he or she looks at each display equally. We measure the infant's acuity by determining the narrowest stripe width that results in preferential looking. The typical results of such an experiment are shown in Figure 1.38. This psychophysical function in an infant is similar to the adult psychophysical curve of Figure 1.15.

Habituation

In the example above, we used the infant's spontaneous looking preference for contours to help us measure acuity. But what if the infant shows no spontaneous preference between two stimuli? If this is the case, how can we get the infant to tell us whether he or she can tell the difference between these two stimuli?

To solve this problem we use the fact that, if infants are given a choice between a familiar

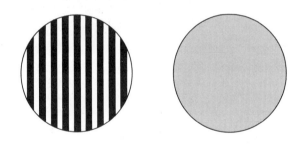

Figure 1.36
Grating stimulus and gray field of the same average intensity.

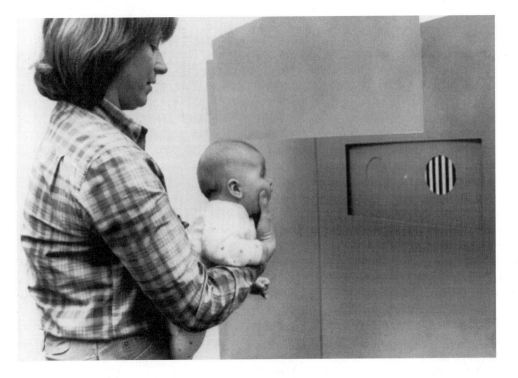

Figure 1.37
An infant being tested by the preferential looking procedure. The mother holds the infant in front of the display: a grating on the right and a homogeneous gray field on the left with the same average intensity as the grating. An experimenter, who does not know which side the grating is on in any given trial, looks through a peephole (barely visible between the grating and the gray field) and judges whether the infant is looking to the left or to the right. (Photograph courtesy of Velma Dobson.)

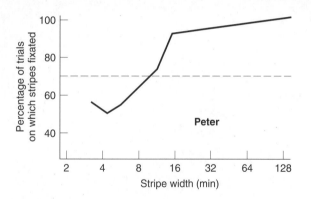

Figure 1.38

Psychophysical function determined by use of the preferential looking technique to determine the acuity of a 5-month-old infant. The function represents the results of many trials in which the infant is presented with a choice between a striped stimulus and a homogeneous gray stimulus. The infant's threshold is defined as the stripe width at which he or she looks at the striped pattern on 70% of the trials (Teller, Morse, Borton, & Regal, 1974).

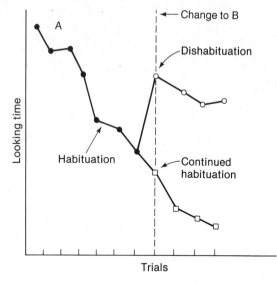
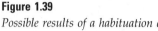
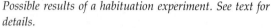

Figure 1.39

Possible results of a habituation experiment. See text for details.

stimulus and a novel one, she or he is more likely to look at the novel one (Fagan, 1976; Slater, Morison, & Rose, 1984). With this fact in hand, we can now *create* a preference for one of the two stimuli by familiarizing the infant with one stimulus but not with the other. In this technique, which is called **habituation**, one stimulus (A) is presented to the infant repeatedly, and the infant's looking time is measured on each presentation. As the infant becomes more familiar with A, he or she habituates to it, looking less and less on each trial (Figure 1.39).

We can see from Figure 1.39 that by the seventh habituation trial the infant is looking much less at A than on the first trial. We now determine whether the infant can tell the difference between A and another stimulus, B, by replacing A with B on the eighth trial. An infant who can tell the difference between A and B will increase her or his looking time to the presentation of B on trial 8 (open circles), since B is a novel stimulus. However, the infant who cannot tell the difference between A and B will continue to habituate to B (since it will not be perceived as novel), as shown by the open squares.

These two psychophysical methods, preferential looking and habituation, have enabled us to show that even newborn infants do possess some perceptual abilities and to measure improvement in these abilities as the infant matures (Granrud, 1987; Slater, Morison, & Rose, 1984; Van Sluyters et al., 1990). The chapters that follow describe research that uses both of these methods to measure infants' ability to perceive qualities such as depth, color, and movement and even their ability to perceive speech.

REVIEW

Perception Does Not Just "Happen"

Outline

- The process of perception consists of a number of steps. In the case of vision, environmental energy enters the eyes and triggers a series of physiological events that ends with perception. This process includes not only physiological steps but also cognitive processes such as thinking and memory.

- In studying the perceptual process, we can ask three different types of questions: the stimulus question, the physiological question, and the cognitive question, each of which offers its own insights and perspectives on the perceptual process.

Questions

1. What are the seven steps listed in the text for the process of perception? (4)
2. How do these steps fall short of doing justice to the complexity of the perceptual process? (4)

3. What three types of information provide "clues" to the identity of environmental stimuli? (4)
4. Describe the three questions we can ask about perception and the relationships associated with each one. (5)

The Physiological Approach to Perception

- Modern ideas about the physiology of perception have evolved from a long line of speculation and research regarding the physiological workings of the mind, beginning with Aristotle and Galen in ancient times, and including 17th-century philosopher Descartes and scientists such as Kepler. Modern approaches began being developed by 18th- and 19th-century scientists.

- By early in the 20th century, the structure of the neuron was known, and the basic components of the physiological basis of perception were established. One of the major advances, the ability to record electrical signals from neurons, occurred in the 1920s.

- Electrical signals in neurons are generated by charged molecules called ions, which flow across the cell membrane in response to changes in the membrane's permeability.

5. What was Aristotle's mistaken idea about the seat of the mind? How do the ideas of Galen, Descartes, and Kepler illustrate the idea that speculations about the brain reflected the technology of the day? (5)
6. What is Müller's doctrine of specific nerve energies? (6)

7. Identify the three parts of the neuron, indicating the function of each part. (6)
8. What basic components of the physiological basis of perception had been established by the early 20th century? (6)

9. What ions are found outside and inside the neuron's axon? (7)

- We can record electrical signals from neurons with microelectrodes. The difference in charge between a recording electrode inside the neuron and a null electrode outside the neuron is the neuron's resting potential. When the neuron is stimulated, the membrane suddenly becomes more permeable to sodium ions, and this starts a sequence of events called the nerve impulse.

- Nerve impulses have a number of basic properties that make them well suited to be carriers of information. These properties enable the fiber to (1) conduct signals over long distances and (2) signal changes in stimulus intensity. In addition, neurons have other properties that limit their rate of nerve firing and create firing even in the absence of environmental stimulation.

- Signals are transmitted from one neuron to another across small gaps called synapses.

- Messages are transmitted across synapses by the action of chemicals called neurotransmitters, which can cause either excitatory or inhibitory effects on the next neuron.

- Specific areas in the brain serve specific functions, a phenomenon called localization of function. Examples of localization of function for the senses are the primary receiving areas for each sense, the areas of the brain that initially receive most of the signals initiated by the receptors.

- The problem of sensory coding asks the question: How do nerve impulses represent characteristics of the environment?

- The mind–body problem asks how physical events within the body are transformed into perceptual experience.

10. What is the resting potential? (7)
11. Describe the flow of ions and changes in electrical charge that occur in the nerve fiber during the nerve impulse. (8)

12. What do we mean when we say that the nerve impulse is a propagated all-or-none response? (9)
13. Describe how nerve impulses change as the intensity of the environmental stimulation is increased. (9)
14. Describe the refractory period and spontaneous activity. (9)

15. What was Golgi's and Ramón y Cajal's disagreement about the nature of the synapse? (10)

16. Describe the action of neurotransmitters at the synapse. Under what conditions does a neurotransmitter cause a voltage change in the postsynaptic neuron? Describe the effect of excitatory and inhibitory electrical responses and how they interact. (10)

17. Where are the primary receiving areas located for vision and hearing? (13)
18. What structure within the brain contains nuclei where neurons for the various senses synapse on their way to their primary receiving areas? (13)

19. Describe two proposals for the way the sensory code might work. (14)

20. What is the difference between the problem of sensory coding and the mind–body problem? How will we be approaching each of these problems in the text? (15)

The Psychophysical Approach to Perception

- The psychophysical approach to perception deals with the stimulus question: How do we use information from the environment to create perceptions? The psychophysical approach provides tools that can be used to help answer this question. One of the pioneers of this approach, Gustav Fechner, published a book, *Elements of Psychophysics*, that described a number of psychophysical methods for measuring the absolute threshold. These methods included the methods of limits, adjustment, and constant stimuli.

- Prior to Fechner's publication of *Elements of Psychophysics*, Ernst Weber had measured the difference threshold, also called the just noticeable difference (JND). The early work of Weber and Fechner helped establish procedures for "quantification of the mind"—an important step in the early history of scientific psychology.

- The psychophysical approach also describes methods for measuring magnitude above threshold. One of these methods is called magnitude estimation.

- Plotting magnitude estimation results on a log-log plot enables us to show that a similar mathematical function describes the relationship between stimulus intensity and perception for all of the senses.

- In this book, the term psychophysics is used in a broad sense to include not only methods for measuring thresholds and magnitude above threshold, but also ways of identifying the kinds of information we use to perceive various perceptual qualities.

21. What was Kant's attitude about the possibility of measuring experiences like perception? (15)
22. What is the absolute threshold? (16)
23. What is the basic idea underlying classical threshold theory? How does the theory explain the gradual transition often observed between not detecting and detecting a stimulus? (16)
24. Describe the procedures involved in the methods of limits, adjustment, and constant stimuli. What errors sometimes occur, and how are they dealt with? (16)
25. What is the difference threshold? How is it measured? (18)
26. How does the JND change with stimulus magnitude? What is Weber's law? When is Weber's law valid? (19)

27. Describe Stevens's magnitude estimation technique. What is response compression? Response expansion? (Be able to illustrate these effects on graphs.) (20)
28. What is a power function? Stevens's power law? What does the exponent of the power law show? (22)

29. Describe some aspects of the environment that have been identified as helping us to perceive depth. (23)

The Cognitive Approach to Perception

- The cognitive approach to perception focuses on how perception is affected by the meaning of a stimulus and by the subject's expectations.

30. Describe the rat–man demonstration. What does it prove? (24)
31. What was the New Look in perception? (24)

- The development of cognitive psychology, beginning in the 1960s, gave impetus to considering the cognitive dimension of perception. One idea behind the cognitive approach is that the mind, like a computer, processes information.

32. Define top-down processing and give an example of it. (25)
33. What is bottom-up processing? (25)

The Approach in This Book

- In this book we will use the physiological, psychophysical, and cognitive approaches to understand the perceptual process. Although these approaches can be described separately, they are closely interrelated.

34. What are some reasons for studying perception? (27)

What Do Other Species Experience?

- There are both similarities and differences between the perceptions of humans and those of other species.

35. What do we mean when we say that just as we have no way of really knowing what other humans are experiencing, we also have no way of knowing what animals are experiencing? (30)

- Even though perception is a private experience for both humans and animals, we can determine characteristics of animals' perception by determining whether they can tell the difference between two stimuli or whether a particular feature of the environment influences their behavior.

36. Describe the following examples of animal perception: hearing in the praying mantis; heat detection by snakes; and the detection of electrical fields by the platypus and magnetic fields by birds. (30)

Infant Psychophysics

- Using psychophysics in infants and animals poses special problems because they can't understand directions or respond verbally. Procedures have been developed, however, that make measurements of infant and animal perceptual capacities possible.

37. Describe the procedures used in the preferential looking technique and the habituation technique. (34)

INTRODUCTION TO VISION: RECEPTORS AND NEURAL PROCESSING

In Chapter 1 we described the perceptions caused by a passing train in order to illustrate a number of commonly experienced perceptual qualities. We now turn to a simpler example, which we will see is actually not so simple when we begin asking some questions about it.

Imagine that you are sitting at your desk when a small red ball enters your field of view from the left and rolls by, moving away from you along a diagonal (cf. Hubel, 1988). Our purpose in this chapter and the next one is to begin answering the question: What happens in your visual system that enables you to perceive the rolling red ball?

Since we will be taking a largely physiological approach to this question, we will begin our search for the answer by doing a hypothetical experiment in which we create a picture of the brain activity caused by perceiving the rolling red ball. We use a device like a PET (positron emission tomography) scanner that creates images that show the bio-

chemical activity in the brain. When we roll the ball past our observer and record her brain activity, the device indicates activity not only in the primary visual receiving area in the occipital cortex, but in many other areas of the brain as well (Figure 2.1). In fact, a large portion of the cerebral cortex, the outer layer of the brain responsible for perception, movement, and thinking, is activated by the ball. Although this exact experiment has not been done, we know from the results of experiments described in the coming chapters that a large number of brain areas, serving different functions, are activated by a stimulus as simple as our rolling ball.

The end result of the activation of these many structures is perception of the ball. In addition to showing that many areas of the brain are activated by a visual stimulus, our observation of the structures activated by the ball contains another important message: Since perception of the ball is based on electrical activation of the brain, *we*

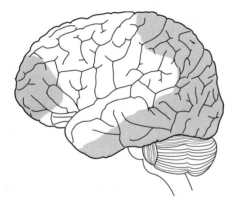

Figure 2.1

Shaded areas show some of the regions of the brain that may be activated by a rolling red ball. In addition to the areas shown, other regions of the cortex, which are folded under and are therefore not visible in this view, are also activated.

perceive the ball indirectly. Our perception is based not on direct contact with the ball, but on the firing of nerve impulses in the brain. This means that there must be information in the nerve firing that stands for "rolling red ball."

What kinds of things must this nerve firing specify? The ball has shape and color, and it starts out at a particular location in space and then moves away from the observer in a specific direction. In this chapter and the next one we will describe the nature of the neural activation that stands for each of these properties. As we do this, we will establish basic principles that we will return to in later chapters when we consider specific visual qualities such as color, form, depth, and movement. We are specifically interested in (1) understanding the anatomy and physiology of the visual system, and (2) relating this anatomy and physiology to perception. In the first third of the chapter we will describe the overall layout of the visual system. In the rest of the chapter we will focus on the beginning of the perceptual process by asking how events that occur within the receptors and other neurons in the eye help determine our perceptions.

OVERALL PLAN OF THE VISUAL SYSTEM

The visual system includes the following elements, which are found in most sensory systems:

1. A structure that collects or modifies the incoming environmental stimuli.

2. Receptors that transform environmental energy into electricity.

3. A series of neurons that transmits signals toward the brain and "processes" them to create signals that can be used to create perceptions.

4. Central neurons in the brain that receive signals, process them further, and eventually result in perceptual experience.

To orient our description of the visual system, let's first look at the overall layout of the system (Figures 2.2–2.5). The visual process begins when light enters the eye, which is the structure that accepts light energy, focuses it into images, and transforms it into the electrical energy of the nervous system (Figure 2.2). Light entering the eye passes through the **cornea** (the transparent front of the eye), then through a hole called the **pupil**, and then through the **lens**. The cornea and the lens focus light onto the **retina,** a layer of neurons that lines the back of the eyeball. Zooming in on the retina, we see a complex network that includes five kinds of neurons (Figure 2.3 and Color Plate 2.3). The "lead" neurons in this network, the **rods** and **cones,** are receptors that generate electrical signals in response to light. These signals are then transmitted through the network of neurons that includes **bipolar cells, horizontal cells, amacrine cells,** and **ganglion cells.**

These electrical signals reach the ganglion cells and then leave the back of the eye in the

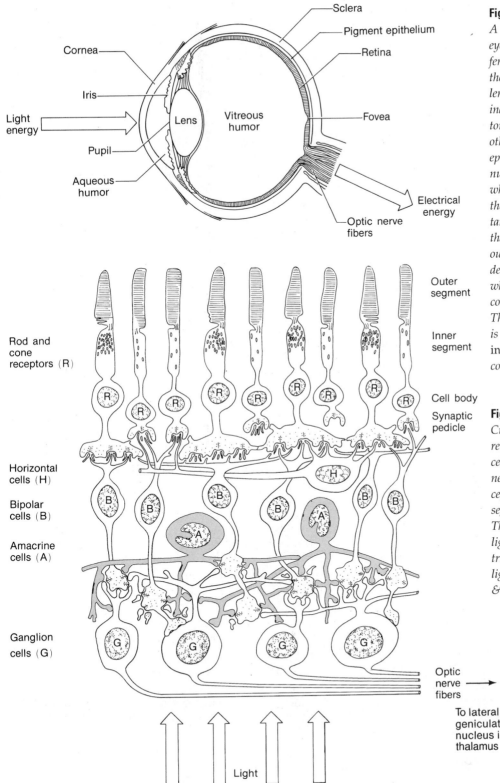

Sclera
Pigment epithelium
Retina
Cornea
Iris
Fovea
Light energy
Lens
Vitreous humor
Pupil
Electrical energy
Aqueous humor
Optic nerve fibers

Rod and cone receptors (R)

Outer segment
Inner segment

Cell body
Synaptic pedicle

Horizontal cells (H)
Bipolar cells (B)
Amacrine cells (A)
Ganglion cells (G)

Optic nerve fibers

To lateral geniculate nucleus in thalamus

Light

Figure 2.2

A cross section of the human eye. Structures we will be referring to in this chapter are the focusing elements (the lens and the cornea); the retina, which contains the receptors for vision as well as other neurons; the pigment epithelium, a layer containing nutrients and enzymes, upon which the retina rests; and the optic nerve, which contains the optic nerve fibers that transmit electrical energy out of the retina. The small depression in the retina, which is called the fovea, *contains only cone receptors. The rest of the retina, which is called the* peripheral retina, *contains both rod and cone receptors.*

Figure 2.3

Cross section of the primate retina showing the five major cell types and their interconnections. Notice that the receptors are divided into inner segments and outer segments. The outer segments contain light-sensitive chemicals that trigger a signal in response to light. (Adapted from Dowling & Boycott, 1966.)

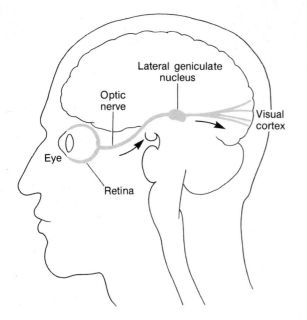

Figure 2.4
A side view of the visual system, showing the three major sites along the primary visual pathway where processing takes place: the retina, the lateral geniculate nucleus, and the visual receiving area of the cortex.

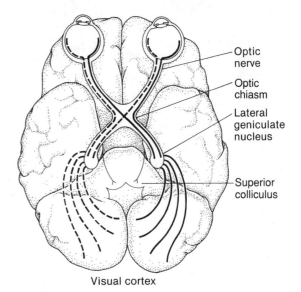

Figure 2.5
The visual system seen from underneath the brain, showing how some of the nerve fibers from the retina cross over to the opposite side of the brain at the optic chiasm. A small proportion of optic nerve fibers goes to the superior colliculus. Most go to the lateral geniculate nucleus and then to the visual receiving area in the occipital lobe of the cortex.

optic nerve (Figures 2.4 and 2.5). Most of the impulses traveling along the optic nerve reach a nucleus in the thalamus called the **lateral geniculate nucleus (LGN)** and from there travel to the occipital lobe of the cortex, which is also called the **visual cortex,** or the **visual receiving area,** of the brain. The journey of these nerve impulses does not, however, end in the occipital cortex. As we will see later, these signals also reach areas in the parietal and temporal lobes (see Figure 1.11).

Now that we have briefly surveyed the overall layout of the visual system, we will look more closely at each of its components, beginning with the front of the eye, where light is focused, and moving to the retina, where electrical signals are initially generated, and then to the lateral geniculate nucleus and the cortex.

FOCUSING THE INCOMING LIGHT

The eye has often been compared to a camera, since both contain optical apparatus for focusing light and creating images of the environment (Figure 2.6). As we will see, the eye, like a camera, does focus light and create an image. However, the similarity ends there because of two important differences between the human eye and a camera: First, the eye and the camera change their focus differently. The camera focuses on objects at different distances by moving its lens back and forth. The human eye changes its focus by changing the shape of its lens. Second, different processes occur after the eye and the camera create their images. For the camera, the film is developed and printed to create an image on photographic paper. For the eye, once electrical signals are generated by the receptors, these signals undertake a long journey through the retina, the lateral geniculate nucleus, and the visual cortex that eventually ends with the creation of a person's conscious visual experience.

The first step in the visual process is focusing the incoming light onto the retina. The eye focuses light with its two focusing elements, the cornea and the lens. Both, working together, sharply focus the light entering the eye onto the retina. To understand how these focusing elements work, let's first consider what happens when we look at a small spot of light located more than 20 feet away. Coming from this distance, light rays that reach the eye are essentially parallel (Figure 2.7a), and these parallel rays are brought to a focus on the retina. If, however, we move our spot closer to the eye, the rays are no longer parallel (Figure 2.7b), and the point at which light comes to a focus moves to behind the retina. Of course, the light never comes to a focus in this situation because it is stopped by the retina, and if things remain in this state, both the image on the retina and our vision will be out of focus.

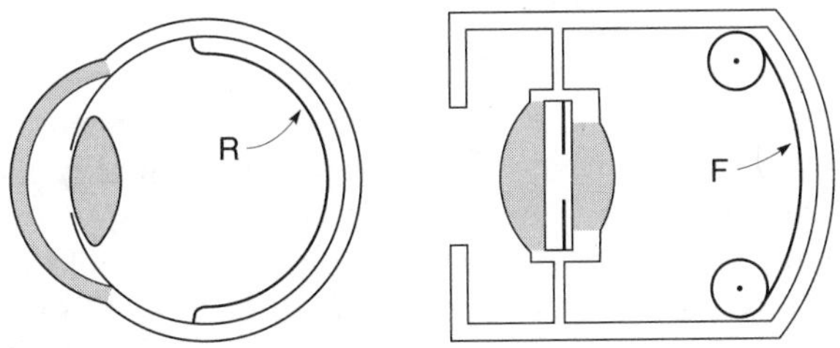

Fortunately, the eye can increase the **focusing power** of the lens to bring the image formed by nonparallel rays of light into focus on the retina. This increase in focusing power is accomplished by a process called **accommodation,** in which tightening the ciliary muscles at the front of the eye increases the curvature of the lens so that it gets fatter (Figure 2.7c). This increased curvature bends the light rays passing through

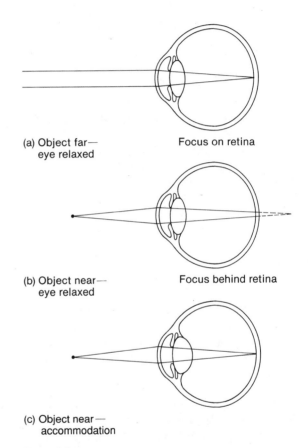

(a) Object far— eye relaxed Focus on retina

(b) Object near— eye relaxed Focus behind retina

(c) Object near— accommodation

Figure 2.7
Focusing of light rays by the normal eye. (a) Parallel rays, from a spot of light farther away than 20 feet, are focused onto the retina. (b) When the spot of light is moved closer to the eye, the rays are no longer parallel, and the focus point of the light is pushed back behind the retina.
(c) Accommodation, indicated by the fatter lens in this picture, pushes the focus point forward onto the retina.

Figure 2.6
There are some similarities between the eye and this old-fashioned box camera. The focusing elements of the eye, the cornea and the lens (shaded), correspond to the two lenses of the camera (shaded). The eye's retina (R) corresponds to the camera's film (F).

Introduction to Vision

the lens more sharply and moves the focus point forward; the result is a sharp image on the retina and, therefore, sharp vision. The beauty of accommodation is that it happens automatically: The eye constantly adjusts the lens's focusing power to keep the image on the retina sharp as we look at objects located at different distances.

DEMONSTRATION

Becoming Aware of
What Is in Focus

Because accommodation occurs unconsciously, you are not normally aware that the lens is constantly changing its focusing power so that you can see clearly at different distances. In fact, this unconscious focusing process works so efficiently that most people assume that everything, near and far, is always in focus. You can demonstrate to yourself that this is not so by closing one eye, looking at a faraway object (at least 20 feet away), and then, while still looking at the far object, moving a pencil toward you while noticing the pencil point. (Don't focus on the point, just "notice" it.) As the pencil gets closer, you should notice that the point becomes blurred and is seen double. When the pencil is about 12 inches away, focus on the point. You now see the point sharply, but the faraway object you were focusing on before has become blurred. Now, bring the pencil even closer until you can't see the point sharply no matter how hard you try. Notice the strain in your eyes as you try unsuccessfully to bring the point into focus.　●

Your exercises in focusing show that accommodation enables you to bring both near and far objects into focus, but that they are not in focus at the same time. You also saw that accommodation has its limits. When you moved the pencil too close, you couldn't see it clearly, even though you were straining to accommodate. The distance at which your lens can no longer adjust to bring close objects into focus is called the **near point.** We will see in Chapter 13 that the distance of the near point increases as a person gets older, a

condition called **presbyopia** (for "old eye") that occurs because aging causes a loss in the ability to accommodate. In Chapter 13 we will also describe other visual problems and how they can be treated.

THE RETINA

The goal of focusing incoming light is to create a clear image on the retina—the network of neurons that covers the back of the eye. As we describe the retina, we will devote most of our attention to the rod and cone receptors, the neurons that transduce the light focused on the retina into electrical signals.

The Rod and Cone Receptors

The rods and cones are named for their shape. The rods are large and rod-shaped, whereas the cones are shorter and cone-shaped, as shown in the 1872 drawing by Max Schultze, who first described these two receptor types (Figure 2.8), and in a modern scanning electron micrograph (Figure 2.9).

The primary purpose of the rod and cone receptors is **transduction**—the transformation of light energy into electrical energy. These receptors accomplish transduction through the action of light-sensitive chemicals called **visual pigments,** which are contained within discs in the outer segment of the receptor (Figure 2.10). As shown in Figure 2.10b and Figure 2.10c, the visual pigment molecule actually makes up part of the structure of the disc membrane, looping back and forth across it seven times. Figure 2.10c shows a part of the visual pigment molecule called **opsin.** Attached to the opsin, at the point shown, is a small light-sensitive molecule called **retinal.** We can appreciate the difference in size

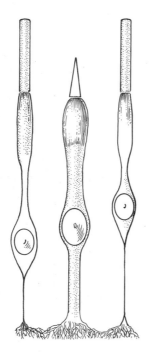

Figure 2.8

A drawing of the rod and cone receptors made in 1872 by Max Schultze. The rod- and cone-shaped parts of the receptors are the outer segments.

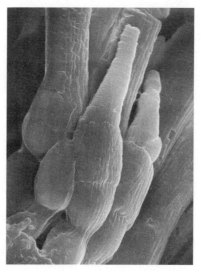

Figure 2.9

Scanning electron micrograph showing the rod and cone outer segments. The rod outer segment on the left is so large that it extends out of the picture, but the cylindrical shape of the rods and the tapered shape of the cones can be clearly seen in this picture (Lewis, Zeevi, & Werblin, 1969).

between the opsin and the retinal by comparing their molecular weights: about 40,000 for the opsin, and only 268 for the retinal.

Despite its small size, retinal is extremely important because it is the part of the molecule that reacts to light. When the retinal absorbs light, it reacts by changing its shape (Figure 2.11). This change in shape transforms the visual pigment molecule into a catalyst—a substance that triggers a chain reaction of chemical events, which leads to the generation of an electrical signal in the receptors (Ranganathan, Harris, & Zuker, 1991).

Although both the rods and the cones transduce light into electricity, they differ in a number of ways in addition to their outward appearance. For one thing, they are distributed differently on the retina. There is one small area in the retina, the **fovea** (see Figure 2.12), that contains only cones. The fovea is located directly on the line of sight, so anytime we look directly at an object, its image falls on the fovea.

There are about 6 million cones in the retina, but since the fovea is so small, only a small fraction of these cones are found in this cone-rich area. Most of the cones are in the **peripheral retina,** the area surrounding the fovea that contains both rods and cones. However, the rods outnumber the cones by about a 20-to-1 ratio, since all 120 million rods in the retina are in the periphery. Figure 2.12 shows the distribution of rods and cones in the retina (also see Color Plate 2.4).

You may have noticed in the cross section of the retina in Figure 2.3 that the rods and cones are facing away from the light, so the light passes through the other neurons in the retina before it reaches the receptors. Why do the receptors face away from the light? One reason is so that they can be in contact with a layer of cells called the **pigment epithelium** (Figure 2.13), which contains nutrients and chemicals called *enzymes* that are vital to the receptors' functioning in ways we will describe later in this chapter. Backward-facing receptors pose little problem for vision, however,

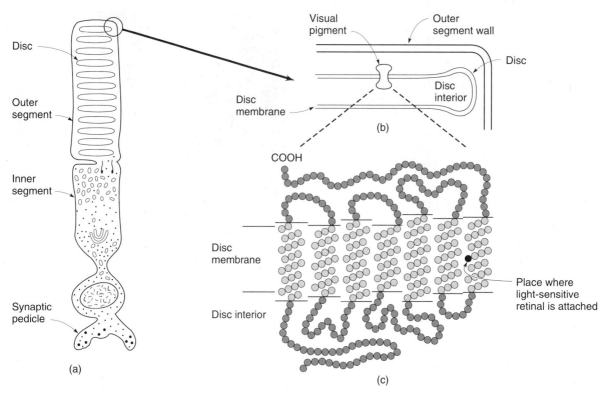

Figure 2.10

(a) Rod receptor showing discs in the outer segment. (b) Close-up showing one disc showing one visual pigment molecule in the membrane. Notice how the molecule straddles the disc membrane. (c) Close-up showing how the protein opsin in one visual pigment molecule crosses the disc membrane seven times. The light-sensitive retinal molecule is attached at the place indicated.

Figure 2.11

Model of a visual pigment molecule. The horizontal part of the model shows a tiny portion of the huge opsin molecule near where the retinal is attached. The smaller molecule on top of the opsin is the light-sensitive retinal. The model on the left shows the retinal molecule's shape before it absorbs light. The model on the right shows the retinal molecule's shape after it absorbs light. This change in shape is one of the steps that accompanies the generation of an electrical response in the receptor.

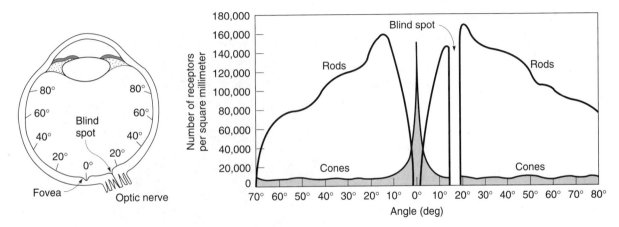

Figure 2.12

The distribution of rods and cones in the retina. The eye on the left indicates locations in degrees relative to the fovea, which are repeated along the bottom of the chart on the right. Notice in the distribution on the right that there are no rods in the fovea, but that the peripheral retina is dominated by rods. Also note that there are no receptors at all at the blind spot, the place where the ganglion cells leave the eye in the optic nerve. (Adapted from Lindsay & Norman, 1977).

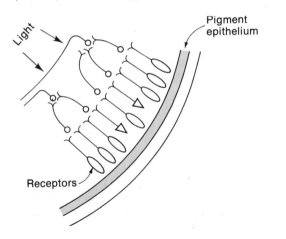

Figure 2.13

Close-up of the retina showing how the receptors face away from the light so the light must pass through the other retinal neurons before reaching the receptors. Since these neurons are transparent, they do not prevent the light from reaching the receptors.

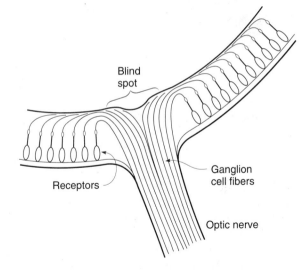

Figure 2.14

There are no receptors at the place where the optic nerve leaves the eye. This enables the receptor's ganglion cell fibers to flow into the optic nerve. The absence of receptors in this area creates the blind spot.

since the light easily passes through the transparent ganglion, amacrine, bipolar, and horizontal cells on its way to the receptors.

The backward-facing receptors do, however, create a problem for the ganglion cells: Since the receptors line the back of the eye, they seem to be blocking the ganglion cells from getting out of the eye. The eye solves this problem, as shown in Figure 2.14, by setting aside a small area where

Introduction to Vision

there are no receptors, and it is here that the eye's 1 million ganglion cell fibers leave the eye in the optic nerve.

Since there are no receptors in the place where the optic nerve leaves the eye, images that fall on this area are not seen. This area is therefore called the **blind spot**. Although you are not normally aware of the blind spot, you can become aware of it by doing the following demonstration.

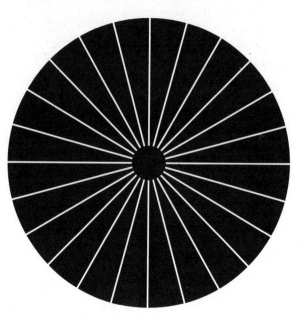

DEMONSTRATION
"Seeing" the Blind Spot

You can demonstrate the existence of the blind spot to yourself by closing your right eye and, with the cross in Figure 2.15 lined up with your left eye, looking at the cross while moving

Figure 2.15

the book (or yourself) slowly back and forth. When the book is 6 to 12 inches from your eye, the circle disappears. At this point, the image of the circle falls on the blind spot. ●

Why aren't we usually aware of the blind spot? There are a number of reasons. First, we usually use two eyes, so when an image falls on the blind spot of one eye, it falls on the receptors of the other. But this explanation doesn't really answer our question, because we usually aren't aware of the blind spot even when we look with only one eye. One reason we aren't aware of it, even with one-eyed vision, is that the blind spot is located off to the side of our visual field, which means, as we will see in this chapter, that we don't see the place where the blind spot is located in sharp focus. Because of this and because we don't know exactly where to look for it (as opposed to the demonstration, in which we know that the circle will disappear), the blind spot is hard to detect.

Figure 2.16
View this pattern as described in the text, and observe what happens when the center of the wheel falls on your blind spot. (From Ramachandran, 1992.)

But perhaps the most important reason that we don't see the blind spot is that some as yet poorly understood mechanism "fills in" the place where the image disappears. Think about what happened when the spot in the demonstration disappeared. The place where the spot used to be wasn't replaced by a "hole" or by "nothingness"; it was filled in by the white page.

DEMONSTRATION
Filling in the Blind Spot

To experience the blind spot's filling-in process in another way, close your right eye and, with the cross in Figure 2.16 lined up with your left eye, move the "wheel" toward you. When the center of the wheel falls on your blind spot, notice how the spokes of the wheel fill in the hole (Ramachandran, 1992). ●

Other Retinal Neurons

The two types of neurons we have discussed so far, the receptors and the ganglion cells, have clear purposes: the transformation of light energy into electrical energy for the receptors and the conduction of nerve impulses out of the eye for the ganglion cells. Interposed between the receptors and the ganglion cells are three other types of neurons: the bipolar cells, which transmit signals from the receptors to the ganglion cells, and the horizontal and amacrine cells, which transmit signals across the retina from one receptor to another and from one bipolar cell to another.

What is the purpose of these neurons that are interposed between the receptors and the ganglion cells? The complexity of the web of connections between horizontal, bipolar, amacrine, and ganglion cells shown in Figure 2.3 (which is greatly simplified compared to the actual situation in the retina) suggests that these neurons do more than simply transmit signals from the receptors to the ganglion cells. As we explore the workings of the visual system in more detail in this chapter and the next one, we will see that these neurons do, in fact, carry out important functions that go beyond just transmitting signals between neurons.

Another suggestion that there is more to these neurons than a way to transmit signals is that these neurons come in different varieties. For example, there are more than a dozen different types of amacrine cells, which differ in structure and in how they are connected to other neurons (Masland, 1988). There are also different types of ganglion cells. There are small ones called *M-cells* and larger ones called *P-cells*. We will see in the next chapter that these two types of ganglion cells serve different visual functions (Shapley & Perry, 1986).

THE LATERAL GENICULATE NUCLEUS

Optic nerve fibers synapse in a number of different structures before their signals reach the brain. About 10 percent go to the superior colliculus, a structure involved in controlling eye movements (Figure 2.5). The rest go to the thalamus, mostly to the lateral geniculate nucleus (LGN). Since most of the optic nerve fibers go to the LGN, we will focus on this structure.

The LGN is a kidney-bean-shaped structure located within the thalamus. Looking at it in cross section, we see that it is organized into six layers (Figure 2.17 and Color Plate 2.7). These layers have two important properties:

1. Each layer receives input from *one* eye, layers 2, 3, and 5 receiving input from the **ipsilateral eye,** and layers 1, 4, and 6 receiving input from the **contralateral eye**. To understand what *ipsilateral* and *contralateral* mean, we need to realize that the LGN, like

Figure 2.17

Cross section of the lateral geniculate nucleus. This is what the LGN looks like when treated with a stain that darkens the cell bodies of the LGN neurons. This darkening shows that there are six layers of cell bodies, each separated by a light band. Layers 1, 4, and 6, marked C, receive input from the contralateral eye, and layers 2, 3, and 5, marked I, receive input from the ipsilateral eye. See the text for details. (From Livingstone & Hubel, 1988.)

Introduction to Vision

many structures in the body, is found on both the left and the right sides of the brain (see Figure 2.5). For a particular LGN, the ipsilateral eye is the eye on the same side of the brain, and the contralateral eye is the one on the opposite side of the brain. Thus, layers 2, 3, and 5 of the LGN in the left hemisphere of the brain receive input from the left (ipsilateral) eye, and layers 1, 4, and 6 receive input from the right (contralateral) eye.

2. Layers 1 and 2 receive input from the M ganglion cells and are called the **magnocellular** (or **magno**) layers. Layers 3, 4, 5, and 6 receive input from the P ganglion cells and are called the **parvocellular** (or **parvo**) layers. (See Color Plate 2.7.) We will see that the magno and parvo layers are responsible for our perception of different visual qualities.

From this description we can see that a basic property of the LGN is that it is *organized*. Optic nerve fibers enter the LGN in different layers, depending on which eye they are from and whether they are M or P ganglion cells. In the next chapter we will see that the LGN is organized not only in terms of ipsilateral and contralateral eyes and magno and parvo layers, but also in another important way: Neurons that originate in the same areas of the retina travel to the same areas of the LGN.

THE VISUAL CORTEX

One and a half million axons stream from each lateral geniculate nucleus toward the occipital lobe of the cortex (see Figure 1.11). Their destination, the visual receiving area in the occipital lobe, is vastly more complex than the LGN, containing over 250 million neurons (Connolly & Van Essen, 1984). The visual receiving area is also

called the **striate cortex** because of the presence of the white stripe (from which the word *striate* derives) of nerve fibers that runs through it (Glickstein, 1988).

Like the LGN, the striate cortex is organized into layers (Figure 2.18). Fibers from the LGN arrive at layer IVc of the cortex, and from there signals are sent to layers above and below this layer. Also as in the LGN, neurons from the same area of the retina meet at the same area of the cortex. We will discuss this important property of the cortex in more detail in Chapter 3.

When the striate cortex was first recognized as a center for seeing, in the late 19th century, it was thought that all visual processes occurred in this area, which accounts for about 15 percent of the cortex (Nakayama, 1990). But later, evidence began accumulating that other cortical areas might also be involved in vision.

One of the most intriguing phenomena that suggests the possibility of a visual role for cortical areas outside the striate cortex—areas we will refer to as **extrastriate** visual areas—is blindsight. **Blindsight** occurs when patients with a damaged striate cortex report that they can't see small spots of light presented to a particular area of their visual field but nonetheless can point to the location of spots of light within this "blind" area. The intriguing thing about blindsight is that even as these patients are accurately pointing to the spots of light, they maintain that they can't see whatever it is they are pointing at (Figure 2.19) (Cowey & Stoerig, 1991; Fendrich, Wessinger, & Gazzaniga, 1992; Weiskrantz, 1986). The exact mechanism responsible for blindsight is still being debated (Gazzaniga, Fendrich, & Wessinger, 1994), but there is some evidence that this fascinating phenomenon may be due to the action of extrastriate cortical areas.

More direct evidence of the existence of extrastriate visual areas comes from anatomical studies, which demonstrate connections between the striate cortex and other areas; ablation studies, which show that the removal of areas outside the striate cortex may result in losses of visual

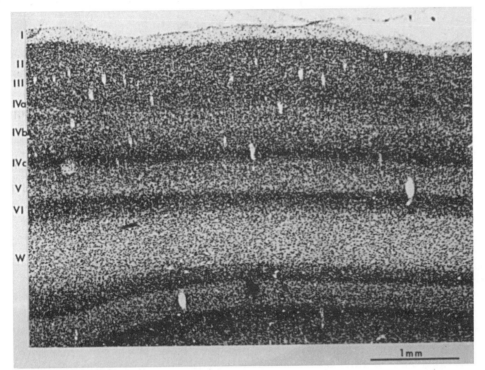

Figure 2.18
The layers of the visual cortex. Fibers from the LGN enter from the bottom, through the white matter (W) below layer VI, and synapse in layer IV. (From Hubel & Wiesel, 1977.)

abilities; and recording studies, which have identified extrastriate neurons that respond to visual stimulation. All of this evidence indicates that the extrastriate cortex makes a huge contribution to vision. Over 30 different extrastriate visual areas have been identified, and it has been shown that about 60 percent of the surface area of the cortex is involved in vision (Color Plate 2.8) (DeYoe & Van Essen, 1988; Felleman & Van Essen, 1991; Maunsell & Newsome, 1987).

Now that we have described the important structures of the visual system, we are going to move back to the eye and, in the rest of the chapter, describe the beginning of the visual process: events that take place in the retina. We will see that these early stages of vision play much more of a role in determining our perceptions than simply transforming light into electricity. We begin by considering the huge role that the rod and cone receptors play in determining the nature of our perceptions.

DUPLICITY THEORY AND PERCEPTION

From our introduction to the rods and cones, we know that these two types of receptors have different shapes and are distributed differently in the retina. As we will discover below, there are other differences between these receptors as well, but perhaps the most important one is that they serve different functions. It is these differences that led J. von Kries to propose the **duplicity theory of vision** in 1896. This theory states that the retina is made up of two types of receptors that not only look different but also operate under different conditions and have different properties.

The existence of two receptor systems with different properties provides us with the opportunity to show how our perceptions are deter-

Figure 2.19

A person with blindsight pointing to a spot of light. Although the person claims he can't see the light, he is able to point to where it is. In an actual testing situation, the person would rest his or her head on a chin rest for more accurate positioning.

mined by the properties of the receptors. One way to illustrate this is by describing a process called **dark adaptation**, the increase in sensitivity that occurs when illumination changes from light to darkness.

Dark Adaptation

You are familiar with dark adaptation from your own experience: When illumination changes from light to darkness, it is difficult to see anything at first, but the longer you spend in the dark, the more your sensitivity increases, and eventually you can see things that at first seemed shrouded in darkness.

Although it is easy to demonstrate that your sensitivity to light increases as you spend more time in the dark, it is not obvious that this increase takes place in two distinct stages: an initial rapid stage and a later, slower stage. We will now describe three experiments that show that the initial rapid stage is due to adaptation of the cone receptors, and that the second, slower stage is due to adaptation of the rod receptors. In our first

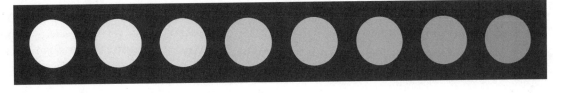

Figure 2.20

experiment, we will describe how to measure a **dark adaptation curve**, a plot of sensitivity versus the time in the dark, which shows the two-stage process of dark adaptation. In our second experiment, we will describe how to measure the dark adaptation of the cones alone. And in our third experiment, we will describe how to measure the dark adaptation of the rods alone. Finally, we will show how the different adaptation rates of the rods and the cones can be explained by differences in the properties of the receptors' visual pigments.

Experiment 1: Determining a Two-Stage Dark Adaptation Curve In all of our dark adaptation experiments, we ask our observer to adjust the intensity of a small, flashing test light so he or she can just barely see it. In the first experiment, our observer looks at a small fixation point while paying attention to a flashing test light that is off to the side (Figure 2.21). Since the observer is looking directly at the fixation point, its image falls on the fovea, and the image of the test light falls in the periphery. Thus, the test light stimulates both rods and cones, and any adaptation measured with this test light should reflect the activity of both the rod and the cone receptors.

To measure dark adaptation, we first expose the observer to a fairly intense light, a process called **light adaptation,** and as the observer is

exposed to this adapting light, we determine her sensitivity to the test light by asking her to adjust its intensity until she can just barely see it (remember from Chapter 1, that this is the psychophysical procedure for measuring the threshold by the method of adjustment). The resulting sensitivity is labeled **light adapted sensitivity** in Figure 2.22.

After determining the light adapted sensitivity, we begin the process of dark adaptation by turning out the adapting light. The test light suddenly appears much brighter, and the observer therefore decreases its intensity back to threshold, so she can again just barely see it. As dark adaptation progresses, the light slowly begins to appear brighter, and the observer therefore decreases its intensity to keep it just at threshold. The solid line of Figure 2.22 shows the dark adaptation curve measured during 28 minutes in the dark. Downward movement of this curve indicates a lower *threshold*, or higher *sensitivity*. (Sensitivity = 1/threshold, so lower thresholds translate into higher sensitivities. This makes sense when we stop to think that a person needs to be highly sensitive to see the low intensities associated with low thresholds.)

We can see from the dark adaptation curve that the observer's sensitivity increases in two phases. It first increases for about 3–4 minutes after the light is extinguished and then levels off; then, after about 7–10 minutes, the sensitivity increases again and continues to do so for another 20–30 minutes. In this experiment, the sensitivity at the end of dark adaptation, labeled **dark adapted sensitivity,** is about 100,000 times greater than the light adapted sensitivity measured before dark adaptation.

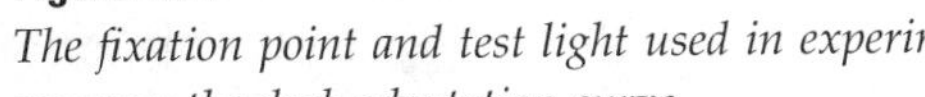

Fixation point X   ◯ Test light

Figure 2.21

The fixation point and test light used in experiments to measure the dark adaptation curve.

Introduction to Vision

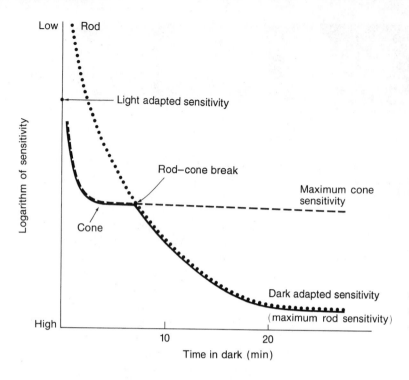

Figure 2.22
Dark adaptation curves. Actually, three curves are shown in this figure. The solid line shows the two-stage dark adaptation curve measured in experiment 1, with a cone branch at the beginning and a rod branch at the end. The dashed line shows the cone adaptation curve measured in experiment 2. The solid and dashed curves actually begin at the point marked "light adapted sensitivity," but there is a slight delay between the time the lights are turned off and the time the measurement of the curves begins. The dotted line shows the rod adaptation curve measured in experiment 3. Note that as these curves go down, sensitivity increases.

Experiment 2: Measuring Cone Adaptation To measure the adaptation of the cones, we repeat the first experiment but have the observer look directly at a test light so small that its entire image falls on the all-cone fovea. The resulting dark adaptation curve, indicated by the dashed curve in Figure 2.22, therefore reflects only the activity of the cones. This curve matches the initial phase of our original dark adaptation curve but does not include the second phase. Does this mean that the second phase is due to the rods? We can show that the answer to this question is "yes" by doing another experiment.

Experiment 3: Measuring Rod Adaptation We know that the dashed curve of Figure 2.22 is due only to cone adaptation because our test light was imaged on the all-cone fovea. To measure a pure rod dark-adaptation curve, we must change to a different observer. The reason is that no area of our "normal" observer's retina contains *only* rods (the fovea contains only cones and the pe-

riphery contains rods *and* cones). Thus, in our third experiment, we measure dark adaptation in a **rod monochromat**—a person who has a retina that, because of a genetic defect, contains *only* rods.

The dark adaptation curve of a rod monochromat is shown by the dotted curve in Figure 2.22 (Rushton, 1961). Note that the light adapted sensitivity of the rods is much lower than that of the cones, and that, as soon as dark adaptation begins, the rods begin to gain sensitivity immediately and continue to do so until reaching their final dark adapted level in about 25 minutes. The fact that the rods begin adapting to the dark immediately after the light is extinguished means that they are adapting during the cone phase of a normal person's dark adaptation curve; however, we don't see this early rod adaptation because the cones are more sensitive than the rods at the beginning of dark adaptation. In our normal observer, rod adaptation becomes visible only after the rods have become more sensitive than the cones, at the **rod–cone break** (Figure 2.22), about 7 minutes after the beginning of dark adaptation.

In addition to showing that the rods are responsible for the second phase of the dark adaptation curve and that they begin adapting immediately after the adapting light is extinguished, the rod monochromat's dark adaptation curve also shows the much slower adaptation of the rods compared to the cones. The rods take 20–30 minutes to achieve their maximum sensitivity, compared to only 3–4 minutes for the cones. We will now show that these differences in the rate of adaptation can be traced to differences in properties of the rods' and cones' visual pigments.

Visual Pigment Regeneration We have seen that the rod and cone receptors contain visual pigments made up of the small, light-sensitive retinal molecule attached to the much larger protein, opsin. When the retinal absorbs light, it changes shape and triggers the transduction process. It then separates from the opsin. This separation causes a change in the color of the retina from its original red color to orange, then to yellow, and finally to transparent (Color Plate 2.6), a process called **pigment bleaching**. Before this bleached molecule can again change light energy into electrical energy, the retinal and the opsin must reunite. This process, which is called **pigment regeneration,** occurs with the aid of enzymes supplied to the visual pigments by the nearby pigment epithelium (Figure 2.13).

Since the visual pigment changes from dark to light as it bleaches, and from light back to dark as it regenerates, we can measure the concentration of pigment in the eye by determining how much light the pigment absorbs. To understand how this measurement is done, look at Figure 2.23. A dim measuring beam with a constant intensity is projected into the eye. This beam passes through the retina, hits the back of the eye, and is reflected. On its way through the retina and back out, much of the beam's light is absorbed by visual pigment in the receptors, by other structures in the retina, and by the black

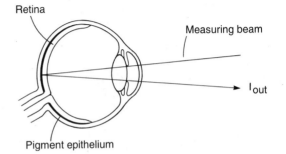

Figure 2.23

The principle underlying retinal densitometry. When visual pigment is exposed to light, the visual pigment molecules in the retina get lighter, so that they absorb less of the measuring beam, and the amount of light reflected from the eye (I_{out}) increases. As the molecules regenerate in the dark, they get darker, absorb more light, and decrease the amount of light reflected from the eye.

pigment epithelium behind the retina. But some light survives this absorption, and a beam with intensity I_{out} is reflected from the eye.

Now consider what happens when we bleach the visual pigment by exposing the eye to light. Bleaching turns the pigment molecules from dark to light. As more pigment molecules bleach, the pigment in the receptors gets lighter (more transparent) and therefore absorb less of the measuring beam. Since less light is being absorbed by the pigment, the intensity of the light reflected from the eye, I_{out}, increases. Therefore, by measuring I_{out}, we can determine how much pigment has been bleached. Conversely, if after bleaching we allow the visual pigment to regenerate in the dark, the pigment gets darker as time passes, and the intensity of the reflected beam, I_{out}, steadily decreases.

William Rushton (1961) used the above procedure, which is called **retinal densitometry,** to measure the concentration of cone and rod pigments during dark adaptation. He determined the rate of cone pigment regeneration by shining his measuring beam onto the fovea of a normal observer, and he determined the rate of rod pigment regeneration by shining his measuring beam onto the retina of an observer who was a rod monochromat. His results show that cone pigment takes 6 minutes to regenerate completely, while rod pigment takes over 30 minutes. Rushton also measured psychophysical dark adaptation curves in both observers and found that the rate of cone dark adaptation matched the rate of cone pigment regeneration, and that the rate of rod dark adaptation matched the rate of rod pigment regeneration.

Thus, Rushton's results support two ideas: (1) Visual pigment regeneration is responsible for the increased sensitivity of both rods and cones that occurs during dark adaptation, and (2) rods adapt slowly because rod pigment regenerates slowly. So, the next time you turn out the lights in your bedroom, remember that both the rod and the cone visual pigments begin regenerating as soon as you turn out the lights and that the regenerating pigments increase your sensitivity. It is this regeneration that enables you, 5 minutes later, to detect the light coming in under the door and, 15–20 minutes later, to detect dimly illuminated objects that were completely invisible just after you turned out the light.

Our dark adaptation experiments show that the ability to detect faint lights depends on whether we are using rod or cone receptors. We have two detector systems with different sensitivities and different rates of adaptation to the dark. The cones, our low-sensitivity detectors, are active in high-intensity situations where high sensitivity is not needed. In fact, a highly sensitive system might not be well suited to vision at high intensities because too much light might overwhelm the system and cause a perception of blinding glare. In contrast, the rods, our high-sensitivity detectors, are active at low light levels, when more sensitivity is needed. This two-detector system is, therefore, constructed to help us perceive across the range of intensities that we encounter in our environment.

In addition to operating best in different intensity ranges, the rods and cones also differ in a property called **spectral sensitivity**—sensitivity to different parts of the visible spectrum.

Spectral Sensitivity

To understand the concept of spectral sensitivity, we need to describe some basic facts about the nature of light. **Wavelength** is a property of light that is related to the fact that light energy travels in waves, much like the waves that are generated by dropping a pebble into a pool of water. The distance between the peaks of these light waves is the wavelength, and the wavelength of visible light is from about 360 nm (nm = nanometer = 10^{-9} m) to about 760 nm. Color Plate 2.1, which shows the **visible spectrum,** indicates that the color of light changes with its wavelength: short-wavelength light appearing blue, medium-wavelength light appearing green or yellow, and long-wavelength light appearing orange or red.

To measure the spectral sensitivity curve, we measure the relative threshold for seeing light at different wavelengths. To determine the threshold for seeing light as a function of wavelength, we have our observer look at test lights of different wavelengths, first 420 nm, then 440 nm, and so on, and at each wavelength we determine the threshold for seeing the light by using one of the psychophysical methods described in Chapter 1. If we do this for wavelengths across the visible spectrum, we obtain the curve in Figure 2.24a, which shows that the threshold for seeing light is lowest in the middle of the spectrum; that is, less light is needed to see wavelengths in the middle of the spectrum than to see wavelengths at either the short- or long-wavelength ends of the spectrum.

We can change threshold to **sensitivity** by our formula, sensitivity = 1/threshold, and if we do this, our relative threshold curve of Figure 2.24a becomes the relative sensitivity curve of Figure 2.24b, which is called a **spectral sensitivity curve.**

Now that we know how to determine the spectral sensitivity curve, let's compare the curve for cone vision with the curve for rod vision. Figure 2.24b is the curve for cone vision, since we determined the person's sensitivity at each wavelength as the person looked directly at the test light, so that it illuminated the fovea and stimulated only cone receptors.

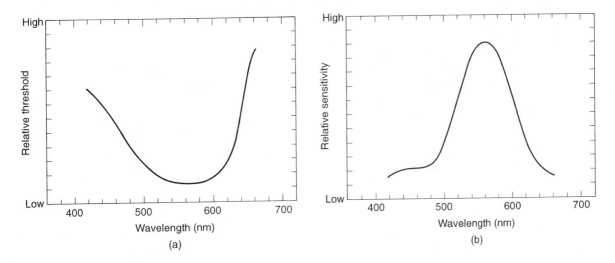

Figure 2.24
(a) The threshold for seeing a light versus wavelength. (b) If we take the reciprocal of the thresholds of the curve in (a) (reciprocal = 1/threshold), the curve turns over and becomes a plot of sensitivity versus wavelength, commonly known as a spectral sensitivity curve. *(Adapted from Wald, 1964.)*

To measure the spectral sensitivity of rod vision, we dark adapt the eye and present test lights to the peripheral retina. If the eye is dark adapted, presentation of threshold flashes results in the **rod spectral sensitivity curve**, shown in Figure 2.25, with the cone curve shown for comparison. This curve shows that the rods are more sensitive to short-wavelength light than are the cones, with the rods most sensitive to light of 500 nm and the cones most sensitive to light of 560 nm. This difference in the sensitivity of the rods and the cones to different wavelengths means that, as our vision shifts from our cones to our rods during dark adaptation, we should become relatively more sensitive to short-wavelength light, that is, light nearer the blue end of the spectrum.

We can illustrate this sensitivity shift by doing dark adaptation experiments using colored test flashes. Figure 2.26 shows dark adaptation curves determined by presenting either red or blue test flashes to the peripheral retina. You can see that the color of the test flash makes a big difference in the dark adaptation curve. Sensitivity measured with a red test flash, which contains only wavelengths above 620 nm, shows just a

small increase after the rod–cone break, while sensitivity measured with a deep blue test flash, which contains only wavelengths shorter than 485 nm, shows a large increase following the rod–cone break. Thus, when rod vision takes over from cone vision during dark adaptation, our sensitivity to short wavelengths increases more than our sensitivity to long wavelengths.

D E M O N S T R A T I O N

Experiencing the Shift from Cone Vision to Rod Vision

You can demonstrate the shift from cone to rod vision to yourself by returning to the closet (see Demonstration, "Spending Some Time in Your Closet") and making the following observations:

1. Before entering the closet, adapt one eye to the dark by closing it for about 10 minutes. Do this in the light so that your opened eye stays adapted to the light while your closed eye is adapting to the dark.

Introduction to Vision

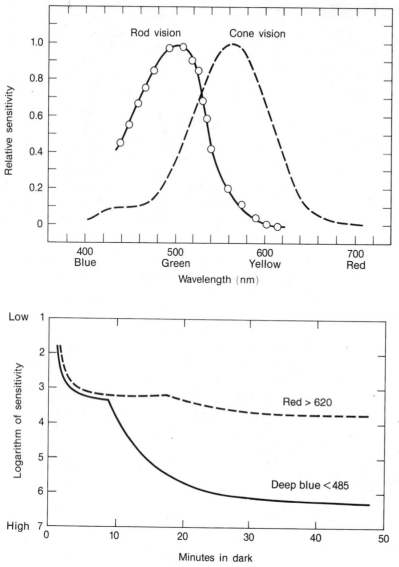

Figure 2.25
Spectral sensitivity curves for rod vision and cone vision. The maximum sensitivities of these two curves have been set equal to 1.0. However, as we saw in Figure 2.22, the relative sensitivities of the rods and the cones depend on the conditions of adaptation: The cones are more sensitive in the light, and the rods are more sensitive in the dark. The circles plotted on top of the rod curve represent the absorption spectrum of the rod visual pigment. (From Wald, 1964; Wald & Brown, 1958.)

Figure 2.26
Dark adaptation curves measured with long-wavelength (red) and short-wavelength (deep blue) test flashes. The red curve has only a small rod branch because the rods are relatively insensitive to red light. (From Chapanis, 1947.)

2. After completing step 1, enter the closet, and with the door open, observe Color Plate 2.5 with your light adapted eye, and compare the brightness of the blue and red flowers. When viewed with your light adapted eye in daylight illumination, the two flowers should appear approximately equal in brightness.

3. Close the door so that the closet is completely dark. Close your light adapted eye and open your dark adapted eye.

4. Slowly crack open the door until enough light is present for you to just see the flowers with your dark adapted eye. If you have kept the light intensity low enough, you will be seeing with your rods, and the flowers should appear gray rather than red and blue (since we perceive in black and white with our rods and in color with our cones, as we will see in Chapter 4). It is important to notice that the flowers' relative brightness should now be different from when you viewed them with your light adapted eye. The flower on the left should now appear slightly brighter than the flower on the right. (If you have forgotten how the flowers looked to your light adapted eye, close your dark adapted eye, open the door, and observe the flowers with your light adapted eye again.) ●

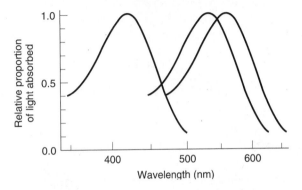

Figure 2.27

Absorption spectra of the three human cone pigments. (From Dartnall, Bowmaker, & Mollon, 1983.)

The brightness of the blue flower compared to the red one increases during dark adaptation because of the rods' greater sensitivity to short-wavelength light. This shift from cone to rod sensitivity is called the **Purkinje** (Pur-*kin*-jee) **shift**, after Johann Purkinje, who described this effect in 1825.

Pigment Absorption Spectra   The difference we have described between the rod and cone spectral sensitivity curves can be explained by differences in the absorption spectra of the rod and cone visual pigments. An **absorption spectrum** is a plot of the amount of light absorbed by a visual pigment versus the wavelength of the light. George Wald, who won the 1967 Nobel prize for his research on visual pigments, determined the absorption spectrum of human rod pigment by chemically extracting the pigment from the retinas of eyes donated to medical research (Wald & Brown, 1958). The resulting solution contained primarily rod pigment, since the rods contain about 99 percent of the visual pigment in the human retina. (Remember that there are 20 times more rods than cones in the retina and that the cones are smaller than the rods.)

When Wald and Paul Brown measured the amount of light absorbed by the pigment solution at wavelengths across the visible spectrum, they obtained the absorption spectrum plotted as open circles in Figure 2.25. The match between the pigment absorption spectrum and the rod spectral sensitivity curve indicates that the spectral sensitivity of rod vision is due to the absorption of light by the rod visual pigment.

How does the spectral sensitivity curve for cone vision compare to the absorption spectrum

of cone visual pigment? To answer this question we need to solve a difficult problem: How can we measure the absorption spectrum of cone pigment if 99 percent of the pigment that we chemically extract from the retina is rod pigment? The solution to this problem was provided by the development of a technique called **microspectro-photometry.**

In microspectrophotometry, rather than shining a beam of light through a solution of visual pigment that has been chemically extracted from millions of receptors, we shine a very small beam of light through the pigment while it is still inside an individual receptor (Brown & Wald, 1964). Figure 2.27 shows the pigment spectra measured using the microspectrophotometry procedure (Dartnall, Bowmaker, & Mollon, 1983). There are three curves because there are three different cone pigments, each contained in its own receptor. The **short-wavelength pigment** absorbs light best at about 419 nm; the **medium-wavelength pigment** absorbs light best at about 531 nm; and the **long-wavelength pigment** absorbs light best at about 558 nm.

How do we get from short-, medium-, and long-wavelength cone pigments that absorb at 419, 531, and 558 nm, respectively, to a psychophysical spectral sensitivity curve that peaks at

Introduction to Vision

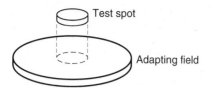

Figure 2.28

Stimulus arrangement for Stiles's two-color threshold method. The small test spot is superimposed on the larger adapting field. The wavelength of the adapting field is kept constant, and the wavelength of the test spot is changed to measure the spectral sensitivity at wavelengths across the spectrum.

560 nm? Apparently these three cone pigments combine to result in the spectral sensitivity curve. This result was demonstrated by comparing the pigment absorption spectra to spectral sensitivity curves determined using the **two-color threshold method** introduced by W. S. Stiles (1953). In this method, the spectral sensitivity curve is measured by determining the sensitivity to test lights presented on top of an **adapting field** (Figure 2.28).

The purpose of the adapting field is to bleach away two of the cone pigments and spare one. For example, an adapting field containing long-wavelength light bleaches the medium- and long-wavelength pigments and leaves the short-wavelength pigment. Each spectral sensitivity curve that Stiles obtained using this method matched the absorption spectra of the cone pigment that wasn't bleached, a result that supports the idea that the spectral sensitivity curve of the cones is due to the combined action of the three cone pigments (Bowmaker & Dartnall, 1980).

From our description of rod and cone spectral sensitivity and dark adaptation, we can see that the properties of rod and cone visual pigments play an important role in shaping our perceptions. The idea that our perceptions are determined by the properties of sensory systems (such as the characteristics of the visual pigments) is a theme that will continue throughout

the book. And we will see that perception is determined not only by the properties of the visual pigments, but by how neurons respond and how they are connected to one another. To describe how neural connections influence perception, we will now introduce the idea that the electrical signals transmitted along nerve fibers are *processed* by these neurons.

THE PROCESSING OF NEURAL SIGNALS

What does it mean to say that neural signals are "processed"? One way to understand the idea of neural processing is to consider what it means to say that *information* is processed. When information is processed it is *analyzed* and *transformed*. For example, consider how a foreign language that you have never heard before sounds to you. Most people perceive an unfamiliar foreign language as an unbroken string of sounds. There is some truth to this perception because, if we analyze the physical speech signal, we find that, unless a person purposely pauses, there are usually no breaks between words.

Compare your perception of the unfamiliar foreign language with your perception of English or any other language you understand. When perceiving your own language, you perceive *individual words*. To accomplish this perception, you have processed the unbroken speech signal by analyzing the sounds and taking the *meanings* of the words into account. This analysis based on meaning has enabled you to transform the sounds you hear into individual units.

This example of processing is taken from speech perception. Neural processing occurs before we actually perceive, but it involves similar principles. Neural signals—the nerve impulses transmitted down nerve fibers—are analyzed

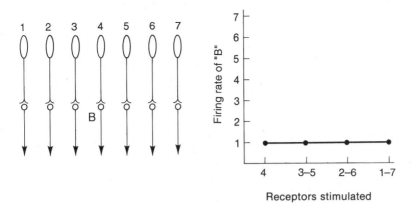

Figure 2.29

A linear circuit (left) and the responses of neuron B generated as we increase the number of receptors stimulated (right). Stimulating receptor 4 causes neuron B to fire, but stimulating the other neurons has no effect since they are not connected with neuron B.

and transformed so that the resulting neural signal becomes easier for the perceptual system to understand and therefore to use in creating perceptions. To illustrate how this neural processing occurs, we will now describe some basic principles of neural circuits.

Introduction to Neural Circuits

In describing the basic structure of a sensory system, we saw that strings of neurons are connected by synapses. These strings of neurons and their synapses enable nerve impulses to travel over long distances, but they also serve another purpose. Synapses are used by the nervous system to "process" electrical signals as they travel from the receptors to the brain. The electrical signals generated in the receptors are processed by the network of nerve fibers, or **neural circuits,** through which the signals travel. To illustrate how this processing works, we will compare how three different neural circuits affect a neuron's response to a light stimulus of different lengths.

We begin with a simple neural circuit and then increase the complexity of this circuit in two stages, noting how this increased complexity affects the circuit's response to the stimulus. In these circuits we represent receptors by ellipses (◯), cell bodies by circles (○), nerve fibers by

straight lines (—), excitatory synapses by Y's (⤙), and inhibitory synapses by T's (⊣). (See page 11 to review excitation and inhibition.) For this example we will assume that the receptors respond to light, although the principles we will establish hold for any form of stimulation.

First, let's consider the circuit in Figure 2.29. We call this circuit a *linear circuit* because the signal generated by each receptor travels straight to the next neuron, and no other neurons are involved. Also, all of the synapses in this circuit are excitatory. We will stimulate the circuit by first illuminating receptor 4 with a spot of light. We then change this spot into a bar of light by adding light to cover receptors 3, 4, and 5 (3–5), then receptors 2–6, and finally receptors 1–7. When we measure the response of neuron B and plot this response in the graph to the right of the circuit, we find that neuron B fires when we stimulate receptor 4, but that stimulating the other receptors has no effect on neuron B, since it is still receiving exactly the same input from receptor 4. For the linear circuit, therefore, the firing of neuron B simply indicates that its receptor has been stimulated and doesn't provide any information about the length of the bar of light.

We now increase the complexity of the circuit by adding **convergence,** as shown in the circuit in Figure 2.30. Convergence occurs when two or more other neurons synapse onto a single neuron.

Introduction to Vision

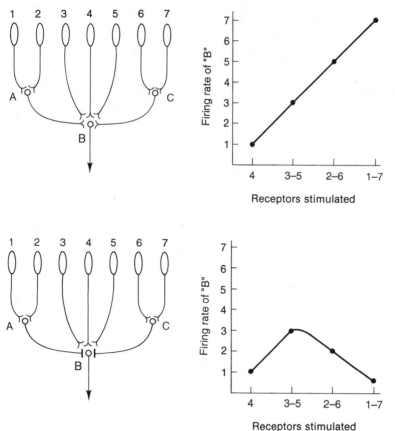

Figure 2.30

When we add convergence to the circuit, so that B receives inputs from all of the receptors, increasing the size of the stimulus increases the size of neuron B's response.

Figure 2.31

When we add inhibition to the circuit, so that stimulation of receptors 1, 2, 6, and 7 now inhibits B, neuron B responds best to stimulation of receptors 3–5.

Thus, in this circuit, receptors 1 and 2 converge onto neuron A; 3, 4, and 5 converge onto B; 6 and 7 converge onto C; and A and C converge onto B. As in the previous circuit, all of the synapses are excitatory, but with the addition of convergence, one cell collects information from a number of other cells. We again focus our attention on neuron B, which, because of convergence, collects information from all of the receptors. When we monitor the firing rate of neuron B as we increase the length of our stimulating light, we find that each time we increase the length of the stimulus, neuron B's firing rate increases, as shown in the graph in Figure 2.30. This occurs because stimulating more receptors increases the amount of excitatory transmitter released onto neuron B. Thus, in this circuit, neuron B's response provides information about the length of the stimulus.

We now increase the circuit's complexity further by adding two inhibitory synapses to create the circuit in Figure 2.31, in which neurons A and C inhibit neuron B. Now consider what happens as we increase the number of receptors stimulated. The spot of light stimulates receptor 4, which, through its excitatory connection, increases the firing rate of neuron B. Extending the illumination to include receptors 3–5 adds the output of two more excitatory synapses to B and increases its firing further. So far, this circuit is behaving similarly to the circuit in Figure 2.30. However, when we extend the illumination further to include receptors 2–6, something different happens: Receptors 2 and 6 stimulate neurons A and C, which, in turn, inhibit neuron B, decreasing its firing rate. Increasing the size of the stimulus further to cover receptors 1–7 increases the inhibition and again decreases the response of neuron B.

In this circuit, therefore, neuron B fires weakly to stimuli that are short (only receptor 4) or long (receptors 1–7) and fires best to a stimulus of medium length (receptors 3–5). By using convergence and inhibition we have created a neuron that responds best to a bar of light of a specific length. The neurons that synapse with neuron B are therefore doing much more than simply transmitting electrical signals; they are also processing the signals in a way that enables neuron B to extract information about the stimulus presented to the receptors. In the next section, we will see how the kinds of neural processing shown in Figures 2.30 and 2.31 actually occur in the retina.

Neural Processing in the Retina: Introduction to Receptive Fields

We have seen that the first action of the retina is to transduce light energy into electrical energy. Once this transduction occurs, signals travel through a network of bipolar, horizontal, and amacrine cells and finally reach the ganglion cells, which then transmit these signals out of the back of the eye. All of the ganglion cell fibers leaving the eye together form the optic nerve.

Inspection of the network of retinal neurons pictured in Figure 2.3 indicates that this circuit contains convergence, with 9 receptors (R) converging onto 6 bipolar cells (B), which converge onto 4 ganglion cells. In actuality, the convergence is much greater than this, since in each human retina 126 million receptors converge onto 1 million ganglion cells (Figure 2.32). Thus, on the average, every ganglion cell receives converging signals from 126 receptors. Inhibition also occurs in the retina, much of it transmitted by the horizontal and amacrine cells.

We can measure the results of the retina's convergence and inhibition by recording from a ganglion cell fiber and determining how that

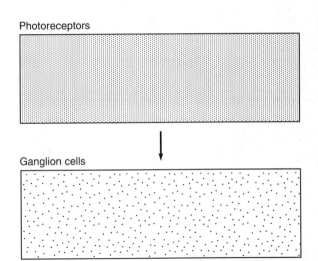

Figure 2.32

Mosaics of retinal neurons in the periphery of the rabbit retina. Each dot in the top panel represents three receptors, and each dot in the bottom panel represents one ganglion cell. The large difference between the number of receptors and the number of ganglion cells means that signals from many receptors converge onto each ganglion cell. (From Masland, 1988.)

fiber responds to stimulation of the receptors. In practice, many experiments like this have been done on cats and monkeys, with a setup like the one shown in Figure 2.33, in which stimuli are presented on a screen at which the animal (a cat, in this case) is looking. Since the cat's eye is kept stationary, presenting stimuli on the screen is equivalent to shining lights on different places on the cat's retina, because for each point on the screen, there is a corresponding point on the cat's retina (Figure 2.34).

When we present the spot of light at different places on the screen, we find that no stimulus presented anywhere in area A causes a change in the activity of our neuron (Figure 2.35a). Eventually, however, we find that any stimulus in area B causes an **excitatory** or **on-response,** an increase in the neuron's firing rate when the light is turned on (Figure 2.35b). We mark this area with +'s to indicate that the response to stimulation from this area

Introduction to Vision

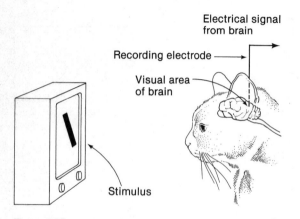

Figure 2.33
Recording electrical signals from the visual cortex of an anesthetized cat. The bar-shaped stimulus on the screen causes nerve cells in the cortex to fire, and a recording electrode picks up the signals generated by these nerve cells. In an actual experiment, the cat is anesthetized and its head is held in place for accurate positioning.

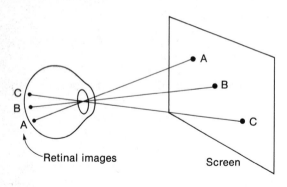

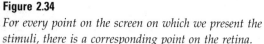

Figure 2.34
For every point on the screen on which we present the stimuli, there is a corresponding point on the retina.

is excitatory. We also find that a stimulus presented anywhere in area C causes an **inhibitory response,** a decrease in nerve firing when the stimulus is turned on, plus an **off-response,** a burst of firing when the stimulus is turned off (Figure 2.35c) (Kuffler, 1953; Schiller, 1992). We mark this area with −'s to indicate that responses

to stimuli from this area are inhibitory. Areas B and C, taken together, are called the **receptive field** of the neuron; that is, *the region of the retina that, when stimulated, influences the firing rate of the neuron.*

The receptive field in Figure 2.35 is called a **center–surround receptive field** because it responds one way to stimulation of the center area and another way to stimulation of the area surrounding this center area. This particular receptive field is an **excitatory-center–inhibitory-surround** receptive field, and there are also **inhibitory-center–excitatory-surround** receptive fields.

The fact that the center and the surround of the receptive field respond in opposite ways causes an effect called **center–surround antagonism.** This effect is illustrated in Figure 2.36, which shows what happens as we increase the size of a spot of light presented to the ganglion cell's receptive field. A small spot that is presented to the excitatory center of the receptive field causes a small increase in the rate of nerve firing (a), and increasing the light's size so that it covers the entire center of the receptive field increases the cell's response, as shown in (b). (Notice that we have used the term *cell* in place of *neuron* here. Since neurons are a type of cell, *cell* is often substituted for *neuron* in the research literature. In this book, we will often use these terms interchangeably.)

However, center–surround antagonism comes into play when we increase the size of the light further, so that it begins to cover the inhibitory area, as in (c) and (d). Stimulation of the inhibitory surround counteracts the center's excitatory response, causing a decrease in the neuron's firing rate. Thus, this neuron responds best to a spot of light that is the size of the receptive field center.

The behavior of this neuron is similar to the behavior of neuron B in the circuit with convergence and inhibition in Figure 2.31, since firing first increases in response to increases in stimulus size but then decreases when the stimulus becomes large enough to create inhibition. The circuit in Figure 2.37 is similar to this circuit, but

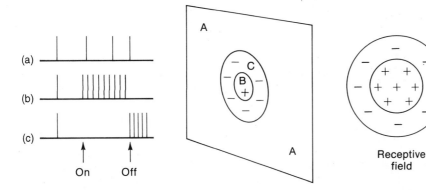

Figure 2.35

Response of a ganglion cell in the cat's retina to stimulation (a) outside the cell's receptive field (area A on the screen to the right); (b) inside the excitatory area of the cell's receptive field (area B); and (c) inside the inhibitory area of the cell's receptive field (area C). The excitatory-center–inhibitory-surround receptive field is shown on the far right without the screen.

we have added another layer of cells to make it more similar to the retina. While still vastly over-simplified compared to the retina's actual cir-cuitry, Figure 2.37 illustrates the convergence and inhibition that, in the retina, produce center–surround receptive fields.

We have seen that neural processing creates the center–surround receptive fields of the ret-ina's ganglion cells. In the next chapter we will see that this neural processing continues as the visual signal travels toward the brain and that this processing creates receptive fields that re-spond best to stimuli far more complex than small spots of light. Before moving on to consider these more complex receptive fields, however, it is important that we keep in mind that this neural

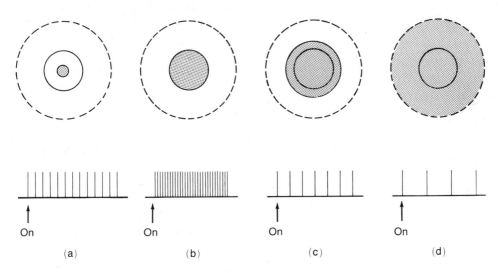

Figure 2.36

Response of an excitatory-center–inhibitory-surround receptive field. The area stimulated with light is indicated by the shading, and the response to the stimulus is indicated by the records below each receptive field. As the stimulus size increases inside the excitatory region of the receptive field in (a) and (b), the response increases. As the stimulus increases further, so that it covers the inhibitory region of the receptive field in (c) and (d), the response decreases. This cell responds best to stimulation that is the size of the receptive field center. (Adapted from Hubel & Wiesel, 1961.)

Introduction to Vision

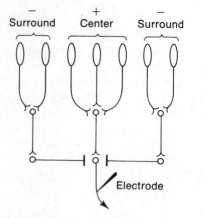

Figure 2.37

A neural circuit that would result in a center–surround receptive field. Signals from the surround receptors reach the cell from which we are recording via inhibitory synapses, while signals from the center receptors reach the cell via an excitatory synapse. Thus, stimulation of the center receptors increases the firing rate recorded by our electrode, and stimulation of the surround receptors decreases the firing rate. In the retina these inhibitory signals are carried by horizontal and amacrine cells.

processing has specific effects on perception. We will therefore end this chapter by considering some of these effects.

NEURAL PROCESSING AND PERCEPTION

When we did our dark adaptation experiments, we saw that after we spent about 15 minutes in the dark, our rod vision became much more sensitive than our cone vision. One reason for this may be that the rod's visual pigments are more sensitive to light than the cone's pigments. However, the major reason for the rod's greater dark adapted sensitivity has to do with differences in the degree of convergence of the rod and cone receptors.

Neural Wiring and Sensitivity

As there are 120 million rods and 6 million cones in the retina, and as the signals from these millions of receptors converge onto the 1 million ganglion cells that carry signals out of the retina in the optic nerve, it is clear that the signals from many rods and many cones must converge onto far fewer ganglion cells. It is also clear from these numbers that rods converge much more than cones; each ganglion cell receives signals from an average of about 120 rods, but from only about 6 cones. This difference between rod and cone convergence becomes even greater when we consider foveal cones, many of which have "private lines" to ganglion cells, so that each ganglion cell receives signals from only one cone—a complete lack of convergence.

How does the difference in rod and cone convergence increase the dark adapted sensitivity of the rods? We can understand how neural wiring contributes to this greater sensitivity by doing some demonstrations with the two circuits in Figure 2.38, in which five rod receptors converge onto one ganglion cell and five cone receptors each synapse on their own ganglion cells. We have left out the bipolar, horizontal, and amacrine cells in these circuits for simplicity, but the conclusions of our demonstrations will not be affected by these omissions.

In our first demonstration we ask the question: How intense must a stimulus be to cause the rods' and cones' ganglion cells to fire? To answer this question, let's assume that we can present small spots of light to individual rods and cones. (Although it isn't possible to do this in the human retina because of the optics of the eye and the small sizes of the receptors, we will assume that we can do it for the purposes of our demonstration.) We will also make the following additional assumptions:

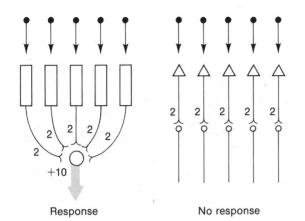

Response   No response

Figure 2.38

The wiring of the rods (left) and the cones (right). The dot and arrow above each receptor represents a "spot" of light that stimulates the receptor. The numbers represent the number of response units generated by the rods and the cones in response to a spot intensity of 2.0. At this intensity the rod ganglion cell receives 10 units of excitation and fires, but each cone ganglion cell receives only 2 units and therefore does not fire. Thus, the rods' greater spatial summation enables them to cause ganglion cell firing at lower stimulus intensities than the cones'.

1. One unit of light intensity causes one unit of response in a receptor.

2. A ganglion cell must receive ten "response units" to fire.

3. When a ganglion cell fires, we see.

We begin our demonstration by presenting to each of our receptors spots of light with intensity = 1.0. In this situation the rod ganglion cell receives 5 response units, 1 from each of the 5 receptors, and each of the cone ganglion cells receives 1.0 response units, 1 from each receptor. Thus, when intensity = 1.0, neither the rod nor the cone ganglion cells fire. If, however, we increase the intensity to 2.0, the rod ganglion cell receives 2.0 response units from each of its 5

receptors, for a total of 10 response units. This total reaches the threshold for the rods' ganglion cell, it fires, and we see the light. Meanwhile, at the same intensity, the cones' ganglion cells are still far below threshold, each receiving only 2 response units. For the cones' ganglion cells to fire, we must increase the intensity to 10.0.

The results of this experiment demonstrate that one reason for the rods' high sensitivity compared to the cones' is the rods' greater **spatial summation;** that is, many rods summate, or add up, their responses by feeding into the same ganglion cell. The cones, on the other hand, summate less, because only one or a few cones feed into a single ganglion cell. The greater spatial summation of the rods is reflected in the greater sizes of the receptive fields in the periphery of the retina, which contains mostly rods, compared to sizes of the receptive fields in the fovea, which contains only cones (Martin, 1991).

Although spatial summation accounts for much of the rods' superior sensitivity, the rods also have other properties that contribute to their high sensitivity. For one thing, the rods are larger than the cones, and therefore a rod receptor absorbs more light than a cone receptor. In addition, individual rods generate larger electrical responses than individual cones (Barlow & Mollon, 1982).

Neural Wiring and Acuity

The reason you often find it difficult to immediately see your friend's face in a crowded room is that, to recognize a face, you must look directly at it. Only all-cone foveal vision has good visual acuity—the ability to see details—so only the particular face at which you are looking is seen in enough detail to be recognized, while the rest of the faces in the crowd fall on the rod-rich peripheral retina and can't be recognized. You find your friend only after you move your eyes to bring the image of his or her face onto your foveas.

Foveal versus Peripheral Acuity

You can demonstrate the superiority of foveal vision to peripheral vision by looking at the X in the line of letters below and, without moving your eyes, seeing how many letters you can see to the left. If you do this without cheating (no fair moving your eyes!), you will find that you can read only a few letters. Because of the low visual acuity of the rods, you cannot read letters that are imaged very far into the periphery.

D I H C N R L A Z I F W N S M Q P Z K D **X**   ●

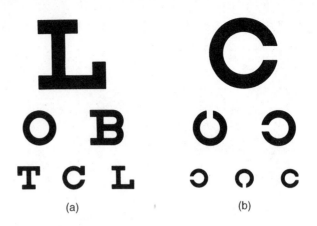

(a)   (b)

Figure 2.39

Snellen letters (a) and Landolt rings (b) used to test visual acuity. (From Riggs, 1965.)

Visual acuity can be measured in a number of ways, one of which is to determine how far apart two dots have to be before a space can be seen between them. We do this measurement by presenting a pair of closely spaced dots and asking whether there are one or two dots. We can also measure acuity by determining how large the elements of a checkerboard or a pattern of alternating black and white bars must be for the pattern to be detected. The letters of the Snellen chart and the Landolt rings in Figure 2.39 are perhaps the most familiar ways of measuring acuity. The observer's task is to identify the Snellen letters or to indicate the location of the gaps in the Landolt rings.

We can measure the differences between rod and cone visual acuity by comparing a person's ability to detect test patterns in the fovea and in the periphery (as in the demonstration above) or by measuring how acuity changes during dark adaptation. When we do this, we find that visual acuity drops (that is, details must be larger in order to be seen) as we move from fovea to periphery and as vision changes from cone to rod function during dark adaptation. Thus, although rod vision is much more sensitive to light than cone vision, it is much worse than cone vision at detecting small details.

To understand how differences in rod and cone wiring explain the cones' greater acuity, let's do another hypothetical demonstration, this time stimulating the circuits in Figure 2.40 with two spots of light, each with an intensity of 10. The question we ask in this experiment is: Under what conditions can we tell that there are two separate spots of light? We begin by presenting the two spots next to each other, as in Figure 2.40a. When we do this, the rod ganglion cell fires and the two adjacent cone ganglion cells fire. The firing of the single rod (ganglion cell) provides no hint that two spots were presented, and the firing of two adjacent cone ganglion cells could have been caused by a single large spot. However, when we spread the two spots apart, as in Figure 2.40b, the output of the cones signals two spots, because there is a silent ganglion cell between the two that are firing, but the output of the rods still provides no information that would enable us to say that there are two spots. Thus, the rods' convergence decreases its ability to resolve details (Teller, 1990).

Perceiving Brightness and Darkness

We have seen how neural processing can explain our ability to detect dim lights and our ability to

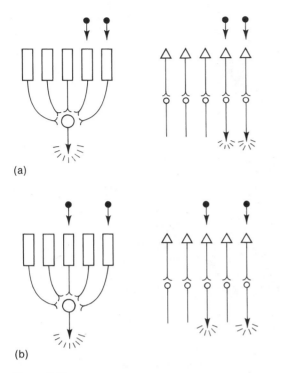

(a)

(b)

Figure 2.40

Neural circuits for the rods (left) and the cones (right). The receptors are being stimulated by two spots of light. See text for details.

detect small details. Both of these cases involve perceptions that occur near threshold. But we can also show how neural processing influences perceptions, such as the brightness of a surface, that occur far above threshold.

DEMONSTRATION

Simultaneous Contrast

When you look at the two center squares in Figure 2.41, the one on the left appears much darker than the one on the right. Now, punch two holes 2 inches apart in a card or a piece of paper, place the two holes over the squares, and compare your perception of the squares as seen through the holes. ●

In this demonstration, you may have been surprised to see that the two squares look the same when their backgrounds are masked by the paper, even though they look very different when the whole figure is visible. Perceiving the two squares on different backgrounds as being

Figure 2.41

Simultaneous contrast. The two center squares reflect the same amount of light into your eyes but, because of the simultaneous contrast effect, look different.

Introduction to Vision

lateral eye →

Figure 2.42

A Limulus, *or horseshoe crab. Its large eyes are made up of hundreds of ommatidia, each containing a single receptor.*

different, even though they are in fact physically identical, is called the **simultaneous contrast** effect. Psychophysically, we can say that this effect is caused by the difference in the backgrounds, but what is the physiological mechanism behind this effect?

This question was answered by Kuffer Hartline, Henry Wagner, and Floyd Ratliff (1956), who used the creature in Figure 2.42—the horseshoe crab, or *Limulus*—to demonstrate an effect of neural processing called **lateral inhibition.** Hartline and his co-workers chose the *Limulus* because of the structure of its eye. The *Limulus* eye is made up of hundreds of tiny structures called *ommatidia,* and each **ommatidium** has a small lens on the eye's surface that is located directly over a single receptor (see Other Worlds of Perception, "Animal Eyes"). Since each lens and receptor is roughly the diameter of a pencil point, it is possible to illuminate and record from a single receptor without illuminating its neighboring receptors.

When Hartline et al. recorded from the nerve fiber of receptor A, as shown in Figure 2.43, they found that illumination of that receptor caused a large response (Figure 2.43a). But when they added illumination to the three nearby receptors at B, the response of receptor A decreased (Figure 2.43b). They also found that increasing the illumination of B further decreased A's response (Figure 2.43c). Thus, illumination of the neighboring receptors *inhibited* the firing of receptor A. This inhibition is called *lateral inhibition* because it is transmitted laterally, across the retina, in a structure called the **lateral plexus.**

What does the result of the Hartline et al. experiment on the *Limulus* have to do with the perception of simultaneous contrast in humans? The answer to this question lies in the similarity between the lateral plexus of the *Limulus* and the horizontal and amacrine cells of the human retina (Figure 2.3). All of these structures transmit signals *across* the retina, thereby providing a pathway for transmitting inhibitory signals from one receptor to another.

Figure 2.44 shows how lateral inhibition can explain the simultaneous contrast effect demonstrated in Figure 2.41. According to the lateral inhibition explanation of simultaneous contrast, the light background on the left darkens our

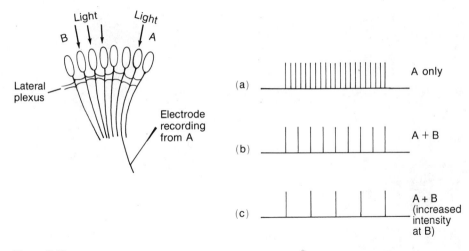

Figure 2.43

A demonstration of lateral inhibition in the Limulus. *The records on the right show the response recorded by the electrode recording from the nerve fiber of receptor A when receptor A is stimulated and (a) no other receptors are stimulated, (b) the receptors at B are stimulated simultaneously, and (c) the receptors at B are stimulated at an increased intensity. (Adapted from Ratliff, 1965.)*

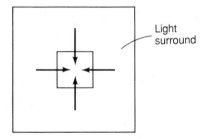

Figure 2.44

The image cast on the retina by the left side of the simultaneous contrast demonstration of Figure 2.41. The light surround stimulates receptors surrounding the dark square, and this stimulation sends lateral inhibition to the area stimulated by the square, as indicated by the arrows. This inhibition decreases the firing caused by the square and makes it appear darker.

perception of its square because the receptors stimulated by this background send inhibition to the receptors stimulated by the square. The dark background on the right does not, however, have

this darkening effect because the receptors stimulated by this background send little inhibition to the receptors stimulated by the square.

Figure 2.45 shows the **Hermann grid**, which illustrates another effect of lateral inhibition. Notice the darkening at the intersections where the white lines intersect. You can prove to yourself that these darkenings are not actually present in the image by looking directly at an intersection, or by covering two of the rows of black squares with pieces of paper. Applying the same principle used to explain simultaneous contrast, you can see that receptors stimulated by the intersections receive lateral inhibition from four sides, whereas receptors stimulated by other parts of the line receive lateral inhibition from only two sides. The greater lateral inhibition received by the receptors at the intersection causes the perceptual darkening.

Another effect that can be explained by lateral inhibition is the **Mach band** effect. This effect was studied in the 1880s by the German scientist Ernst Mach, who studied displays like the one in

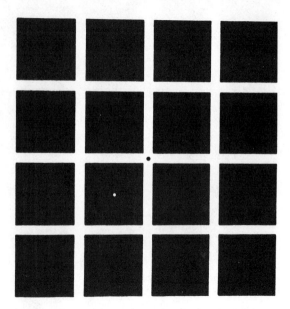

Figure 2.45

Hermann grid pattern. See text for viewing instructions.
(From Verheijen, 1961.)

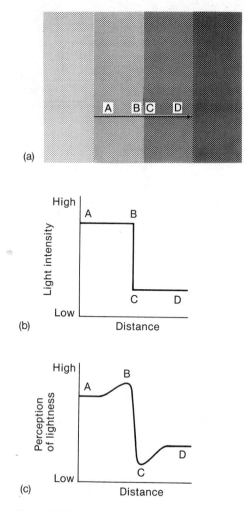

(a)

(b)

(c)

Figure 2.46

(a) Mach bands at a contour. Just to the left of the contour, near B, a faint light band can be perceived, and just to the right at C, a faint dark band can be perceived. (b) A plot showing the physical intensity distribution of the light, as measured with a light meter. (c) A plot showing the perceptual effect described in (a). The bump in the curve at B indicates the light Mach band, and the dip in the curve at C indicates the dark Mach band. Note that the bumps are not present in the physical intensity distribution (b).

Figure 2.46a. If we measure the intensity across the stripes in Figure 2.46a with a light meter by starting at A and measuring the amount of light reflected by the stripes between A and D, we obtain the result shown in Figure 2.46b. We see that the intensity distribution between A and B is flat; that is, the same amount of light is reflected across the entire distance between A and B. Then, the intensity drops sharply at the border and stays at a constant lower level between C and D.

Although our light meter tells us that the intensities remain constant across the two stripes, we *perceive* something very different. At B there appears to be a band that is brighter than the rest of the left stripe, and at C there is a band that is dimmer than the rest of the right stripe. These bright and dim bands, which are the Mach bands, are represented graphically in Figure 2.46c.

THE VISUAL PROCESS

The stimulus for vision is visible light, a small band of energy contained within the electromagnetic spectrum. The electromagnetic spectrum stretches from X-rays, which have wavelengths as short at 10^{-12} meters, to radio waves, which have wavelengths as long as 10^{+4} meters (Plate 2.1). Located between these extremes, visible light has wavelengths on the order of 10^{-6} meters. Expanding this visible part of the electromagnetic spectrum reveals the familiar array of colors seen by humans with normal color vision (see text pages 58 and 134).

The visual process begins when visible light enters the eye and forms images on the retina, a thin layer of neurons lining the back of the eye (Plate 2.2). The magnified view of the retina shown to the right in Plate 2.2 reveals that the retina consists of a number of different types of neurons, including the rod and cone receptors, which transform light energy into electrical

energy, and fibers that transmit electrical energy out of the retina in the optic nerve. (See Figure 2.3 on page 43 for a more detailed picture of the different retinal neurons.)

The cross section of the rhesus monkey retina in Plate 2.3 illustrates the layered nature of the retina. In this picture, light is coming from the top, and the receptors are facing the dark-colored pigment epithelium (shown here in the lower-right corner) that lines the back of the retina. We can clearly see the layering by looking at the cell bodies of the retinal neurons. The red circles near the bottom of the picture are the cell bodies of the receptors (labeled R in Figure 2.3), the circles in the next layer are the cell bodies of the bipolar cells (labeled B in Figure 2.3), and the circles in the top, bluish layer are the cell bodies of the ganglion cells (labeled G in Figure 2.3). (Page 43)

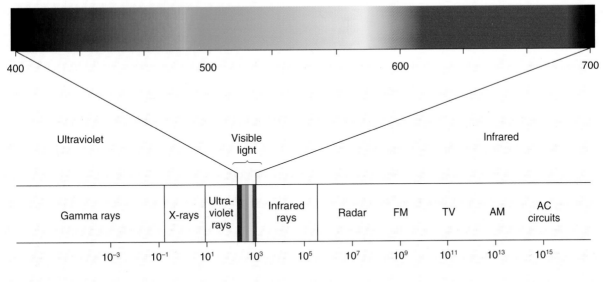

Wavelength (nm)

Plate 2.1

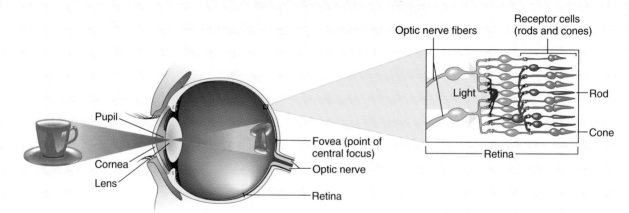

Plate 2.2

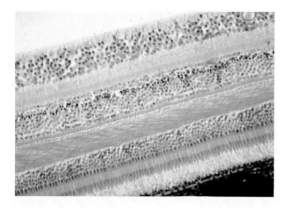

Plate 2.3

Looking down on the receptors reveals the "mosaic" of rods and cones shown close up in Plate 2.4a and over a larger area in Plate 2.4b. In these pictures of the periphery of a monkey's retina, the rods are the small circles and the cones are the larger circles. The cones appear larger because the retina has been sliced across the receptors' inner segments (see Figure 2.3, page 43, and Figure 2.8, page 47), which are fatter in the cones than in the rods. Since this is the peripheral retina, there are many more rods than cones (page 49). A special dye, which affects only the cones that absorb light at the short-wavelength end of the spectrum, has stained them yellow. These cones, as well as the cones which absorb longer wavelengths, are discussed on pages 61, 138, and 142–143.

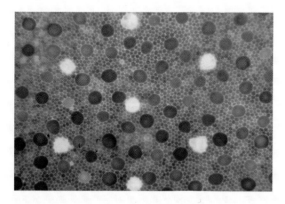

Plate 2.4a

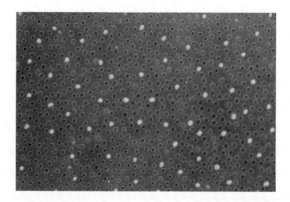

Plate 2.4b

Plate 2.5

The rods and cones have different properties, with the rod system being more sensitive to shorter wavelengths than the cone system. You can demonstrate this perceptually by following the Demonstration, "Experiencing the Shift from Cone Vision to Rod Vision," on page 59. If you close one eye to adapt it to the dark while leaving the other eye open, your perception of the brightness of the red and blue flowers in Plate 2.5 should change when you alternate eyes. When viewed with the dark adapted eye, the blue flower should appear brighter compared to the red one than it does when viewed with the light adapted eye. This shift in perception is caused by the shift from cone to rod vision that occurs during dark adaptation.

Both the rod and cone receptors contain light-sensitive visual pigment that reacts to light by changing shape and generating an electrical signal. This change in shape is accompanied by a change in the color of the pigment, which is called *bleaching*. In Plate 2.6, the left photograph shows a frog retina taken immediately after a light was turned on, so little bleaching has occurred and the retina appears red. When the retina is placed on a flat surface, as shown here, its edges bend over, causing a double layer of retina and a deeper red color around the edges. The black spots are small pieces of the pigment epithelium, the cell layer on which the retina rests when in the eye. The middle photograph was taken after some bleaching, so the retina is

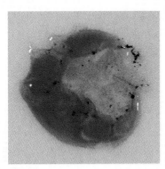
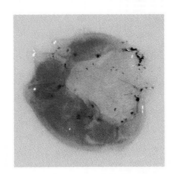
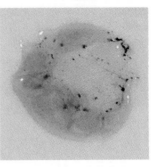

Plate 2.6

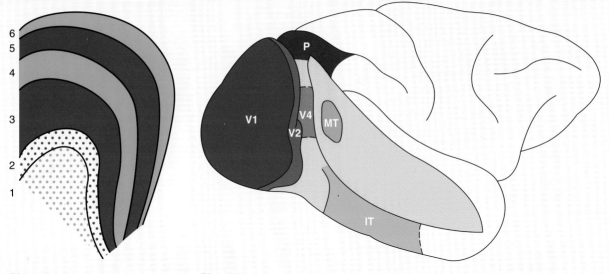

Plate 2.7　　　　　　　　　　　**Plate 2.8**

lighter red; in the right photograph, further bleaching has resulted in a light orange appearance. When bleaching is complete, the orange fades and the retina becomes transparent. If this retina were still in the frog's eye, the transparent retina would regain its red color as the pigment regenerated in the dark; however, little regeneration occurs when the retina is dissected from the eye, as in these photographs. (pages 48 and 57)

The signals generated in the receptors trigger electrical signals in the next layer of the retina, the bipolar cells, and these signals are transmitted through the various neurons in the retina, until eventually they are transmitted out of the eye by ganglion cell fibers. These ganglion cell fibers flow out of the back of the eye and become fibers in the optic nerve. Most of these optic nerve fibers reach the lateral geniculate nucleus (LGN), the first major way station on the way to the brain. The LGN, shown in cross section in Plate 2.7, has been colored to indicate two types of organization: (1) *Organization by eye*. Layers 2, 3, and 5 (red) receive inputs from the ipsilateral eye, the eye on the same side of the body as the LGN, and layers 1, 4, and 6 (blue) receive inputs from the contralateral eye, the eye on the opposite side of the body; (2) *Organization by type of ganglion cell*. Layers 1 and 2 (dots), called the *magno* layer, receive inputs from the large M-ganglion cells; layers 3, 4, 5, and 6 (solid), called the *parvo* layer, receive inputs from the smaller P-ganglion cells. (pages 51–52)

From the LGN, fibers stream to the primary visual receiving area, the striate cortex or V1, in the occipital lobe. Plate 2.8 shows the location of this area as well as a number of the major extrastriate areas that are involved in processing visual information. In this view of the monkey brain, part of the temporal lobe has been removed to show structures underneath. Areas that are labeled correspond to those described in Chapters 2 and 3 that are associated with the parietal and temporal extrastriate pathways (see Figures 3.18–3.20, pages 105–107). IT stands for inferotemporal cortex; MT for medial temporal area; and P for the part of the parietal area associated with vision. The yellow area represents other parts of the cortex that are also associated with vision. Area V3 is not visible, since it is hidden by a fold in the cortex.

Light band

Dark band

Figure 2.47
Shadow-casting technique for observing Mach bands. Illuminate a sheet of white paper with your desk lamp and then cast a shadow with another piece of paper.

DEMONSTRATION

Creating Mach Bands in Shadows

In Figure 2.46 we created Mach bands with gray stripes. You can also create Mach bands by casting a shadow, as shown in Figure 2.47. When you do this, you will see a dark Mach band near the border of the shadow and a light Mach band on the other side of the border. The light Mach band is often harder to see than the dark band. ●

If Mach bands do not exist in the intensity distribution, where do they come from? Mach's answer to this question was based on his observation that covering all but one of the stripes in a display like the one in Figure 2.46a eliminates the bands. If you try this for yourself, you will see that without the influence of the adjacent stripes, the uncovered stripe appears the same all the way across, just as its intensity distribution indicates.

Mach's observation that the bands vanish when the adjacent stripes are covered led him to propose a physiological mechanism to explain Mach bands. The light and dark bands must, according to Mach (1914), be caused by "an organic reciprocal action of the retinal elements on one another" (p. 218). Mach's hypothesis is that illumination of one area of the retina affects the response of receptors in another nearby area of the retina.

Mach's hypothesis is important both because it is correct and because it is an example of a physiological conclusion based on a psychophysical observation. Remember that Mach proposed his hypothesis in the late 1800s, long before Hartline et al.'s research on lateral inhibition.

A Neural Circuit for Mach Bands We can see how lateral inhibition can explain Mach bands by looking at the neural circuit in Figure 2.48, which shows four receptors, each of which sends lateral inhibition to its neighbors on both sides. To show how this circuit could cause the perception of Mach bands, let's illuminate these receptors so that A and

75

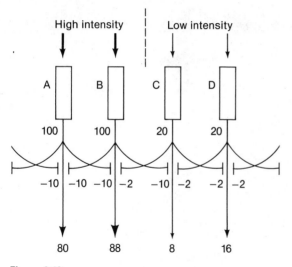

Figure 2.48

Four receptors that inhibit each other. If we know the initial output of each receptor and the amount of lateral inhibition, we can calculate the final output of the receptors. (See the text for a description of this calculation.)

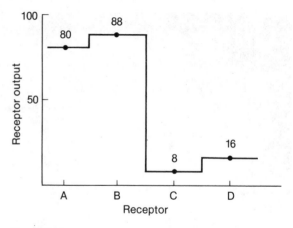

Figure 2.49

A plot showing the final receptor output calculated for the circuit of Figure 2.48. The bump at B and the dip at C correspond to the light and dark Mach bands, respectively.

B receive intense illumination and C and D receive dim illumination, analogous to the stimulus we would create by illuminating all four receptors and then casting a shadow on receptors C and D. Let's assume that receptors A and B generate responses of 100, whereas C and D generate responses of 20, as shown in Figure 2.48. Thus, without inhibition, A and B generate equal responses, and C and D generate equal responses. We can show, however, by means of the following calculation, that lateral inhibition can modify the initial responses of these receptors to produce a physiological effect that mimics the perception of Mach bands.

1. Start with the initial response of each cell: 100 for A and B and 20 for C and D.

2. Determine the amount of inhibition that each cell receives from its neighbor on each side. For the purposes of our calculation, we will assume that each cell sends inhibition to its neighbor equal to one-tenth of that cell's initial output. Thus, cells A and B will send

$100 \times 0.1 = 10$ units of inhibition to their neighbors, and cells C and D will send $20 \times 0.1 = 2$ units of inhibition to their neighbors.

3. Determine the final output of each cell by subtracting the amount of inhibition from the initial response. Remember that each cell receives inhibition from its neighbor on either side. (We assume here that receptor A receives 10 units of inhibition from an unseen receptor on its left and that D receives 2 units of inhibition from an unseen receptor on its right.) Here is the calculation for each cell in Figure 2.48:

Cell A: Output = 100 − 10 − 10 = 80

Cell B: Output = 100 − 10 − 2 = 88

Cell C: Output = 20 − 10 − 2 = 8

Cell D: Output = 20 − 2 − 2 = 16

The graph of these responses in Figure 2.49 looks very similar to Figure 2.46b, where there is an increase in nerve firing on the light side of the border at B and a decrease on the dark side at C. The lateral inhibition in our circuit has therefore created "Mach bands" in the neural response. A circuit similar to this one, but of much greater complexity, is probably responsible for the Mach bands that we see.

Some Perceptual Phenomena in Search of Physiological Explanations

As we have explored the physiology of vision, we have been able to offer some physiological explanations. We are just beginning, however, to understand the physiological mechanisms responsible for most perceptual phenomena. We will now describe two cases that are noteworthy because the perceptions we experience pose a puzzle for explanations based on neural circuits in the retina. To experience the first example, try the following demonstration, which was originally proposed by Ernst Mach.

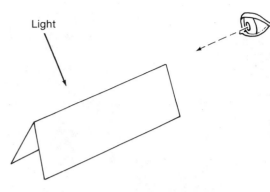

Figure 2.50
How to view the Mach card.

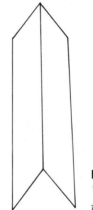

Figure 2.51
What the Mach card looks like when it perceptually "flips."

DEMONSTRATION
The Mach Card Demonstration

Fold a 3 × 5 or 4 × 6 card as shown in Figure 2.50, and orient it so that the left side is illuminated slightly less than the right (the light should be coming from the right). When viewed with two eyes at about a 45-degree angle from above, both sides of the card look white, the left side appearing slightly shaded. Now, close one eye and view the card until your perception "flips" so that the card appears to stand on end like an open book with its inside toward you, as in Figure 2.51. When this happens, notice that something else also happens. The shadowed left side of the card gets much darker, and the illuminated right side may even appear luminous. ●

What's going on here? Consider what happens to the Mach card's image on the retina when it flips from one orientation to another. Since the card never actually moves, the perceptual flip is not accompanied by any change in the pattern of light and dark on the retina. This effect poses problems for a neural explanation based on the activity of retinal receptors or on lateral inhibition. The next demonstration shows two patterns reported by David Knill and Daniel Kersten (1991) that also defy explanation in terms of receptor activity or lateral inhibition.

DEMONSTRATION
Surface Curvature and Lightness Perception

Compare the two displays in Figure 2.52. The one at (a) looks like a flat surface, and the one at (b) looks like a curved surface. In addition to their difference in surface

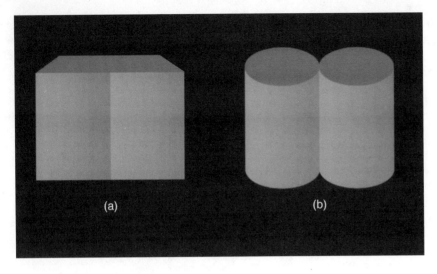

Figure 2.52

The light distribution is identical for (a) and (b), though it appears to be different. See text for further details. (Figure courtesy of David Knill and Daniel Kersten.)

curvature, they also appear to be shaded differently. The flat surface in (a) appears to be darker on the left than on the right, whereas the curved surface in (b) appears more evenly shaded. But now, take two pieces of paper and cover the top and bottom edges of (b) so it has straight edges as in (a). What do you see?　●

Perhaps you were surprised to see that when you turned the curved edges of (b) into straight lines, the left and right sides became much more like those in (a). This is actually not surprising because the intensity distributions of (a) and (b) are, in fact, identical. Since the intensities of the displays are identical, any explanation based only on stimulation of the receptors or on lateral inhibition would predict that the shading of the two patterns should look identical. But this does not occur. Apparently, the way we perceive the curvature of a surface can influence the way we perceive its shading. Exactly how this works is not clear, but it is clear that explanations based only on networks of retinal neurons cannot explain this effect (also see Adelson, 1993, for a similar demonstration).

The demonstrations we have presented show that we can't explain all perceptual phenomena by means of the interaction of neurons in the retina. Of course, we also know that the retina is just the beginning of the perceptual process. In the next chapter we will see that a great deal of processing and many additional perceptual mechanisms operate in the lateral geniculate nucleus and in the striate and extrastriate areas of the cortex. The demonstrations above have still not been explained at any level of the visual system, but when an explanation is finally discovered, it is likely that it will involve these higher visual centers.

THE BEGINNINGS OF THE PERCEPTUAL PROCESS

This chapter has been predominantly about the visual receptors and the neural wiring associated with these receptors. The receptors mark the beginning of a complex sequence of events called the *perceptual process,* which takes place extremely rapidly, and largely "behind the scenes" of a person's awareness, so as far as the person is concerned, she or he just looks at a visual stimulus and sees it.

We have begun to discover, however, how events that occur during the perceptual process shape what we see. We have found, for example, that visual perceptions are affected by events in the receptors and their neural circuits in the following ways:

- The receptors respond only to light energy to which they are sensitive. Thus, human vision is restricted to the visible spectrum, between 380 and 760 nm. Also, the region within the visible spectrum to which we are most sensitive depends on whether the rods or the cones are controlling our vision.

- The receptors and their neural wiring determine how sensitive we are to light. We can see dimmer lights with our rods than with our cones.

- The receptors and their neural wiring determine how much detail we see. We can see detailed stimuli with our cones, and only broader, less detailed aspects of the visual scene with our rods.

- The receptors and their wiring can modify our perceptions of light and dark, so what we perceive does not always correspond exactly to the pattern of stimulation on the

retina. Thus, we perceive Mach bands and the dark spots of the Hermann grid even though these patterns are not present in the incoming stimulation.

It is clear from these examples that the perceptual process is not simply a passive recording of images or of light and dark areas of images. Instead, it is a process consisting of mechanisms that first transform environmental stimuli into nerve impulses and then process the information contained in these nerve impulses.

As we continue our exploration of this process, we will discover that one way that the visual system operates is to analyze a visual stimulus into various properties. Thus, the red ball that rolled across our field of view at the beginning of the chapter is analyzed into properties (such as color, movement, and shape) that are all coded in neural impulses that are eventually combined to create our perception of the ball. In this chapter we have observed just the beginning of this process. The next chapter takes us on a journey up the visual pathway to the LGN, to the striate cortex, and to the extrastriate cortex. We will see that in these higher-level structures the information leaving the back of the eye in the optic nerve is processed further to create the neural code that stands for various properties of the stimuli in our environment.

ANIMAL EYES

All animals have a similar problem to solve: how to sense objects in the environment. For the majority of animals, one of the solutions to that problem involves eyes: a sheet of receptors on which an image is formed and that is designed for sensing light energy. In some animals this image is extremely crude, as in those that see with an open eye cup, an arrangement that provides the ability to sense light and dark areas in the environment, but not the ability to see details (Figure 2.53).

However, in the vast majority of animals the eye includes a focusing element such as a lens, which creates a sharp image of the environment on the receptor's surface. There are two basic arrangements for lens eyes. In the **single lens eye,** a single lens collects light from a wide area. This is the human model and is also called the *camera eye.* In **multiple lens eyes,** many smaller lenses, each contained within a structure called an **ommatidium,** collect light from small areas. This is the insect model and is also called the **compound eye**. Single lenses are designed to focus light onto a concave sheet of receptors, whereas multiple lenses focus light onto receptors arranged on a convex surface (Figure 2.54).

Within these two basic types of eye there are numerous variations, based on the animal's behavior, habitat, and patterns of activity. We will look at a few examples of single lens eyes to show how the eyes of different animals have evolved to serve their specific needs. One of the most obvious differences in animals, which is mirrored in the structure of their eyes, is whether they are active during the day or at night.

Diurnal (Day) and Nocturnal (Night) Eyes

Diurnal animals, which are active during the day, such as lizards, ground squirrels, chipmunks, and prairie dogs, have eyes that provide good acuity. These eyes achieve this acuity in two ways: (1) They have cone-dominated retinas that provide sharp resolution because of the small size of the cone receptors and their lack of convergence, and (2) they are large eyes, so the image on the retina is large and covers many receptors. Thus, birds, which achieve good acuity with their cone-dominated retinas, further increase their acuity with huge eyes that take up most of the space in their heads. The eyes of many birds are so large that they actually touch each other, making it possible to stimulate one eye by shining light through the wall of the other (Levine, 1955).

Nocturnal animals, such as flying squirrels, rats, and owls, achieve high sensitivity by having all-rod eyes with large lenses. Compare the large lens and cornea of the nocturnal opossum to the much smaller lens and cornea of the diurnal ground squirrel (Figure 2.55) (Tansley, 1965). Another way nocturnal animals increase their sensitivity is through a reflecting surface called the **tapetum**, located behind the retinas of some animals. By reflecting light back through the retina, the tapetum increases the amount of light hitting the receptors. The glow you see when you shine light into a cat's eye is light reflected from the cat's tapetum.

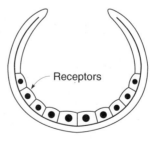

Figure 2.53
Open eye cup consisting of light-sensitive receptors in an open cup.

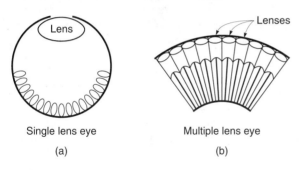

Single lens eye | Multiple lens eye
(a) | (b)

Figure 2.54

(a) Single lens eyes, such as the human's, focus light onto a concave sheet of receptors. (b) Multiple lens eyes, like the compound eyes of insects, focus light onto receptors arranged on a convex surface. Each of the lenses of the compound eye sits atop a structure called an ommatidium, *which contains a visual receptor.*

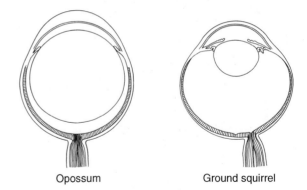

Opossum | Ground squirrel

Figure 2.55

Eyes of the nocturnal opossum and the diurnal ground squirrel.

If a nocturnal animal wants to venture out into the daylight, it must have a way to protect its sensitive eyes. This protection is accomplished in some nocturnal animals by a pupil that becomes a vertical slit when it contracts in response to light. A slit pupil protects the retina against light better than a round pupil because it can close all the way, whereas a round pupil can never close completely. Thus, an animal that is active at night can sun itself on a rock during the day, with its sensitive eyes protected by its completely closed pupil. Katherine Tansley (1965) points out, however, that truly nocturnal animals, such as the owl, have rounded pupils because they never venture into the bright daylight and therefore don't need to protect their retinas from the light.

Eyes for Underwater Vision

Living in the water poses a focusing problem. In air-living animals most of the focusing is done by the cornea; however, when the eye is submerged in water, which has physical properties similar to those of the cornea, the cornea loses most of its ability to bend light. Thus, fish and other animals that live in the water have rounded lenses that provide extra focusing power for seeing underwater.

The eyes of the "four-eyed" fish *Anableps* illustrate an ingenious solution to its visual environment. It swims along the surface of the water, so half of its eye sees through the air and half sees through the water. This fish has therefore evolved an eye that is optically adapted to both air and water vision simultaneously (Figure 2.56). A horizontal pigmented stripe divides the eye into top and bottom halves, so the eye has two pupils: an upper one, which admits light from the air, and a lower one, which admits light from underwater. The secret of how the *Anableps* eye can focus light simultaneously from these two different environments is revealed by looking at the positioning of its lens. For light coming from the water, the lens is positioned so that it is elliptical, with greater focusing power to compensate for the cornea's loss of focusing power underwater. For light coming from the air, the lens is flattened and has

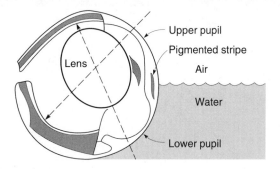

Figure 2.56

Eye of the Anableps. *Light from the water passes through the lower pupil and is focused by the powerful elliptical axis of the lens. Light from the air passes through the upper pupil and is focused by the less-powerful flattened axis of the lens (Sivak, 1976).*

less focusing power, since the cornea can now help with the focusing.

Eyes with Areas for Detail Vision

From our description of the human eye, we know that the fovea is the area of sharpest vision. This is so both because of the high density of cones and because of the lack of neural convergence, so that there is a high density of ganglion cells carrying messages from the fovea. The eagle and the falcon provide an example of foveas with higher cone densities than those in humans; these higher cone densities increase acuity to two to three times that of humans—an asset for detecting small prey from a vantage point high in the sky (Fox, Lehmukuhle, & Westendorf, 1976; Reymond, 1985).

Whereas humans, eagles, and falcons have small pit-shaped foveas, other animals have areas of high-detail vision that are spread out over a larger area. The red-eared turtle provides an example of such an arrangement: it has a hori-

zontal area of high receptor density called the **area centralis** (Brown, 1969). This linear area centralis has a property well suited to the turtle's view of the world since it is lined up with the horizon. This arrangement serves the turtle well because most of the visual stimuli that are important to the turtle, such as potential predators, appear on the horizon, where the turtle's vision is sharpest. Many other animals that live near to the ground have a linear area centralis, as well as some birds that also depend on the horizon for orientation as they are flying.

Animals' eyes are adapted in many ways besides the examples we have described here. For example, the wavelengths at which light-sensitive visual pigments absorb light are often shifted toward wavelengths that match the light environment. Thus, fish that live in murky water, in which longer wavelengths predominate, have pigments that are more sensitive at long wavelengths (Ali & Klyne, 1985; Lythgoe & Partridge, 1989). Another adaptation is eye placement. Some animals, such as cats and humans, have frontal eyes with overlapping fields of view that provide good depth perception, and others, such as rabbits, birds, lizards, and rodents, have lateral eyes on the sides of their heads that provide a more panoramic view of the world, an especially important adaptation for monitoring the environment for the presence of predators (Figure 2.57). When eyes see different areas of the environment, as in lateral-eyed animals, the eyes sometimes move independently, as in some birds and lizards, so that they can look for the most important objects on the left and the right simultaneously. In contrast, most frontal-eyed animals use "yoked" or coordinated eye movements to focus on one thing at a time.

We close our discussion of different types of eyes with an interesting fact. The visual pigments contained in all eyes are based on the same general plan: a large protein called *opsin* and a small,

Figure 2.57
Frontal eyes such as those of the cat have overlapping fields of view that provide good depth perception. Lateral eyes such as those of the rabbit provide a panoramic view, but poorer depth perception.

light-sensitive molecule called *retinal*. Thus, all animals share visual pigments that belong to the same general family of chemicals, but these similar chemicals are contained within a wide range of different packages, each one designed to deliver the intensity and pattern of light to the visual pigments in a way that will best fit each animal's visual requirements.

VISUAL ACUITY AND THE NEWBORN'S CONES

Visual acuity is poorly developed at birth but improves rapidly over the first six months of life. Researchers have measured infants' visual acuity by using the psychophysical preferential looking technique described in the Developmental Dimension in Chapter 1. They have also used a physiological technique in which electrical signals are recorded by small disk electrodes placed on the back of the infant's head, over the visual cortex. The infant looks at a gray field, which is briefly replaced by either a field of alternating black-and-white stripes or a checkerboard pattern. If the stripes or checks are large enough to be resolved by the visual system, a response called the **visual evoked potential (VEP)** is generated in the visual cortex; however, if the pattern cannot be resolved, no response is generated. Thus, the VEP provides an objective measure of the resolving power of the visual system and is therefore well suited to studies of the development of visual acuity.

The results of visual acuity measurements using both preferential looking (PL) and VEP measurements indicate that acuity is poor at first (about 20/400 to 20/600 at 1 month),[1] and then rapidly increases over the first six months to just below the adult level of 20/20 (Banks & Salapatek, 1978; Dobson & Teller, 1978; Harris, Atkinson, & Braddick, 1976; Salapatek, Bechtold, & Bushness, 1976). This improvement in acuity with age is shown in Figure 2.58, which shows a series of

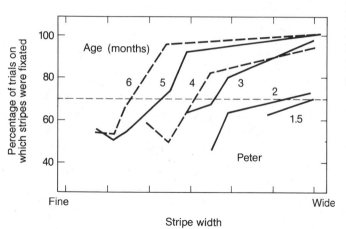

Figure 2.58

A series of psychophysical functions obtained by the preferential looking technique for a single subject at ages 1.5–6 months. Each of these functions represents the results of many trials in which the infant was presented with a choice between a striped stimulus and a homogeneous gray stimulus. The subject's threshold is defined as the stripe width at which he looked at the striped pattern on 70 percent of the trials. The fact that the functions moved to the left as the infant got older indicates that he could perceive finer and finer stripes (Teller et al., 1974).

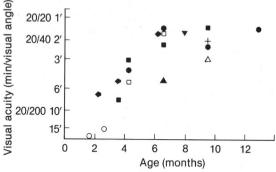

Figure 2.59

The improvement of acuity over the first year of life, as measured by the VEP technique. The numbers on the vertical axis indicate the smallest stripe width that results in a detectable evoked response. Snellen acuity values (see Chapter 13) are also indicated on this axis. The different symbols represent measurements of different subjects (Pirchio, Spinelli, Florentini, & Maffei, 1978.)

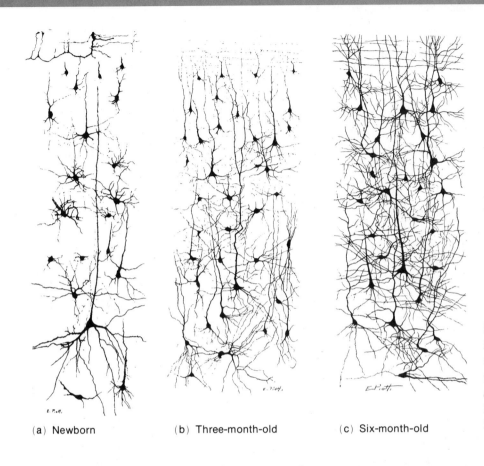

(a) Newborn   (b) Three-month-old   (c) Six-month-old

Figure 2.60

Drawings of neurons in the visual cortex of the newborn, the 3-month-old, and the 6-month-old human infant (Conel, 1939, 1947, 1951).

psychophysical functions of one subject measured by the PL technique, and Figure 2.59, which shows the acuities of a number of subjects measured by the VEP technique. The rapid improvement of acuity until the sixth month is followed by a leveling-off period, and full adult acuity is not reached until sometime after 1 year of age.

Why is acuity so low at birth? One reason is that the infant's visual cortex is not fully developed. Figure 2.60 shows the state of cortical development at birth, at age 3 months, and at 6 months (Conel, 1939, 1947, 1951). These pictures indicate that the visual cortex is only partially developed at birth and becomes more developed at 3 and 6 months, the time when significant improvements in visual acuity are occurring.

However, the state of the cortex is not the whole explanation of the infant's visual acuity. If we look at the newborn's retina, we find that, although the rod-dominated peripheral retina appears adultlike in the newborn, the all-cone fovea contains widely spaced and very poorly developed cone receptors (Abramov et al., 1982).

Figure 2.61 compares the shapes of newborn and adult foveal cones. The newborn's cones have fat inner segments and very small outer segments, whereas the adult's inner and outer segments are larger and are about the same diam-

[1] The expression 20/400 means that the infant must view a stimulus from 20 feet to see the same thing that a normal adult observer can see from 400 feet. (See Chapter 13.)

eter (Banks & Bennett, 1988; Yuodelis & Hendrickson, 1986). These differences in shape and size have a number of consequences. The small size of the outer segment means that the newborn's receptors contain less visual pigment and therefore do not absorb light as effectively as adult cones. In addition, the fat inner segment creates the coarse receptor lattice shown in Figure 2.62a, with large spaces between the outer segments. In contrast, the thin adult cones are closely packed, as in Figure 2.62b, creating a fine lattice that is well suited to detecting fine details. Martin Banks and Patrick Bennett (1988) calculated that the cone receptors' outer segments effectively cover 68 percent of the adult fovea but only 2 percent of the newborn fovea. This means that most of the light entering the newborn's eyes is lost in the spaces between the receptors and is therefore not useful for vision.

Another possible cause of the newborn's poor acuity is the optics of the eye. As it turns out, however, the optical quality of the newborn's lens and cornea is quite good, so light enters the eye easily. The infant's low acuity, therefore, is due to the underdeveloped state of the visual cortex and to the inability of the receptors to make efficient use of the entering light. The rapid development of both retina and cortex over the first six months of life opens the window of detailed vision to the infant.

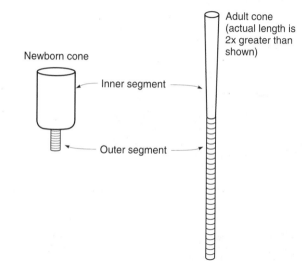

Figure 2.61

Idealized shapes of newborn and adult foveal cones. (Real cones are not so perfectly straight and cylindrical.) Foveal cones are much narrower and longer than the cones elsewhere in the retina, so these look different from the ones shown in Figures 2.3 and 2.8. The adult cone is actually twice as long as shown here. See text for details. (From Banks & Bennett, 1988.)

Figure 2.62

Receptor lattices for (a) newborn and (b) adult foveal cones. The newborn cone outer segments, indicated by the dark circles, are widely spaced because of the fat inner segments. In contrast, the adult cones, with their slender inner segments, are packed closely together. (Adapted from Banks & Bennett, 1988.)

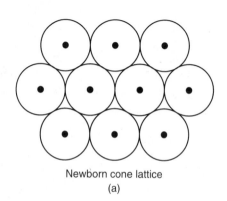

Newborn cone lattice
(a)

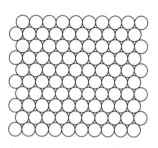

Adult cone lattice
(b)

REVIEW

Overall Plan of the Visual System

Focusing the Incoming Light

The Retina

The Lateral Geniculate Nucleus

- Most neurons leaving the retina synapse in the lateral geniculate nucleus (LGN) in the thalamus. A basic property of the LGN is that it is organized.

8. How many layers does the LGN have, and how are they organized in terms of ipsilateral and contralateral, and magnocellular and parvocellular? (51)

The Visual Cortex

- The cortex is an extremely complex structure, which, like the LGN, is layered. About 60 percent of the surface area of the cortex is involved in vision.

9. What is the striate cortex? The extrastriate cortex? What evidence suggests that visual functions occur outside the striate cortex? (52)

Duplicity Theory and Perception

- The duplicity theory of vision states that the retina consists of two types of receptors that operate under different conditions and have different properties.

10. What is dark adaptation? How is it measured? Describe three experiments that distinguish between rod and cone dark adaptation. Be sure you understand Figure 2.22. Why can't we measure a pure rod dark-adaptation curve in the periphery of a normal observer? (54)

- When visual pigments absorb light, the opsin and retinal separate, a process called bleaching because it is accompanied by a change in color. The reverse of bleaching—pigment regeneration—occurs when the two parts reunite.

11. Describe how the process of pigment bleaching and regeneration can be measured by means of retinal densitometry. What did Rushton find, using this technique? (57).

- The rods and the cones are most sensitive to wavelengths in different regions of the visible spectrum.

12. Describe the rod and the cone spectral-sensitivity curves. What is the Purkinje shift? What is the relation between pigment absorption spectra and spectral sensitivity? (58)

The Processing of Neural Signals

- When we say that a neural signal is processed, we mean that it is analyzed and transformed so that the resulting neural signal carries information that can be used by the perceptual system. Processing occurs by networks of nerve fibers called neural circuits.

- Convergence and inhibition in the retina create receptive fields with excitatory and inhibitory areas.

13. Describe how each of the three circuits in Figures 2.29, 2.30, and 2.31 process information. What is the role of convergence and inhibition in processing? (63)

14. Define receptive field. What is a center–surround receptive field? Center–surround antagonism? Be able to draw a circuit that results in a center–surround receptive field. (66)

Neural Processing and Perception

- Perception is closely linked to neural processing. One reason the rods and the cones cause different perceptions is the differences in their neural circuits.

- Neural processing not only affects perceptions near threshold, such as sensitivity and acuity, but also affects perceptions that occur above threshold, such as the brightness of a surface.

- Although some perceptions can be explained by retinal circuits, others cannot.

15. What is the difference between rod and cone neural circuits? How can this difference explain differences in rod and cone sensitivity and acuity? (68)

16. What is the simultaneous contrast effect? Describe Hartline et al.'s research on the *Limulus* that provided a physiological explanation of simultaneous contrast. Be sure you understand how lateral inhibition affects perception. (71)

17. What is the Hermann grid? Mach bands? How can perception of the grid and Mach bands be explained by lateral inhibition? Understand how the circuit in Figure 2.48 operates. (73)

18. Describe why the perceptions of the Mach card demonstration and Figure 2.52 are difficult to explain based only on retinal circuits. (77)

The Beginnings of the Perceptual Process

- One of the major messages of this chapter is that visual perceptions can be affected by neural processing—specifically, processing that occurs in the retina.

19. Cite four examples of how properties of the receptors affect our perceptions. (79)

Animal Eyes

- There are many different types of eyes and varieties within each type. In many cases we can show how an animal's eyes have evolved to meet its needs.

20. Describe how animals' eyes have been adapted to deal with the following conditions: diurnal and nocturnal vision; underwater vision; detail vision; vision in murky water. Also describe the different properties of frontal and lateral eyes. (80)

Visual Acuity and the Newborn's Cones

- Infants have poor visual acuity, but their acuity improves rapidly over the first six months of life, as indicated by measurements using the preferential looking and VEP techniques.

21. Describe how cortical wiring and the state of the foveal cones at birth can explain the human newborn's low acuity. (85)

INTRODUCTION TO VISION: CENTRAL PROCESSING

Processing in the Lateral Geniculate Nucleus

Processing in the Striate Cortex

The Relationship between Physiology and Perception

Processing Past the Striate Cortex

Some Challenges for Physiological Research

In Chapter 2 we saw how the receptors and the other neurons in the retina process the electrical signals generated when light is absorbed by the visual pigments. Our task in this chapter is to follow these electrical signals as they flow along the optic nerve to the lateral geniculate nucleus and the other visual areas of the brain, and to determine how these signals are processed on their journey from retina to cortex and how the resulting cortical signals are related to perception.

Our rolling red ball, as we know from Chapter 2, activates a large area in the cortex. We will now see that the reason for this widespread activity is that different areas process information related to different properties of the stimulus. Thus, one area or series of areas may be concerned with the ball's shape, another with its movement, another with its color, and so on. However, before the electrical signals arrive at these cortical areas, they must pass through the lateral geniculate nucleus. We take up our story there.

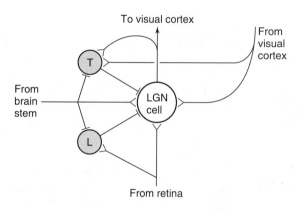

Figure 3.1

Inputs and outputs of an LGN neuron. In addition to the incoming signals carried in optic nerve fibers from the retina, this neuron is also receiving signals from the cortex, from a nucleus elsewhere in the thalamus (T), from another LGN neuron (L), and from the brain stem. Excitatory synapses are indicated by Y's (<) and inhibitory ones by T's (⊣). (Adapted from Kaplan, Mukherjee, & Shapley, 1993.)

PROCESSING IN THE LATERAL GENICULATE NUCLEUS

The lateral geniculate nucleus (LGN), strategically placed between the retina and the visual cortex, is the first place in which most of the 1 million fibers in each optic nerve synapse after leaving the retina. Neurons in the LGN receive signals from incoming optic nerve fibers and also from the visual cortex, the brain stem, and nuclei in the thalamus (Figure 3.1).

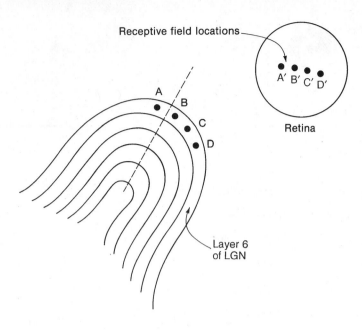

Receptive field locations

A' B' C' D'

Retina

A

B

C

D

Layer 6
of LGN

Figure 3.2

Retinotopic mapping of neurons in the LGN. The neurons at A, B, C, and D in layer 6 of the LGN have receptive fields located at positions A', B', C', and D' on the retina. The receptive fields of neurons encountered along an electrode track perpendicular to the surface of the LGN (dashed line) all have approximately the same location on the retina.

Although a great deal of neural processing does occur in the LGN, the receptive fields of LGN neurons have the same center–surround configuration as those of retinal ganglion cells (Figure 2.35). The major function of the LGN is apparently to regulate the flow of information as it travels from the retina to the visual cortex (Casagrande & Norton, 1991; Humphrey & Saul, 1994). One example of this regulation is that for every 10 nerve impulses that reach the LGN from the retina, only about 4 nerve impulses leave the LGN for the cortex. This slowing down of firing in the LGN may help protect cortical cells from becoming overstimulated. In addition, the firing of LGN cells is sensitive to the organism's state of arousal: Sleep slows down LGN firing, and heightened alertness increases its firing (Kaplan et al., 1993).

The LGN also organizes the information reaching it from the retina. We have already seen that the LGN consists of six layers, each one receiving input from only one eye (Figure 2.17). We also know that ganglion cells near each other in the retina travel to sites near each other in the LGN, creating a map of the retina in the LGN.

Maps of the Retina in the LGN

The map of the retina in the LGN is called a **retinotopic map.** This means that each location on the LGN corresponds to a location on the retina, and neighboring locations on the LGN correspond to neighboring locations on the retina. We can demonstrate this organization by determining the location of the receptive fields of neurons A, B, C, and D in layer 6 of the LGN. When we do this, we find that their receptive fields are also adjacent to each other at A', B', C', and D' on the retina (Figure 3.2).

Having determined that layer 6 of the LGN contains a retinotopic map, let's now look at the other layers. When we do this, we find that these layers also contain retinotopic maps, and that the maps in the other layers are lined up with one another. In other words, if we lower an electrode through the LGN along the track indicated by the dashed line in Figure 3.2, we find that all of the neurons along that track have receptive fields in the same location on the retina. These aligned retinotopic maps caused the anatomist Gordon Walls (1953) to compare the LGN to a club sandwich, and to note that a toothpick piercing the LGN's "sandwich" layers would encounter neurons that all received information from the same place on the retina (Mollon, 1990). This is an amazing feat of organization: One million ganglion cell fibers from each eye travel to the LGN, and on arriving there, each fiber goes to the correct LGN layer (remember that fibers from each eye go to different layers) and finds its way to a location next to other fibers that left from the same place on the retina. Meanwhile, all of the other fibers are doing the same thing in the other layers of the club sandwich!

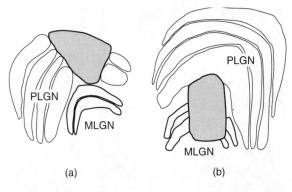

(a)   (b)

Figure 3.3

The areas of the LGN destroyed by Schiller and his co-workers are indicated by the shaded areas: (a) destruction of neurons in the parvocellular layers (PLGN); (b) destruction of neurons in the magnocellular layers (MLGN). (From Schiller, Logothetis, & Charles, 1990.)

The Magno and Parvo Layers of the LGN

Another example of organization in the LGN is that layers 1 and 2 receive input from the M ganglion cells, and that layers 3, 4, 5, and 6 receive inputs from the P ganglion cells. We described this organization of the LGN into magno layers (layers 1 and 2) and parvo layers (layers 3, 4, 5, and 6) in Chapter 2 and noted that the neurons in these layers are responsible for our perception of different visual qualities. Let's now look at the evidence that supports this statement by considering an ingenious experiment done by Peter Schiller, Nikos Logothetis, and Eliot Charles (1990), which asked how destroying the magno or parvo layers in the monkey LGN would affect a monkey's ability to perceive various visual qualities.

Schiller and his co-workers first tested rhesus monkeys behaviorally to determine their ability to perceive movement, pattern, shape, color, and depth. After training the monkeys to perform tasks that required them to respond to these qualities, Schiller et al. anesthetized the monkeys and then destroyed part of the magno layers in some monkeys and part of the parvo layers in other monkeys by injecting the neurotoxin ibotenic acid

into these layers (Figure 3.3). After recovering from the operation, the monkeys that had magno lesions had lost their ability to detect movement, and the monkeys that had parvo lesions had lost their ability to detect color, fine textures and patterns, and the depth of small or finely detailed objects. Schiller and his co-workers therefore concluded that neurons in the magno and parvo layers represent two channels: The magno channel sends information about motion to the cortex, and the parvo channel sends information about color, texture, shape, and depth to the cortex. Returning to our rolling red ball, we can say that information about the ball's motion is carried in the magno channel and that information about its roundness, its redness, and its distance from us is carried in the parvo channel.

What happens to this information when it is transmitted to the cortex? We will see in the next section that the cortex represents a further stage of processing in which receptive fields become more complicated and in which the separation of neural pathways with different functions continues.

Figure 3.4
*David Hubel (left) and Torsten
Wiesel (right), who won the 1981
Nobel prize in physiology and
medicine for their research on the
physiology of vision. The results
of their research established the
groundwork for much of our
knowledge of visual physiology.*

PROCESSING IN THE
STRIATE CORTEX

How is information processed in the striate cortex? Signals from the magno and parvo layers of the LGN enter the striate cortex at two different locations within layer IVc (see Figure 2.18). Later in this chapter we will look at information processing in the cortex by considering how signals travel along these two streams. For now we will describe the properties of the receptive fields of cortical neurons. We begin by looking at research that took place in the laboratory of David Hubel and Torsten Wiesel beginning in the late 1950s (Figure 3.4). At that time it was known that retinal ganglion cells had center–surround receptive fields, and Hubel and Wiesel wanted to determine the types of stimuli that caused cortical neurons to fire.

In the address he gave on accepting the 1981 Nobel prize in physiology and medicine that he and Wiesel received for their research on the visual cortex, Hubel (1982) reported that, at first, he and Wiesel had had a difficult time eliciting responses from cortical neurons. They were projecting spots of light onto a screen with a slide projector to stimulate different areas of a cat's

visual field but were having little luck. Even though these same spot stimuli had generated good responses from retinal ganglion cells, they were generating little or no response from the cortex.

After attempting to elicit cortical responses for a number of hours, Hubel and Wiesel experienced something startling: As they were inserting a glass slide containing a spot stimulus into their projector, a neuron "went off like a machine gun." They later discovered that the machine-gun-like response was a neuron responding to the image of the straight edge of the slide that was moving downward on the screen as the slide was lowered into the projector. After testing many more neurons, Hubel and Wiesel proposed that cortical neurons respond best to barlike stimuli that are oriented in a specific direction. We will now look at the results that led them to this conclusion.

Receptive Fields of Neurons
in the Striate Cortex

Hubel and Wiesel identified three major types of neurons, classifying them according to the type of stimuli to which they responded best. These neurons have been recorded from the striate cortex and, in some cases, from the extrastriate cortex, as well (Hubel, 1982).

Simple Cortical Cells **Simple cortical cells** have receptive fields that, like center–surround receptive fields, have excitatory and inhibitory areas. However, these areas are arranged side-by-side rather than in the center–surround configuration (Figure 3.5). The receptive field of a simple cortical cell is arranged so that this cell responds best to a bar of light oriented in a particular direction. A large response results when the bar is oriented along the length of the receptive field, as in Figure 3.5a; a smaller response results when the bar is tilted, as in Figure 3.5b; and no response results when the bar is perpendicular to the orientation of the receptive field, as in Figure 3.5c (Hubel & Wiesel, 1959).

This preference of simple cortical cells for bars with particular orientations is shown graphically in Figure 3.6. This **orientation tuning curve,** determined by measuring the responses of a simple cortical cell to bars with different orientations, shows that this cell responds with 25 nerve impulses per second to a vertically oriented bar. The cell's response decreases, however, as the bar is tilted away from the vertical, until a bar that is tilted 20 degrees from the vertical elicits only a small response. (We can appreciate the narrowness of this tuning by noting that the angle between 12:00 and 12:04 on a clock face is 24 degrees.) While this particular simple cell responds best to a bar with a vertical orientation, Hubel and Wiesel found other simple cells that responded best to bars with horizontal or diagonal orientations.

Complex Cortical Cells Like simple cells, **complex cells** respond best to bars of a particular orientation. Unlike simple cells, complex cells don't respond well to small spots of light or to stationary stimuli. Most complex cells respond when a correctly oriented bar of light *moves* across the entire receptive field. Further, many complex cells respond best to a particular *direction* of movement (Figure 3.7).

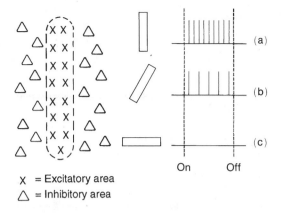

X = Excitatory area
△ = Inhibitory area

Figure 3.5
The receptive field of a simple cortical cell. This cell responds best to a vertical bar of light that covers the excitatory area of the receptive field (a) and responds less well as the bar is tilted so that it covers the inhibitory area (b and c). (Adapted from Hubel & Wiesel, 1959.)

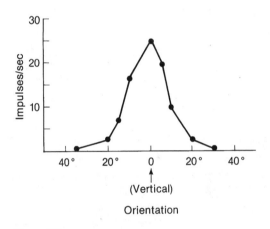

Figure 3.6
An orientation tuning curve of a simple cortical cell. This cell responds best to a vertical bar (orientation = 0) and responds less well as the bar is tilted in either direction.

End-Stopped Cells **End-stopped cells** (which Hubel and Wiesel originally called "hypercomplex cells") fire to moving lines of a specific length or to moving corners or angles. The cell in Figure 3.8 responds best to a corner that is moving upward across the receptive field, as shown

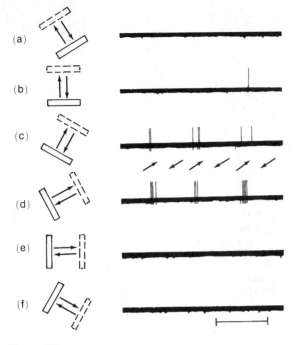

Figure 3.7

Response of a complex cell recorded from the visual cortex of the cat. The stimulus bar is moved back and forth across the receptive field. The records on the right indicate that the cell fires only when the bar is moved at a specific angle. The cell does not respond when the bar is oriented as in (a), (b), (e), and (f). A slight response occurs in (c). The best response occurs in (d), but even when the bar is at this optimal orientation, a response occurs only when the bar is moved from left to right, as indicated by the arrows above the records. No response occurs when the bar moves from right to left. The horizontal bar at the lower right represents 1 second. (From Hubel & Wiesel, 1959.)

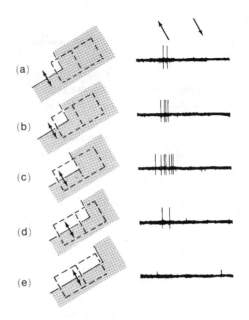

Figure 3.8

Response of an end-stopped cell recorded from the visual cortex of the cat. The stimulus is indicated by the light area on the left. This cell responds best to a light corner moving up (see the arrows above the records); there is no response when the corner moves down. Note that, as the corner is made longer as we progress from (a) to (b) to (c), the cell's firing rate increases, but that, when the length is increased further, as in (d) and (e), the firing rate decreases. (From Hubel & Wiesel, 1965a.)

in Figure 3.8c. While the length of the stimulus does not affect complex cells, end-stopped cells will not fire if the stimulus is too long. If we extend the length of this stimulus, as in Figure 3.8e, the cell no longer fires (Hubel & Wiesel, 1965a).

We have now come a long way from the retinal receptors to the visual cortex, and we have seen that the information processing that occurs between the receptors and the cortex has created cortical neurons that fire in response to specific features of the stimulus, such as orientation or direction of movement. For this reason, these neurons are sometimes called **feature detectors**. Table 3.1, which summarizes the properties of the various types of neurons we have described so far, makes clear an important fact about neurons in the visual system: As we travel farther from the retina, neurons require more specific stimuli to fire. Retinal ganglion cells respond to just about any stimulus, whereas end-stopped cells respond only to bars of a certain length that are moving in a particular direction. Later, we will see that this specialization increases even further as we move into other visual areas of the cortex.

The Organization of the Visual Cortex

One thing that is clear from our description of the properties of cortical neurons is that a substantial amount of neural processing occurs in the cortex. Neurons outside the cortex respond equally well to most orientations, whereas most neurons within the cortex respond selectively to specific orientations, to movement, and to the direction of movement.

The sophisticated responses of cortical neurons are accompanied by sophisticated cortical organization. We will show how this cortical organization was discovered by describing some experiments in which Hubel and Wiesel determined how neurons with common characteristics

Table 3.1

Cell	Characteristics
Optic nerve fiber (ganglion cell)	Center–surround receptive field. Responds best to small spots but will also respond to other stimuli.
Lateral geniculate	Center–surround receptive fields very similar to the receptive field of a ganglion cell.
Simple cortical	Excitatory and inhibitory areas arranged side by side. Responds best to bars of a particular orientation.
Complex cortical	Responds best to movement of a correctly oriented bar across the receptive field. Many cells respond best to a particular direction of movement.
End-stopped cortical	Responds to corners, angles, or bars of a particular length moving in a particular direction.

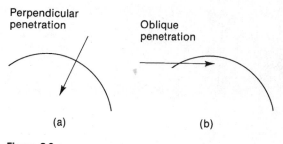
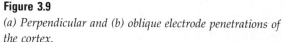

Figure 3.9
(a) Perpendicular and (b) oblique electrode penetrations of the cortex.

are organized in the cortex. To do this, they penetrated the cortex with electrodes oriented either *perpendicularly* to the cortical surface, as in Figure 3.9a, or *obliquely* to the cortical surface, as in Figure 3.9b. As they penetrated the cortex, Hubel and Wiesel stopped at closely spaced intervals and determined the properties of neurons along the electrode track. The first question they asked was: Where are the receptive fields of these neurons located on the retina?

Location Columns and Retinal Maps When Hubel and Wiesel lowered an electrode perpendicularly into a monkey's cortex, they found that the neurons they encountered had receptive fields either on top of each other or very close together on the retina, as shown in Figure 3.10a. They concluded from this result that the cortex is therefore organized into **location columns,** and that the neurons within a location column have their receptive fields at the same location on the retina.

When Hubel and Wiesel penetrated the cortex obliquely and recorded from neurons separated by 1 mm along the electrode track, they found that the receptive fields were systematically displaced, and that neurons close to each other along the electrode track corresponded to receptive fields close to each other on the retina (Figure 3.10b). Thus, as in the LGN, there is a retinotopic map of the retina in the visual cortex.

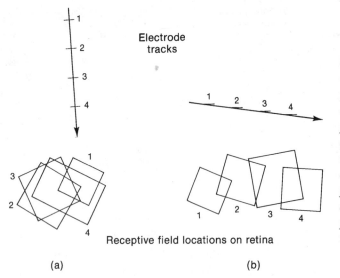

Electrode
tracks

Receptive field locations on retina

(a)

(b)

Figure 3.10

(a) When an electrode penetrates the cortex perpendicularly, the receptive fields of the neurons encountered along this track overlap. The receptive field recorded at each numbered position along the electrode track is indicated by a correspondingly numbered square. (b) When the electrode penetrates obliquely, the receptive fields of neurons recorded from the numbered positions along the track are displaced, as indicated by the numbered receptive fields; neurons near each other in the cortex have receptive fields near each other on the retina.

As Hubel and Wiesel determined the receptive field locations of neurons along the oblique track, they measured how far apart the receptive fields moved on the retina every time they advanced their electrode 1 mm. They found that their results depended on the electrode's location in the cortex. When recording from an area of cortex that received signals from receptors near the fovea, moving the electrode 1 mm across the cortex caused only a small shift in the location of receptive fields, as shown by arrow A in Figure 3.11. If, however, they were recording from an area that received input from a more peripheral area of the retina, moving the electrode 1 mm caused a much larger shift in the location of receptive fields, as shown by arrow B in Figure 3.11. Thus, the same distance on the cortex represents a small distance on the retina near the fovea and a larger distance on the retina in the periphery.

We can appreciate the importance of this result by looking at the relationship between distance on the cortex and distance on the retina in another way. Figure 3.12 shows that a small retinal area near the fovea is allotted more space in the cortex than the same-sized retinal area in the periphery. This effect is called the **magnification**

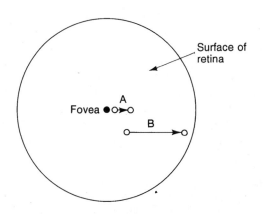

Figure 3.11

How receptive field location (open circles) changes on the retina when recording from two neurons separated by 1 mm on the visual cortex. Arrow A shows the small shift that occurs in the locations of the receptive fields for two cortical neurons that receive inputs from an area of the retina on or near the fovea. Arrow B shows the larger shift in location that occurs when the two cortical neurons receive inputs from a more peripheral area of the retina.

factor, since the foveal representation in the cortex is *magnified* compared to the representation of the periphery.

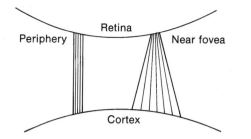

Figure 3.12
The relationship between the area on the retina and the area in the cortex. In this illustration, two equal-sized areas on the retina are served by different-sized areas on the cortex, with the area near the fovea being allotted more space than the area in the periphery. (Based on data from Hubel & Wiesel, 1974.)

The Magnification Factor   Although the fovea accounts for only 0.01 percent of the area of the retina, it accounts for 8 percent of the neurons in the striate cortex. We can understand why this magnification factor occurs by considering how neurons are packed in the retina and in the cortex. In the retina, the foveal receptors are packed very closely together, whereas the peripheral receptors are much more widely spaced. These differences in the packing of the receptors are mirrored by the ganglion cells that receive signals from these receptors: There are about 50,000 ganglion cells per square millimeter of retina near the fovea but fewer than 1,000 cells per square millimeter in the peripheral retina (Stone, 1965; Wassle et al., 1990).

When we move to the cortex, however, we see that the density of neurons in different cortical areas remains constant. Consider what this means: Since a small area of fovea sends signals from many more ganglion cells to the cortex than the same sized area of peripheral retina, the signals from the foveal ganglion cells will require more space in the cortex. The result is the magnification factor: More cortical space is allotted to parts of the retina that send more ganglion cell signals to the cortex. In fact, recent research shows that the magnification factor occurs not only because the fovea sends more ganglion cell signals per unit area to the cortex than does the peripheral retina, but also because each foveal input is given extra space in the cortex. A ganglion cell from near the fovea is allotted three to six times more cortical tissue than a ganglion cell from the periphery (Azzopardi & Cowey, 1993).

This magnified representation of the fovea in the cortex is related to perception. As we know from our discussion of the rods and the cones in Chapter 2, the fovea is the part of the retina you use for high-acuity tasks such as reading this book or picking your friend's face out of a crowd. We now see that this high acuity is achieved not only because of the way the cones are wired in the retina but also because of the large amount of cortical space devoted to the fovea. Azzopardi and Cowey (1993) suggest that this extra cortical space may be used for neural circuits that provide additional neural processing for the stimuli that fall on the fovea.

We have been describing how the visual cortex is organized in terms of location. The cortex is also organized in another way, which Hubel and Wiesel also discovered when lowering electrodes perpendicular to the surface of the cortex.

Orientation Columns   In the process of discovering simple, complex, and end-stopped cells in the cortex, Hubel and Wiesel observed an interesting phenomenon. When they lowered their electrode so that its path was perpendicular to the surface of the cortex, as shown in Figure 3.13, they encountered all three types of cells along the electrode path—simple, complex, and end-stopped—but the cells had something in common: Not only were the locations of their receptive fields the same, but they preferred similar stimulus orientations. Thus, all cells encountered along the electrode track at A in Figure 3.13 respond best to horizontal lines, whereas all those along electrode track B respond best to lines oriented at about 45 degrees. Thus originated the idea that the cortex is organized into **orientation columns,** with each column containing cells that respond best to a particular orientation.

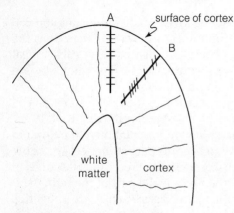

A   surface of cortex

B

white matter   cortex

Figure 3.13

Electrophysiological evidence of orientation columns in the visual cortex. The microelectrode tracks (A and B), which are both perpendicular to the surface of the cortex, encounter simple, complex, and end-stopped cells along their paths, but all of these cells have the same preferred stimulus orientation (indicated by the lines cutting across each electrode track).

The finding that cortical cells with the same orientation preference are organized into columns is consistent with a proposal made by Hubel and Wiesel that complex cells are constructed from inputs from a number of simple cells with the same preferred orientation, and that end-stopped cells are constructed from a number of complex cells with the same preferred orientation. If this idea is correct, grouping cells with similar preferred orientations would make the construction process much easier.

This columnar organization of the cortex, which Hubel and Wiesel discovered while doing electrophysiological experiments, has been confirmed anatomically by means of the **2-deoxyglucose technique.** This technique is based on the following facts:

1. Brain cells depend on glucose as a source of metabolic energy.

2. Cells that are more active use more glucose.

3. 2-Deoxyglucose (2-DG) can masquerade as glucose, so it is taken up by active cells as glucose is.

4. After 2-DG is taken up by the cell, it begins to be metabolized, but the resultant metabolite can't cross the membrane of the cell's wall and so accumulates inside the cell.

These properties of 2-DG enabled Hubel, Wiesel, and Michael Stryker (1978) to do the following experiment. After injecting radioactively labeled 2-DG into a monkey, they stimulated the monkey's visual system by moving black and white vertical stripes back and forth in front of the animal for 45 minutes. This stripe movement increased activity in the cells that prefer vertical orientations, causing them to increase their uptake of radioactive 2-DG. After this stimulation the monkey was sacrificed, and when its brain was examined, Hubel, Wiesel, and Stryker found that the cortex contained the regularly spaced narrow bands of radioactivity shown in Figure 3.14. These narrow bands, which were caused by the high activity of the cells that respond best to vertical stripes, showed anatomically what had previously been demonstrated electrophysiologically: The visual cortex is made up of columns that contain cells with the same preferred orientation.

In addition to demonstrating that the visual cortex is made up of columns of cells with the same preferred orientation, Hubel and Wiesel showed that adjacent columns have similar, but slightly different, orientations. They showed this by moving an electrode through the cortex obliquely, as in Figure 3.9b, so that the electrode cut across orientation columns. As they did this, they found that the neurons' preferred orientations changed in an orderly fashion, and that, within each millimeter they moved across the cortex, they encountered cells that respond to the entire 180-degree range of orientations.

Ocular Dominance Columns In addition to being organized for location and orientation, neu-

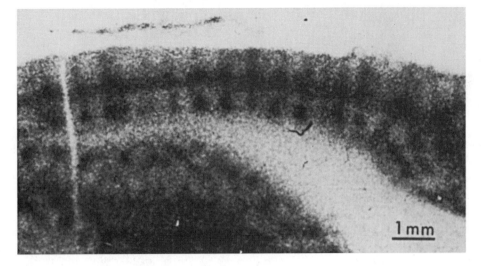

Figure 3.14
Magnified picture of a slice of visual cortex that has taken up radioactive 2-DG as described in the text. The dark vertical bands, produced by the radioactive 2-DG, are orientation columns. The dark horizontal band is layer 4 of the cortex. Neurons in this layer receive inputs from the LGN and respond to all orientations. (From Hubel, Wiesel, & Stryker, 1978.)

1 mm

rons in the cortex are also organized in terms of the eye to which they respond best. About 80 percent of the neurons in the cortex respond to stimulation of both the left and the right eyes. However, most cells respond *better* to one eye than to the other. This preferential response to one eye is called **ocular dominance,** and cells with the same ocular dominance are organized into **ocular dominance columns** in the cortex.

Hubel and Wiesel observed these columns during their oblique penetrations of the cortex. They found that a given area of cortex usually contains cells that all respond best to one of the eyes, but when the electrode was moved about 0.25–0.50 mm, the dominance pattern changes to the other eye. Thus, the cortex consists of a series of columns which alternate in ocular dominance in a left-right-left-right pattern.

Hypercolumns We have seen that the visual cortex is organized into columns in terms of three different properties of the stimulus:

1. Its *location* on the retina: Cortical neurons serving the same retinal location are found in columns about 1 mm wide.

2. Its *orientation* on the retina: Cortical neurons responding to the same orientation are found in columns, which are arranged so that all possible orientations are included within about 1 mm of cortex.

3. Its presentation to the *left or right eye:* Cortical neurons that respond best to each eye are located in 0.25- to 0.50-mm-wide alternating columns.

One of the things that may strike you about the summary above is the similarity of the sizes of the three types of columns. Location columns are about 1 mm wide, orientation columns are about 1 mm wide, and the left- and right-eye-dominance columns together are about 1 mm wide.

What this means, according to Hubel and Wiesel, is that a 1-mm block of cortex can serve as a **processing module** for a particular area of the retina. This processing module, which Hubel and Wiesel called a **hypercolumn,** is shown schematically in Figure 3.15. The cortex is made up of thousands of these hypercolumns, each one serving a small area of the retina. (Remember that there is a retinotopic map of the retina on the cortex.) Thus, if we present a bar of light oriented at a 45-degree angle to a small area of the retina of the left eye, we will activate neurons in the hypercolumn serving that location on the retina,

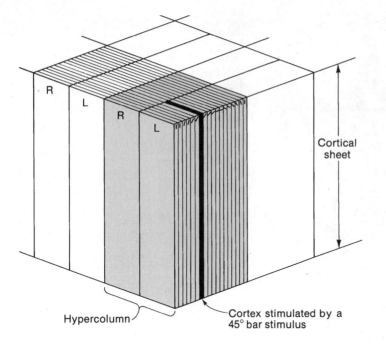

R L R L

Cortical sheet

Hypercolumn

Cortex stimulated by a 45° bar stimulus

Figure 3.15

A very diagrammatic picture of a hypercolumn. The shaded area is a hypercolumn, consisting of a left- and right-ocular-dominance column that receives inputs from the same retinal location. Within each ocular-dominance column is a complete set of orientation columns. When a bar of a particular orientation is presented to the retinal area served by a particular hypercolumn, the orientation column in that hypercolumn is activated. The activation that occurs in response to a bar oriented at 45 degrees presented to the left eye is indicated in this picture by the darkened 45-degree orientation column in the left-ocular-dominance columns.

and within that hypercolumn, neurons will respond in the left-ocular-dominance column and in the 45-degree orientation column, as shown in Figure 3.15. If we make this bar longer so that it also stimulates neurons in other location columns, we will activate more hypercolumns and more neurons in left-ocular-dominance columns and 45-degree orientation columns.

One thing is clear from Hubel and Wiesel's work on cortical organization: The information that specifies "long-bar-shape" is translated into a pattern of cortical stimulation that differs greatly from the actual shape of the stimulus. Although this result may be surprising, it simply confirms a basic property of our perceptual system: Our perception is based on electrical signals that bear little actual resemblance to the environmental stimuli that they represent. Remember that the electrical signals in the visual system *represent* the environment in coded form, and that there is no particular reason that the code must resemble the thing it stands for.

Thus, the cortical representation of a stimulus presented to the retina does not have to resemble the stimulus; it just has to contain information that *represents* the stimulus. A long bar on the retina is represented not by a bar on the cortex but by the firings of many neurons in different cortical columns. Of course, before we perceive the bar, the information from these different columns must be combined. We will discuss how this combination may occur later in the chapter, but first, let's consider evidence regarding the role of striate cortex neurons in perception.

THE RELATIONSHIP BETWEEN PHYSIOLOGY AND PERCEPTION

Our discussion so far has focused on the stimulus–physiology relationship from Figure 1.2. From this focus we have gained a great deal of knowledge about the physiology of the visual system, but we have neglected the relationship between physiology and perception. It is often difficult to measure this relationship directly because in animals, in which we can monitor physiological responding, it is difficult to measure perception, and in humans, in whom we can measure perception more easily, it is difficult to measure physiological responding. Thus, researchers often infer the relationship between physiology and perception by measuring the two relationships that are more accessible: (1) the stimulus–physiology relationship and (2) the stimulus–perception relationship.

We can illustrate this procedure by describing an experiment on the sense of taste in which both psychophysical and physiological functions were measured in humans. G. Borg and his co-workers (1967) recorded from the chorda tympani nerve in five patients undergoing middle ear operations. (The chorda tympani, which carries nerve fibers from the tongue, passes through the middle ear on its way toward the taste area of the thalamus.)

Borg et al. determined the stimulus–perception relationship two days before the operation by flowing various concentrations of citric acid, sucrose, and sodium chloride over a person's tongue and having the person make magnitude estimates of the intensity of the taste sensation for each concentration (see page 20 in Chapter 1 to review magnitude estimation). The result for citric acid, shown in Figure 3.16a, is a power function with a slope of 0.5.

To measure the stimulus–physiology relationship, Borg et al. flowed the same taste solutions over the tongue and recorded the response of the chorda tympani. The result, shown in Figure 3.16b, is also a power function with a slope of 0.5. The fact that the stimulus–perception and the stimulus–physiology functions are similar supports the idea that there is also a relationship between physiology and perception. In this case, that relationship is between the rate of nerve firing and the magnitude of taste sensation.

We will now apply a similar approach to the visual system to investigate the possibility that

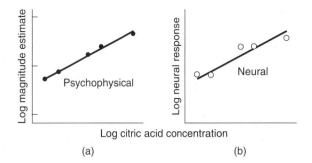

Figure 3.16

(a) Psychophysical response to citric acid. The relation between the log magnitude estimates of the taste sensation and the log citric acid concentration is a straight line with a slope of 0.5. (b) Physiological response to citric acid. The relationship between log neural firing and log concentration is also a straight line with a slope of 0.5. In both graphs the distance between each tick mark on the vertical axis represents one log unit, or a change in the magnitude estimate or the firing rate of a factor of 10. (From Borg et al., 1967.)

there is a relationship between the firing of orientation-selective neurons and the perception of orientation. To do this, we will describe some psychophysical experiments that use a stimulus called a *grating*, which consists of alternating stripes (Figure 3.17). The first step in our experiment is to determine an observer's **contrast sensitivity** to gratings of different orientations. Contrast sensitivity = 1/contrast threshold, where the contrast threshold is the smallest intensity difference between the light and dark bars that enables the observer to detect the bars.

After determining the contrast sensitivity by using one of the psychophysical methods of Chapter 1 for a number of different orientations, we adapt the observer to a high-contrast vertical grating by having her observe the grating for about one minute. This is called **selective adaptation,** since looking at the vertical orientation adapts the observer *selectively* to that orientation. After the observer is adapted to the vertical grating, we remeasure the person's contrast sensitivity to all of the orientations. When we do this, we find that her sensitivity to the vertical

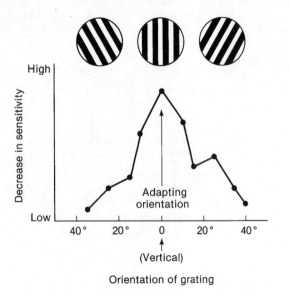

Figure 3.17

Top: Some of the grating stimuli used in the selective adaptation experiment. After measurement of the subject's contrast sensitivity to gratings with different orientations, the subject is adapted to the vertical grating (orientation = 0 degrees). The subject's contrast sensitivity to all of the gratings is then remeasured to determine the effect of the adaptation. Bottom: The curve in this graph shows that the subject's adaptation to the vertical grating causes a large decrease in her ability to detect the vertical grating when it is presented again, but that this adaptation has less effect on gratings that are tilted to either side of the vertical. Gratings tilted more than about 35 degrees from the vertical are essentially unaffected by adaptation to the vertical grating.

grating has decreased; that is, for the observer to see the vertical grating, we must increase the intensity difference between the light and the dark bars. The observer's sensitivity to the other gratings has also decreased, though not as much as to the vertical grating. This result is shown by the graph in Figure 3.17.

If the psychophysically determined curve of Figure 3.17 looks familiar, it is because it is similar to the physiological orientation tuning curve for simple cortical cells (Figure 3.6). This similarity between the psychophysically measured selective adaptation curve and the electrophysiological tuning curve suggests a possible explanation for the selective adaptation result: Looking at the vertical adapting grating stimulates the neurons that respond best to vertical lines. This stimulation fatigues these neurons, so that the subject finds it harder to see vertical orientations when we present another grating. Our psychophysical curve therefore shows the greatest decrease in sensitivity for the vertical orientation and drops off for other orientations, just as does the electrophysiological tuning curve. This parallel between psychophysical and electrophysiological functions is not perfect, since the selective adaptation curve is wider than the physiological curve, but the similarity still suggests that the responding of orientation-sensitive neurons may play a role in our perception of orientation.

Here and in Chapter 2 we have been able to demonstrate some connections between physiology and perception. We have explained visual acuity and sensitivity in terms of rod and cone pigments and wiring, and the perception of orientation in terms of the firing of cortical orientation detectors. These parallels between physiology and perception represent the first steps toward our goal of determining the physiological mechanisms of perception, but it is important to acknowledge that our ability to explain perception in physiological terms is still primitive. For example, the evidence we have presented linking the firing of orientation detectors and the perception of orientation is indirect evidence based on selective adaptation, rather than on the actual perception of orientation. Ideally, we would eventually like to be able to demonstrate a direct link between the firing of specific neurons and the perception of specific orientations. It is also important to realize that to explain perception in physiological terms we need to look past the striate cortex. We will therefore now continue our journey through the visual system by looking at the anatomy and physiology of visual areas "past" the striate cortex.

Processing Past the Striate Cortex

As recently as the 1960s and 1970s researchers thought that the striate cortex was the sole "perceptive center" in humans, and that the surrounding cortex was involved in higher-order processes such as visual memory (Zeki et al., 1991). In the 1970s, however, this view began to change, as researchers began discovering areas outside the striate cortex, which they called **extrastriate areas,** that respond to visual stimulation. Today we know that over half of the cortex can be activated by visual stimuli (Mishkin, 1986).

In this section we will describe these extrastriate visual areas by asking questions such as: How do neurons in these areas respond? How are the different areas organized? What is their role in perception? We will see that neurons in different areas respond to different features or qualities of the environment and that there is a rationale for how these areas are linked to one another. We begin by looking at how cortical pathways are organized, in terms of both anatomical connections and the way different functions are segregated into different areas.

Organization of the Extrastriate Pathways

A good way to begin our description of organization is by returning to the research of Peter Schiller and his co-workers described earlier in this chapter. This research showed that lesions of the magno and parvo layers of the LGN had different perceptual outcomes. Destroying magno neurons affected movement perception, whereas destroying parvo neurons affected the perception of color, form, and depth. We have also noted that magno and parvo neurons synapse in different locations within area 4C of the striate cortex. We could assume, therefore, that, if we were to follow the visual pathways further in the cortex, we

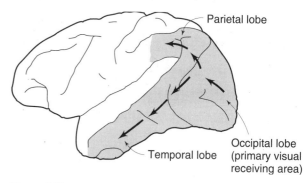

Figure 3.18

The monkey cortex, showing pathways from the primary visual receiving area, in the occipital lobe, to the parietal and temporal lobes. The sequences of arrows indicate that there are a number of synapses along these pathways.

might expect to find at least two pathways corresponding to the magno and parvo layers that serve different functions.

As we will see, a large amount of evidence supports the idea of multiple visual pathways. A good starting point for describing these pathways is research by Leslie Ungerleider and Mortimer Mishkin (1982), which showed that two separate pathways extend from the striate cortex in the occipital lobe to the parietal and temporal lobes (also see Mishkin, Ungerleider, & Macko, 1983). These pathways, shown in Figure 3.18, serve two different functions. The one reaching the temporal lobe is crucial for *identifying* objects, whereas the one reaching the parietal lobe is crucial for *locating* objects.

We can understand the conclusion that these two areas serve different functions by looking at Ungerleider and Mishkin's experiments, which used two different kinds of problem-solving tasks: object discrimination and landmark discrimination. Let's first consider an *object discrimination* problem. A monkey is familiarized with one object—say, a rectangular solid—and is then presented with a two-choice task like the one shown in Figure 3.19a. To receive a reward, the monkey must pick the "familiar" object, in this case the rectangular solid. Normal monkeys and

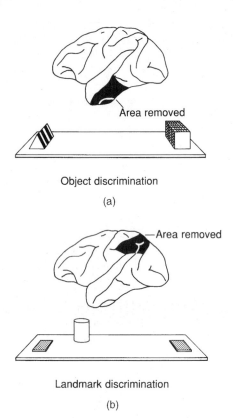

Figure 3.19

The two types of discrimination tasks used by Ungerleider and Mishkin. (a) In the object discrimination task the monkey had to pick the correct object. Monkeys with an area of their temporal lobes removed (shaded area of brain) had difficulty with this task. (b) For the landmark discrimination, the monkey had to pick the food well closer to the cylinder. Monkeys with an area of their parietal lobes removed found this task difficult. (From Mishkin, Ungerleider, & Macko, 1983.)

monkeys with their parietal lobes removed can do this easily. However, removal of an area of the temporal lobes turns this into an extremely difficult task.

A different type of problem, called *landmark discrimination,* is shown in Figure 3.19b. Here, the monkey is rewarded for choosing the covered food well closer to the tall cylinder. This task can

be done by a normal monkey or by one with its temporal lobe removed, but it is difficult for monkeys lacking part of the parietal lobe.

Both of these problems are examples of higher-order visual functioning that goes beyond the analysis carried out by neurons in the striate cortex. The end result of processing in the temporal lobe is information about an object's physical properties that enables us to identify it when it is seen from different viewpoints and in different areas in space. The end result of processing in the parietal lobe is information about the object's location.

The conclusion from these experiments is that there are two extrastriate pathways, a **temporal pathway** concerned with *what* an object is, and a **parietal pathway** concerned with *where* an object is. These pathways are therefore sometimes called the *what* and *where pathways.* (One way to remember this is to notice that *what* contains a *t,* for *temporal.*)

Anatomists, physiologists, and psychologists have studied these pathways and the structures associated with them and have expanded on the "what" or "where" idea. Figure 3.20 is an extremely simplified diagram showing the general results of this research (also see Color Plate 2.8). Notice that the parietal, or "where," pathway begins with the retinal M ganglion cells and the LGN magno layers, and that the temporal, or "what," pathway begins with the retinal P ganglion cells and the LGN parvo layers. Also note that the striate cortex has been labeled *V1* in this diagram and that, in order to simplify our picture of the visual system, we have omitted many of the 25 or so extrastriate areas and their connections. We will consider some of the implications of these omissions later. However, for now we will use this simplified diagram because it captures the essence of the idea of multiple pathways and structures and provides a good reference point for describing the research that looks at the functions of the structures in these pathways. (See Casagrande, 1994, for a more detailed diagram and evidence for a third visual pathway, which she calls the "K pathway").

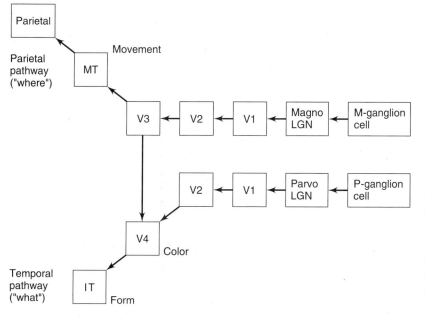

Figure 3.20
Simplified diagram of the visual pathways. Signals flow from right to left, starting with the M and P ganglion cells on the far right, which feed into the parietal and temporal pathways, respectively. V1 is the striate cortex, and V2, V3, and V4 are extrastriate visual areas; other extrastriate areas are IT, inferotemporal cortex; MT, medial temporal cortex; and Parietal, which refers to other areas in the parietal lobe. The visual qualities most strongly associated with areas MT, V4, and IT are indicated.

Functions of Extrastriate Structures in Monkeys

The research we will consider asks the question: What is the function of specific structures in the visual system? Most of the research on this question has been carried out in monkeys by means of three basic techniques: (1) brain lesioning, which asks how the removal of a particular structure influences the animal's perception; (2) brain stimulation, which asks how stimulating a structure influences the animal's perception; and (3) recording from neurons, which asks what kinds of stimuli cause neurons in a structure to fire.

We will look at research on three brain areas: the medial temporal area in the parietal pathway, and area V4 and the inferotemporal area in the temporal pathway. After describing the results of monkey research we will then look at evidence that the human visual system is also organized into "what" and "where" processing streams.

Medial Temporal Area (Movement)   Lesioning, recording and electrical studies provide strong

evidence of the role of the medial temporal (MT) area in movement perception. Let's consider each type of evidence.

Lesioning. William Newsome and Edward Paré (1988) developed an ingenious technique for determining a monkey's threshold for detecting the direction of movement. They used a stimulus that consisted of a random pattern of moving dots created by a computer, which varied the degree to which the dots moved in the same direction (Figure 3.21). For example, Figure 3.21a represents zero correlation in the direction of the dots' movement, so that all dots moved randomly, much like the "snow" you see when your TV set is tuned between channels. Figure 3.21b represents 50 percent correlation, so that at any point in time half of the dots were moving in the same direction. Figure 3.21c represents 100 percent correlation, so that all of the dots were moving in the same direction.

When monkeys were trained to indicate the predominant direction of the dots' movement, they could detect the direction in patterns with correlations as low as 1–2 percent. However, after area MT was lesioned, the monkeys could detect

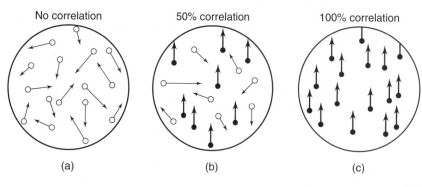

No correlation   50% correlation   100% correlation

(a)   (b)   (c)

Figure 3.21
Stimuli used by Newsome and Paré. The dots on the left moved randomly, with no connection to one another. The ones in the center were partially correlated, half (the black dots) always moving in the same direction. The ones on the right were fully correlated, all moving in the same direction. (From Newsome & Paré, 1988.)

the direction of movement only if the correlation was 10–20 percent or more. Thus, lesioning MT causes an increase in the threshold for detecting the direction of movement (also see Movshon & Newsome, 1992; Pasternak & Merigan, 1994).

Recording. We have already seen that cortical neurons such as the complex and end-stopped cells in V1 respond best to a particular direction of movement. This directional selectivity is seen in about 90 percent of the neurons in area MT, while in area V4, which is not involved in motion perception, less than 5 percent of the neurons are directionally selective (Figure 3.22) (Merigan & Maunsell, 1993).

Stimulation. C. Daniel Salzman and co-workers (1990, 1992) used a recording electrode to locate a group of neurons in area MT with the same directional selectivity and then stimulated these neurons by passing a weak electrical current through the tip of their electrode. This technique, which is called **microstimulation,** since only a small number of neurons is stimulated, was carried out while monkeys were being behaviorally tested with random dot patterns (see Figure 3.21) to determine their threshold for detecting the direction of movement.

How did the microstimulation affect the monkeys' judgments? The monkeys were able to more easily perceive movement in the direction that matched the preferred direction of the stimulated neurons. Thus, the microstimulation of neurons in MT lowers the threshold for perceiving movement in the direction preferred by the stimulated neurons.

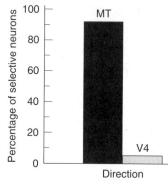

Figure 3.22
Most of the neurons in area MT (black bar) are directionally selective, whereas few in area V4 (shaded bar) are. (Adapted from Felleman & Van Essen, 1987.)

Area V4 (Color) Whereas area MT is specialized for perceiving movement, area V4 is specialized for perceiving color. (Although, as we will see, many neurons in area V4 also respond to other qualities.) The major evidence for this specialization comes from recording experiments. About 60 percent of the neurons in area V4 respond to color, compared to close to 0 percent in area MT (Figure 3.23). Semir Zeki (1983a, 1983b, 1984) has recorded from neurons in area V4 that respond best to specific colors of objects, irrespective of lighting conditions. For example, a particular neuron may fire to the redness of our ball, even when it is illuminated

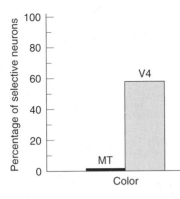

Figure 3.23
About 60% of the neurons in area V4 respond to color (shaded bar), whereas close to 0% in area MT respond to color. (Adapted from Felleman & Van Essen, 1987.)

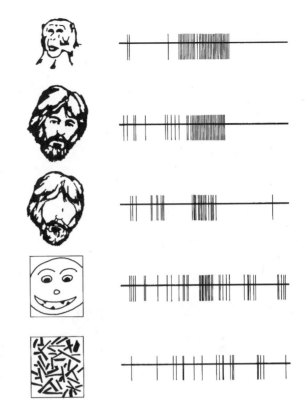

Figure 3.24
Responses of a neuron in a monkey's area IT to various stimuli. This neuron responds best to a full face, as shown by its response to monkey and human faces in the top two records. Removing the eyes or presenting a caricature of a face reduces the response. This neuron does not respond to a random arrangement of lines. (From Bruce, Desimone, & Gross, 1981.)

by light of different colors. That is, the neuron responds to the actual color of the ball and ignores the color of the illumination. We will discuss this important property of V4 neurons in more detail in Chapter 4, when we describe a phenomenon called *color constancy*—our tendency to perceive the colors of objects as remaining the same, no matter what the illumination.

Inferotemporal Cortex (Form) As we moved up the visual pathway from the retina to the cortex, we saw that the neurons responded best to more and more specialized stimuli. This trend reaches an extreme in the inferotemporal (IT) area of the cortex, in which neurons have been found that respond to very specialized stimuli, such as pictures of faces (Figure 3.24) (Bruce, Desimone, & Gross, 1981; Rolls, 1992). It has been proposed that neurons that respond to specialized stimuli are responsible for our perception of complex forms. For example, Tanaka (1993) has found neurons in the temporal lobe that respond best to shapes like the ones shown in Figure 3.25. He proposes that a complex form would stimulate a number of these neurons, each one responding to a different part of the form, and that we perceive the form when the information from all of these neurons is combined.

Extrastriate Structures and Pathways in Humans

The research we have just described indicates that various extrastriate structures in the monkey are specialized to respond best to different aspects of a visual stimulus. It is likely that the same situation exists in humans, given the similarity between the monkey and human visual systems, but we need direct evidence from re-

Figure 3.25
Some of the stimuli that elicit the best response from neurons in the temporal lobe (Tanaka, 1993).

parietal ("where") pathway. In general, the PET studies have obtained these predicted results (Haxby et al., 1991; Ungerleider & Haxby, 1994).

Clinical Studies Clinical studies of people who have suffered brain damage due to accidents or strokes have also generally confirmed the idea of specialized structures in separate extrastriate pathways. For example, J. Zihl and his co-workers

search with humans indicating that this is the case. Since we can't do lesioning, recording, or stimulation experiments on humans, researchers have used other techniques (e.g., PET scans, clinical studies of patients who have suffered brain damage, and psychophysical research) to determine whether specialized extrastriate structures also exist in humans.

PET Scans Positron emission tomography (PET) is a technique that enables researchers to determine the areas of the brain that are active in awake, behaving humans (Figure 3.26). A number of studies have been carried out recently in which people do tasks that would be expected to activate different visual pathways. For example, a face recognition task would be expected to activate the temporal ("what") pathway, whereas a task involving determining the location of a dot within a larger pattern would be expected to activate the

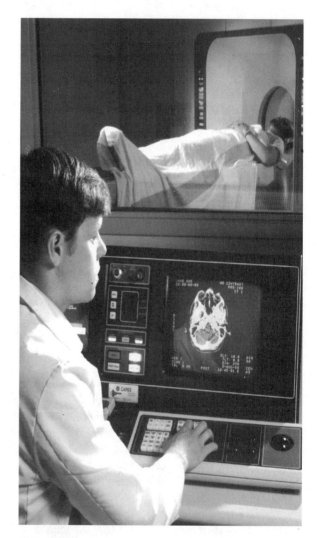

Figure 3.26
A person in PET scan apparatus in the background, with the control room in the foreground.

(Zihl, von Cramon, & Mai, 1983; Zihl et al., 1991) reported the case of a woman who was admitted to the hospital after complaining of severe headaches, dizziness, and nausea. A brain scan and other testing indicated damage to an area of the cerebral cortex around the border of the occipital and temporal lobes. The result of this damage, an inability to see movement in many situations, is described as follows in the report of her case:

> The visual disorder complained of by the patient was a loss of movement vision in all three dimensions. She had difficulty, for example, in pouring tea or coffee into a cup because the fluid appeared to be frozen, like a glacier [Figure 3.27]. In addition, she could not stop pouring at the right time since she was unable to perceive the movement in the cup (or a pot) when the fluid rose. Furthermore the patient complained of difficulties in following a dialogue because she could not see the movements of the face, and, especially, the mouth of the speaker. In a room where more than two other people were walking she felt very insecure and unwell, and usually left the room immediately, because "people were suddenly here or there but I have not seen them moving." The patient experienced the same problem but to an even more marked extent in crowded streets or places, which she therefore avoided as much as possible. She could not cross the street because of her inability to judge the speed of a car, but she could identify the car itself without difficulty. "When I'm looking at the car first, it seems far away. But then, when I want to cross the road, suddenly the car is very near." She gradually learned to "estimate" the distance of moving vehicles by means of the sound becoming louder. (Zihl et al., 1983, p. 315)

It is clear from this description, as well as from the results of psychophysical testing, that this patient had a severe disorder of movement perception called **motion agnosia,** and that this condition appears to be caused by damage in an area of the brain that may correspond to the area identified with movement in the monkey: the MT cortex.

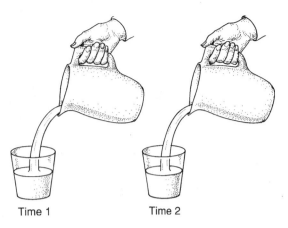

Time 1   Time 2

Figure 3.27
Zihl et al.'s patient, who may have had damage in an area equivalent to the monkey's area MT, perceived no change in the level of water being poured into a cup.

Other research on clinical cases has studied patients with **prosopagnosia,** an inability to identify faces. People with this condition are unable to visually recognize people they have known for years, such as friends and relatives, although they can see well and can identify these people based on the sound of their voices (Farah, 1990). One person with this disorder recalled sitting in his club and wondering why another member was staring so intently at him. When he complained to one of the waiters, he discovered he had actually been viewing his own face in a mirror (Farah, 1992)! Prosopagnosia is usually associated with damage to the temporal lobe, just as we would expect from the location of monkey face-selective neurons in the IT cortex (Damasio, Tranel, & Damasio, 1990).

Psychophysical Experiments One prediction of the idea of specialized visual areas is that the activation of just the color-sensitive areas should not result in motion perception. This idea has been tested psychophysically by the use of moving grating stimuli in which the alternating bars have a property called **equiluminance.** An equiluminant stimulus is one in which the brightness of the alternating bars is the same. Thus, an equiluminant "black-and-white" grating wouldn't actually be a grating at all, because bars of equal brightness would be either all white, all black, or all the same shade of gray. However, an equiluminant grating in which the bars are of different colors—say, red and green—will still appear to be a grating since, even though the equiluminant red and green bars have the same brightness, they look different because of the difference in their color.

Now let's consider what happens when we present a moving red and green grating in which the red bars start out being much brighter than the green bars. As the grating moves, the brightness difference between the bars stimulates the movement-sensitive system (presumably neurons in the parietal pathway), and the person sees the grating move. If, however, we decrease the brightness of the red bars until the red and the green bars become equiluminant, then only a color difference remains between the two bars, and this difference should not stimulate the movement system, which responds only to the brightness difference. When Patrick Cavanaugh, Christopher Tyler, and D. E. Favreau (1984) did this experiment, they found that, at equiluminance, either the moving bars appeared to stop moving or the impression of movement was greatly decreased. This is the result we would predict if the equiluminant colored bars were not able to stimulate the visual system's "movement area" (Livingstone, 1990; Livingstone & Hubel, 1987, 1988). (See Logothetis et al., 1990, for an argument against using equiluminant stimuli to separate the different visual pathways.)

If we consider all of the research we have surveyed, from the center–surround receptive fields of retinal ganglion cells all the way up to the specialized areas for movement, color, and form in the extrastriate visual areas, we can see that, beginning with the relatively simple responses of the retinal ganglion cells, neural processing endows higher-order neurons with a selectivity that causes them to respond to specialized stimuli. We will have more to say about these specialized neurons in the chapters on color, form, movement, and depth perception.

We will see, for example, that although we have not yet mentioned neurons that respond to depth, such neurons do exist. We will also see that researchers have identified different kinds of movement-selective neurons: some that respond to the overall movement of a pattern and others that respond to the movement of individual components within the pattern.

Now that we have followed neural signals from their origin in the rods and the cones all the way to the firing of specialized extrastriate neurons, we are ready to return to our rolling red ball. We now know that, as the ball rolls by, its movement activates MT neurons, its redness activates neurons in area V4, and its roundness activates neurons in the IT cortex. This neural picture of the red ball is correct up to a point, but we still have more to say about it. For one thing, our description is somewhat simplified. We acknowledged this when we noted that we were going to focus on only 3 of the 25 or so extrastriate visual areas that have been discovered. Thus, our ball stimulates many more extrastriate areas than just the MT, V4, and IT. In addition, it turns out that, although extrastriate neurons are specialized to respond best to one type of stimulus, some of these neurons respond to other qualities as well. For example, some neurons in the temporal cortex respond not only to complex forms but also to the movement of these forms (Sary, Vogels, & Orban, 1993).

One reason these neurons respond to more than one quality is that there are many interconnections between them (Boussourd et al., 1990; Nakamura et al., 1993; Ungerleider & Haxby, 1994). These anatomical connections create "cross-talk" between the pathways so that they are not quite as separated as they appear in Figure 3.20. For example, signals from the magno and parvo layers of the LGN are not totally segregated in the parietal and temporal pathways as is implied in the figure (Merigan & Maunsell, 1993). Also, evidence from a number of lesioning studies indicates that lesioning area V4 in the monkey causes some problems in color perception but can have even stronger effects on form perception (Schiller, 1993, 1994). Thus, the picture we have been presenting of channels that serve specific functions is generally correct, but the idea of totally separate and independent channels for different qualities is an oversimplification.

The results outlined in Chapter 2 and in this chapter illustrate the impressive achievements of the physiological approach to perception. As impressive as our present knowledge is, there are still numerous challenges ahead, among them simply finding out more about how neural responding signals various qualities. To end this chapter, we focus on a few additional problems facing researchers who are working toward a physiological understanding of perception.

SOME CHALLENGES FOR PHYSIOLOGICAL RESEARCH

In this section we briefly describe two topics that pose interesting puzzles for researchers working on the physiology of perception.

The Active Observer: The Physiology of Attention

One thing you may have noticed all through our discussion of the visual system's response to our red ball is that the visual system is extremely active. Signals travel along numerous pathways and neural processing causes neurons to become more and more specialized, so that even something as simple as our rolling red ball generates simultaneous activity in many different structures. But one thing that has been missing from our discussion is perhaps the most important component of all: the person doing the perceiving. In our single-minded devotion to discussing neural processing, we have forgotten the person who is seeing our ball.

The reason it is important to consider the person is that, from the point of view of the perceiver, perception is an extremely active process. In most cases we do not sit by passively, paying no attention to the things happening around us. Instead, we actively seek out things in the environment that interest us, and this affects what we perceive and what we remember. We would assume that these perceptual and cognitive effects are reflected in brain activity, and in fact research has shown that focusing of attention does affect the activity of specific brain structures. Attention, therefore, adds another dimension to our consideration of visual processing.

The problem of visual attention is one that has been recognized since the beginnings of scientific psychology, as illustrated by the following quote from William James's 1890 textbook, *The Principles of Psychology*:

> Millions of items . . . are present to my senses which never properly enter my experience. Why? Because they have no *interest* for me. *My experience is what I agree to attend to.* . . . Everyone knows what attention is. It is the taking possession by the mind, in clear and vivid form, of one out of what seem several simultaneously possible objects of trains of thought. . . . It implies withdrawal from some things in order to deal effectively with others. (italics in the original)

In this quote James captured the experience of attention: When confronted with a large number of items, we withdraw from most and focus our attention on just a few. Modern physiological research has shown that the process described by James is reflected in the way information is processed in the nervous system. Things we attend to are physiologically enhanced, and those that we don't attend to are not enhanced or may even be inhibited.

To examine this process, let's look at an experiment by Jeffrey Moran and Robert Desimone (1985). Moran and Desimone trained monkeys to keep their eye fixated on a dot such as the one shown in Figure 3.28. As they recorded from a neuron in area V4 of a monkey that was steadily

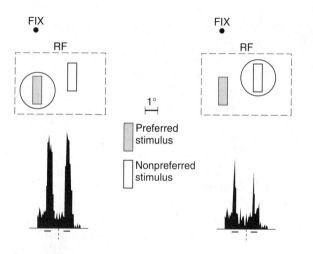

Preferred
stimulus

Nonpreferred
stimulus

Figure 3.28

*The effect of selective attention on the response of a neuron
in area V4; the receptive field (RF) is indicated by the
dashed line. The monkey kept its eyes fixed on the dot.
When the monkey paid attention to the neuron's preferred
stimulus, as indicated by the "spotlight" on the left
display, the neuron fired (see records at the lower left).
When the monkey paid attention to the nonpreferred
stimulus, as indicated by the spotlight on the right display,
the neuron fired less vigorously (see the record at the lower
right). (Adapted from Moran & Desimone, 1985.)*

fixating on the dot, Moran and Desimone presented two stimuli that fell within the neuron's
receptive field. These two stimuli differed in an
important way: One, which we will call the *preferred stimulus*, was a color that caused the V4
neuron to fire vigorously, and the other, which
we will call the *nonpreferred stimulus*, was a color
that caused little or no response in the neuron.

While recording from this V4 neuron, Moran
and Desimone signaled the monkey to pay attention to either the preferred or the nonpreferred
stimulus on different trials. The results show that
where the monkey attended had a large effect on
the neuron's response (Figure 3.28): Attention to
the preferred stimulus caused a good response,
whereas attention to the nonpreferred stimulus
caused a smaller response. The important thing to
remember about this experiment is that in both

cases *the stimulus remained on the same place on the
retina* (since the monkey never moved its eyes).
Therefore the enhanced response in the left record
was due solely to the monkey's attentional state.
Moran and Desimone also obtained similar results
for neurons in the IT cortex. These results add
another dimension to our story of neural processing by showing that the visual system's neurons
are responsive to what the person is interested in
and by emphasizing the importance of taking the
observer's actions into account when we are
studying the physiology of perception.

Combining Parts and Qualities into Wholes: The Binding Problem

Another problem facing physiological researchers is related to the fact that many neurons in the
visual system are specialized to process information about specific qualities. Thus, when our red
ball rolls by, the visual system separates the ball
into its different qualities, as activity occurs in
separate neurons that respond to the ball's movement, color, and shape. However, we experience
the ball more as a "whole"—we see a rolling red
ball, not separate "rolling," "redness," and
"roundness." This raises an important question:
How are the ball's motion, color, and shape combined, so that we perceive a unified rolling red
ball rather than separate independent qualities?
This problem, which is called the *binding problem*,
has become a hot topic in visual research.

To begin dealing with the question of how
the visual system combines parts and qualities of
an object to create the perception of a whole
object, we return to our discussion of how neurons in the striate cortex (V1) respond to a long
bar with a particular orientation. We saw that
presentation of the bar to the retina causes activity in each of the hypercolumns that process information from the receptors that the bar
stimulates. Thus, the electrical picture of, say, a
long bar oriented at 45 degrees might look like
Figure 3.29: The bar generates responses in the

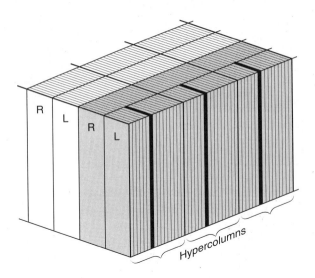

Figure 3.29

The possible response patterns in the visual cortex to a long bar oriented at 45 degrees and presented to the left eye. This bar covers an area of the retina served by three hypercolumns, so it generates activity in a number of separated areas in the cortex. Activity occurs in neurons in the 45-degree-angle orientation columns in the left-ocular-dominance column in each hypercolumn (dark areas).

45-degree orientation columns in each of the hypercolumns that are activated.

The way the bar is represented—split up into electrical activity in separated places in the cortex—raises an important question: How is the information in each of these areas combined to result in a perception of the whole bar? This is called the **binding problem** because it asks how we can bind separated information together to create a perceptual whole.

One possible answer to the binding problem may be that the separated orientation columns can somehow communicate with each other. There is, in fact, evidence that a network of neurons connects these columns (Gilbert & Wiesel, 1989). This is a first step toward solving the problem, but we need to go a step further, by asking what kinds of messages these neurons might send from one column to another.

A description of the possible nature of the column-to-column messages has been proposed in a bold hypothesis by a number of German researchers (Engel et al., 1991a; Engel, Konig, & Singer, 1991b; Engel et al., 1992; Gray & Singer, 1989; Singer et al., 1993). Their hypothesis is that objects are represented in the visual system by groups of neurons that they call **cell assemblies,** and that these assemblies become activated when the firing of the neurons in these assemblies generates oscillatory responses (alternating bursts of high and low rates of firing) that become synchronized with one another. To examine what this means, let's look at an experiment described by Andreas Engel and his co-workers (1992).

Engel used two electrodes to simultaneously record activity from two neurons, separated by 7 mm in the striate cortex, that both responded best to vertically oriented bars. Figure 3.30 shows three different ways that stimuli were presented to the neurons' receptive fields (top records) and shows plots called *cross-correlograms* (bottom graphs) that indicate whether the neurons were firing in synchrony with each other.

Figure 3.30a shows the cross-correlogram when a single long bar was swept across the two receptive fields. The wavy record means that the neurons both fired in bursts separated by quieter periods (oscillatory responding) and that the two neurons' bursts were synchronized. When two smaller bars were swept across the receptive fields, as in Figure 3.30b, the synchronization of the two neurons' responses became weaker, and when the two bars were moved in opposite directions, as in Figure 3.30c, the flatness of the cross-correlogram indicates that the synchronization had totally disappeared. In other words, the firing of these two neurons oscillated in a synchronized manner when a whole bar moved across their receptive fields, but their response was less synchronized if the bar was split, and not synchronized at all if the two halves were moving in opposite directions. Synchrony of response therefore signals the presence of a whole object. Another way to describe this result is to say that synchrony is the "glue" that binds together re-

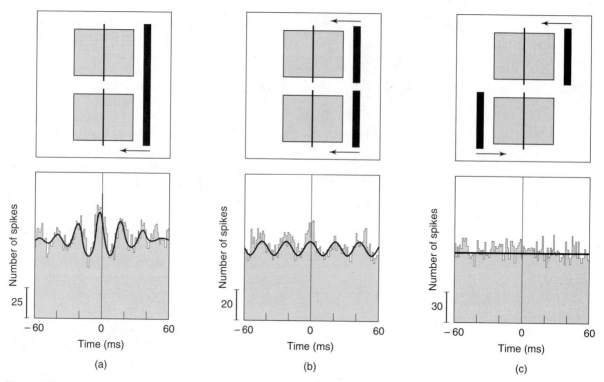

Figure 3.30

The top diagrams show the following three ways that a bar was swept across the receptive fields of two neurons in the cat's striate cortex: (a) the whole bar; (b) the bar split in two; and (c) the bar split and the parts moved in opposite directions. Each neuron responded with an oscillatory response (one that alternates between bursts of high and low firing). The bottom diagrams are cross-correlograms for each stimulus condition. Larger peaks and troughs, as in (a), indicate that the firing patterns generated by the two neurons were synchronized with each other. (Adapted from Engel et al., 1992.)

sponses that occur in different places in the cortex but that are generated by the same object.

This idea of synchrony as a "binding" agent has great potential because it also works with neurons that have receptive fields with different preferred orientations (they don't both have to respond best to the same orientation, as in Figure 3.30). Synchrony has also been demonstrated between striate and extrastriate neurons. It has also been proposed that synchrony may occur between neurons representing different qualities of an object. According to this idea, if neurons that respond to the color, the movement, and the shape of our ball fire in synchrony with each other, this synchronized firing would indicate that all three qualities belong to the same object (Stryker, 1989).

It is important to acknowledge that this "synchronization" explanation of how binding occurs is a hypothesis that has just recently been proposed. The final explanation of the binding problem may be quite different from this one. The important point is that any object causes widespread activity in the brain, so that, before we can say we understand the connection between neural responses and perception, we need to discover how all of these many separated signals somehow combine their information to create our perception of meaningful objects.

In this chapter and in Chapter 2 we have provided a general overview of the physiological events that occur in the visual system in response to our rolling red ball. In the chapters that follow, we will fill in many of the details of this process by describing how the visual system processes specific qualities, such as color, shape, depth, and movement. As we focus on these specific qualities, we will see that in some cases we can draw close parallels between neural firing and the perception of these qualities, but that much remains to be learned about the physiological processes involved in perceiving even simple stimuli. We will also begin moving away from purely physiological explanations of perception and moving toward explanations based on the stimulus and cognitive approaches, which have many important things to tell us.

In this chapter we have seen that the monkey's visual system, and presumably the human's as well, contains many neurons that respond selectively to stimuli with a specific orientation. These "orientation detectors" probably play a role in our ability to see features of shapes, objects, and visual patterns.

Researchers have wondered how insects are able to see orientations. Do they use primatelike orientation detectors, which can detect the orientation of objects even if they are stationary, or do they use a mechanism that detects orientation by analyzing the movement of patterns across the their receptors? It makes sense that insects may combine orientation detection with movement detection, because their extremely small and primitive visual system is capable of far less neural processing than is that of the monkey or the human.

However, recent behavioral research has shown that bees can detect orientation separately from movement. M. V. Srinivasan, S. W. Zhang, and B. Rolfe (1993) demonstrated this ability by training honeybees to negotiate a Y-maze to receive sugar water. The bees entered the maze through a small hole and could see two patterns in the arms of the maze: one with vertical bars and the other with horizontal bars (Figure 3.31). If the bee approached the rewarded pattern, it received sugar water from a feeder behind the pattern. If it approached the unrewarded pattern, it found no sugar water. When one pattern was consistently rewarded, the bees approached it on 87 percent of the trials, indicating their ability to discriminate horizontal from vertical bars.

But were the bees making this discrimination based on information provided by movement of the bars' image across their receptors as they flew toward the patterns? To answer this question, Srinivasan and co-workers flashed the stripes for

ORIENTATION DETECTORS IN INSECTS

25/1,000 second every half second, thereby decreasing the possibility that the bars could create motion by sweeping across the bees' receptors. Since the bees still picked the rewarded pattern on 62 percent of the trials, the bees were apparently discriminating orientation based on geometrical cues and not on the basis of image motion. According to Srinivasan et al. (1993), these results "suggest the existence of orientation channels analogous in mechanism to those in the mammalian visual cortex" (p. 540).

This idea of mammalian-like orientation detectors in insects is bolstered by David O'Carroll's (1993) finding that there are feature-detecting neurons in the optic lobe of the dragon-

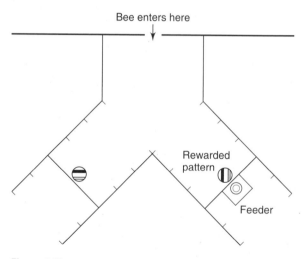

Figure 3.31

Top view of the maze used to determine a bee's ability to detect orientation. From the entryway, the bees could see the vertical and horizontal patterns at the ends of the left and right arms of the maze. In this example, the rewarded pattern was in the left arm of the maze. If the bee chose this arm, it gained access to the feeder behind the pattern. (Adapted from Srinivasan, Zhang, & Rolfe, 1993.)

fly. Some of these neurons respond only to small targets, and others respond only to long bars, a property similar to the end-stopped cells in the primate visual cortex. In addition, some of these cells respond to only a narrow range of orientations, another property that is similar to those of neurons in the cat and monkey visual cortex.

The fact that orientation detectors have been discovered in dragonflies, combined with Srinivasan's psychophysical results in bees, strengthens the possibility that similar orientation detectors may exist in bees. But let's go a step further in speculating about possible physiological detectors in bees, by considering what stimuli are important to bees. Flowers are particularly important to bees, and psychophysical experiments by M. Lehrer and coworkers (1995) show that bees do, in fact, prefer flower-like patterns. In these experiments, bees were released in the middle of a circular enclosure which contained a number of patterns displayed on the walls. Figure 3.32a and b shows two sets of these patterns and the percentage of trials on which bees spontaneously flew toward each pattern. Notice that the bees were more likely to fly toward the radiating pattern that resembles a single flower, as in (a) or to the pattern that resembles a group of flowers, as in (b).

Does showing that bees prefer flower-like patterns mean that they posses flower-detecting neurons? Not necessarily, since it is unlikely that organisms have specialized detectors for every shape they can perceive. However, when specialized detectors do exist, they are usually tuned to respond best to stimuli that are especially important to the animal, such as neurons in the monkey that respond best to faces (see Figure 3.24).

Another example of a neuron specialized for an animal's needs are the neurons reported by

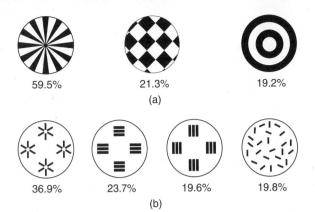

Figure 3.32

Stimuli used to test bees' preference for various patterns. The numbers below each pattern indicate the percentage of trials on which the bees flew toward that pattern. In (a) three patterns were presented simultaneously, and in (b) four patterns were presented simultaneously. In both cases the bees preferred the patterns that resembled flowers. (Adapted from Lehrer, et. al., 1995.)

Jerome Lettvin and his coworkers (1959) in a classic paper that described "bug detectors" in the frog's retina that responded best to small moving bug-like shapes. Given the importance of flowers to the bee, it is not unreasonable to speculate that the bee might have neurons that respond best to flower-like stimuli. We can't say whether this is the case until physiological results are available, but when the physiological experiments are carried out, it would certainly make sense to look both for basic orientation detectors similar to those found in the dragonfly, and for more specialized "flower detectors" that are specifically tailored to the bee's needs.

SENSITIVE PERIODS IN PERCEPTUAL DEVELOPMENT

The process of perceptual development can be strongly influenced by the environment within which an animal develops, and this influence is strongest during an early period in the animal's life, called the **sensitive period.** David Hubel and Torsten Wiesel demonstrated the existence of this sensitive period by showing that changing the early experience of cats and monkeys influences the number of binocular neurons in their visual cortex (Wiesel, 1982).

Binocular cortical neurons are neurons that respond to the stimulation of both eyes. Hubel and Wiesel first determined that most of the neurons in the visual cortex of the newborn kitten are binocular neurons, and they then raised the kittens under the following two conditions that disrupted the coordinated stimulation that would normally have reached each kitten's two eyes: (1) monocular deprivation, in which one eye was sutured shut, so that the kitten could see details out of only one eye, and (2) image misalignment, in which the kitten's eye muscles were cut so that the eyes were looking in different directions.

The Effect of Monocular Deprivation

The effect of monocular deprivation on binocularity is illustrated by **ocular dominance histograms,** such as those in Figure 3.33. These histograms are determined by recording from a large number of cells and then rating each cell's ability to respond to stimulation of both the contralateral eye (the eye on the opposite side of the head from the cell) and the ipsilateral eye (the eye on the same side as the cell). Each cell is placed in one of seven categories according to the degree of **ocular dominance,** as listed in Table 3.2.

The histograms in Figure 3.33 show the striking effect of monocular deprivation on the way the kitten's corticle cells responded to stimulation of each eye. Whereas most of the cells in the normal cat respond to both eyes, and therefore fall into categories 2–6 of the histogram, all the cells in the deprived kitten responded only to stimulation of the undeprived eye and are placed in category 7.

Hubel and Wiesel found that the longer kittens were monocularly deprived, the greater were the abnormalities in their ocular dominance histograms; however, if the deprivation was postponed until the kittens became adult cats, even long periods of monocular deprivation had no effect on their ocular dominance histograms. This finding led Hubel and Wiesel to propose a sensitive period, early in the kitten's life, during which monocular deprivation has a large effect; once this period is past, however, deprivation has little effect.

To investigate this idea, Hubel and Wiesel (1970) monocularly deprived kittens at various

Figure 3.33

(a) An ocular dominance histogram of recordings from 223 neurons in the visual cortex of adult cats. Numbers refer to the categories described in Table 3.2. Note that a large number of cells respond to the stimulation of both eyes. (b) Ocular dominance histogram of 25 cells recorded from the visual cortex of a 2 1⁄2-month-old kitten that was reared with its right eye occluded until the time of the experiment. The dashed bar on the right indicates that 5 cells did not respond to the stimulation of either eye. The solid bar indicates that all 20 cells that did respond to stimulation responded only in the eye that was opened during rearing (Wiesel & Hubel, 1963). See the text for further explanations.

times after birth. They found that deprivation for only three days between the fourth and fifth weeks of life caused a large change in the ocular dominance histograms. But deprivation started after about the eighth week caused smaller effects, until even long periods of deprivation at four months caused no effect. Hubel and Wiesel concluded that the sensitive period for suscepti-

bility to monocular deprivation begins in the fourth week and extends to about 4 months of age. Later research, using longer periods of deprivation and more sensitive tests of brain function, has shown that monocular deprivation can cause effects as late as the sixth month in cats (Figure 3.34) (Cynader, Timney, & Mitchell, 1980; Jones, Spear, & Tong, 1984; Olson & Freeman, 1980).

The large effects of monocular deprivation on the kitten's visual system also led researchers to investigate how binocularity is influenced by misalignment of the images in the two eyes.

The Effect of Image Misalignment

Misalignment of the images in the two eyes can be accomplished by either cutting the eye muscles or fitting the animal, with a helmet that contains small optical prisms. Cutting the eye muscles causes the eyes to become misaligned, as shown in Figure 3.35, and optical prisms, shown

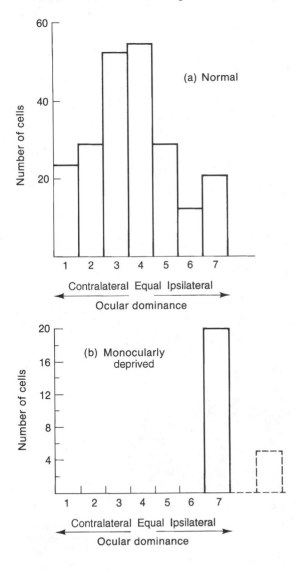

Table 3.2

Categories of binocular response

Category	Description
1	Cell responds only to stimulation of the contralateral eye. Thus, if the cell is in the right hemisphere, it responds only to stimulation of the left eye.
2	Cell responds much more to stimulation of the contralateral eye than to stimulation of the ipsilateral eye.
3	Cell responds slightly more to stimulation of the contralateral eye.
4	Cell responds equally to stimulation of each eye.
5	Cell responds slightly more to stimulation of the ipsilateral eye.
6	Cell responds much more to stimulation of the ipsilateral eye.
7	Cell responds only to stimulation of the ipsilateral eye.

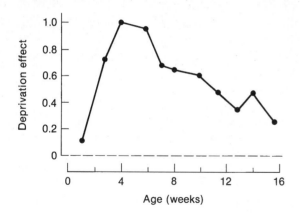

Figure 3.34

Profile of the sensitive period for monocular deprivation in kittens. "Deprivation effect" (the vertical axis) indicates how severely binocularity was disrupted by 10–12 days of monocular deprivation imposed at the ages on the horizontal axis. This curve indicates that monocular deprivation causes substantial effects as long as four months after birth. Other measurements indicate that deprivation effects continue to occur up to about 6 months of age. (From Olson & Freeman, 1980.)

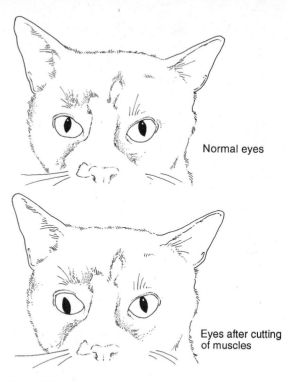

Figure 3.35

The appearance of a normal cat's eyes and the eyes of a cat that have been misaligned by cutting of the eye muscles.

in Figure 3.36, change the direction of the light entering the eyes. Both procedures cause effects similar to those observed after monocular deprivation. Whereas 80 percent of visual cortical cells in normal cats respond to stimulation of both eyes, only 20 percent of the cells in cats with cut eye muscles respond to stimulation of both eyes (Hubel & Wiesel, 1965b). Similarly, M. L. J. Crawford and G. K. von Noorden (1980) found that 70 percent of cortical cells in normal monkeys respond to stimulation of both eyes, but less than 10 percent of the cells in monkeys that had worn prism helmets for 60 days respond to stimulation of both eyes.

All of the experiments we have discussed so far show that the visual systems of young cats and monkeys are very sensitive to changes in the visual environment. This sensitivity to the envi-

Figure 3.36

A monkey wearing an optical prism helmet, which causes a misalignment of the images in the two eyes (Crawford & von Noorden, 1980).

ronment has been called **cortical malleability** because the visual cortex is malleable (changeable) for a long period after birth. This malleability has important implications for the vision of young children with visual problems.

The Effect of Visual Cortical Malleability in Children

In Hubel and Wiesel's monocular rearing experiments, cats that had one eye sutured shut between 4 and 8 weeks of age essentially lost the use of that eye, as indicated behaviorally and by the fact that no cortical cells would fire to stimulation of the previously occluded eye. There is increasing evidence that a condition called **amblyopia**—a large reduction in the visual acuity in one eye that is not caused by a physical problem in the eye—may occur in humans because, as young children, they had reduced use of one eye due to patching following an eye operation.

Shinobu Awaya and co-workers (1973) investigated the histories of 19 patients with amblyopia and found that all had had their amblyopic (low-visual-acuity) eye closed early in life, following an eye operation; most of the closures had occurred during the first year after birth. This type of amblyopia has therefore been called **stimulus deprivation amblyopia,** a term that distinguishes it from amblyopia due to other causes (von Noorden & Maumanee, 1968). It seems likely that the same mechanisms are responsible for stimulus deprivation amblyopia and the loss of vision in Hubel and Wiesel's monocularly reared kittens.

Another cause of reduced vision in one eye is **strabismus,** an imbalance in the eye muscles that upsets the coordination between the two eyes. We have seen that upsetting the coordination between the eyes of kittens by cutting the eye muscles causes a loss of binocular neurons, just

as in monocular deprivation. Numerous investigators have recently found evidence of a similar lack of binocular cells in people who had strabismus as young children. Strabismus can be corrected by a muscle operation that restores the balance between the two eyes. However, if this operation is not performed until the child is 4–5 years old, a loss of binocularly driven cells can occur similar to that observed in monocularly deprived cats or in cats with artificially produced strabismus.

How do we know that people who had early strabismus lack binocularly driven cells? Obviously, we can't record from single neurons in the human cortex. We can, however, use a perceptual effect, called the **tilt aftereffect,** that enables us to estimate the binocularity of a person's cortical neurons.

D E M O N S T R A T I O N
The Tilt Aftereffect

You can illustrate the tilt aftereffect to yourself by covering up the pattern on the right in Figure 3.37 and staring for about 60 seconds at the adaptation lines on the left. As you stare, move your eyes around the pattern slowly. Then, when you see the pattern begin to "shimmer," cover up the left side of the figure and shift your gaze to the test lines on the right. If the aftereffect is successful, you will see the lines on the right as being slightly tilted to the left even though, in reality, they are vertical. ●

The tilt aftereffect has been used to measure binocularity by making use of the phenomenon of **interocular transfer.** If an observer looks at the adaptation lines with one eye and then looks at the test lines with the other eye, the aftereffect will transfer from one eye to the other. This transfer, which causes an effect about 60–70 percent as strong as the effect that occurs if the adaptation and the test lines are viewed with the same eye, indicates that information from one eye must be shared with the other. Since the first place that neurons carrying signals from the left and the right eye meet is the visual cortex (remember that little or no interaction between the eyes occurs in the lateral geniculate nucleus), this information sharing between the two eyes must take place at the level of the visual cortex, or higher. The degree of transfer of the tilt aftereffect, therefore, can be used to assess the state of binocularly driven cells in the visual cortex (Aslin & Banks, 1978; Mitchell, Reardon, & Muir, 1975; Mitchell & Ware, 1974; Ware & Mitchell, 1974).

Armed with the tilt aftereffect, Martin Banks, Richard Aslin, and Robert Letson (1975) measured the degree of interocular transfer in people who had had strabismus early in life. Figure 3.38 plots the magnitude of interocular transfer as a function of the age at which 12 people born with strabismus had had corrective surgery. When the surgery had been carried out early in the person's life, interocular transfer was high, indicating good binocular function, but if the surgery had been delayed, interocular transfer was poor, indicating poor binocular function. Based on the results in Figure 3.38, other data from their experiments, and data from similar experiments by A. Hohmann and Otto Creutzfeldt (1975), Aslin and Banks (1978) concluded that a sensitive period for binocular development in humans begins during the first year of life, reaches a peak during the second year, and decreases by 4–8 years of age.

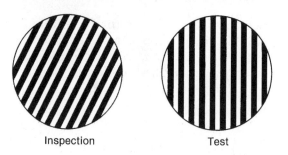

Inspection   Test

Figure 3.37

Stimuli for measuring the tilt aftereffect. Cover the test pattern on the right, and stare at the pattern on the left for about 60 seconds, moving your eyes around the pattern during that time. Then cover the lefthand pattern, and transfer your gaze to the test lines on the right. If you see the test lines as tilted to the left, you are experiencing the tilt aftereffect.

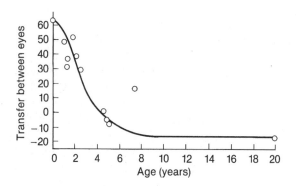

Figure 3.38

The degree of interocular transfer of the tilt aftereffect as a function of the age at which surgery had been performed to correct strabismus. (From Banks, Aslin, & Letson, 1975.)

REVIEW

Processing in the Lateral Geniculate Nucleus

Outline

- The lateral geniculate nucleus (LGN) is the first place most of the fibers leaving the retina synapse.

- There is a map of the retina on the LGN called a retinotopic map. This means that each point on the LGN corresponds to a point on the retina and that neighboring points on the LGN correspond to neighboring points on the retina.

- The M ganglion cells synapse in layers 1 and 2 of the LGN (magno layers), and the P cells synapse in layers 3, 4, 5, and 6 (parvo layers).

Questions

1. What is the major function of the LGN? Cite some evidence to support your answer. (92)

2. Describe the organization of the retinotopic maps in each of the layers of the LGN. Why did Gordon Walls compare the LGN to a club sandwich? (92)

3. How did Schiller et al. determine that the magno and parvo layers of the LGN serve different functions? What functions are served by the magno and parvo layers? (93)

Processing in the Striate Cortex

- Hubel and Wiesel identified three major types of neurons in the visual cortex: simple, complex, and end-stopped.

- The visual cortex is organized into location columns, with neurons within each location column having receptive fields in the same location on the retina.

- The magnification factor refers to the fact that a given area of foveal receptors is allotted more space on the cortex than the same-sized area of peripheral receptors.

4. Describe the properties of simple, complex, and end-stopped neurons. (95)
5. What is an orientation tuning curve? (95)
6. How did Hubel and Wiesel determine that location columns existed in the cortex? (97)
7. How do receptive field locations shift when an electrode is moved along an oblique track in the cortex? Compare this shift for receptive fields near the fovea and further into the periphery. (98)
8. Explain why the magnification factor occurs in terms of the density of neurons in the retina and the cortex. (99)
9. What additional factor increases magnification of the fovea on the cortex? What is the relationship between magnification and perception? (99)

- Orientation columns are columns in which all cells respond best to the same stimulus orientation.

- Ocular dominance columns are columns in which all neurons respond best to the same eye.

- A hypercolumn consists of a location column, a set of orientation columns, and a pair of ocular dominance columns.

- A basic property of the visual system is that perception is based on electrical signals that bear little resemblance to the stimuli they represent.

10. How did Hubel and Wiesel demonstrate orientation columns? How are orientation columns for all orientations arranged relative to each other? Describe the 2-deoxyglucose technique. What does it tell us about orientation columns? (99)

11. How are columns for the left and right eyes arranged in the cortex? (101)

12. What is the basis for calling a hypercolumn a processing module? (101)

13. Describe how the striate cortex is activated when a long bar oriented at 45 degrees is presented to the left eye. (102)

The Relationship between Physiology and Perception

- It is often difficult to directly determine the relationship between physiology and perception. This relationship can be determined indirectly from the relationship between the stimulus and physiology and between the stimulus and perception.

- Psychophysical selective-adaptation experiments have been used to help determine the relationship between physiology and perception. In such an experiment, the person is adapted to one stimulus value (such as a particular orientation), and then the effect of this adaptation on a range of orientations is determined.

14. Describe Borg et al.'s experiment on the taste system. What do their results tell us about the relationship between nerve activity and the perception of citric acid? (103)

15. What is a grating stimulus? Contrast sensitivity? (103)

16. Describe the experiment in which observers were selectively adapted to orientation. What do the results of this experiment tell us about the link between physiology and perception? (103)

Processing Past the Striate Cortex

- Extrastriate areas that respond to visual stimulation account for a large fraction of the cerebral cortex. These areas are organized into streams that process different types of visual information.

- The functions of specific structures in the extrastriate pathways have been determined by three basic techniques: brain lesioning, brain stimulation, and recording from neurons.

- Most research on extrastriate pathways has been carried out on monkeys. However, there is some evidence to support the idea that the human visual system also has separate extrastriate pathways.

17. Describe Ungerleider and Mishkin's experiment showing that there are two separate visual processing streams in the cortex. (105)
18. Describe the two extrastriate pathways. (106)
19. Describe lesioning, recording, and stimulation experiments that indicate the function of the MT cortex. (107)
20. What do recording experiments tell us about the functions of area V4 and the IT cortex? (108)
21. Describe the results of PET scans, clinical studies, and psychophysical experiments that support the idea of multiple visual channels. (110)
22. Describe the structures activated by the rolling red ball. (112)
23. Why is a description of the visual system in terms of two separated extrastriate channels an oversimplification? (112)

Some Challenges for Physiological Research

- Perception is an extremely active process. Observers actively seek out information in the environment by directing their attention to objects in which they are interested.

- The fact that a particular object triggers activity in a large number of separate structures creates the following problem: How is this activity combined to create a perceptual whole? This is called the binding problem.

24. Describe Moran and Desimone's experiment, which showed that neural responding is influenced by attention. (113)

25. Describe the proposed solution to the binding problem that involves the oscillatory firing of neurons in cell assemblies. (114)

Orientation Detectors in Insects

- Behavioral and physiological research indicates that insects can detect orientation separately from movement and have mammalian-like orientation detectors.

26. Describe the behavioral experiments that demonstrated the bee's ability to detect orientation, and their preference for flower-like patterns. Describe physiological experiments on dragonfly feature-detecting neurons. What do these results suggest about the possibility of feature-detecting neurons in the bee? (118)

Sensitive Periods in Perceptual Development

- Perceptual development can be influenced by the environment within which an animal develops, and this influence is especially strong during a period early in the animal's life called the sensitive period.

27. Describe how monocular deprivation and image misalignment affect the responding of binocular cells in kittens and cats. What do these results tell us about the cat's sensitive period? What is cortical malleability? (120)

28. How have the animal results been generalized to human amblyopia? What is the sensitive period for binocular development in humans? (123)

④

PERCEIVING COLOR

Color is one of the most obvious and pervasive qualities in our environment. We interact with it every time we note the color of a traffic light, when we choose clothes that are color-coordinated, or when we enjoy the colors of a painting. But the importance of color extends beyond helping us drive safely or providing aesthetic experiences. Color has important functions that relate to our ability to perceive forms accurately, to identify objects, and to carry out tasks that are important to survival (Jacobs, 1993; Mollon, 1989; Wurm et al, 1993).

FUNCTIONS OF COLOR VISION

Two of the most important functions of color vision are (1) creating perceptual segregation and (2) signaling.

Perceptual Segregation

Perceptual segregation, the process of determining the boundaries of objects that overlap, is something most people take for granted. But the ability to tell one object from another and especially to see small objects against a varied background, such as flowers in a field or individual people in a crowd, is greatly facilitated by the ability to see in color. In fact, this ability is crucial to the survival of many species. Consider, for example, a monkey foraging for fruit in the forest. A monkey with good color vision easily detects red fruit against a green background (Color Plate 4.1a), but a color-blind monkey would find it difficult to find the fruit (Color Plate 4.1b).

Some researchers have proposed that monkey and human color vision evolved for the express purpose of detecting fruit in the forest (Mollon, 1989; Walls, 1942). This suggestion sounds reasonable when we consider the difficulty color-blind human observers have when confronted with the seemingly simple task of picking berries. Knut Nordby (1990), a totally color-blind visual scientist who sees the world in shades of gray, described his experience: "Picking berries has always been a big problem. I often have to grope around among the leaves with my fingers, feeling for the berries by their shape" (p. 308). If Nordby's experience is any indication, a color-blind monkey would have difficulty finding berries or fruit and would be less likely to survive than monkeys with color vision.

Colors not only provide the contrast that helps us see objects against a background, as in the case of berries in a bush, but also provide a cue that tells us that parts of an object that are separated by overlapping objects actually belong together and also prevent us from being confused by shadows, reflections, or uneven illumination. Although we take our ability to perceive objects in shadows for granted, changing illumination can create **illumination contours** that may be mistaken for the contours of an object, so a person who is completely color-blind may think that an object that is half in shadow and half in the light is two separate objects. One reason that people with normal color vision are rarely fooled by these illumination contours is that changes in lighting caused by shadows have little or no effect on their perception of color.

Signaling

When we stop at a red traffic light, we are responding to a color's signaling function. Certain colors have specific meanings. Some are learned, as in the case of humans responding to traffic signals, and others are instinctive, as in the case of a female robin responding to a male robin's red breast or a stickleback fish using the red belly of its potential mate as a signal to initiate a complex underwater "mating dance." Color also indicates whether fruit is ripe or spoiled; it can be used as a health index such as a person's skin color, or as a signal that indicates emotions such as fear (flushed skin) or embarrassment (a red blush). It is clear that color serves a number of

functions, which for some animals may be crucial to survival. But here our main interest in color is to determine the mechanisms that make it possible for us to perceive it in the first place.

Color is the first visual quality we discuss in detail not because it is obvious in our environment or because of its importance to survival, but because it provides a model system that uses many of the principles we have introduced in the first three chapters. This chapter also establishes new principles that we will apply in the remainder of the book. One of the goals of the chapter is to illustrate how researchers have used both psychophysical and physiological approaches to determine a perceptual mechanism. Another goal is to introduce some basic principles of sensory coding that apply not only to color, but to other perceptual qualities as well. We begin our discussion of color perception by considering how we describe our experience of color.

DESCRIBING COLOR EXPERIENCE

Imagine the following situation: You awaken early in the morning, and although it is still dark, you are unable to go back to sleep, so you get up. It is about 30 minutes before sunrise, with only a hint of lightness in the sky, and as you look out the window, you see only fuzzy, ill-defined grayish forms. Keeping the lights off, you continue observing the slowly lightening scene in your yard. Even though you know the trees outside are green and the flowers are red, yellow, lavender, and orange, you see none of these colors. It is still dark, and gray is your predominant perception (Color Plate 4.2a). As the sun comes up and the sky lightens further, your perceptions begin to shift from shades of gray to varied colors. The trees' leaves become green, and the flowers take on their familiar colors. In addition, another change occurs: Shapes that initially appeared fuzzy and ill-defined are now sharply outlined (Color Plate 4.2b).

This change in perception from fuzzy grays to sharply defined reds, greens, and yellows is the Purkinje shift we described in Chapter 2. As your vision shifts from rod vision to cone vision with the increase in illumination, you perceive things more sharply and in color. This change in perception illustrates a number of important things about color perception.

One thing this shift illustrates is the distinction between achromatic colors and chromatic colors. Whites, blacks, and shades of gray are **achromatic colors.** Blues, reds, greens, and yellows are examples of **chromatic colors.** Another term for chromatic color is **hue**, but this term is rarely used in everyday language. We usually say, "The color of the fire engine is red" rather than "The hue (or chromatic color) of the fire engine is red." Therefore, throughout the rest of this chapter, we will use the word *color* to mean "chromatic color" or "hue," and we will use the term *achromatic color* to refer to white, gray, or black.

In addition to illustrating the difference between achromatic and chromatic color, the perceptual shift that occurs with the change from rod vision to cone vision raises a number of questions about the relationship between perception and neural processing. What is it about the neural processing in the rod and cone systems that accounts for the shift from achromatic to chromatic vision? Specifically, what is it about the cones that adds chromatic color to our perceptions? We will answer these questions soon. But first, let's pose two questions about color: (1) How many colors can we see? (2) Are there a few colors that psychologists focus on in color vision research?

One approach to the question "How many colors can we see?" is to start at one end of the visible spectrum (Color Plate 2.1) and slowly increase the wavelength until the observer indicates that he or she can discriminate a difference in color. When we do this, we find that observers can discriminate about 200 steps in the visible spectrum (Gouras, 1989). We can multiply these 200 discriminable colors in two ways. First, we can vary the intensity of each step. Changing the intensity usually changes the brightness of the color, and if we slowly increase the intensity of one color, we can distinguish about 500 steps of brightness. Second, we can vary the saturation of each step. If we start with a 640-nm light, which appears red, and then add white to it, we say that the resulting pink color is less saturated than the original red. **Saturation** is inversely related to the amount of whiteness in a color—that is, the more saturated a color, the less whiteness it contains. Taking into account that each of the 200 discriminable colors has up to 500 values of brightness and 20 values of saturation, we can discriminate about $200 \times 500 \times 20 = 2,000,000$ different colors (Gouras, 1989).

Another approach to determining the number of colors we can see is to determine how many names for colors there are. The worlds of advertising, paint manufacturing, and cosmetics expose us to such names as "crushed strawberry," "azure blue," "Kelly green," and "Chinese red." Although the ingenious names invented to describe different shades of paint, lipstick, floor tile, and fabric are far from 2 million, the number of such names is still impressively high. One compilation, published by the National Bureau of Standards, lists 7,500 different color names (Judd & Kelly, 1965). Obviously, 2 million or even 7,500 are far too many colors for us to deal with, and this brings us to our second question: Are there a few colors that psychologists focus on in color vision research? The answer to this question is yes, since color scientists prefer to deal with just a few basic colors.

Research shows that we can describe all the colors we can discriminate by using the terms *red, yellow, green, blue,* and their combinations (Abramov & Gordon, 1994; Hurvich, 1981). When people are presented with many different colors and are asked to describe them, they can describe all of them if they are allowed to use all four terms, but they can't if one of these is omitted. Furthermore, other colors, such as orange, violet, purple, and brown, are not needed to achieve these descriptions (Fuld, Wooten, & Whalen, 1981; Quinn, Rosano, & Wooten, 1988). Thus, red, yellow, green, and blue are considered to be basic colors by color researchers. These colors can be arranged in a color circle, as shown in Figure 4.1 and Color Plate 4.3, so that each is perceptually similar to the one next to it. Thus, as we move around the circle, we see the colors change gradually from one to the next. Since they are arranged in a circle, we eventually return to where we started.

Hurvich (1981) described the experience of moving around the circle in this way: If we start with red at 12 o'clock and move clockwise around the circle, the colors become increasingly yellow, passing through various shades of orange, until we reach pure yellow at 3 o'clock. We call this *pure yellow* because it contains no trace of the red we just left or of the green we will approach as we move further around the circle. As we continue, the colors become greener, until we reach a pure green at 6 o'clock. After green, blue becomes stronger until we reach a pure blue at 9 o'clock, and then the blue turns to violet as red begins to reappear. Finally, we come back to pure red at the top of the circle. Though we encounter many different colors as we travel around the circle, we recognize that these other chromatic colors consist of various proportions of the four basic colors: red, yellow, green, and blue.

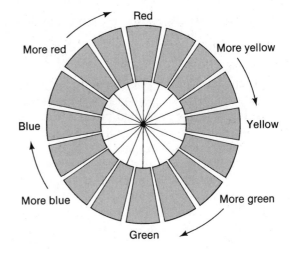

Figure 4.1

The color circle. In this circle, also shown in Color Plate 4.3, we arrange colors by placing perceptually similar colors next to each other. When we do this, we find that the colors can be arranged in a circle with the four basic colors at 12, 3, 6, and 9 o'clock on the circle. (From Hurvich, 1981.)

These four colors are considered basic not only because all of the colors in the color circle can be described in terms of these colors, but for other reasons as well. Cross-cultural studies show that, although different cultures vary in the number of terms used to describe colors, the sequence of color terms always enters the language in the sequence shown in Figure 4.2. All cultures use names that stand for the equivalent of black and white, and red, yellow, green, and

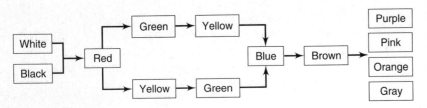

Figure 4.2

Colors named by different cultures follow the pattern shown here, the colors being added in the order shown. Thus, cultures with just two colors use black and white; cultures with three colors use black, white, and red; and cultures with four colors use black, white, and red, plus either green or yellow.

blue are added before any others (Berlin & Kay, 1969; Boynton & Olson, 1987, 1990). After sifting through all of the evidence regarding the names people assign to different colors, researchers have concluded that only the terms in Figure 4.2 are used consistently by people, and that there must therefore be a universal, shared physiologi-

cal basis for the experiences associated with these colors (Abramov & Gordon, 1994; Pokorny, Shevell, & Smith, 1991). In this chapter we will focus on the nature of this physiological process. The first step is to answer the question: Which physical stimulus quality is most closely related to color perception? The answer to this question begins in Isaac Newton's room at Cambridge University in 1704.

Color and Wavelength

In his room at Cambridge University, Isaac Newton placed a prism so that sunlight shining through a hole in the shutter of his window entered the prism (Figure 4.3). He observed that, as the sunlight passed through the prism, it was transformed by its passage through the prism

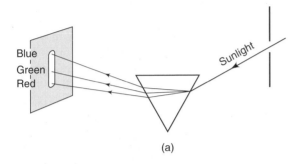

(a)

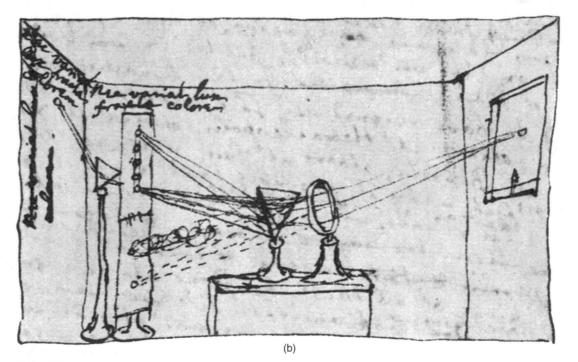

(b)

Figure 4.3

(a) When Isaac Newton passed sunlight through a prism he observed that the white sunlight was separated into the colors of the spectrum. (b) His original sketch of the experiment.

Perceiving Color

into a spectrum of colors like the one in Color Plate 2.1. When Newton recombined the spectral colors with a lens, he re-created the sunlight with which he started. On the basis of this and other experiments, Newton concluded that sunlight is made up of all of the spectral colors. Later work showed that these spectral colors differ in wavelength: Wavelengths between about 400 and 450 nm appear violet; 450–500 nm, blue; 500–570 nm, green; 570–590 nm, yellow; 590–620 nm, orange; and 620–700 nm, red. Thus the wavelength of light is the physical property connected with color perception, and knowing the wavelength of a light gives us a good idea of its color.

In our everyday experience, however, we are rarely exposed to single wavelengths. Light sources that illuminate the objects in our environment give off many different wavelengths, and the objects reflect many wavelengths into our eyes. Let's first describe the wavelengths given off by two sources of light: the sun and incandescent light bulbs.

Figure 4.4 shows the **wavelength distributions** of two important light sources: **tungsten light,** the light emitted by incandescent light bulbs (named after the bulb's tungsten filament), and sunlight. The wavelength distribution of

tungsten light contains much more intensity at long wavelengths than at short wavelengths, as indicated by the dashed line, and so appears yellow. The wavelength distribution of sunlight is relatively flat, indicating that sunlight contains an approximately equal intensity of each wavelength across the spectrum. Light that has equal intensity at all wavelengths in the spectrum is called **white light.**

Light from light bulbs or the sun can reach our eyes directly if we look at the light sources (not recommended in the case of the sun!), but most of the light we see is reflected from objects in the environment. To understand why objects have different colors, we must look at the reflectance curves of the objects themselves. **Reflectance** is the percentage of the light falling on an object that is reflected from the object. A **reflectance curve** is a plot of reflectance versus wavelength. Figure 4.5 shows reflectance curves for white, gray, and black paper and for blue and green pigments. Notice that for the three achromatic colors reflectance is approximately equal across the spectrum, but that chromatic colors reflect some wavelengths and not others. This reflection of only some of the wavelengths in the spectrum, which is called **selective reflection,** is

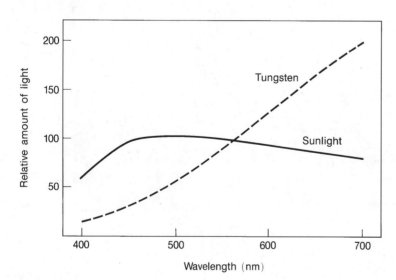

Figure 4.4

The wavelength distribution of sunlight and of light from a tungsten light bulb. (Based on Judd, MacAdam, & Wyszecki, 1964.)

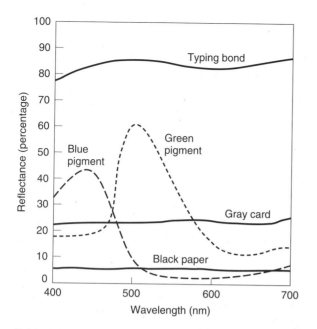

Figure 4.5

Reflectance curves for surfaces that appear white, gray, and black, and for blue and green pigments. (Adapted from Clulow, 1972.)

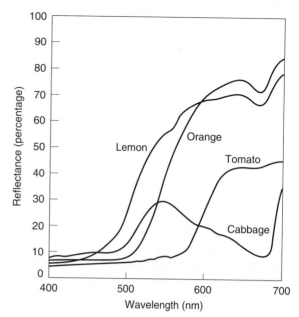

Figure 4.6

Reflectance curves of some common foods. Knowing which wavelengths are reflected enables us to roughly predict the pigment's color by consulting Table 4.1. Try this prediction for these foods and for the pigments in Figure 4.5. (Adapted from Clulow, 1972.)

shared by all objects that appear colored. The reflectance curves for the blue and green pigments in Figure 4.5 and the curves for the foods in Figure 4.6 show that the region of the spectrum reflected determines the object's color. Table 4.1 indicates the relationship between the color perceived and the wavelengths reflected.

The objects we have described so far reflect some wavelengths and absorb the rest, but what about translucent things, such as liquids, plastics, and glass? The relationship between wavelength and color shown here also holds for these substances, except that they *transmit* rather than reflect light, and if they transmit certain wavelengths selectively, they appear colored. For example, cranberry juice selectively transmits long-wavelength light and appears red, while limeade selectively transmits medium-wavelength light and appears green.

Establishing the connection between color and wavelength is the first step in understanding the physiological mechanisms responsible for color perception, because understanding this

Table 4.1

Relationship between predominant wavelengths reflected and color perceived

Wavelengths Reflected	Perceived Color
Short	Blue
Medium	Green
Long	Red
Long and medium	Yellow
Long and a little medium	Orange
Long and short	Purple
Long, medium, and short	White

Perceiving Color

relationship is the first step in determining the sensory code for color. In Chapter 1, we defined the *sensory code* as the characteristics of nerve impulses that represent various characteristics of the environment. Since we know that wavelength is the crucial physical property for determining color, the search for the sensory code for color has focused on answering the question: How do nerve impulses in the visual system signal the wavelength of light?

Determining the sensory code is a central concern of sensory psychologists and physiologists, not only for color vision, but for all other perceptual qualities. Thus, before looking at research on the sensory code for color, we will describe some basic principles of sensory coding that hold for color, and for other qualities as well.

The Search for the Sensory Code

How does the firing of neurons signal properties of the environment? We saw in Chapter 1 that, in searching for the answer to this question, researchers have generally distinguished between two different ways that neural coding can represent stimulus properties: specificity coding and across-fiber pattern coding.

Specificity Coding

The basic idea behind specificity coding is that the firing of specifically tuned neurons provides information about specific qualities in the environment. For example, if specificity coding were the mechanism used to represent different colors, each color would be signaled by a receptor that was tuned to fire only to that specific color. To evaluate this idea, let's consider the possibility

that there are receptors tuned to single wavelengths, as shown in Figure 4.7. Since our perception of color is closely linked to wavelength (see the visible spectrum, Color Plate 2.1), receptors that respond selectively to single wavelengths could signal the hundreds of different colors we can perceive. The idea of hundreds of color receptors, one for each color, encounters problems, however, because we can see a wide range of colors even in a spot of light so small that it covers only a few receptors on the retina. If we can see many colors based on the firing of just a few receptors, the idea of hundreds of narrowly tuned receptors cannot be the explanation for the range of colors we perceive.

Specificity coding encounters similar problems for other perceptual qualities. Consider, for example, the almost limitless number of different forms we can perceive. Robert Erickson (1984) calculated that 100 billion possible figures can be produced with just half a dozen lines of differing location, length, orientation, and color. Thus, there are simply too many colors and forms, and also tastes and smells, for our perceptions to be explained in terms of neurons that fire only to specific perceptual qualities.

Another argument against specificity coding for color is that the firing of an individual visual receptor is influenced by a range of wavelengths and by light intensity as well. This means, as we

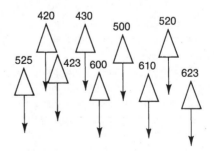

Figure 4.7

A hypothetical array of visual receptors, each tuned to respond to light of only a single wavelength.

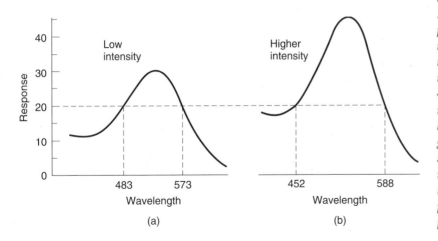

Figure 4.8

Response curve of the 531-nm cone pigment. (a) The curve for a low-intensity light. The dashed lines indicate that at this intensity the receptor has a response of 20 to 483- and 573-nm lights. (b) The receptor's response to a higher-intensity light. At this intensity the receptor generates a response of 20 to 452- and 588-nm lights. Because the receptor responds to a range of wavelengths and is influenced by stimulus intensity, a particular response does not signal a particular wavelength.

will see below, that a particular response of the receptor does not signal a specific wavelength. Consider, for example, one of the cone receptors that we described in Chapter 2. The response curve of Figure 4.8a indicates that this cone responds best at about 531 nm. However, this cone also responds to wavelengths above and below 531 nm, and its response is also influenced by stimulus intensity. We can see from Figure 4.8b that this cell's response increases at all wavelengths when we increase the intensity, so wavelengths that elicit a poor response at low intensity might now elicit a good response at the higher intensity.

These two properties of cone receptors—(1) they respond to a range of wavelengths and (2) their response is influenced by stimulus intensity—mean that a given response does not unambiguously indicate wavelength. For example, we can see from the curves in Figure 4.8 that a response of 20 may be due to either 483- or 573-nm lights at the low intensity, or 452- or 588-nm lights at the higher intensity.

The problems we have just described make it unlikely that specificity coding is the answer to the problem of sensory coding for color vision. The answer appears, instead, to be the other proposed coding mechanism: across-fiber pattern coding.

Across-Fiber Pattern Coding

The basic idea behind across-fiber pattern coding is that different qualities are signaled to the brain by the *pattern* of activity across a population of neurons. Looking at the curves for the three cone pigments in Figure 4.9, we see how across-fiber pattern coding may indicate the wavelength of a light. Cone S responds *best* to 419 nm, cone M to 531 nm, and cone L to 558 nm.

Let's consider how each of these three cones would respond to two different stimuli: stimulus A, a 440-nm light, and stimulus B, a 490-nm light. Figure 4.10 shows how cones S, M, and L respond to the two stimuli. To stimulus A, cone S responds best, and cones M and L respond less well. To stimulus B, cone S now responds least strongly, and cones M and L respond far more. The *pattern* of response to stimuli A and B differs greatly across the three types of cones.

Thus, the brain could differentiate between two wavelengths by registering the *pattern* of firing across a number of neurons. The pattern of firing is a strong candidate for a potential sensory code because it is unaffected, or affected only slightly, by changes in stimulus intensity. Increasing the intensity of A or B increases the firing rate of all three neurons but leaves the *patterns* of

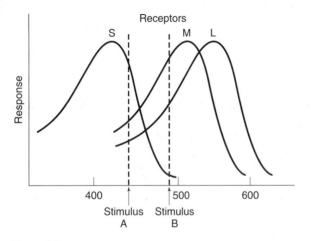

Figure 4.9

Response curves for three types of cone receptors: S, M, and L. We can determine the response of each type of receptor to a particular wavelength of light by drawing a vertical line at that wavelength and noting where that line crosses each curve. The responses generated by stimulus A and stimulus B shown in this figure are indicated in Figure 4.10.

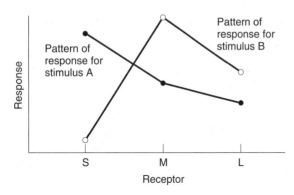

Figure 4.10

The patterns of response of the S, M, and L receptors in Figure 4.9 to stimuli A and B. The pattern for each stimulus provides information about the identity of the stimulus.

response to the two stimuli (S > M > L for A and M > L > S for B) unchanged.

As we will see below, the sensory code for color is created by the response pattern of three

kinds of cone receptors, which are sensitive to different portions of the spectrum. This code was discovered in a search that began in earnest in the 19th century. The story of this search is one that illustrates how both the psychophysical and the physiological approaches can work in concert to uncover a perceptual mechanism. We will tell this story in two parts. First, we consider the early psychophysical observations that led to the proposal of two different theories of color vision. Then, we consider modern physiological research that confirmed and added detail to these two theories.

PSYCHOPHYSICAL RESEARCH ON COLOR VISION

In this section we will establish an important principle that holds not only for color perception, but also for the perception of other qualities as well: *Psychophysical results can be used to determine physiological mechanisms.* The story of how the sensory code for color was discovered illustrates this principle. For color vision, the tactic of using psychophysics to predict physiology was borne of necessity because theorists in the 1800s had none of the physiological tools that would enable them to measure neural activity. They were clever enough, however, to realize that, by doing the right psychophysical experiments, they could make educated guesses regarding the physiological mechanisms.

This story of how psychophysics was used to discover the physiology of color vision is really two stories, each created by different people who looked at two different sets of psychophysical evidence and came to two different physiological conclusions. We will look at both of these stories, and we will then show how later physiological research proved that both were correct.

COLOR PERCEPTION

The world of color is a world of yellow Miatas, brightly painted window shutters, orange-red sunsets, and multicolored football jerseys. But what does color do for us other than create aesthetic experiences, moods, and easier identification of opposing teams? For a monkey searching for food in the forest, color vision makes red, yellow, or orange fruit easily visible against the green of the foliage (Plate 4.1a). In black and white, this fruit becomes much more difficult to detect (Plate 4.1b), so a monkey without color vision would find food gathering difficult, a result with negative consequences for the monkey's survival. (page 129)

Plate 4.2 shows the change in color perception that occurs as illumination changes from dawn to daylight. The view in (a) shows the scene as it would be perceived under the dim illumination of early dawn. The scene lacks color because the rods are responsible for vision under dim illumination. As the scene lightens, as shown in (b), the cones become active and colors emerge that both enhance the beauty of the scene and add contrast that makes it easier to make out the scene's components. One of the many functions of color is to enhance the contrast between objects. (page 131)

Plate 4.1a

Plate 4.1b

Plate 4.2a

Plate 4.2b

Plate 4.3

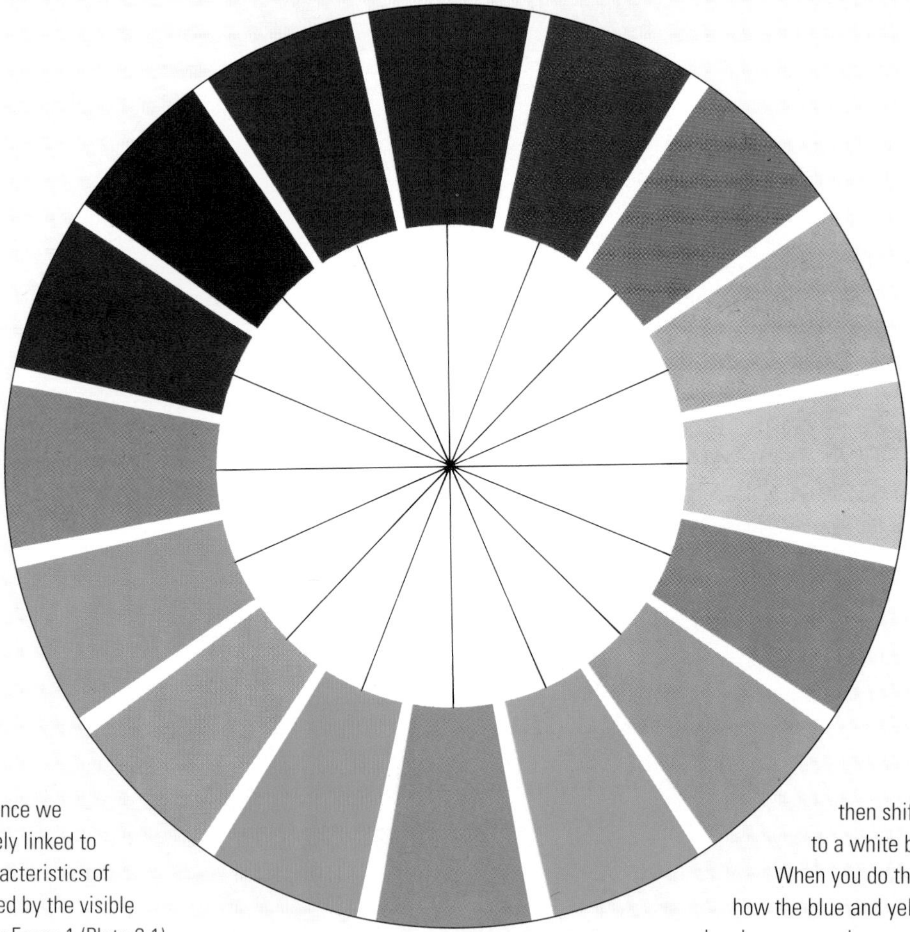

The experience we call color is closely linked to the spectral characteristics of light, as illustrated by the visible spectrum in Color Essay 1 (Plate 2.1). Another way to organize the perceptual experience of color is by using the color circle, which places colors in the same order as they appear in the spectrum but arranges them in a circle (Plate 4.3). This arrangement helps show that all colors consist of various proportions of red, yellow, green, and blue — the colors that appear at 12, 3, 6, and 9 o'clock on the circle. (page 132)

We can study some of the mechanisms of color vision by noting how our perception of color changes under different viewing conditions. For example, the cones synapse with other neurons in the retina to form opponent cells that fire in opposite ways to blue and yellow and to red and green. You can experience the opponent responses of blue and yellow and of red and green by looking at the center of Plate 4.4 for 30 seconds and then shifting your gaze to a white background. When you do this, observe how the blue and yellow and the red and green panels reverse positions in the resulting afterimage (see Demonstration, "Opposing Afterimages," on page 140).

Another way to demonstrate the opponent nature of the visual system is to place a small square of white paper within one of the squares in Plate 4.4 and follow the viewing instructions in the Demonstration, "Afterimages and Simultaneous Contrast," on page 140). You will observe an effect called *simultaneous contrast*, in which a surrounding field induces a color into the area that is surrounded. The simultaneous contrast effect is also illustrated in Plate 4.5, which is a composition by Josef Albers, an artist who often used simultaneous contrast in his paintings. Although one X looks yellow and the other looks gray, they are actually the same, as you can see by looking at the place where they are connected.

Plate 4.4

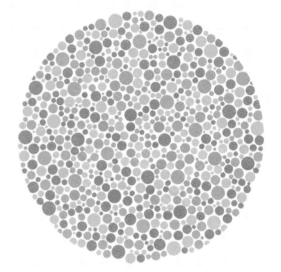

Plate 4.6

Plate 4.5

Plate 4.7

Plate 4.8

Color is by no means universally experienced. Many animals experience no colors, and others perceive fewer than humans (see Other Worlds of Perception, "Color Experience in Animals," on pages 163–166). Even among humans, about 4 percent of males and a much smaller percentage of females are color deficient and therefore perceive a reduced palette of colors. One way to diagnose color deficiency is through a display such as the one in Plate 4.6, which is called an Ishihara plate (page 151). The 74, which is visible to people with normal color vision, cannot be seen by people with a form of red-green color deficiency. You can induce a mild (and temporary) form of color deficiency in yourself by doing the following demonstration: Illuminate Plate 4.7 with bright sunlight or a desk lamp and view it with one eye open and the other closed for about a minute. Then blink back and forth; you will notice that reds viewed with the eye that was open appear more washed out than reds viewed with the eye that was closed. The reason for this is that viewing the red field selectively bleached cone pigments sensitive to long wavelengths, making them less sensitive. People with red-green color deficiency are missing either their medium- or long-wave cone pigment. (page 152)

Adapting the eye to one color, as you did when you looked at the red field, is called *chromatic adaptation*. For an explanation of how chromatic adaptation can partially explain color constancy (see page 153), see the Demonstration, "Adapting to Red," on page 158. Research has also shown that color constancy works best if an object is surrounded by objects with many different colors. This research, which has investigated how color perception is influenced by complex visual displays, has used multicolored "Mondrian" displays like the one in Plate 4.8 as stimuli. (page 159)

CREATING COLOR BY SUBTRACTION OR ADDITION

Newton's prism demonstration, in which he split white light from the sun into all of the colors of the spectrum, contains an important message regarding our perception of chromatic colors. We see white when we are stimulated by equal intensities of all wavelengths in the spectrum simultaneously and we see chromatic colors when we are stimulated by only a portion of the spectrum.

CHROMATIC COLOR CREATED BY SUBTRACTION FROM WHITE

One way to interpret Newton's result is that the perception of chromatic color occurs when some wavelengths are subtracted from white light. There are a number of ways that this subtraction can occur. One way, which we can observe in our natural environment, is by the scattering of light by the atmosphere. This is illustrated by the way light from the sun is scattered by particles in the air to create perceptions of the blue sky and yellow sun during the day, and of the red sun at sunset.

Sunlight entering the atmosphere encounters many small particles, which scatter the light. When these particles are small in relation to the wavelength of the light, a condition known as **Rayleigh scattering** occurs, in which short wavelengths are scattered more than long wavelengths. As shown on the left side of Plate 4.9, this causes short wavelengths to be subtracted from the light entering the atmosphere, and it is these short wavelengths that cause us to see the sky as blue. The scattered light also causes objects in the distance to appear blue, since we must look through scattered short-wavelength light to see the object (Plate 4.10).

With short wavelengths scattered in the sky, the remaining light, which passes directly through the atmosphere, is rich in long wavelengths, so the sun appears yellow. This effect is exaggerated at sunset (Plate 4.9, right), when the light from the setting sun travels a greater distance through the atmosphere than it does at noon, thereby increasing the amount of short and medium wavelengths scattered and leaving only the longest wavelengths, which we perceive as the red setting sun.

Another way chromatic color is created by subtraction is illustrated by objects that appear colored because the substances they are made of subtract some wavelengths by a process called *absorption*, and reflect others by *selective reflection* (described on page 135). Thus, a ripe tomato appears red because the tomato absorbs short and medium wavelengths and reflects long wavelengths (Figure 4.6, page 135).

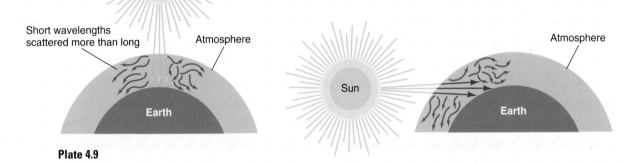

Plate 4.9

Plate 4.10

The process of absorption also explains the colors we see when we mix paints — a process called **subtractive color mixture.** For example, many people have had the experience of mixing blue and yellow paints to create green (see page 143). We can understand how subtraction causes blue and yellow together to make green by first considering the wavelengths that are subtracted from white by the blue paint and the yellow paint separately (Plate 4.11).

Blue paint absorbs wavelengths associated with yellow, orange, red, and some of the green, and reflects blue and a little green. Yellow paint absorbs blue, orange, red, and some of the green, and reflects yellow and a little green. When we mix these two paints together, both paints still absorb the same colors they absorbed when alone. This means that the mixture of blue and yellow paints will absorb *all* the blue (since yellow paint by itself absorbs blue), *some* of the green (blue and yellow paints each absorb some green), *all* the yellow (absorbed by blue paint), and *all* the orange and red (absorbed by both blue paint and yellow paint). After all this absorbing, what's left? The only color that remains is the green reflected by both blue and yellow. (Remember that these paints don't absorb all the green.) *The only colors reflected from a mixture of paints are the colors reflected by both paints in common.* Another way to put this is that the color we see when we mix paints is created by the wavelengths that are *not* subtracted by the paints in the mixture.

The reason that our blue and yellow mixture resulted in green was that there was a little green in each of the paints. If our blue paint reflected only blue and our yellow paint reflected only yellow, these paints would have no colors reflected in common, so mixing them would result in little or no reflection across the spectrum, and the mixture would appear black. It is rare, however, for paints to reflect light in only one region of the spectrum. Most paints reflect a broad band of wavelengths. If paints didn't reflect a range of wavelengths, then many of the **color mixing** effects that painters take for granted would not occur.

CHROMATIC COLOR CREATED BY ADDITION OF OTHER CHROMATIC COLORS

Chromatic colors can also be created by adding together two or more other chromatic colors. This process occurs when we superimpose two or more colored lights (Plate 4.12). Mixing lights is called **additive color mixture,** because all the wavelengths

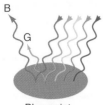

Blue paint   Yellow paint   Blue paint
                                          + Yellow paint

Plate 4.11

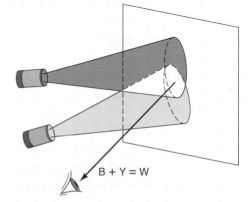

B + Y = W

Plate 4.12

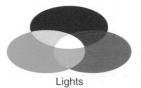
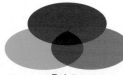

Lights   Paints

Plate 4.13

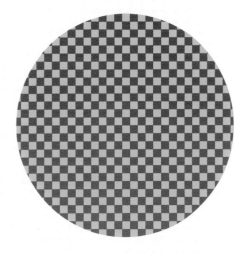

Plate 4.14

contained in each light still reach the eye when the lights are superimposed. Consider what happens when we look at blue and yellow lights that have been superimposed on a white projection screen. The short wavelengths of the blue light are reflected from the screen into our eyes, and the medium and long wavelengths of the yellow light are also reflected from the screen into our eyes. The result? Short, medium, and long wavelengths reach our eyes and we perceive white.

We can appreciate the difference between creating chromatic colors by addition (mixing lights) and by subtraction (mixing paints) by noting that every time we superimpose a *light* onto another light, we add to the amount of light reflected from the screen into the observer's eye. However, every time we add an additional glob of *paint* into a mixture of paints, we subtract from the amount of light reflected. This opposite nature of additive and subtractive color mixture is perhaps best illustrated by comparing the color that results from mixing blue, green, and red *lights* to the color that results from mixing blue, green, and red *paints*. Mixing the lights results in white, while mixing the paints results in black (Plate 4.13).

Finally, there is another way that chromatic colors can be created by addition. This is a process called **optical color mixing,** in which colors add in the eye when small spots with different colors are viewed from a distance. You can experience this effect by propping up your book and slowly walking back from Plate 4.14. As you increase your distance, you are eventually unable to resolve the green and red dots, which add in your eye just as if they were lights projected on top of one another to create a perception of yellow. This technique, which in painting is called **pointillism,** was used by French

painters such as George Seurat and Paul Signac to create optical color mixing effects and to create shimmering effects often associated with natural light. An example of pointillism is illustrated by Signac's painting in Plate 4.15, in which the foreground is made up of tiny blue and orange dots. Move back from this picture and notice how the appearance of the foreground changes as it becomes more difficult to see the individual dots.

Plate 4.15

Plate 6.1

When viewed correctly, an autostereogram such as the one shown here creates a convincing illusion of three-dimensionality. See pages 249–251 for directions on viewing the autostereogram and for an explanation of how it works. Another autostereogram is shown on page 252.

Trichromatic Theory: Color Matching

Two eminent 19th-century researchers, Thomas Young (1773–1829) and Hermann von Helmholtz (1821–1894), used the results of a procedure called *color matching* to propose a theory of color vision. In these **color-matching experiments,** observers were asked to adjust the proportions of three other wavelengths in a mixture so that the color of the mixture looked identical to that of another, single wavelength. For example, as shown in Figure 4.11, the observer might be asked to mix together 420-nm, 560-nm, and 640-nm lights in a comparison field to match the color of a 500-nm light presented in the test field. Observers with normal color vision can do this and, in fact, can match *any* wavelength in the test field by mixing these three wavelengths in the appropriate proportions. (Any three wavelengths can be used in the comparison field, as long as we can't match any one of them by mixing the other two.) Most observers cannot, however, match all test wavelengths if they are provided with only two other wavelengths. For example, if we were given only the 420-nm and 640-nm lights to mix, observers would be unable to match certain colors.

Because at least three wavelengths are needed to match any wavelength in the test field, Thomas Young (1802) proposed the **trichromatic theory of color vision.** This theory, which was later championed by Helmholtz (1852; Figure 4.12) and is also called the **Young–Helmholtz theory of color vision,** proposes that color vision depends on three receptor mechanisms, each with different spectral sensitivities.

According to this theory, light of a particular wavelength stimulates the three receptor mechanisms to different degrees, and the pattern of activity in the three mechanisms results in the perception of a color. Each wavelength is therefore coded in the nervous system by its own pattern of activity in the three receptor mechanisms, an arrangement identical to the one we used to illustrate across-fiber pattern theory in Figures 4.9 and 4.10.

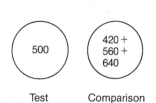

Figure 4.11

Test and comparison fields used in a color-matching experiment. In this experiment, a 500-nm light is being matched by mixing lights of 420 nm, 560 nm, and 640 nm.

Figure 4.12

Hermann von Helmholtz (1821–1894), who championed the trichromatic theory of color vision.

The proposal that more than one receptor type is involved in coding for wavelength makes sense when we remember from our discussion of specificity theory that just one type of receptor cannot unambiguously indicate the wavelength of a light. In a single receptor, any wavelength could generate any response, depending on the light's intensity. However, two or more cone receptor mechanisms can provide an across-fiber pattern that signals which wavelength is present, independent of intensity, by generating a particular pattern of activity that stays relatively constant even when we change the intensity.

The way that Young and Helmholtz reasoned that a minimum of three wavelengths are needed to match all wavelengths in the spectrum and concluded that color vision is based on three receptor mechanisms shows how psychophysics can predict physiology. However, before we consider the physiological data that support the Young–Helmholtz theory, let's look at another example of how psychophysics can predict physiology. This example is provided by Ewald Hering's phenomenological approach to the study of color vision.

Perceiving Color

Figure 4.13
Ewald Hering (1834–1918), who proposed the opponent-process theory of color vision.

two squares and look at it for about 30 seconds. If you then look at a piece of white paper and blink, the image you see, which is called an **afterimage**, is colored. Notice the position of the red and green areas in the afterimage. Then repeat this procedure for the blue and yellow squares. ●

Hering observed that viewing a red field generates a green afterimage, that viewing a green field generates a red afterimage, and that we get analogous results for blue and yellow.

Opponent-Process Theory: Phenomenological Observations

Although trichromatic theory explains a number of color vision phenomena, including color matching and color mixing, there are some color perceptions that it cannot explain. These color perceptions can be demonstrated through **phenomenological observations**, observations in which we simply present a stimulus and ask the observer what he or she perceives. Ewald Hering (1834–1918; Figure 4.13), another eminent physiologist who was working at about the same time as Helmholtz, made a number of phenomenological observations, which showed that the colors red and green are perceptually paired with one another and the colors blue and yellow are paired with one another. This pairing of red and green and of blue and yellow is illustrated by the following three demonstrations.

D E M O N S T R A T I O N
"Opposing" Afterimages

Cover the blue and yellow squares in Color Plate 4.4 with a piece of white paper, and illuminate the red and green squares with your desk lamp. Pick a spot on the border between the

D E M O N S T R A T I O N
Afterimages and Simultaneous Contrast

Cut out a 1/2-inch square of white paper and place it in the center of the green square in Color Plate 4.4. Cover the other squares with white paper, and stare at the center of the white square for about 30 seconds. Then look at a white background, and blink to observe the afterimage. What color is the outside area of the afterimage? What color is the small square in the center? Repeat your observations on the red, blue, and yellow squares in Color Plate 4.4. ●

When you made your observations using the green square, you probably confirmed your previous observation that green and red are paired, since the afterimage corresponding to the green area of the original square is red. But the color of the small square in the center also shows that green and red are paired: Most people see a green square inside the red afterimage. This green afterimage is due to **simultaneous color contrast**, an effect that occurs when surrounding an area with a color changes the appearance of the surrounded area. In this case, the red afterimage surrounds a white area and causes the white area

Table 4.2

Results of afterimage and simultaneous contrast demonstration

Original Square	Color of Outside Afterimage	Color of Inside Afterimage
Green	Red	Green
Red	Green	Red
Blue	Yellow	Blue
Yellow	Blue	Yellow

to become green (see Color Plate 4.5 for another demonstration of simultaneous contrast).

Table 4.2 indicates this result and the results that occur if we repeat this demonstration on the other squares. All of these results show a clear pairing of red and green, and of blue and yellow. Another way to illustrate this pairing is by visualizing mixtures of colors.

◢ D E M O N S T R A T I O N
Visualizing Colors

We can illustrate the pairing of red and green and of blue and yellow by trying to visualize certain colors. Start by visualizing the color red. Attach this color to a specific object such as a fire engine if that makes your visualizing easier. Now visualize a reddish yellow and then a reddish green. Which of these two combinations is easiest to visualize? Now do the same thing for blue. Visualize a pure blue, then a bluish green and a bluish yellow. Again, which of the combinations is easiest to visualize? ●

Most people find it easy to visualize a bluish green or a reddish yellow but find it difficult (or impossible) to visualize a reddish green or a bluish-yellow. This inability to visualize red and green together or blue and yellow together was demonstrated by more quantitative methods in

an experiment by James Gordon and Israel Abramov (1988; also see Abramov & Gordon, 1994). They presented single wavelengths and asked their observers to state the percentage of blue, green, yellow, and red they perceived at each wavelength. Whatever percentage they assigned, they had to be sure that the total added to 100 percent for all four colors at each wavelength. The results of this experiment, shown in Figure 4.14, should be no surprise. Blue dominates at short wavelengths, green in the middle of the spectrum, and yellow and red at long wavelengths, just as we would expect from the visible spectrum. However, the important result for opponent-process theory is that there is very little overlap between the blue and yellow curves and the red and green curves—just as our visualization experiments would predict.[1]

These observations, plus Hering's observation that people who are color-blind to red are also blind to green, and that people who can't see blue also can't see yellow, led Hering to the conclusion that red and green are paired and that blue and yellow are paired. Based on this conclusion, he proposed the **opponent-process theory of color vision** (Hering, 1878/1964, 1905/1964).

The basic idea underlying Hering's theory is shown in Figure 4.15. He proposed three mechanisms, each of which responds in opposite ways to different intensities or wavelengths of light. The Black (−)–White (+) mechanism responds positively to white light and negatively to the absence of light. Red (+)–Green (−) responds positively to red and negatively to green, and Blue (−)–Yellow (+) responds negatively to blue and positively to yellow. According to Hering, these positive and negative responses represented the buildup and breakdown of chemicals in the retina: White, yellow, and red cause a reaction that results in a buildup of the chemicals;

[1] Although there does appear to be some overlap between these curves, it occurs because the curves represent the judgments of many observers. When we consider the perceptions of individual observers, there is no overlap between red and green and between blue and yellow.

Perceiving Color

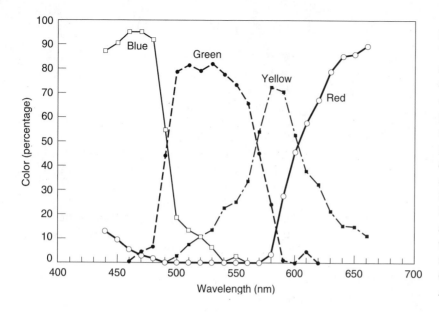

Figure 4.14

The results of a color-scaling experiment. After viewing each stimulus light, the subject rates her or his color sensation by assigning percentages to blue, green, yellow, or red so that they add up to 100 percent. These data, which are averages from a number of subjects, indicate very little overlap between blue and yellow and between red and green. Even this small amount of overlap decreases when we consider the results of individual subjects. (Adapted from Gordon & Abramov, 1988; also see Abramov & Gordon, 1994.)

black, green, and blue cause a reaction that results in a breakdown of the chemical. Although chemicals don't build up or break down as Hering proposed, later research, which we will describe in a moment, showed that these colors do cause physiologically opposite responses.

We have seen that the proposal of the opponent-process and trichromatic mechanisms was based on psychophysical observations made in the 1800s. We are now going to move ahead to the 1950s and 1960s to look at physiological research that supports these theories and shows that color vision is based on the simultaneous operation of both the trichromatic and the opponent-process mechanisms.

PHYSIOLOGICAL RESEARCH ON COLOR VISION

Over 70 years after the proposal of the trichromatic and opponent-process theories, physiological research showed that both theories are correct and can be combined at the physiological level. Before describing how this combining occurs, let's look at each line of physiological evidence separately.

Trichromatic Theory: Receptors and Pigments

The question facing the physiological researchers who were working to identify the receptor mechanisms proposed by trichromatic theory was: Are there three mechanisms, and, if so, what are their physiological properties? This question was answered in the 1960s, when researchers were able to measure the absorption spectra of the cone visual pigments (Brown & Wald, 1964). Dartnall et al. (1983) found human cone pigments with maximum absorption in the short- (419-nm), middle-

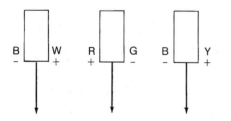

Figure 4.15
The three opponent mechanisms proposed by Hering.

(531-nm), and long-wavelength (558-nm) regions of the spectrum (S, M, and L in Figure 4.9). Schnapf, Kraft, and Baylor (1987) obtained similar results by electrophysiological recording from single middle- and long-wavelength human cones.

If color perception is based on the pattern of activity of these three receptor mechanisms, we should be able to determine which colors will be perceived if we know the response of each of the receptor mechanisms. Figure 4.16 shows the relationship between the responses of the three kinds of receptors and our perception of color. In this figure, the responses in the S, M, and L receptors are indicated by the size of the receptors. For example, blue is signaled by a large response in the S receptor, a smaller response in the M receptor, and an even smaller response in the L receptor. Yellow is signaled by a very small response in the S receptor and large, approximately equal responses in the M and L receptors.

Thinking of wavelengths as causing certain patterns of receptor responding helps us to predict which colors should result when we combine lights of different colors. For example, what color should result if we project a spot of blue light onto a spot of yellow light? The patterns of receptor activity in Figure 4.16 show that blue light causes high activity in the S receptors, and that yellow light causes high activity in the M and L receptors. Thus, combining both lights should stimulate all three receptors equally, and we should perceive white. This is exactly the result we achieve if we mix blue and yellow lights. (However, a different result occurs if we mix blue and yellow *paints*. The reason we achieve different results from lights and paints is explained in Color Essay 3.)

The idea that our perception of colors is determined by the pattern of activity in different kinds of receptors says something important about the relation between neural responding and perception. Combining two or more wavelengths so they perceptually match a single wavelength creates two *physically different* fields that *appear identical*. For example, when we mix a 620-nm red light and a 530-nm green light, we can create a yellow that matches the color associated with a 580-nm light (Figure 4.17). The 580-nm light and the mixture of the 620-nm and 530-nm lights appear identical because even though they are physically different, they create the same pattern of activity in the cone receptors.

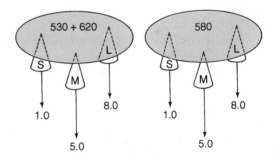

Figure 4.17

The proportions of 530- and 620-nm lights in the field on the left have been adjusted so that the mixed lights appear to be identical to the 580-nm light in the field on the right. The numbers, which indicate the responses of the short-, medium-, and long-wavelength receptors, show that there is no difference in the responses of the two sets of receptors. The identical neural responding causes the two fields to be perceptually indistinguishable.

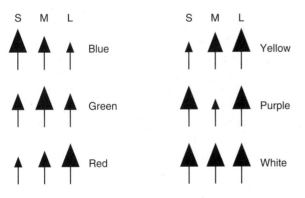

Figure 4.16

Patterns of firing of the three types of cones to different colors. The size of the cone symbolizes the size of the receptor's response.

Perceiving Color

The 530-nm green light causes a large response in the M receptor, and the 620-nm red light causes a large response in the L receptor. Together, they result in a large response in the M and L receptors and a much smaller response in the S receptor. This is the pattern for yellow and is the same as the pattern generated by the 580-nm yellow light. Thus, as far as the visual system is concerned, these lights are identical.

Two lights that have different wavelength distributions but are perceptually identical are called **metamers.** The basic principle of metamers is as follows: *Two lights with different wavelength distributions appear to be the same color if they stimulate the receptors in the same ratios.* Putting this another way, we can say: *If two stimuli cause the same neural response, they will appear to be identical even if they are physically different.*

Another important advance in our understanding of the physiology of color vision came in the 1980s, when researchers were able to determine the detailed structure of the visual pigment molecules (Mollon, 1989, 1993; Nathans, Thomas, & Hogness, 1986). We saw in Chapter 2 that the pigment molecule consists of a large protein, opsin, and a small, light-sensitive molecule, retinal (Figures 2.10 and 2.11). The retinal molecule is identical in all of the visual pigments, but different types of pigments have different sequences of the small molecular groups called amino acids that make up the protein. These differences in the amino acids cause the differences in the absorption spectra of the different pigments: More similar amino acid sequences result in more similar absorption spectra. Thus, the spectra of the middle- and long-wavelength cones, which differ by only 27 nm in their wavelength of maximum absorption, have about 96 percent identical amino acid sequences, whereas the short- and middle-wavelength cones, which are separated by about 112 nm, have only 44 percent of their amino acid sequences in common.

The discovery of the link between amino acid sequences and absorption spectra led to the finding that, in the M and L pigments, a difference in one amino acid causes a shift of 5–7 nm in the peak of the absorption spectrum (Neitz, Neitz, & Jacobs, 1993). Thus, changing just one amino acid could create new M and L cone pigments with absorption spectra shifted slightly from the "normal" M and L pigments. In fact, research has shown that some subjects with normal trichromatic vision have four different cone pigments: the three "standard" ones and an additional shifted one. For reasons we don't yet understand, their vision is still trichromatic, rather than tetrachromatic (i.e., based on four kinds of cones). Perhaps the responses of two cones with slightly different spectra are combined neurally by converging on the same neurons, so the psychophysical response appears to be from a single type of pigment (Dartnall et al., 1983; Neitz, Neitz, & Jacobs, 1993).

Opponent-Process Theory: Neural Responding

Although numerous psychophysical observations supported Hering's opponent-process theory, it has only recently been taken as seriously as trichromatic theory. One reason for its slow acceptance was that people couldn't imagine a physiological process that resulted in either the buildup or the breakdown of a chemical substance. This poor acceptance of opponent-process theory is illustrated by the amount of coverage given the theory in Yves LeGrand's 1957 book *Light, Color and Vision*, a standard reference on vision. Though 25 pages are devoted to trichromatic theory, opponent-process theory is dealt with in less than a page.

It wasn't until solid physiological evidence became available that opponent-process theory began to gain equal footing with trichromatic theory. This evidence took the form not of chemicals that were either broken down or built up by different wavelengths, as Hering proposed, but by neurons that respond with electrical signals

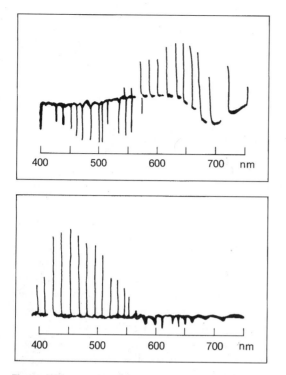

Figure 4.18

S-potentials recorded from the fish retina. The vertical lines are the responses generated by test flashes; the wavelengths are indicated on the horizontal scale. (From Svaetichin, 1956.)

that react in opposite ways to different wavelengths.

Opponent Cells in the Retina and the Lateral Geniculate Nucleus Evidence for opposing electrical signals was provided by research on two animals with excellent color vision: the rhesus monkey and fish from the carp family. In the fish, Gunnar Svaetichin (1956) discovered neurons in the retina that responded to light by slowly changing their electrical charge, a response he called the **S-potential**. This electrical response had a property that supported the opponent-process theory: The neurons responded positively to light at one end of the

spectrum and negatively to light at the other end of the spectrum, as is illustrated in Figure 4.18. The top record is from a cell that responds negatively to short wavelengths and positively to long wavelengths. The bottom record is from a cell that responds positively to short wavelengths and very little to long wavelengths.

A few years after Svaetichin's discovery of opposing S-potentials, Russell DeValois (1960) found cells in the lateral geniculate nucleus (LGN) of the rhesus monkey that responded to light at one end of the spectrum with an increase in nerve firing, and to light at the other end of the spectrum with an inhibition of spontaneous activity. The firing of four such cells, which are called **opponent cells**, is shown in Figure 4.19. For each cell, spontaneous activity is indicated in the top record, and the responses to 450-nm (blue), 510-nm (green), 580-nm (yellow), and 660-nm (red) lights are shown in the other records. The B+Y− cell responds to the 450-nm light with an increase in firing and to the 580-nm light with an inhibition of spontaneous activity. The G+R− cell increases its firing to the 510-nm light and decreases its firing to the 660-nm light. The Y+B− and R+G− cells also show opponent responses, but they are inhibited by short wavelengths and are excited by long wavelengths.

The results of Svaetichin's and DeValois's experiments made believers of researchers who had doubted the physiological reality of opponent mechanisms in the visual system, and opened the way for other researchers to determine the detailed properties of these opponent mechanisms not only in the retina and the LGN, but also in the cortex.

Opponent Cells in the Cortex A number of types of opponent cells have been discovered in the monkey striate cortex (Derrington, Lennie, & Krauskopf, 1983; DeValois & Jacobs, 1984; Gouras, 1990; Hubel & Livingstone, 1990; Zrenner et al., 1990). Most of these cells have one thing in common: They are excited by wavelengths at one end of the spectrum and are inhibited by

Perceiving Color

	B+Y–	G+R–	Y+B–	R+G–
Spontaneous				
450 nm (blue)				
510 nm (green)				
580 nm (yellow)				
660 nm (red)				

Figure 4.19

Responses of opponent cells in the monkey's lateral geniculate nucleus. These cells respond in opposite ways to blue and yellow (B+Y– or Y+B–) and to red and green (G+R– or R+G–). (From DeValois & Jacobs, 1968.)

wavelengths at the other end of the spectrum. We will focus on two of these cortical opponent cells. The first, called a *type 1 color-opponent cell*, is like the LGN neuron: It is a center–surround cell that is inhibited by one band of wavelengths presented to the surround and is excited by another band presented to the center (or vice versa).

Another type of opponent cell found in the cortex is a **double color-opponent cell**. The receptive field of a double color-opponent cell recorded from layer IVc of the monkey's cortex is shown in Figure 4.20. The center of this cell's receptive field has an R+G– opponent response, and the surround has an R–G+ opponent response. The reason for the name *double color-opponent cell* is that the cell responds in an opponent fashion, but in opposite ways, depending on whether the center or the surround is stimulated.

Margaret Livingstone and David Hubel (1984) observed that these types of double color-opponent cells (R+G– center and R–G+ surround) are by far the most common types of color cells in the monkey, and they suggest that there may be a functional reason. In their natural habitat, monkeys need to perceive brightly colored fruit, usually red or orange, on a green leafy background. If the red fruit stimulates the R+ center of one of the monkey's double color-opponent cells and the green leaves stimulate the G+ surround, the cell will fire vigorously. Perhaps, suggested Livingstone and Hubel, the dou-

ble color-opponent cells help create a high-contrast display that the monkey can see easily.

Livingstone and Hubel also observed that these double color-opponent cells are concentrated in cortical areas they called **blobs,** so called because these areas show up as bloblike shapes when the cortex is treated with a special stain. These blobs, which appear to receive inputs from the opponent cells in layer IVc (Michael, 1986), contain cells that respond to colors but not to orientation, unlike most other cells in the visual cortex, which prefer particular orientations. This segregation of color-sensitive cells within the blobs and orientation-sensitive cells outside the blobs is consistent with the idea of parallel processing in the visual system that we introduced in Chapters 2 and 3, color being processed in the

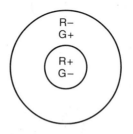

Figure 4.20

The receptive field of a double color-opponent cell in the monkey cortex. This neuron has an R–G+ response in the surround and an R+G– response in the center.

P (or temporal) channel and motion being processed in the M (or parietal) channel.

Not only is color processed separately in the blob areas of the striate cortex, but within the blobs, opponent neurons are organized in columns, so only blue–yellow or red–green neurons are found within a particular column (Ts'o, 1989). This discovery of color columns in the cortex has led to a revision of the hypercolumn scheme we introduced in Figure 3.15, in which a hypercolumn was pictured as consisting of location, orientation, and ocular dominance columns. We now modify this scheme by adding color col-

umns, as shown in Figure 4.21 (Livingstone & Hubel, 1984).

The existence of color-opponent cells raises two questions: (1) How do neural circuits result in opponent neurons? (2) Why are these neurons necessary for color vision? We will consider each of these questions in turn.

The How and the Why of Opponent Cells Figure 4.22 shows a neural circuit in the retina that creates opponent cells from the signals generated by the three types of cone receptors. To understand this circuit, let's first focus on the R+G– cell. This cell receives inhibitory input from the M cone and excitatory input from the L cone. Thus, light in the middle of the spectrum, which preferentially stimulates the M cone, causes an inhibitory response in this cell. Similarly, light at the long-wavelength end of the spectrum, which preferentially stimulates the L cone, causes an excitatory response in this cell. The opponent response of the R+G– cell, therefore, occurs because of the opposing inputs from the M and L cones.

The B+Y– cell is slightly more complex because it receives an excitatory input from the S cone and an inhibitory input from cell A, which sums the inputs from the M and L cones. This arrangement makes sense if we remember that

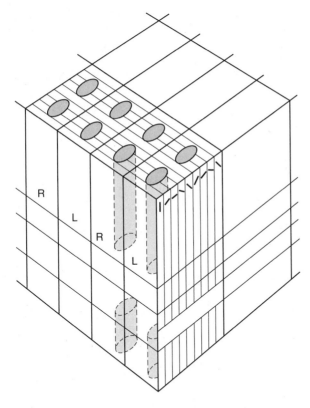

Figure 4.21

The hypercolumn organization of the cortex introduced in Chapter 3 (see Figure 3.15), with the addition of columns of color-opponent cells (shaded). These areas are called blobs *because of their appearance when the cortex is stained. (Adapted from Livingstone & Hubel, 1984.)*

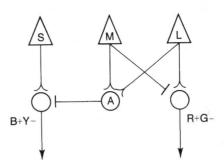

Figure 4.22

Neural circuit showing how the blue–yellow and red–green mechanisms can be created by excitatory and inhibitory inputs from the three types of cone receptors. See text for details.

Perceiving Color

we perceive yellow when both the M and the L receptors are stimulated. Thus, cell A, which receives inputs from both of these receptors, causes the "yellow" response of the B+Y− mechanism. For this reason the B+Y− cell is also called a B+(R+G)− cell.

Although this diagram is greatly simplified, it illustrates the basic principles of the neural circuitry for color coding in the retina (see DeValois & DeValois, 1993, for examples of more complex neural circuits that have been proposed to explain opponent responding). The important thing about this circuit is that its response is determined not only by the arrangement of inhibitory and excitatory synapses, but also by the properties of the receptors that send signals to these synapses. We can think of the processing in this circuit as taking place in two stages: first, in the receptors, which respond with different patterns to different wavelengths, and then, at the later neurons, which process the signals received from the receptors.

Having described a circuit that causes neurons to respond in opposite ways to different regions of the spectrum, let's now consider our second question: Why are these neurons necessary? Doesn't the firing pattern of the three types of cone receptors contain adequate information to signal which wavelength has been presented? The answer to this question is yes, but processing this information further changes it into a form that signals the presence of specific wavelengths more clearly.

To understand what this means, let's consider what an opponent cell does with the information it receives from the receptors by looking at the response of the opponent R+G− cell in Figure 4.23b. This cell takes the *difference between* the responses of the L and the M receptors by subtracting the inhibitory signal of the M recep-

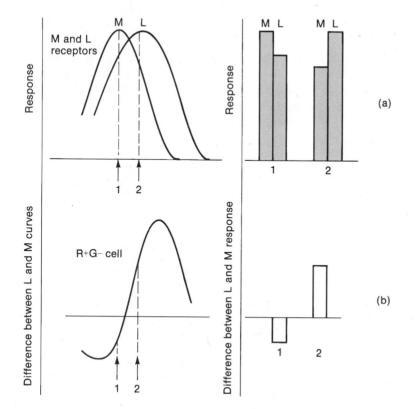

(a)

(b)

Figure 4.23

(a) Left: Response curves for the M and L receptors. Right: Bar graph indicating the size of the responses generated in the receptors by wavelengths 1 (left pair of bars) and 2 (right pair). (b) Left: Response of an R+G− cell that receives excitatory input from the L receptor and inhibitory input from the M receptor. Right: Bar graph showing the opponent response of the R+G− cell to wavelengths 1 and 2. The response to 1 is inhibitory, and the response to 2 is excitatory.

tor from the excitatory signal of the L receptor (Figure 4.23a). This transforms the M and L receptor responses shown in the upper left panel of Figure 4.23 are transformed into the opponent response of the R+G− cell shown in the lower left panel of the figure.

What does taking this difference accomplish? We can answer this question by looking at how the receptors and the opponent cell respond to two nearby wavelengths, labeled 1 and 2 in Figure 4.23. The top right panel, which shows how the M and the L receptors respond to these two wavelengths, indicates that there is information in these responses that signals the difference between wavelengths 1 and 2. When wavelength 1 is presented, receptor M responds more than receptor L, and when wavelength 2 is presented, receptor L responds more than receptor M. The lower right panel of the figure shows how the opponent cell responds to the two wavelengths. The R+G− cell is inhibited by wavelength 1 and is excited by wavelength 2.

To compare these two ways of responding to wavelengths 1 and 2, look at Figure 4.23 and ask yourself this question: Which information is simpler: the receptor information in the upper right panel or the opponent information in the lower right panel? Clearly, the opponent information in the lower panel is simpler, and this simplicity makes it easier to tell the difference between the neural responses generated by each of the wavelengths. In fact, some researchers have suggested that we perceive red when R+G− cells are excited, green when G+R− cells are excited, blue when B+Y− cells are excited, and yellow when Y+B− cells are excited (Abramov & Gordon, 1994). If this is so, then the response of our neuron in Figure 4.23 would result in the perception "red" when excited by wavelength 2 and no perception when inhibited by wavelength 1. For wavelength 1 to cause a "perceive green" signal it would have to excite a G+R− neuron. We don't know if this idea is correct, but we do know that whatever the mechanism that actually signals different color perceptions, the opponent neurons transform the neural information generated by the receptors into a simpler form that probably enhances the visual system's ability to distinguish between different wavelengths.

Before leaving our consideration of opponent neurons, let's consider the link between the firing of these neurons and our perception of color. From our description so far you may think that there is a direct link between the firing of opponent neurons and color perception. After all, we have demonstrated opponent responding both in the firing of these neurons and in the perception of afterimages, simultaneous contrast, and the appearance of colors. However, when we look more closely at how the opponent neurons fire, we find that the details of their firing don't match the perceptual results.

For example, measured psychophysically, the red–green response drops to zero at around 580 nm. You can see that this is so by referring back to Figure 4.14 and noting that subjects rarely see red or green at this wavelength. However, the response of many red–green opponent neurons does not drop to zero at this wavelength, as you can see from the second column in Figure 4.19. Notice that this G+R− neuron responds vigorously at 580 nm.

Another argument against the idea that the firing of these opponent neurons leads directly to color perception is that most of these neurons fire not only to chromatic light, but to white light as well. If these neurons were actually the ones directly responsible for color vision, they should not respond to lights that do not cause color perceptions (Abramov & Gordon, 1994). Thus, while opponent neurons in the striate cortex are involved in processing information that leads to color perception, the actual perception of color probably occurs further downstream. In fact, there is evidence that many of the neurons in area V4 of the cortex respond to color. Some of these neurons have interesting properties that make them particularly important for color perception. We will discuss the properties of these neurons later in the chapter when we describe a phenomenon called *color constancy*.

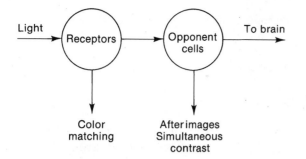

Light → **Receptors** → **Opponent cells** → To brain

Color matching

Afterimages
Simultaneous contrast

Figure 4.24

Our experience of color vision is shaped by physiological mechanisms both in the receptors and in the opponent neurons. The existence of three different kinds of cone receptors is responsible for the fact that we need a minimum of three wavelengths to match any wavelength in the spectrum. The opponent cells are responsible for perceptual experiences such as afterimages and simultaneous contrast. Note that, although the activity in the receptors and other neurons early in the visual system may shape our perception of color, color perception doesn't actually occur until sometime after the signals from these early neurons reach the brain.

Our description of the physiological mechanisms of color vision in the retina, the LGN, and the cortex verifies one of the major themes of this book: *Perception is shaped by neural processing.* We have seen that perceptual experience is both trichromatic (as measured by color-mixing experiments) and opponent (as observed phenomenologically). The idea that these different types of color experience are related to different physiological mechanisms is shown in Figure 4.24. At the beginning of the visual system, the receptors determine our ability to match colors by mixing wavelengths. Later in the system, opponent neurons determine experiences such as the perception of afterimages and simultaneous contrast.

The idea that processing at various stages in the visual system leaves its mark on our perception means that we do not have to deal with the problem facing early color-vision researchers, who felt that they had to choose between the competing trichromatic and opponent-process theories. We now know that both mechanisms influence our perception of color—the trichromatic mechanism operating at the receptors, and the opponent-process mechanism operating at neurons further downstream.

COLOR DEFICIENCY

It has long been known that some people have difficulty perceiving certain colors. Perhaps the most famous early report of **color deficiency,** an inability to perceive some colors that people with normal color vision can perceive, was provided by the well-known 19th-century chemist John Dalton (1798/1948), who described his own color perceptions as follows: "All crimsons appear to me to consist chiefly of dark blue: but many of them seem to have a tinge of dark brown. I have seen specimens of crimson, claret, and mud, which were very nearly alike" (p. 102).

Dalton's descriptions of his abnormal color perceptions led to the early use of the term *Daltonism* to describe color deficiency. More recent measurements, using the color-matching procedure to determine the minimum number of wavelengths needed to match any other wavelength in the spectrum, have revealed the following three types of color deficiency:

1. A **monochromat** can match any wavelength in the spectrum by adjusting the intensity of any other wavelength. Thus a monochromat needs only one wavelength to match any color in the spectrum.

2. A **dichromat** needs only two wavelengths to match all other wavelengths in the spectrum.

3. An **anomalous trichromat** needs three wavelengths to match any wavelength, just

as a normal trichromat does. However, the anomalous trichromat mixes these wavelengths in different proportions from a trichromat, and an anomalous trichromat is not as good at discriminating between wavelengths that are close together.

The results of these color-matching measurements provide an objective way of distinguishing between people with different types of color vision. Another way to determine whether someone is color-deficient is to use color vision tests like the ones shown in Color Plate 4.6, which are called **Ishihara plates**. Subjects who have dichromatic vision perceive either different numbers from a person with trichromatic vision or no numbers at all, as explained in the Color Essay.

After we have determined whether a person's vision is color-deficient, we are still left with the question: What colors does a person with color deficiency see? When I pose this question in class, someone inevitably suggests that we can answer this question by pointing to objects of various colors and asking someone who is color-deficient what he sees. This method does not, however, really tell us what the person perceives because a color-deficient person may say "red" when we point to a strawberry simply because he has learned that people call strawberries "red." For all we know, however, the person may be having an experience similar to what a person with normal color vision would call "yellow."

A better way to tell what a color dichromat perceives is to locate a **unilateral dichromat**—a person with trichromatic vision in one eye and dichromatic vision in the other eye. Since both eyes are connected to the same brain, it would be possible for this person to look at a color with the dichromatic eye and then determine which color it corresponds to in the trichromatic eye. Although they are extremely rare, the few unilateral dichromats who have been tested have helped us determine the nature of a dichromat's color experience (Alpern, Kitahara, & Krantz, 1983; Graham

et al., 1961; Sloan & Wollach, 1948). Let's now look at the nature of the color experience of both monochromats and dichromats.

Monochromatism

Monochromatism is a rare form of color blindness that is usually hereditary and occurs in only about 10 people out of 1 million (LeGrand, 1957). Monochromats usually have no functioning cones; therefore their vision has the characteristics of rod vision in both dim and bright lights. Monochromats see everything in shades of lightness (white, gray, and black) and can therefore be called *color-blind* (as opposed to dichromats, who see some chromatic colors and therefore should be called *color-deficient*).

In addition to a loss of color vision, monochromats have poor visual acuity and are so sensitive to bright lights that they often must protect their eyes with dark glasses during the day. The reason for this sensitivity is that the rod system is not designed to function in bright light and so becomes overloaded in strong illumination, creating a perception of glare.

Dichromatism

Dichromats experience some colors, though a lesser range than trichromats. There are three major forms of dichromatism: protanopia, deuteranopia, and tritanopia. The two most common kinds, protanopia and deuteranopia, are inherited through a gene located on the X chromosome (Nathans et al., 1986). Since males (XY) have only one X chromosome, a defect in the visual pigment gene on this chromosome causes color deficiency through a loss of either the M or the L cone pigments. Females (XX), on the other hand, with their two X chromosomes, are less likely to become color-deficient, since only one normal gene is required for color vision. These forms of color vision are therefore called *sex-linked* because

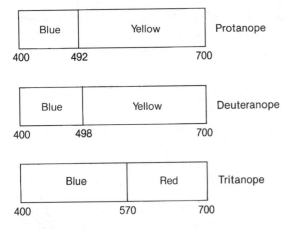

Figure 4.25
The color perceptions of the three kinds of dichromats. The number under the dividing line indicates the wavelength of the neutral point, the wavelength at which gray is perceived.

women can carry the gene for color deficiency without being color-deficient themselves, and they can pass the condition to their male offspring. Thus, many more men than women are protanopes or deuteranopes.

Protanopia **Protanopia** affects 1 percent of males and 0.02 percent of females and results in the perception of colors across the spectrum indicated in Figure 4.25. A protanope perceives short-wavelength light as blue, and as wavelength is increased, the blue becomes less and less saturated until, at 492 nm, the protanope perceives gray. The wavelength at which the protanope perceives gray is called the **neutral point.** At wavelengths above the neutral point, the protanope perceives yellow, which becomes increasingly saturated as wavelength is increased, until at the long-wavelength end of the spectrum the protanope perceives a saturated yellow.

Deuteranopia **Deuteranopia** affects about 1 percent of males and 0.01 percent of females and

results in the perception of colors across the spectrum as shown in Figure 4.25. A deuteranope perceives blue at short wavelengths, sees yellow at long wavelengths, and has a neutral point at about 498 nm (Boynton, 1979).

Tritanopia **Tritanopia** is very rare, affecting only about 0.002 percent of males and 0.001 percent of females. As indicated in Figure 4.25, a tritanope sees blue at short wavelengths, sees red at long wavelengths, and has a neutral point at 570 nm (Alpern, Kitahara, & Krantz, 1983).

Physiological Mechanisms

What are the physiological mechanisms of color deficiency? Most monochromats have no color vision because they have just one type of cone or no cones. Dichromats are missing one visual pigment. Using his retinal densitometry technique (described on page 57) to measure the visual pigments in protanopes and deuteranopes, William Rushton (1964) found that the protanope is missing the long-wavelength cone pigment and that the deuteranope is missing the medium-wavelength cone pigment. Because of the tritanope's rarity and because of the low number of short-wavelength cones, even in normal retinas, it has been difficult to measure the visual pigments of the tritanope, but it appears that the tritanope is missing the short-wavelength pigment.

More recent research has identified differences in the genes that determine visual pigment structure in trichromats and dichromats (Nathans et al., 1986), and it has been suggested that anomalous trichromats probably match colors differently from normal trichromats and have more difficulty discriminating between some wavelengths because their M and L pigment spectra have been shifted so they are closer together (Neitz, Neitz, & Jacobs, 1991).

Perceptual Constancy

In this section we introduce a concept called *perceptual constancy* that is important not only for understanding color perception, but for understanding other types of perception as well. **Perceptual constancy** is our perception that properties of objects remain constant even when the conditions of stimulation are changed. To examine perceptual constancy, let's consider the example we cited at the beginning of the first chapter: your perception of the shape of your desktop as you walk past it. Let's consider for a moment what's happening as you view your desktop from different angles. Although your desktop has a rectangular shape, it casts a trapezoidal image on the retinas when viewed from most angles, and the shape of this image changes constantly as you walk past the desk (Figure 4.26). *Perceptual constancy* means that even while the desktop's image on your retinas is changing, you continue to perceive it as rectangular. You perceive its true shape rather than the many different shapes that the desktop casts on your retinas as you walk past it. Your constant perception of your desktop's shape as you view it from different angles is called **shape constancy.**

We will now describe two other examples of perceptual constancy that, like shape constancy, involve situations in which aspects of the stimulus change but observers continue to perceive the properties of the stimulus in the same way. These phenomena are color constancy and lightness constancy. **Color constancy** is our perception of an object's color as remaining relatively constant even when it is illuminated by lights with different wavelength distributions. **Lightness constancy** is our perception of an object's achromatic colors—white, gray, or black—as remaining constant even when it is illuminated by lights with different intensities. We will first discuss lightness constancy, then color constancy.

Lightness Constancy

To experience lightness constancy, do the following demonstration.

 DEMONSTRATION

Lightness Perception under Changing Illumination

Illuminate a piece of white paper with your desk lamp and select the square on the gray scale in Figure 4.27 that appears to be of the same whiteness. Without changing the illumination on your gray scale, turn off the lamp that illuminates the white paper, so that it is now illuminated only by the general light level in your room. Repeat your lightness judgment. ●

Figure 4.26
Three views of the image that a rectangular desktop would cast on the retinas as an observer walks past it. The fact that the observer continues to perceive the desktop as rectangular even though its image is changing on the retinas is an example of shape constancy. Analogous constancy phenomena occur for color and lightness, as explained in the text.

Grays ——→ Increasing blackness

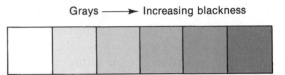

Figure 4.27
Gray scale.

Most people find that changing the illumination has little or no effect on lightness. Even though you decreased the illumination substantially by turning off the lamp, the white paper continues to appear white; it doesn't become dark gray. Lightness constancy means that we see the true achromatic properties of an object no matter what the illumination is. The white page of this book is seen as white in a dimly lit room or in bright sunlight, and the black print on the page is seen as black, no matter what the illumination. It's a good thing that lightness constancy occurs because, without it, the lightnesses of the objects around us would be constantly changing. Taking a piece of coal from inside to outside would change it from black to white, and it would become meaningless to say, "This coal is black" or "This paper is white," because their lightnesses would change every time we changed the illumination.

What is responsible for lightness constancy? We will consider two explanations.

Lightness Constancy and Relationships Look at Figure 4.28. The two squares in this figure are physically different but appear the same (or nearly the same) because they are on different backgrounds. (To eliminate the effect of the backgrounds, view the small squares through two holes punched in a card.) The principle behind this effect is called the **ratio principle** (Jacobsen & Gilchrist, 1988; Wallach, 1963). According to this principle, two areas that reflect different amounts of light will look the same if the ratios of their intensities to the intensities of the surrounds are kept constant (Figure 4.29).

We can understand how the ratio principle helps explain lightness constancy by considering how you perceive the black letters on the pages of this book. The letters look black whether viewed under dim or under intense illumination because, even if we change the illumination, the ratio of the light intensity reflected from the let-

Figure 4.28

The two small squares reflect different amounts of light but appear close in lightness. To appreciate the actual physical difference between these squares, punch two holes 1½ inches apart in a card and look at the two squares with their backgrounds masked.

ters to the light intensity reflected from the paper remains the same (Figure 4.30).

An experiment by Gelb (1929) demonstrates the importance of relationships in the perception of lightness constancy. Figure 4.31, the setup for Gelb's experiment, shows a disk of low reflectance suspended in completely black surroundings. The key feature of this experiment was the presence of a hidden light that illuminated only the disk. When viewed from the observer's position, the disk, which would look black in your living room or outdoors, looked white. This result occurred because the only stimulus present,

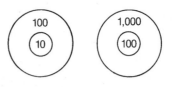

Figure 4.29

How simultaneous contrast can make two different disks appear identical. If light intensities were as indicated by the numbers in the outer rings and inner disks, the inner disks would appear identical because the ring-to-disk ratio is 10 to 1 in both cases. (Based on Wallach, 1963.)

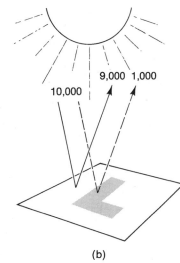

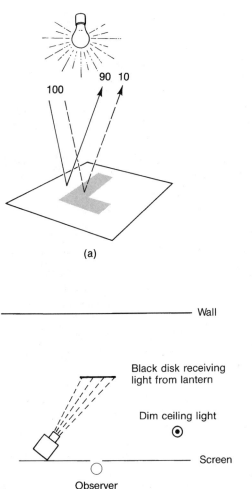

Figure 4.30
What happens to the amount of light reflected from a sheet of white paper and from a black letter L on the paper when viewed (a) under low illumination in which the intensity equals 100, and (b) under high illumination in which the intensity equals 10,000. In both cases, the paper reflects 90 percent of the light and the letter reflects 10 percent, so that the ratio of the light intensities reflected from the paper and the letter remains at 9 to 1 under both levels of illumination.

Figure 4.31
The setup of Gelb's concealed illumination experiment, seen from above. The observer could not see the light on the left, which was projected only onto the black disk. The background, which was also black, was dimly illuminated by the ceiling light. (Adapted from Hochberg, 1971.)

other than the disk, was the black background, which reflected only a small amount of light compared to the illuminated disk. This percep-

tion of a black disk as white is consistent with the idea that relationships are important in determining lightness. But Gelb wasn't satisfied just to turn a black disk white; he also wanted to make it turn black again. He did this by placing a small piece of white paper partially in front of the disk so that it became illuminated by the hidden light. As soon as the white paper was introduced, the disk turned black! This new relationship, with the white paper reflecting much more light than the disk, caused the disk to look dark.

Gelb's experiment shows that lightness constancy breaks down—that is, an ordinarily black object appears white—if the ordinarily black object has the highest intensity in the field. This effect occurs only under special conditions such as those used by Gelb: a hidden light and no other comparison objects in the field. As soon as a comparison object is placed in the light with the black disk, the relationship between the comparison object and the disk reinstates the lightness constancy, and the disk becomes black.

Let's ask this question about Gelb's experiment: What effect does the observer's knowledge of the situation have on his or her perception? Once the white paper is presented, the observer becomes aware that the disk is really black. You may think that, once the truth is known, the disk would always be perceived as black, but this is not the case. When the small piece of white paper is removed, the black disk turns white again, and no amount of knowledge will make it turn black. In this example, the observer's knowledge of the situation does not affect her or his perception.

Lightness Constancy and Perceived Illumination
A number of experiments have shown that an observer's interpretation of how an object is illuminated affects his or her perception of the object's lightness. For example, when the card in the Mach card demonstration from Chapter 2 (page 77) perceptually "flipped," your perception of the card's surfaces changed, so the previously shaded side appeared darker than it had before the flip, and the lighter side appeared lighter, even luminous (repeat this demonstration to observe the effect). The "flipping" of the card eliminated lightness constancy: Both sides of the card originally appeared white, but afterward one side appeared dark and the other appeared light (Figure 4.32).

We can explain the Mach card effect by considering how we register the illumination relative to the card. Before the card flips, we perceive the right side of the card as illuminated and the left side as in shadow. Our perceptual system apparently takes the illumination conditions into account, and both sides of the card appear white. That is, lightness constancy is working. After the card flips, however, the apparent illumination conditions change. Now the shadowed left side appears to be facing toward the light and the illuminated right side appears to be facing away from the light. This change creates the following problem for the perceptual system: Although the left side appears to be facing *toward* the light, only a small amount of light is reflected from that side. Similarly, although the right side appears to be facing *away from* the light, a large amount of light is reflected from that side. The perceptual system's solution: The left side must be made of a low-reflectance material such as dark gray paper, and the right side must be made of a high-reflectance material such as white paper. Thus, the erroneous information about the flipped card's orientation relative to the direction of the light causes observers to perceive the two sides as being made of different kinds of paper.

The change in lightness perception we experience when the Mach card flips illustrates how our perception of illumination can affect our perception of lightness. Another way to show this is illustrated in the next demonstration.

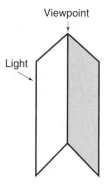

D E M O N S T R A T I O N
Lightness at a Corner

Stand a folded index card on end so that it resembles the outside corner of a room, and illuminate it so that one side is illuminated and the other is in shadow. When you look at the corner, you can easily tell that both sides of the corner are made of the same white material, but that the nonilluminated side is shadowed. Now punch a hole in another card, and with the hole a few inches from the corner of the folded card, view the corner with one eye about a foot from the hole. If, when viewing the corner through the hole, you perceive the corner as a flat surface, your perception of the left and right surfaces will change. ●

Viewpoint

Light

Figure 4.32
When the Mach card, viewed from the top, perceptually "flips" so it looks like an opened book standing on end (even though it is actually lying horizontally, as shown in Figure 2.50), the left side takes on a darker appearance. See text for a possible explanation.

In this demonstration, eliminating your perception of depth at the corner eliminates information about the conditions of illumination and therefore eliminates lightness constancy, so that the light side appears lighter and the dark side appears darker. Some people even perceive the dark side as dark gray or black—a very different perception from when they saw the two sides as part of a three-dimensional corner.

What is the physiological explanation of lightness constancy? Although lateral inhibition may be part of the answer, especially to explain the effect of the surround in Figure 4.30, it is unclear what physiological mechanism explains the effects you have observed in the Mach card and "lightness-at-a-corner" demonstrations. (Remember that we introduced the Mach card demonstration in Chapter 2 to demonstrate a phenomenon that could not be explained by lateral inhibition.) Does this mean that physiological explanations for these phenomena don't exist? Not necessarily. We just haven't discovered them yet.

Color Constancy

We now consider the related phenomenon of color constancy, and as before let's start with a simple demonstration.

 D E M O N S T R A T I O N

Color Perception and Changing Illumination

View Color Plates 4.2b and 4.4 so that they are illuminated by natural light by taking them outdoors or illuminating them with light from a window, and then illuminate them with the tungsten light bulb of your desk lamp. Notice whether the colors change and, if so, how much they change. ●

In this demonstration you may have noticed some change in color as you changed the illumination, but the change was probably much less than would be predicted from the change of illumination. We can understand this phenomenon by remembering that, when you observed, for example, the blue square in Color Plate 4.4 under sunlight, it was receiving approximately equal energy at all wavelengths (solid curve in Figure 4.4), and so it reflected mainly short wavelengths into your eyes. But when you viewed it under tungsten light, which contains much more energy at long than at short wavelengths (dashed curve in Figure 4.4), it now reflected more long-wavelength light than it did when outside. Nonetheless, it still appeared blue.

Dorthea Jameson (1985) calculated that the wavelengths reflected from a blue color chip illuminated by tungsten light can match the wavelengths reflected by a yellow color chip illuminated by sunlight. But even though changing the illumination on a blue chip from sunlight to tungsten illumination greatly increases the relative amount of long-wavelength light reflected from it, we perceive little or no change in the color of the chip. As Jameson put it, "A blue bird would not be mistaken for a goldfinch if it were brought indoors" (p. 84).

This relative constancy of perceived color under different conditions of illumination is color constancy. It is important to note, however, that although our perception of colors does not change as much as we might expect under different conditions of illumination, color constancy is not complete; some changes do take place. On a recent visit to the art museum, I noticed that one of my favorite paintings had been moved from a location where it had received mostly natural light to one where it received mainly artificial light. Its colors had not changed so much that I could really say that the blues had become greener or the greens yellower, but the painting somehow looked different than it had before. In fact, experiments have shown that fluorescent lighting alters our perception of colors (Helson,

Judd, & Wilson, 1956), and many people have found, unhappily, that their new clothes, which looked exactly right in the fluorescently lit store, do not appear the same color at home (Hurvich, 1981).

Since our color perception changes a little when we change the illumination, we usually experience *approximate* color constancy. Even though only approximate, color constancy is still an impressive phenomenon. An object's color is determined primarily by its reflectance curve—the *percentage* of light reflected from the object at each wavelength (Figure 4.5)—not by the actual *amount* of light that reaches the observer's eye at each wavelength.

Why does color constancy occur? Psychophysical studies have identified a number of factors, including chromatic adaptation, the surroundings, and the observer's knowledge of the characteristic colors of objects, that apparently work together to achieve this effect. Let's consider each of these factors.

Chromatic Adaptation One mechanism responsible for color constancy is chromatic adaptation, an effect you can experience for yourself.

 D E M O N S T R A T I O N
Adapting to Red

Illuminate the red field of Color Plate 4.7 with a bright light from your desk lamp; then, with your left eye close to the page and your right eye closed, look at the field with your left eye for about 30–45 seconds. At the end of this time, look up and around, first with your left eye and then with your right. ●

This demonstration shows that color perception can be changed by **chromatic adaptation**—prolonged exposure to chromatic color.

Adaptation to the red light selectively affects your long-wavelength cone pigment, which decreases your sensitivity to red light and causes you to see the reds and oranges viewed with your left (adapted) eye as less saturated and bright than those viewed with the right eye.

We can understand how chromatic adaptation contributes to color constancy by considering what happens when you walk into a room illuminated with tungsten light. The eye adapts to the long wavelengths that predominate in the tungsten light, and this chromatic adaptation decreases your eye's sensitivity to long wavelengths. This decreased sensitivity causes long-wavelength light reflected from objects to have less effect than before adaptation, thus compensating for the greater amount of long-wavelength light reflected from these objects. The result is a negligible change in your perception of color.

If this explanation of color constancy is valid, then the light in our tungsten-illuminated room should appear more yellow if we do not adapt to it. You can test this idea by standing outside at night and observing the window of an illuminated room from a distance. Since you are not standing in the room, you are not adapted to its light; therefore, the light you see through the window looks more yellow than when it is seen from inside the room. Although chromatic adaptation partially explains color constancy, it isn't the whole answer, because color constancy also occurs when an object is seen too briefly for adaptation to have had an effect.

Memory Color **Memory color** refers to the fact that an object's characteristic color influences our perception of that object's color. This idea is supported by the results of an experiment done by John Delk and Samuel Fillenbaum (1965). They showed observers shapes like the ones in Figure 4.33, all of which were cut from the same sheet of orange-red cardboard. Shapes such as the heart and the apple are characteristically red, while others, such as the bell and the mushroom, are not. The observer's task was to match the color of

Figure 4.33
Some of the stimuli used in Delk and Fillenbaum's (1965) experiment on memory color. Although all of the stimuli were cut from the same orange-red paper, the apple and the heart were judged to appear slightly redder than the mushroom and the bell.

each object to that of a background field by adjusting the amount of redness in the background field. The result, in agreement with the idea of memory color, was that characteristically red objects, such as the heart and the apple, were matched with a redder background field than were nonred objects, such as the bell and the mushroom.

While memory color is a real effect, it is also a small one and plays only a minor role in color constancy, since objects without a characteristic color, such as a sweater or a piece of colored paper, also stay about the same color under changing illumination. More important than the characteristic color of an object are its surroundings.

The Surroundings   As illustrated by the following demonstration, color constancy is also affected by an object's surroundings.

   D E M O N S T R A T I O N

Masking the Surroundings

We can illustrate the effect of the surroundings on color constancy by a simple demonstration. Illuminate the green quadrant of Color Plate 4.4 with tungsten light; then look at it through a small hole punched in a piece of paper, so that all

you see through the hole is part of the green area. Now repeat this observation while illuminating the same area with daylight from your window.   ●

When the surroundings are masked, most people perceive the green area to be slightly more yellow under the tungsten light than in daylight. The fact that color constancy works less well when we mask the surroundings has been researched by a number of investigators, who have shown that color constancy works best when an object is surrounded by objects of many different colors. Much of this research has used displays like the one in Color Plate 4.8, which is called a *Mondrian display,* because of its similarity to works created by the Dutch painter Piet Mondrian (Land, 1983, 1986; Land & McCann, 1971). Much of the research using these displays has led to the proposal of mechanisms for explaining color constancy that involve complex calculations that take into account how light is reflected from many areas of a scene. For more details on these mechanisms see Brainard and Wandell (1986), Land (1983, 1986), and Pokorny, Shevell, and Smith (1991).

Physiological Mechanisms   We can explain color constancy at the physiological level by returning to color-sensitive neurons in area V4. Semir Zeki (1983, 1984) studied these neurons by using Mondrian displays. In a typical experiment, Zeki positioned a square of this display that looked green and reflected predominantly medium-wavelength light onto the receptive field of a monkey's G+R− striate neuron and onto the receptive field of a V4 neuron. When Zeki illuminated the display with white light, he found that both the G+R− neuron and the V4 neuron fired in response to the green area. However, when he illuminated the display with long-wavelength light so that the green patch reflected more long-wavelength light than medium-wavelength light, the G+R− neuron was inhib-

Perceiving Color

Table 4.3

Response of striate and V4 cells to a "green" patch under two illuminations

	White Illumination	Long-Wavelength Illumination
G+R− striate neuron	+	−
V4 cell	+	+

ited, but the V4 neuron continued to respond (Table 4.3).

The G+R− neuron behaved just as we would expect a G+R− neuron to behave: It fired when the retina was stimulated with medium-wavelength light and was inhibited when the retina was stimulated with long-wavelength light. The response of the V4 neuron, however, corresponded not to the wavelength distribution of the light, but to the color that the patch appeared to the experimenter. Because the patch was part of a complex display, color constancy caused the patch to look green under both white and long-wavelength illumination, and the V4 neuron fired similarly in both cases. Zeki (1983, 1984) suggests that neurons such as this one represent the physiology behind color constancy and perhaps color perception in general. It is, however, unlikely that these V4 neurons are the final answer to color perception, since they respond to white light, and since receptive fields for these neurons are not found outside the central 30 degrees of the visual field, an area in which people experience color (Abramov & Gordon, 1994).

Our discussion of lightness constancy and color constancy shows that our perception of an object is based not only on stimulation coming directly from that object, but also on stimulation from other objects in the environment. This is a basic perceptual principle that we will see holds for qualities in addition to lightness and color. We now end this chapter by reviewing some of the principles that we have discussed and that we will encounter in other chapters.

SOME PERCEPTUAL PRINCIPLES

In this chapter we have applied many of the basic principles of neural processing to color perception. Five of these principles are listed in Table 4.4, along with examples from Chapters 2 and 3 and examples from our consideration of color perception in this chapter.

In addition to showing how basic principles of neural processing are involved in color perception, we have also illustrated the following perceptual principles:

1. *We can explain perception both psychophysically and physiologically.* In Chapter 1 we introduced the idea that perception can be explained in terms of both psychophysics and physiology. This idea of different kinds of explanations is beautifully illustrated by the history of research on color vision, which has been marked by important discoveries using both psychophysical and physiological methods.

2. *Physiological mechanisms can be deduced from psychophysical observations.* Not only can perception be explained both psychophysically and physiologically, but these approaches interact with one another. Color vision research provides an excellent example of psychophysics' predicting physiology.

3. *Our perceptions are created by the way our sensory systems operate.* In Chapter 2 we saw how properties of the rods and cones and their circuits influence sensitivity, acuity, and adaptation. This chapter illustrates how physiological processes create perceptions in the following ways:

   a. Properties of the receptors determine perceptions. The three types of cone pigments create trichromatic perceptions.

Table 4.4

Examples of basic principles of neural processing from Chapters 2 and 3 and from this chapter

Neural Mechanisms	Chapters 2 and 3	Color Perception
Response selectivity *Neurons respond to selected aspects of the environment.*	Directionally selective neurons respond best to specific directions of movement.	S, M, and L cone pigments respond best to different regions of the spectrum. LGN and striate neurons respond to selected regions of the spectrum.
Convergence *One neuron receives inputs from many other neurons.*	Rod summation. Center–surround receptive fields.	Cone receptive fields.
Excitation and inhibition *Signals can oppose and, sometimes, cancel each other.*	Center–surround antagonism.	Color-opponent neurons in retina, LGN, and cortex.
Columnar organization *Neurons responsive to similar properties are arranged in columns in the cortex.*	Location columns. Ocular dominance columns. Orientation columns.	Color columns in the striate cortex.
Parallel pathways *There are two pathways, temporal and parietal, which process different stimulus properties.*	Color is processed in the temporal pathway, motion in the parietal pathyway.	Color-sensitive neurons are segregated in blobs.

People with only two types of cones (dichromats) perceive colors differently from people with three types of cones (trichromats).

b. The wiring of neurons affects perceptions. Opponent-process neurons, which respond in opposite ways to different parts of the spectrum because of the interplay of excitation and inhibition at the synapse, cause color-opponent perceptions.

c. Identical neural responses can result in identical perceptions, even if different physical stimuli created these responses. This is the principle behind metamers in color vision, in which two fields can look identical even if they consist of different wavelengths, because they cause identical patterns of firing of the three types of cone receptors and therefore cause identical firing further downstream in the visual system.

4. *People may not have exactly the same perceptions.* We know this is true from descriptions of color deficiency, but it is likely that this principle is true even of people with "normal" vision. Recent studies on how pigment absorption shifts slightly because of differences in just one or two amino acids in the pigment's protein molecule show that even people with normal color vision may have slightly different visual pigments. This is probably why some people, classified as having normal color vision, use different proportions of red and green lights when matching a yellow light (Neitz, Neitz, & Jacobs, 1993; Rayleigh, 1881). Reflecting the idea that these differences in perception are probably caused by very small differences in the structure of the visual pigments, John Mollon (1992) stated that "the difference of a single nucleotide places people in distinct phenomenal worlds."

5. *Mechanisms exist that keep perception constant in the face of changing stimulation.* Color constancy and lightness constancy illustrate how the properties of objects (their chromatic color or lightness in this case) remain stable even if the illumination changes. This perceptual constancy enables us to perceive the stable qualities of the world.

Although we have used examples from color vision to illustrate each of these five principles, we will see in the chapters that follow that both the neural mechanisms in Table 4.4 and our five perceptual principles apply to qualities in addition to color. For example, in the next chapter we will return to the idea that some neurons respond to specific qualities as we search for a physiological explanation of object perception, and in the chapter on depth perception we will again encounter the phenomenon of perceptual constancy. One of the messages of this book is that, although we perceive many different perceptual qualities, these qualities are, for the most part, created by similar mechanisms.

COLOR EXPERIENCE IN ANIMALS

We have seen that our perceptions are shaped by the way our nervous system operates. We can, however, go even further than this and say that *the basic nature of an organism's experience* is created by its nervous system. To understand what this means, let's consider the following statement about color vision made by Sir Isaac Newton (1642–1727) in his book *Optiks*:

> The Rays to speak properly are not coloured. In them there is nothing else than a certain Power and Disposition to stir up a Sensation of this or that Colour. . . . So Colours in the Object are nothing but a Disposition to reflect this or that sort of Rays more copiously than the rest.

Newton was saying that the colors that we see in response to different wavelengths are not *contained* in the rays of light themselves. Rather, colors are *created* by our nervous system, and although specific colors are related to specific wavelengths, the connection between wavelength and the experience we call color is an arbitrary one. There is nothing intrinsically "red" about long wavelengths or "blue" about short wavelengths. In fact, the light rays are simply energy and actually have no color at all.

We can find similar examples by looking at other senses. We hear in response to pressure changes in the air. But why do we perceive rapid pressure changes as high-pitched and slow pressure changes as low-pitched? Is there anything intrinsically "high-pitched" about rapid pressure changes? Or consider the sense of smell. We perceive some substances as "sweet" and others as "rancid," but where is the "sweetness" or "rancidity" in the molecular structure of the substances that enter the nose? Again, the answer is that these perceptions are not in the molecular structure. They are created by our nervous system.

The idea that our actual *experience* is created by our nervous system is hard for some people to understand. "After all," they say, "aren't we simply seeing what's out there?" It comes as a surprise to them that we experience things such as colors, sounds, tastes, or smells by a process in which our nervous system is stimulated by environmental energy and then adds the experience.

This idea becomes easier to appreciate when we ask the question: What do animals perceive? When we ask this, we find many examples of situations in which animals are capable of perceiving energy that humans can't perceive at all. Consider, for example, the honeybee (Figure 4.34). The honeybee has trichromatic vision, but its three kinds of receptors are spread out over more of the spectrum than are human receptors (Figure 4.35). Honeybees are sensitive to light in the ultraviolet region of the spectrum (very short wavelengths) that humans can't see, because one of the honeybee's receptors absorbs maximally at 335 nm (Menzel & Backhaus, 1989; Menzel et al., 1986). What "color" do you think bees perceive at these short wavelengths? You are free to guess, but you really have no way of knowing. Since, as Newton stated, "The rays are not colored," there is no color in the wavelengths, so the bee's nervous system creates its experience of color. For all we know, the honeybee's experience of color is quite different from ours, even for wavelengths that we perceive well. We do know, however, that the bee's sensitivity to very short wavelengths is likely to be particularly useful in helping bees to detect different flowers.

The pigeon is another example of an animal with color vision that is different from humans'. Pigeons may have pentachromatic color vision (based on five different color mechanisms), although this has not been definitely proved

Figure 4.34
The honeybee relies on its ability to perceive in the short-wavelength region of the spectrum to distinguish between different kinds of flowers.

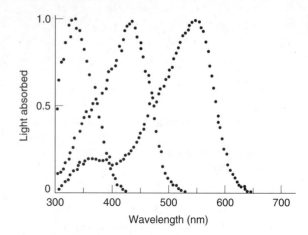

Figure 4.35
Absorption curves of the honeybee's three cone pigments. From these curves we can infer that the honeybee's vision extends into the ultraviolet (very-short-wavelength) region of the spectrum. (Adapted from Menzel et al., 1986.)

(Varela, Palacios, & Goldsmith, 1993). This idea that another species' color vision may surpass humans' makes the point that color vision is relative. A human dichromat is considered color-deficient compared to a trichromat since trichromats perceive a wider range of colors. Using similar reasoning, we can hypothesize that a trichromat is color-deficient compared to a tetrachromat (having four color mechanisms) or a pentachromat (having five color mechanisms). It is possible that an animal with more than three mechanisms sees a wider range of colors than an animal with "only" trichromatic vision.

Although there is no way for us to know what various animals' color experiences are like, we can determine whether or not animals have color vision (Jacobs, 1993). This is, however, an extremely difficult task, because in order to demonstrate color vision behaviorally, we need to show that an animal can tell the difference between two lights that have different wavelengths, but that are equated for brightness. Some early research, which claimed to demonstrate animal color discrimination by showing that the animals could be trained to respond to one hue and not to another, failed to take brightness into account, so they simply demonstrated that the animal could discriminate between a bright light and a dim light. To be sure that brightness plays no role in making a discrimination, we must measure an animal's spectral sensitivity curve (see Figure 2.24) and, based on this curve, adjust the intensity of stimuli of different wavelengths so that they appear equally bright to the animal.

Such a procedure was followed by Jacky Emmerton and Juan Delius (1980), who presented a pigeon with a pair of wavelengths equated for brightness based on the pigeon's spectral sensitivity function. The pigeons were trained by being rewarded with food for pecking a key illuminated with one of the wavelengths, designated the test wavelength, and by not being rewarded for pecking at the key illuminated with the other wavelength, designated the comparison wavelength. Once the pigeons mastered that discrimination, the comparison wavelength was changed so that it was closer to the test wavelength, and the procedure was repeated until the test and comparison wavelengths were so close that the pigeons could no longer tell the difference between them. This procedure was repeated for test wavelengths across the spectrum, and the results (Figure 4.36) show that the pigeon can discriminate between two wavelengths even if

there is no brightness difference between them (Varela et al., 1993).

Another way to approach the question of whether an animal sees colors is to consider its physiology. If an animal has only one visual pigment, color vision is unlikely. If an animal has more than one visual pigment, this condition suggests, but does not guarantee, that color vision is present. The only way to prove that an animal has color vision is by testing the animal's behavioral response to different wavelengths, as described above.

The goldfish is a good example of a case in which both physiological and behavioral evidence indicate the presence of color vision. The goldfish has three kinds of cone pigments (Marks, 1965; Tomita et al., 1967), its retina generates opponent S-potentials (Svaetichin, 1956; see Figure 4.19), and behavioral experiments indicate that goldfish have trichromatic vision (Yager & Thorpe, 1970).

Finally, we can look to an animal's environment and behavior for clues to the presence of color vision (Tansley, 1965). If color is a feature of one sex or is used in a species' mating or threat displays, it is likely that members of the species can perceive these colors. For example, that a territory-holding male robin attacks an intruder because of its red breast suggests that the robin has color vision. Similarly, it seems likely that peacocks have color vision, so the female can perceive the male's colorful plumage.

By means of all the methods described above, it has been determined that most birds have color vision, some being trichromatic (Varela et al., 1993), and that many fish also have trichromatic color vision, especially those that swim in shallow water and therefore receive a wide range of wavelengths. (Since water filters out visible light, fish that swim in deeper water are less likely to have color vision; Levine & MacNichol, 1982.)

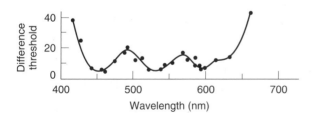

Figure 4.36

Wavelength discrimination in the pigeon. This curve indicates the difference threshold at wavelengths across the spectrum. For example, at 500 nm the difference threshold is about 18 nm, so the pigeon can tell the difference between 500-nm and 518-nm lights that have the same brightness. (From Emmerton & Delius, 1980.)

The most common type of color vision in mammals is dichromatic vision (Jacobs, 1993). Though cats were originally thought to be color-blind (Tansley, 1965), recent behavioral and electrophysiological results indicate that they may be dichromats (Mello & Peterson, 1964; Meyer & Anderson, 1965; Pearlman & Daw, 1970; Sechzer & Brown, 1964), and similar results have recently shown that dogs also have dichromatic vision (Jacobs et al., 1993; Neitz, Geist, & Jacobs, 1989). Another mammal that may be a dichromat is the squirrel (Michael, 1969; Tansley, 1965).

Monkeys have the best color vision among nonhuman primates. New World monkeys such as the *Cebus* are dichromats (Grether, 1939), whereas female squirrel monkeys have vision that corresponds to that of a human anomalous trichromat, and the male's vision is dichromatic (DeValois & Jacobs, 1968; Jacobs, 1993). The color vision of the Old World rhesus monkey is excellent, being nearly identical to humans'. This finding is supported by psychophysical experiments and by microspectrophotometry, which has isolated three types of cone pigments similar to those of humans (DeValois & Jacobs, 1968; Marks, Dobelle, & MacNichol, 1964). Thus, the human and the rhesus monkey have the best color vision of the mammals, and we must look to birds and fish to find comparable color vision in other species.

INFANT COLOR VISION

Can infants see colors? If they can, how do their perceptions compare to adults'? These are difficult questions to answer, for the same reason that assessing animal color vision is difficult: We must somehow test vision without the luxury of being able to use language to communicate with our subjects. However, researchers have devised a number of ingenious methods for testing color vision in infants and have found that infants have some color vision early in life and that they develop trichromatic vision by at least 2–3 months of age.

Marc Bornstein, William Kessen, and Sally Weiskopf (1976) assessed infant color vision by asking whether infants perceive the same color categories in the spectrum as adults. People with normal trichromatic vision see the spectrum as a sequence of color categories, starting with blue at the short-wavelength end, and followed by green, yellow, orange, and red, with fairly abrupt transitions between one color and the next.

Bornstein and his co-workers used the habituation procedure diagrammed in Figure 4.37 to determine whether the color vision of 4-month-old infants follows this pattern. They first presented a 510-nm light—a wavelength that appears green to a trichromat. As the infant viewed

the 510-nm light for a number of trials, it habituated, looking less and less at the light. Once the infant's looking time had decreased to less than half its original level, Bornstein presented either a 480-nm light, which looks blue to a trichromat, or a 540-nm light, which is on the other side of the blue–green border and therefore appears green. Bornstein picked 480 and 540 nm as his test wavelengths because the 540-nm light is in the same perceptual category as the 510-nm light (both appear green to adults), whereas the 480-nm light is in a different category (it appears blue to adults).

When presented with the 540-nm light, the infant's looking time changed only slightly from its habituated response to the 510-nm light, but the looking time increased greatly when the infant saw the 480-nm light. The 540-nm light apparently looks about the same as the 510-nm light to the infant, but 480 nm looks different. From this result and from experiments in other regions of the spectrum, Bornstein concluded that 4-month-old infants categorize colors the same way trichromats do.

Later experiments have asked more precise questions about infant color vision. For example, Russell Hamer, Kenneth Alexander, and Davida Teller (1982) wondered whether 1-, 2-, and 3-month-old infants have both medium- and long-wavelength cone pigments. The starting point for these authors' experiment was the fact that dichromats, who have only the medium- or the long-wavelength pigment but not both, can't distinguish between two lights with wavelengths above 550 nm if these lights have the same brightness. We can understand why this is so by looking at the cone pigment absorption spectra in Figure 4.9. Notice that only the medium- and long-wavelength pigments absorb light above 550 nm. Thus, if one of these kinds of pigments is missing, the person is left

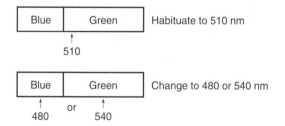

Figure 4.37

Habituation procedure in the Bornstein, Kessen, and Weiskopf (1976) experiment. See text for details.

with only one kind of pigment in this part of the spectrum and, without the minimum of two kinds of pigments required for color vision, will confuse wavelengths above 550 nm if they have the same brightness.

Do infants have operational medium- and long-wavelength receptors? Hamer and co-workers answered that question by using the preferential looking technique and the display in Figure 4.38, in which a red test square was presented on either the left or the right side of a yellow background on different trials. An infant who could see the red square indicated his or her perception by looking at the square. By monitoring the infant's looking behavior, Hamer et al. determined whether the infant could discriminate the red square from the yellow background. But remember that they needed to show that the infant could make this discrimination even if the red and yellow lights were of the same brightness. Since the researchers had no way of telling how bright these lights appeared to the infants, they presented the red square at a wide range of intensities, rea-

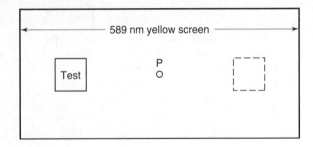

Figure 4.38

The stimulus used by Hamer, Alexander, and Teller (1982) to determine whether infants can tell the difference between two wavelengths above 550 nm that have the same brightness. A test square that appears red to an adult is presented either on the left or on the right side of a yellow screen. The infant's looking behavior is monitored by an observer who views the infant through the peephole, P.

soning that at least one of the intensities within this range would match the brightness of the yellow background.

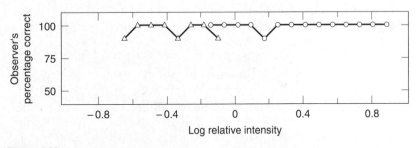

Figure 4.39

Results of the Hamer, Alexander, and Teller experiment for a 4-week-old infant. The infant's ability to detect the red test square was measured at a range of intensities of the test square, indicated along the horizontal axis. The intensity marked 0 represents the intensity at which the red and the yellow have the same brightness for an adult. Since the infant's performance ranged from 80% to 100% correct at all intensities, we can infer that she was, in fact, able to distinguish the red square from the yellow background on the basis of color alone.

Hamer et al. found that about one half of the 1-month-old infants could discriminate between red and yellow at all intensities, and that by 3 months, almost all of the infants could make this discrimination (Figure 4.39). Based on this result, Hamer et al. concluded that some 1-month-old infants, most 2-month-old infants, and all 3-month-old infants have operational medium- and long-wavelength receptors.

Researchers have also asked whether infants have short-wavelength receptors. Using a procedure similar to Hamer's, but too complex to describe here, D. Varner and co-workers (1985) tested infants' ability to see short-wavelength light and found that, by 2 months of age, infants have functioning short-wavelength cones. Our conclusion from the Hamer et al. and Varner et al. experiments is that all three types of cones are present by at least 2–3 months of age, and that some infants show evidence of three-cone vision even earlier. This infant trichromatic vision may not be identical to normal adult color vision, but it does seem likely that infants as young as 2 or 3 months old experience a wide range of colors.

REVIEW

Functions of Color Vision

Outline

- Color serves a number of functions, including creating perceptual segregation and signaling.

Questions

1. How does color vision create perceptual segregation? Give some examples of the signaling function of color. (129)

Describing Color Experience

- In dim illuminations we perceive the world in shades of gray. In brighter illumination, we perceive chromatic colors.

- We can describe all of the colors we can discriminate by using combinations of four basic colors—red, green, yellow, and blue—plus black and white.

- Wavelength is the physical property most closely related to color.

2. Define chromatic color and achromatic color. (131)

3. How many colors can humans discriminate? How many color names are there? Describe the color circle. What are some reasons for considering red, green, yellow, and blue basic colors? (131)

4. Describe the relationship between wavelength and perceived color. Describe the wavelength distributions that are associated with some common light sources, objects, and dyes. (133)

The Search for the Sensory Code

- Researchers have proposed two basic ways that neural coding can represent stimulus properties: specificity coding and across-fiber pattern coding.

5. How could specificity coding determine color perception? Why is specificity coding an unlikely code for color? Describe how an across-fiber pattern code could be the sensory code for color. (136)

Psychophysical Research on Color Vision

- Thomas Young and Hermann von Helmholtz proposed the trichromatic theory of color vision, based on the results of color-matching experiments.

6. What is the trichromatic theory? Describe how the results of color-matching experiments provided evidence for this theory. (139)

- Ewald Hering proposed the opponent-process theory of color vision, based on phenomenological observations that involved afterimages, simultaneous contrast, and visualizing colors.

7. Which colors are paired in opponent-process theory? Describe the phenomenological evidence for this pairing and Gordon and Abramov's color-naming experiment. (140)
8. What is the basic idea behind opponent-process theory? (141)

Physiological Research on Color Vision

- In the 1960s researchers used microspectrophotometry to show that in the human there are three types of cone pigments that absorb light in different parts of the spectrum. These pigments are called the short-, medium-, and long-wavelength pigments.

- Physiological research has determined the molecular structures of the visual pigments.

- The discovery of opponent S-potentials in the fish retina and opponent neurons in the monkey LGN provided physiological evidence that supports the opponent-process theory.

- Opponent cells have also been discovered in the cortex, with double color-opponent cells concentrated in areas called blobs.

- Opponent cells are created by the way the cones are connected to other neurons in the retina.

9. What is the relationship between the pattern of response of the three types of cone receptors and color perception? How can we use this information to predict what colors will result from mixing lights? (142)
10. What are metamers? What is the physiological principle underlying metamers? (144)
11. What is the relationship between the molecular structure of visual pigments and the pigment's absorption spectrum? (144)
12. Describe how opponent cells in the retina and the LGN respond to different wavelengths. (144)
13. Describe type 1 color-opponent cells and double color-opponent cells. Why would certain double color-opponent cells be well suited to helping monkeys find fruit in the forest? (146)
14. How are double color-opponent cells organized within the blobs? Relate this organization to hypercolumns. (146)
15. Describe a simple circuit that would create opponent responses from the inputs of the three types of cone receptors. (147)

- Information about wavelengths that is processed to create opponent responses changes the information provided by the receptors into a form that signals the presence of specific wavelengths.

16. What is the difference in how information is represented by the responding of the three types of cones and by opponent neurons? (148)
17. How likely is it that there is a direct link between perception and the firing of opponent neurons in the striate cortex? (149)
18. Explain how trichromatic and opponent-process theories can both be correct. (150)

Color Deficiency

- Color deficiency is an inability to perceive or discriminate some of the colors that people with normal color vision can perceive or discriminate. We can determine what people with dichromatic vision see by asking a person who is a unilateral dichromat (having dichromatic vision in only one eye) to compare the color perceptions in the color-deficient and normal eyes.

- Most color deficiency is caused by the absence of one or more cone pigments, or by the presence of pigments that are different from normal ones.

19. Describe how people who are monochromats, dichromats (protanopes, deuteranopes, and tritanopes), and anomalous trichromats (a) perform in color-matching experiments and (b) perceive colors. (150)
20. Why are some forms of color deficiency sex-linked? (151)

21. Which cone pigments are missing for each type of color deficiency? Why do anomalous trichromats match colors differently from normal trichromats? (152)

Perceptual Constancy

- Perceptual constancy is our perception that properties of objects remain constant even when the conditions of stimulation are changed.

- When an object is illuminated by light of different intensities, the achromatic color of the object remains constant or changes only slightly. This relative constancy of achromatic color under different conditions of illumination is called lightness constancy. One of the things that helps establish lightness constancy is the relationships between the reflectances of adjacent areas.

22. What do shape constancy, color constancy, and lightness constancy have in common? (153)

23. Describe the ratio principle. How does it help to explain lightness constancy? (154)
24. Describe Gelb's experiment and its relationship to lightness constancy. (154)

- Lightness constancy is influenced by the observer's interpretation of how an object is illuminated.

- When an object is illuminated with lights of different wavelengths, such as sunlight and tungsten light, the perceived color of the object changes only slightly. This relative constancy of chromatic color under different conditions of illumination is called color constancy.

- A number of explanations have been proposed for color constancy, including chromatic adaptation, memory color, and the effect of the surroundings.

25. Describe how perception of the Mach card changes when it perceptually flips. What is the explanation for this change in perception? (156)
26. Why does perception of the lightness of two surfaces forming a corner change when a person's perception of depth at the corner is eliminated? (156)
27. What is the difference between complete color constancy and approximate color constancy? (157)
28. An object's chromatic color is determined primarily by what? (158)

29. How is color constancy explained by chromatic adaptation, memory color, and the effect of the surroundings? (158)
30. Describe how the response of cells in area V4 provide an explanation of color constancy at the physiological level. Why is it unlikely that the response of V4 cells is the final answer to color perception? (159)

Some Perceptual Principles

- Many of the perceptual principles introduced in Chapters 2 and 3 also hold for color perception.

31. Describe the five basic principles listed in Table 4.4, giving examples from Chapters 2 and 3 and this chapter that illustrate each principle. (160)
32. Describe five additional perceptual principles described at the end of this chapter. (160)

Color Experience in Animals

- The basic nature of an organism's experience is created by its nervous system. The nervous system creates the perception of color from different wavelengths.

33. What do we mean when we say that the relationship between wavelength and the experience of color is arbitrary? (163)
34. How is the color vision of the honeybee and the pigeon different from human color vision? In what sense could we say that a human with trichromatic vision is color-deficient? (163)

- To demonstrate color vision in animals, we need to show that the animal can tell the difference between two lights with different wavelengths that are equal in brightness. Other ways of investigating whether color vision exists include determining which types of cone pigments are present and studying the animal's environment and behavior.

35. How did Emmerton and Delius test color vision in the pigeon? Describe color vision in the following animals, giving the reasons for this conclusion, where applicable: goldfish, robins, peacocks, birds, cats, dogs, and monkeys. Which nonhuman mammal has the best color vision? (165)

Infant Color Vision

- Studying infant color vision poses problems similar to those encountered in the study of animal color vision. Researchers have shown that young infants have some color vision and that some form of trichromatic vision is present by 2–3 months of age.

36. Describe the experiments of Bornstein et al. on the perception of color categories, and of Hammer et al. on whether infants have medium- and long-wavelength cone functions, citing both procedures and results. What did Varner et al. conclude about the presence of short-wavelength cone function in infants? (167)

PERCEIVING OBJECTS

When you try asking people what they see in a room, you will probably hear responses like "A chair, some books on the desk, pictures on the wall." Perception, for most people, is first and foremost the perception of objects. How can we study the process of perceiving these objects? So far, our discussion of perception has focused on neural information processing in the visual system and neural coding, that is, the connection between neural responding and specific visual qualities. For example, we emphasized the search for connections between neural responding and visual qualities in Chapter 4 on color vision, as we identified connections between the wavelength of the stimulus and the responding of neurons in the retina, the lateral geniculate nucleus, and the cortex.

In this chapter we take a different approach by placing less emphasis on neural responding, which has dominated our discussion so far. Another difference between the approach here and in the previous chapter is that here we don't have the luxury of being able to focus our attention on one particular physical characteristic, such as wavelength. There is no agreement that there is just one

physical property that explains how we perceive objects. Instead, different researchers have focused on a variety of different physical properties and on different aspects of object perception. This chapter, therefore, provides an opportunity to see how researchers and theorists have approached a problem in a number of different ways. Our plan is to look first at some of the problems involved in perceiving objects. We will then list a number of questions that have been posed by various researchers. In the remainder of the chapter, we will describe how these researchers have answered each of these questions.

THE PROBLEM OF OBJECT PERCEPTION

Why is object perception a "problem"? Like other kinds of perception, it appears to be effortless. We look at a chair and, with no particular effort, see a chair, unless it is extremely dark or

Figure 5.1
"Mystery object" behind wall.

the chair is hidden from view. And even when most of the chair is not visible, we can often still identify it (Figure 5.1).

Given the ease with which we perceive objects, we might assume that the process of object perception is simple. But we can appreciate that there is nothing simple about object perception by considering the difficulties involved in programming a computer to recognize even simple scenes.

Problems for Computer Vision

Although many of the early researchers in computer vision thought that it wouldn't be very

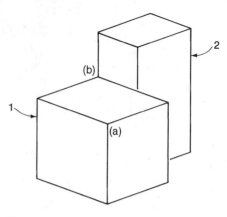

Figure 5.2

difficult to design systems that could recognize objects or scenes, they soon found that, although seeing is easy for humans, it is an extremely difficult task for computers. Even now, after decades of work on computer vision, most sophisticated computer programs can recognize simple shapes like those in Figure 5.2 but cannot correctly identify most of the varied objects that we see easily every day.

Why is the perception of objects so difficult for a computer? We can answer this question by considering the block scene in Figure 5.2. The computer's task is to use the two-dimensional information in images like the one in the figure to determine the three-dimensional layout of the scene. To do this, the computer must deal with the following problems:

1. Transforming a two-dimensional representation into a perception of three-dimensional objects. The problem arises when we realize that a given two-dimensional representation can be caused by many different three-dimensional objects. For example, the two-dimensional image shown in Figure 5.3a could be caused by a circle of rocks, as appears to be the case based on this picture, or it could be caused by viewing the arrangement of rocks shown in Figure 5.3b from a specific vantage point.

(a)   (b)

Figure 5.3

An environmental sculpture by Thomas Macaulay. (a) When viewed from exactly the right vantage point (the second-floor balcony of the Blackhawk Mountain School of Art, Black Hawk, Colorado), the stones appear to be arranged in a circle. (b) Viewing the stones from the ground floor reveals a truer picture of their configuration. These figures show that a two-dimensional representation does not always accurately represent a three-dimensional object or scene. In this example, the view in (a) creates the erroneous impression that the rocks are arranged in a circle. (Photographs courtesy of Thomas Macaulay)

2. Deciding whether three intersecting lines are part of the same object or are created by two different objects. For example, in Figure 5.2 the intersection at (a) is the corner of object 1, but the intersection at (b) is created by objects 1 and 2 together.

3. Determining the shapes of objects that are partially hidden. Although we assume that object 2 in Figure 5.2 is a rectangular solid, we do this by making an assumption about what is happening behind object 1 (just as we make an assumption that there is a rocking chair behind the wall in Figure 5.1). This problem also extends to single objects. For example, although we may see shape 1 as a solid cube, for all we know it is open at the back.

These are only a few of the problems facing computer vision. Things become even more complex when we consider the many varied shapes we see in the real world. (For more detailed discussions of the problems involved in computer vision, see Barrow & Tannenbaum, 1986; Beck, Hope, & Resenfeld, 1983; Brown, 1984; Hanson & Riseman, 1978; McArthur, 1982; Poggio, 1986; Winston, 1975.)

The point of this brief foray into computer vision is that, although we are presented with the same information as the computer, in the form of a two-dimensional image of the scene on our retina, we are able to translate this image into a correct perception of the scene much more easily than even the most powerful computer. Although we are sometimes fooled (perhaps shape

2 in Figure 5.2 is not really a rectangular solid), most of the time we are able to solve effortlessly the complexities of object perception and to arrive at a correct perception of objects and the scenes within which these objects exist.

Another way to appreciate the complexity of object perception is to consider what happens when we view objects that are degraded or ambiguous.

Perceiving Degraded or Ambiguous Images

We have seen that people can easily see things that a computer has difficulty dealing with; however, perceiving objects becomes difficult, even for a person, if the stimuli to be perceived are partially obscured or ambiguous. For example, most people see Figure 5.4a as an array of meaningless shapes. However, these shapes are actually fragments of B's, as we can see in Figure 5.4b (Bregman, 1981). Or consider the following demonstration:

D E M O N S T R A T I O N
Finding Faces in a Landscape

Consider the picture in Figure 5.5. At first glance this scene appears to contain mainly trees, rocks, and water. But on closer inspection you can see some faces in the trees in the background, and if you look more closely, you can see that a number of faces are formed by various groups of rocks. There are, in fact, 13 faces in this picture. If you have trouble seeing all of them, try looking at the picture from a few feet away. From this distance previously unseen faces sometimes become visible.   ●

In this demonstration some people find it difficult to perceive the faces at first, but once they succeed, they find it difficult to return to their previous perception of rocks and trees. Your perceptions of Figures 5.4 and 5.5 illustrate a few of the problems facing psychologists interested in studying object perception. Figure 5.4 illustrates a problem in perceptual organization: Why do the shapes become organized into B's when the black "blob" is added? Figure 5.5 illustrates, among other things, that we have to take more than just the pattern of light and dark on the page into account when explaining object perception, since the same stimulus can create more than one perception: One moment it creates rocks, another moment faces.

Researchers who study object perception are interested in explaining perceptions of objects like the ones in Figures 5.4 and 5.5 that may be difficult to see, and they are also interested in explaining how we perceive things that are easier to see, such as the objects you can see as you look around your environment right now. In searching for these explanations, these researchers have posed a number of questions:

Asking Questions about Object Perception

Here are a few questions that have been posed by researchers interested in explaining object perception.

1. How do we organize small elements into larger patterns or meaningful objects, and how do we tell the difference between objects and their backgrounds?

2. What happens in the mind during the process of perceiving an object? This question focuses on mental processes.

3. How do we recognize three-dimensional shapes? Like question 2, this question is related to mental processes, but it focuses specifically on three-dimensional stimuli.

4. How would the brain accomplish object perception if it analyzed the image on the retina as a computer would?

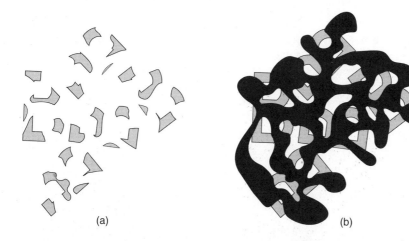

(a)

(b)

Figure 5.4
The gray areas are the same in (a) and (b), but they become perceptually organized into five B's when an occluding blob fills in the missing parts of the letters. (From Bregman, 1981.)

Figure 5.5
The Forest Has Eyes *by Bev Doolittle (1985). Can you find 13 faces in this picture?*

5. How do neurons participate in object perception? This question involves many of the physiological principles we introduced in Chapters 2 and 3.

As we see how researchers have answered these questions in the sections that follow, we will become more sensitive to how different researchers describe the basic nature of the perceptual process. We will see that some explanations of perception are based entirely on characteristics of the stimulus (Question 1), whereas other explanations focus on mental processes (Questions 2 and 3). Still others see the perceptual process as involving a mechanistic computer-like process (Question 4), while others see object perception in terms of the firing of neurons in the brain (Question 5). We begin with the first question.

PERCEPTUAL ORGANIZATION: THE GESTALT APPROACH

The questions "How do we group things into objects?" and "How do we tell the difference between objects and their backgrounds?" are concerned with a problem called **perceptual organization**—the grouping of small parts into larger units. When my son Adam was 6 years old, he regularly provided examples of perceptual organization at breakfast when he would tell me that he was about to eat an elephant, or some other animal, that had appeared in his scrambled eggs. Adam's perception of an elephant in his scrambled eggs meant that the pieces of egg on his plate had become perceptually organized so that they looked like an elephant.

Seeing animals in scrambled eggs or, for that matter, animals or other objects in the clouds is not limited to 6-year-olds. Many adults have these perceptions, too, and we routinely carry out this process of perceptual organization because it is one of the essential ways we make sense of the world. When we saw the train along the roadside in Chapter 1, the process of organization enabled us to separate the train from the trees in the background. Similarly, when we talk with a friend in a noisy room, the process of organization enables us to differentiate the friend's voice from the jumble of other sounds in the room. In the 1920s a group of psychologists founded an approach to psychology called **Gestalt psychology**, which is especially concerned with the process of percep-

tual organization. These psychologists were the first to establish some of the basic principles governing this process.

The Beginnings of Gestalt Psychology

Gestalt psychology was a reaction to an idea proposed by psychologists that advocated an approach called *structuralism*, which was popular in the early 1900s. According to **structuralism**, perceptions are built up of tiny building blocks called *sensations*, just as each of the dots in the face in Figure 5.6 add together to create our perception of a face. Max Wertheimer, one of the founders of Gestalt psychology (Figure 5.7), proposed the following argument against structuralism. Consider the situation diagrammed in Figure 5.8. A light on the left is flashed on and off, followed by 50 msec (50/1,000 sec) of darkness; then the line on the right is flashed on and off. This sequence of flash-darkness-flash causes a phenomenon called **apparent movement**—the perception of movement from left to right through the dark space separating the two flashed lights. How, asked Wertheimer, is it possible to explain our perception of a line moving through the dark empty space in terms of sensations? Since there is no stimulation whatsoever in that space, no sensations are present to provide an explanation. With this demonstration and others, Gestalt psychology rejected the structuralists' idea of perceptions being built from tiny sensations and in its place proposed the idea that

Figure 5.6
According to structuralism, a number of sensations (represented by the dots) adds up to create our perception of the face.

Figure 5.7
Max Wertheimer (1880–1943), whose experiments and theoretical writings stimulated the founding of the Gestalt school of psychology.

illusory because they aren't actually present in the physical stimulus. The absence of physical contours becomes obvious if you imagine that the black circles are holes and that you are looking at the cube through these holes. When you arrive at this perception, you wil see the cube as floating in dark space behind a surface full of holes, but without the illusory contours. The fact that we sometimes perceive illusory contours supports the idea that our perception of parts of a stimulus

(a)	(b)	(c)	(d)
Flash line on left	50 msec of darkness	Flash line on right	Perception: movement from left to right

Figure 5.8
Wertheimer's experiment in movement perception.

"The whole is different from the sum of its parts."

Much of the evidence supporting the idea that the whole is different from the sum of its parts comes from examples showing that our perception of one part of a stimulus depends on the presence of other parts of the stimulus. Look, for example, at Figures 5.9 and 5.10. We interpret the horse in Figure 5.9 as rearing back, but we see the identical horse in Figure 5.10 as moving forward. The presence of the rider in Figure 5.9 and of the lead horse in Figure 5.10 make the same horse look different in the two pictures.

Or consider Figure 5.11. As you view this figure, imagine that it is a cube floating in space in front of black circles. When you view the figure in this way, you may see faint **illusory contours** that represent the edges of the cube (Bradley & Petry, 1977). These contours are called

Figure 5.9
A rearing horse. (From Arnheim, 1974.)

Figure 5.10
One horse following another horse. (From Arnheim, 1974.)

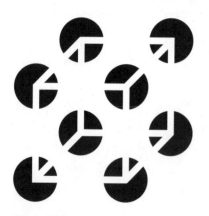

Figure 5.11

This figure can be seen as a cube floating in front of eight disks or as a cube seen through eight holes. In the first case, the edges of the cube appear as illusory contours. (From Bradley & Petry, 1977.)

depends on the overall stimulus configuration. The contours of the cube are not physically present; they are caused by the black circles and by the white lines inside the circles. No theory proposing that perceptions are constructed from individual sensations can explain this result.

Look at the two vases in Figure 5.12. The one on the left has a glossy finish, and the one on the right a dull finish. Or do they? If you cover up the highlights on the left vase with your finger, it becomes the same as the right vase, because both vases are identical except that the highlights have been removed from the right vase. In this example, as in the previous ones, the perception of parts of an object is determined by the other parts of the object.

The Gestalt psychologists were interested not only in demonstrating that the whole is different from the sum of its parts but also in determining the rules that specify how we organize

Figure 5.12

Two vases, showing how highlights on the surface on the left make the whole surface appear glossy. (From Beck, 1972.)

small parts into wholes. Look at Figure 5.13. What do you see? If you see a dog, then you have succeeded in organizing a mass of black and white shapes into a Dalmatian! How does this particular arrangement of black and white shapes enable us to differentiate the spotted dog from the spotted background? A Gestalt psychologist would answer this question by referring to the **laws of perceptual organization.**

The Laws of Perceptual Organization

The laws of perceptual organization are a series of rules that describe what your perception will be, given certain stimulus conditions. Let's look at the six most important Gestalt laws.

Pragnanz *Pragnanz*, roughly translated from the German, means "good figure." The **law of Pragnanz**—the central law of Gestalt psychology (it is also called the **law of good figure** or the **law of simplicity)** states: *Every stimulus pattern is seen in such a way that the resulting structure is as simple as possible.* According to the law of simplicity, you should perceive Figure 5.14a as a square and an elliptical object as in Figure 5.14b because these two objects are simpler than some of the other possible perceptions shown in Figures 5.14c and 5.14d. Similarly, Figure 5.15 is perceived as a triangle overlapping a rectangle, and not as a complicated 11-sided figure.

Similarity Most people perceive Figure 5.16a as either horizontal rows of circles, vertical columns of circles, or both. But when we change some of the circles to squares, as in Figure 5.16b, most people perceive vertical columns of squares and circles. This perception illustrates the **law of similarity:** *Similar things appear to be grouped together.* This law causes the circles to be grouped with other circles and the squares to be grouped

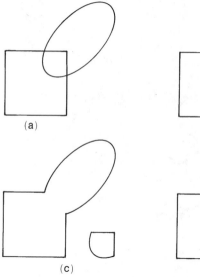

(a)

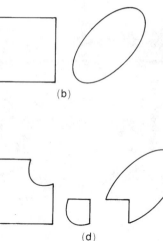

(b)

(c)

(d)

Figure 5.14
The displays in (b), (c), and (d) indicate the possible perceptions of the components of the display (a). According to the law of Pragnanz, (b) is the preferred perception because it is the simplest.

Figure 5.15
According to the law of Pragnanz, we perceive this as a rectangle and a triangle.

with other squares. Grouping can also occur because of similarity of lightness (Figure 5.17), hue, orientation (Figure 5.18), or size.

Grouping also occurs for auditory stimuli. For example, notes that have similar pitches and that follow each other closely in time become perceptually grouped. We will consider this and other auditory grouping effects when we describe the organizational processes in hearing in Chapter 9.

Good Continuation The series of points starting at A in Figure 5.19 flows smoothly to B. It does not go to C or D, because that path would involve making sharp turns and would violate the **law of good continuation,** which states:

Points that, when connected, result in straight or smoothly curving lines are seen as belonging together, and lines tend to be seen in such a way as to follow the smoothest path.

Good continuation is illustrated by the bridge and the smokestack in Camille Pissarro's painting *The Great Bridge at Rouen,* shown in Figure 5.20. Although the smoke cuts the bridge in two and cuts the smokestack into three pieces, we assume, because of good continuation, that the various parts belong together, and the bridge and the smokestack, therefore, do not fall apart. Good continuation also comes into play in helping us to perceive a smoothly curving elliptical shape and a square in Figure 5.14a.

Proximity or Nearness Figure 5.21a is perceived as horizontal rows of circles. This illustrates the **law of proximity:** *Things that are near to each other appear to be grouped together.* And although every other circle is changed to a square in Figure 5.21b, we still perceive horizontal rows; in this case the law of proximity overpowers the law of similarity (also see Figure 5.22).

Common Fate The two dancers in Figure 5.23 form a group by virtue of their nearness and

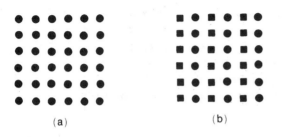

(a) (b)

Figure 5.16
(a) Perceived as horizontal rows or vertical columns or both. (b) Perceived as vertical columns.

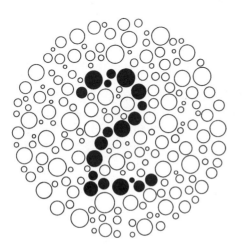

Figure 5.17
Grouping due to similarity of lightness. The light objects form one group, and the dark objects form another group.

Figure 5.18
Grouping due to similarity of orientation. In this pas de deux from The Nutcracker *the perceptual unity of the two dancers is greatly enhanced by the similarity of their arm and body orientations. Top: The curve of the dancers' arms and bodies match closely. Middle: The dancers' arms and legs become a series of parallel lines. Bottom: The dancers' legs are parallel, and the mirror images of their arms further enhance the perceptual grouping. (Photographs courtesy of the Pittsburgh Ballet Theater.)*

similar orientation, but perhaps most important is their "common fate"—the fact that they are moving in the same direction. The **law of common fate** states: *Things that are moving in the same direction appear to be grouped together.* This law often comes into play in ballet and modern dance. When one group of dancers moves together in one direction, it is perceived as a group separated from other dancers who are stationary or are moving in another direction.

Meaningfulness or Familiarity The **law of familiarity** states: *Things are more likely to form*

Perceiving Objects

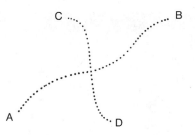

Figure 5.19
Good continuation.

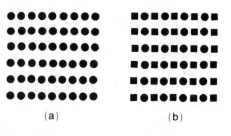

(a)   (b)

Figure 5.21
Two examples of the law of nearness. (a) Perceived as horizontal rows of circles. (b) Still perceived as horizontal rows, even though half of the circles have been changed to squares.

groups if the groups appear familiar or meaningful (Helson, 1933; Hochberg, 1971, p. 439). This law is illustrated by the "rocks-and-faces" picture in Figure 5.5. When your perception changes from "rocks in a stream" or "trees in a forest" into components of faces, the perceptual organization of the rocks and the trees changes as well. Two rocks that are initially perceived separately in a stream become associated with each other when they become the left and right eyes of a face. In

fact, once you perceive a particular grouping of rocks as a face, it is often difficult *not* to perceive them in this way: They have become permanently organized into a face.

Meaningfulness also helps us separate the horses from their background in Figure 5.24. But there are other Gestalt laws at work here as well.

Figure 5.20
The Great Bridge at Rouen *by Camille Pissarro (1896). (Museum of Art, Carnegie Institute, Pittsburgh.)*

Figure 5.22

This picture illustrates a number of laws of organization. Nearness splits the soccer players into a large group on the left and a single person on the right. At the same time, however, all of the players are grouped together by the similarity of their uniforms and of the orientations of their legs and of the outstretched arms bridging the open space on the right.

Good continuation (the contours of the horses' backs and legs) and similarity (the similar shading of the horses' legs and bodies) also help us perceive the horses as separate from their background. This separation of an object from its background, which is called **figure–ground segregation**, was of great interest to the Gestalt psychologists, because they saw figure–ground segregation as crucial to our ability to perceive objects.

Figure–Ground Segregation

In studying figure–ground segregation, the Gestalt psychologists considered patterns like the one in Figure 5.25, which was introduced by Danish psychologist Edgar Rubin in 1915. This is

called a **reversible figure–ground** pattern, because it can be perceived either as two black faces looking at each other, in front of a white background, or as a white vase on a black background. Some of the properties of the figure and ground are that:

1. The figure is more "thinglike" and more memorable than the ground.

2. The figure is seen as being in front of the ground.

3. The ground is seen as unformed material and seems to extend behind the figure.

4. The contour separating the figure from the ground appears to belong to the figure.

Perceiving Objects

Figure 5.23

Grouping due to common fate. The perceptual grouping of these dancers is enhanced both by their similarity of orientation and by their common fate, that is, the fact that they are both moving in the same direction at the same speed. (From Mercuric Tidings. *Photograph courtesy of the Pittsburgh Ballet Theater.)*

You can demonstrate these properties to yourself by looking at Rubin's face–vase reversible figure–ground in Figure 5.25. Note that when the vase is seen as figure, it appears to be in front of the black background, and when the faces are figure, they are on top of the white background. Also notice that, when you are perceiving the vase as figure, it is difficult, if not impossible, to simultaneously perceive the faces. Remember that the ground is seen as "unformed material"; as soon as you perceive the white area as figure, the vase is seen in front and the black area becomes "unformed material" that extends behind the vase.

D E M O N S T R A T I O N

Determinants of Figure and Ground

Look at the following figures and decide, as quickly as possible, which areas you see as the figure and which as ground:

Figure 5.26: On the left side, which area is figure, white or black? Which area is figure on the right side?

Figure 5.27: The white area or the black area?

Figure 5.28: The wide-blade propeller shape of the "cross figure" or the narrow-blade propeller shape of the "plus figure"?

Figure 5.29: The upright propeller shape or the tilted propeller shape?

Figure 5.30: The black areas or the white areas?　●

There are no "correct" answers to these questions, but experiments have shown that certain properties of the stimulus influence which areas are seen as figure and which are seen as ground. Symmetrical areas tend to be seen as figure, so in Figure 5.26 the symmetrical black areas on the left and the symmetrical white areas on the right are seen as figure. Also, convex (outwardly bulging) shapes tend to be seen as figure, and convex-

Figure 5.24
Pintos *by Bev Doolittle (1979).*

ity usually overpowers symmetry, as shown in Figure 5.27, in which the convex white areas tend to be perceived as figure over the symmetrical black areas.

The Gestalt psychologists also found that stimuli with comparatively smaller areas are more likely to be seen as figure, so the plus figure in Figure 5.28 is more likely to be seen as figure than is the cross figure (Kunnapas, 1957; see also Oyama, 1960). Vertical or horizontal orientations are more likely to be seen as figure than are other orientations. Thus, the vertical-horizontal propeller shape in Figure 5.29 is more likely to be seen as figure than is the tilted propeller shape. Finally, as we saw in looking at Figures 5.5 and

5.24, meaningful objects are more likely to be seen as figure. Thus, the black areas in Figure 5.30, which include three arrows, tend to be seen as figure (the smaller size of the black areas compared to the white areas also helps make the black into "figures"). However, adding two more black areas on either side, as in Figure 5.31 on page 192, makes it easier to see that the white areas spell a word (WIN), so that these areas dominate our perception.

From our description of the Gestalt approach, we can see that the Gestalt psychologists explained perception by focusing on characteristics of the stimulus. Our perceptions, according to the Gestalt psychologists, can be explained in

Perceiving Objects

Figure 5.25
A version of Rubin's reversible face–vase figure.

Figure 5.26
Symmetry and figure ground. Look to the left and to the right, and observe which colors become figure and which become ground. (Adapted from Hochberg, 1971.)

Figure 5.27
The black columns are symmetrical and the white columns are convex. Which are seen as figure (Kanizsa, 1979)?

terms of factors such as the lightness, shape, color, size, and spacing of small units that create larger stimulus patterns. Even though this approach to perception was first proposed over 75 years ago, it is still considered a valuable one today, and the idea that the whole is different from the sum of its parts is still an important principle of perceptual psychology.

While today's perceptual psychologists continue to be influenced by many of the principles originated by the Gestalt psychologists, they have also criticized the Gestalt approach on a number of grounds. We will now consider a few of these criticisms.

Current Reactions to the Gestalt Approach

One criticism of the Gestalt approach is that, while the laws of organization seem to work well when applied to the examples picked to illustrate them, the operation of some of the laws is not always as straightforward as in the examples. Consider, for example, the law of simplicity. How do we tell if one figure is simpler than another? We can see that this is not an easy question to answer by considering the following demonstration.

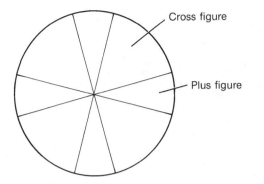

Cross figure

Plus figure

Figure 5.28
The effect of area on figure–ground perception. Which is more likely to be seen as figure, the wide-blade propeller shape of the cross figure or the narrow-blade propeller shape of the plus figure?

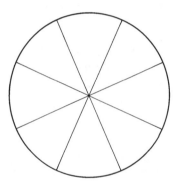

Figure 5.29
The effect of orientation on figure–ground perception. Which is easier to see as a figure, the vertical-horizontal propeller shape or the tilted propeller shape? What is your initial perception? Allow your perception to flip back and forth between the two alternatives. Which perception is present the longest?

 D E M O N S T R A T I O N

Figures That Can Be Seen in More Than One Way

Many figures can be seen in more than one way. Look at Figures 5.32 and 5.33 and decide (1) how you perceive them

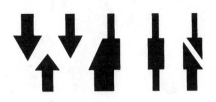

Figure 5.30
Which do you see as figure, the black area or the white area? After deciding, turn to Figure 5.31 on page 192.

initially and (2) which other perceptions are possible. Is Figure 5.32 two overlapping rectangles, or something else? Is Figure 5.33 a flat six-pointed star, or can you see alternative perceptions? ●

Most people perceive Figure 5.32 as two overlapping rectangles, but it could be a rectangle and an upside-down L-shaped object in the same plane. Which of these two perceptions is "simpler?" Does the fact that the perception of two rectangles involves three rather than two dimensions make this perception more simple or more complex than the perception of a rectangle and an L-shaped object? Since the law of simplicity provides us with no rules for determining which is simpler, it is hard to answer this question except to say that most people tend to see this figure in three dimensions, with one rectangle positioned in front of the other.

Figure 5.33 is often initially perceived as a flat six-pointed star; however, after looking at it for a while people often see a number of alternative perceptions. Did you see the two intersecting *V*'s, one right side up and one upside down, as in Figure 5.34a (the upside-down *V* is shaded), or the three-finned propeller on top of a triangle? To see the propeller, try to perceive the shaded area of Figure 5.34a as the triangle and the light area as the three-finned propeller. (Or the other way around.) Finally, look at 5.34b and imagine that the shaded areas on the left and right represent the pages of opened books.

Perceiving Objects

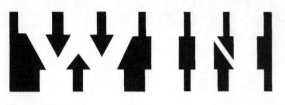

Figure 5.31
In this version of Figure 5.30, which area is figure, white or black? Hint: Look for a three-letter word.

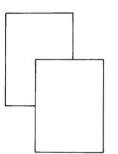

Figure 5.32
What is this?

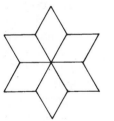

Figure 5.33
What is this?

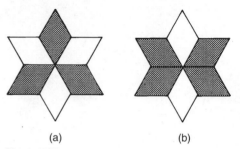

(a)   (b)

Figure 5.34
Alternate perceptions of Figure 5.33.

T T L

Figure 5.35
Which is more similar to the T, the tilted T or the L?

not provide enough information about what simplicity is for us to know what it predicts about perception in situations like Figures 5.32 and 5.33.

Another example of difficulty in applying a Gestalt law is illustrated by the following demonstration:

DEMONSTRATION
Similarity and Grouping

Look at Figure 5.35. Which is more similar to the T, the tilted T or the L? After deciding on your answer, look at Figure 5.36. Which array of letters appears to be grouped with the T's, so that it is harder to see the dividing line between them? ●

In response to the first question, many people pick the tilted T as the most similar to the T. If that is so, it should follow from the Gestalt law of similarity that the T's and the tilted T's should be

Obviously there are many possible perceptions of Figure 5.33 (in fact, my students have discovered others in addition to those described here: Can you find two chairs, each missing its legs on one side?). Although we might expect the law of simplicity to predict that the simplest perception would be the flat, symmetrical star, people often see the seemingly more complex perceptions suggested by Figure 5.34. In fact, many people find that their perceptions change between two or even three different objects as they continue to look at this figure. Can something be simple one minute and not simple the next? Unfortunately, the law of simplicity does

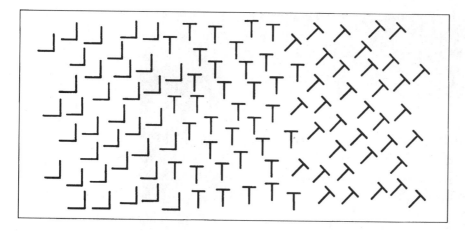

Figure 5.36

The tilted T's form a group even though they are very similar in form to the upright T's. Orientation is a powerful force responsible for perceptual grouping. (From Beck, 1966.)

perceived as forming a group in Figure 5.36. But is this what happens? Most people see the T's and L's as forming one group, while the tilted T's appear to be separated from that group.

This result tells us that similarity, as judged by comparing one stimulus to another, as in Figure 5.35, is not a sure way to determine the stimulus properties responsible for perceptual grouping in larger areas, as in Figure 5.36. In Figure 5.36 the relevant property is *orientation*, a property that, in other experiments, has also been shown to be important in determining perceptual grouping.

Another criticism of the Gestalt approach is that it offers mainly after-the-fact explanations. For example, when we see Figure 5.32 as two overlapping rectangles, Gestalt law tells us that this is so because two rectangles in depth are simpler than a rectangle and an L-shaped figure. A humorous example of this kind of after-the-fact explanation is provided by the "weather-forecasting stone" shown in Figure 5.37. If the stone is wet, the "forecast" is rain; if it is white on top, "snow"; and so on. What we need in both weather forecasting and perception are ways to *predict* what is going to happen before it happens, not simply descriptions of what has already happened.

This tendency of the Gestalt approach to *describe* rather than to *explain* has led many present-

day researchers to question the Gestalt approach. For example, James Pomerantz (1981) described the Gestalt approach as the "look-at-the-figure-and-see-for-yourself" method: An observer looks at a figure and reports what he or she sees. Pomerantz and others have argued that we need a more quantitative approach to the Gestalt principles. To accomplish this, a number of people have begun to apply a more experimental approach to the study of the Gestalt laws.

An example of a modern experimental approach to Gestalt psychology is provided by Naomi Weisstein and Eva Wong (1986), who conducted an experiment to test the idea that different kinds of perceptual analysis occur in regions seen as figure and as ground. According to Bela Julesz (1978), analysis of the figure is concerned with seeing fine details whereas analysis of the ground is concerned with seeing larger areas.

If "figure analysis" concerns details, then we should see sharply focused objects more easily when they are superimposed on the figure than when they are superimposed on the ground. To test this idea, Weisstein and Wong flashed vertical lines and slightly tilted lines onto a line drawing of Rubin's faces–vase reversible picture (Figure 5.38) and asked subjects to decide whether the line they saw was vertical or tilted. Since Rubin's figure is reversible, sometimes the

Perceiving Objects

Figure 5.37
*A weather-forecasting stone.
See text for details.*

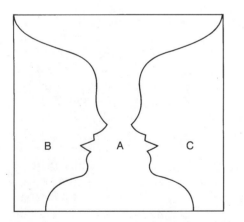

Figure 5.38
Rubin's faces–vase reversible figure used by Weisstein and Wong (1986). In their experiment, described in the text, vertical or tilted lines were flashed at locations A, B, or C. The lines' tilt, or lack of it, was more easily detected when the area on which the line was flashed was perceived as figure.

faces (areas B and C) were seen as figure and sometimes the vase (area A) was seen as figure. On each trial, the subject indicated whether the vase or the faces were the figure, and the line was then flashed randomly on one of the areas. Subjects were three times more accurate in determining whether the line was tilted when it appeared on the figure. Thus, it does indeed appear that the process of figure analysis concerns processing information about detail.

Studies such as this one, plus many others (for further examples of present-day approaches to Gestalt, see Beck, 1993; Peterson, 1994; Rock & Brosgle, 1964; and Rock & Palmer, 1990), go beyond the early Gestalt psychologists' "look-at-the-figure-and-see-for-yourself" method and have begun to study **perceptual processing**— perception as the end product of a sequence of mental operations. This brings us to our second question about perception: What happens in our mind during the perceptual process? This question forms the major focus of an approach called the **constructivist approach to perception**.

PERCEPTION AS A CONSTRUCTIVE PROCESS: THE CONSTRUCTIVIST APPROACH

Rather than focusing on the relationship between the stimulus pattern and perception, as the Gestalt psychologists did, psychologists who take a constructivist approach are more interested in how perceptions are *constructed* by the mind. This approach takes a number of different forms, including research on the connection between perception and neural processing and research on how perception is determined by mental processing. We introduce the constructivist approach in this section. In the sections that follow this one we will describe a number of ways perception has been explained in terms of perceptual processing, all of which are examples of the constructivist approach to perception.

Approaching perception by asking what the mind does during the perceptual process is not a new idea. Like Gestalt psychology, its roots go back to the 19th century, when Hermann von Helmholtz (of the trichromatic theory of color vision) proposed the **likelihood principle:** We will perceive the object that is most likely to be the cause of our sensory stimulation. According to this principle, if a number of possible objects could have caused a particular pattern of light and dark on the retina, we will perceive the object that is *most likely* to occur in *that particular situation.*

A modern descendant of Helmholtz's likelihood principle is Richard Gregory's (1973) idea that perception is governed by a mechanism Gregory calls **hypothesis testing**. He states that "we may think of sensory stimulation as providing *data for hypotheses* concerning the state of the external world" (p. 61). Thus, you might hypothesize that the shadowy object in that dimly lit corner across the room is a small table. However, after looking at the corner more closely, you realize that this hypothesis is incorrect and, based on the new data garnered from your closer inspection, realize that the "table" is actually a toy drum.

In this example the process of selecting the hypothesis to pick the most likely object is conscious: You are aware of each of the hypotheses that leads, eventually, to your perception of the drum. But hypothesis testing does not always occur at a conscious level. We will see, as we discuss other ideas about perceptual processing, that we are usually not aware of the complex mental processes that occur as we perceive forms and objects.

The idea that mental operations occur during the perceptual process is illustrated by a classic early study by Külpe (1904), who briefly presented displays of various colors and told his subjects to pay attention to a particular aspect of the display, such as the positions of certain letters. But when he then asked his subjects to describe another aspect of the display, such as the color of a particular letter, they were unable to do so. This demonstration shows that, even though all of the information from the display reached the subject's eye, a selection process took place somewhere between the reception of this information and the subject's perception, so that only part of the information was actually perceived and remembered. This simple demonstration, which has since been repeated in many different ways, shows that perception depends on more than simply the properties of the stimulus, and that the observer makes his or her contribution to the process.

When we introduced the idea of processing in Chapter 2, our emphasis was on processing at the neural level. But when we talk about the likelihood principle, or hypothesis testing, or mental operations, we are adding a cognitive dimension to perceptual processing. Another way this cognitive aspect of processing has been approached is by considering the eye movements people make when observing an object. Julian Hochberg (1971) points out that, as a person looks at a scene, he or she takes in information by a series of **fixations**—pauses of the eye that occur one to three times every second as an observer examines part of the

Perceiving Objects

Figure 5.39
A picture of The Wave *by Katsushika Hokusai (1760–1850) that was presented to observers by Buswell (1935) in his study of eye movements. The record below the picture indicates the pattern of fixations and eye movements made by an observer viewing this picture. (Also see Yarbus, 1967.)*

stimulus—and **eye movements,** which propel the eye from one fixation to the next. These are both shown in Figure 5.39, a record of the fixations and eye movements made by a subject observing Katsushika Hokusai's picture *The Wave.*

These eye movements are necessary if we are to see all of the details of the scene, because a single fixation would reveal only the details near where we are looking. According to Hochberg (1970), these eye movements also have another purpose: The information they take in about different parts of the scene is used to create a "mental map" of the scene by a process of "piecing together" or "integration." The idea that we create a mental map from the information taken in by eye movements is supported by our response

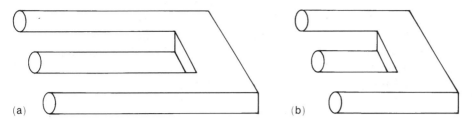

Figure 5.40

(a) An impossible object. Since we cannot attend to the entire object at once, we need to compare the parts of the object before we realize that it is impossible. (b) It is easier to see that this smaller version of the object is impossible because we don't have to distribute our attention over such a large area.

to objects like the one in Figure 5.40. When we first look at this object it appears to be a reasonable three-pronged shape. We become aware that it is actually an **impossible object,** one that could not exist in the three-dimensional world, only after we attempt to create a mental map of this object by comparing the information taken in as we fixate different parts of the object.

The idea that taking in information by using eye movements is an important aspect of perception is the basis of the following demonstration.

 D E M O N S T R A T I O N

Where You Look Makes a Difference

Look at point 1 in Figure 5.41, and decide which shape appears in front, X or Y. Then shift your gaze to point 2, and again decide which is in front. ●

Mary Peterson and Julian Hochberg (1983) found that, when subjects look at point 1, they tend to see X in front, and when they look at point 2, they tend to see Y in front. The results of Peterson and Hochberg's experiments with this figure and a number of others show that our

perception of an object depends on where on the object we look. For the stimulus in Figure 5.41 we base our perception on **local depth information**—information at one point on a figure that indicates depth. If local depth information is important in determining our perception, then, according to Peterson and Hochberg, we need to rethink the Gestalt idea that our perceptions are determined by the whole stimulus rather than by its parts.

Helmholtz's likelihood principle, Gregory's idea of hypothesis testing, and Hochberg's idea that our perceptions are affected by local depth information all treat perception as involving an active observer who processes stimulus information. But what exactly is happening as an observer processes information from the stimulus? Recently a number of researchers have begun to study the problem of information processing in

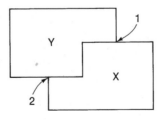

Figure 5.41

Stimulus used by Peterson and Hochberg (1983), originally from Ratoosh (1949). See text for details.

197

Perceiving Objects

perception in more detail. The basic conclusion of much of this research, which is also in the constructivist tradition, is that our perception of a whole object is constructed from information taken in from smaller parts. Specifically, this research says that, in perceiving a stimulus, we analyze it into components or attributes and that this process takes place in a series of stages.

PERCEIVING OBJECTS IN STAGES: PREATTENTIVE AND FOCUSED PROCESSING

The idea that we perceive objects in a number of stages has been embraced by a number of people. The general idea is that in a first stage, called the **preattentive stage of processing**, a stimulus is broken down into **primitives**—elementary components of the stimulus—and that in a second stage, called the **focused attention stage of processing**, these primitives are combined to form a whole. If an object is broken down into elemen-

tary units, or primitives, what are the units? Different people have offered answers to this question, but there is some agreement among them.

Determining the Primitives

Bela Julesz (1981) proposed that the primitives for object perception are units called **textons**. He illustrated their existence by presenting displays like the ones in Figure 5.42, which create **texture segregation**—the perceptual separation of fields with different textures. Julesz asked what it is about the components of these fields that is responsible for the perceptual separation. In Figure 5.42a, texture segregation occurs because the components have different orientations. In Figure 5.42b, segregation occurs because one component (the +'s) has "line crossings" and the other (the *L*'s) does not.

Julesz hypothesized that the properties that cause texture segregation are textons, which are basic units that operate during the initial, preattentive stage of vision. This preattentive stage happens rapidly and automatically, and conscious focused attention is not required. Thus,

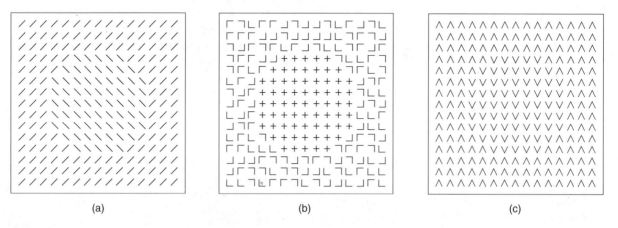

(a) (b) (c)

Figure 5.42
Texture segmentation by texton differences. (a) Difference in orientation. (b) Difference in line crossings. In (c) there is no texton difference, so texture segregation does not occur. (From Nothdurft, 1990.)

texture formation happens almost instantaneously—we see the different areas in Figures 5.42a and 5.42b as soon as we look at the pattern—and these cues can be perceived even when presented in exposures as brief as 160 milliseconds (Julesz, 1984). If two areas do not differ in textons, as in Figure 5.42c, in which the areas differ in the orientation of their angles (not a texton), then texture segregation does not occur. In addition to orientation and line crossings, Julesz also proposed that "terminators"—the ends of lines, as well as "blobs," which are small dots or larger circles—are also textons. (For some recent research investigating Julesz's proposed textons, see Enns, 1986; Northdurft, 1990.)

How do these primitives actually result in object perception? Ann Treisman (1987, 1993) answered this question in her **feature integration theory** (FIT), which proposes the sequence of stages shown in Figure 5.43. FIT proposes that perception occurs as follows:

1. Primitives are identified in the rapid preattentive stage.

2. The primitives are combined in the slower focused-attention stage.

3. We perceive a three-dimensional object.

4. We compare that object to a representation that is stored in our memory.

5. If we find a match, we identify the object.

Let's consider each of these stages in more detail, beginning with the preattentive stage.

In describing the operation of the preattentive stage, Treisman deals with the same problem that Julesz did: identifying the primitives. One way she does this is to use texture segregation, as Julesz did, asking what differences in texture fields lead to immediate perceptual segregation, as in Figures 5.42a and 5.42b, a process she calls the formation of **pop-out boundaries**. Treisman also uses a visual search task (also described in Julesz, 1984), which you can experience in the following demonstration.

DEMONSTRATION

Visual Search

Find the target in each of the displays in Figures 5.44 and 5.45. For each display, notice how long it takes you to find the target. ●

You probably identified the O in the first display almost instantaneously. It pops out because the O's property of curvature differs from the V's property of straight lines. It probably took you longer to find the R in the second display (unless by chance you happened to look at it right away). The longer search time for the R occurs because the target letter, R, contains a vertical line and a curved

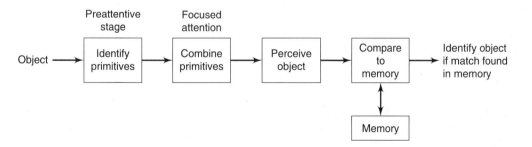

Figure 5.43

Flow diagram showing steps in Treisman's feature integration theory of object perception.

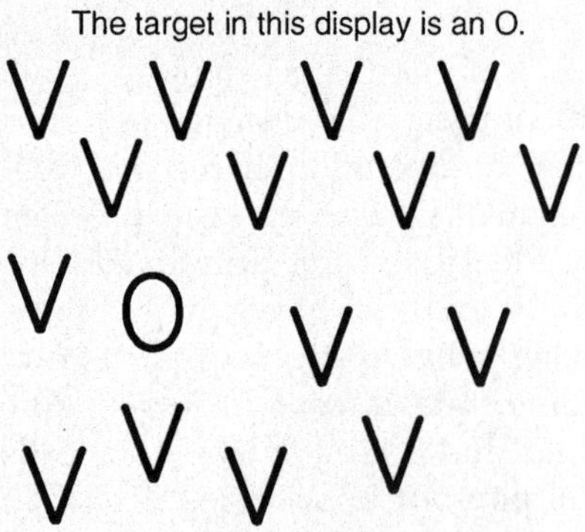

The target in this display is an O.

Figure 5.44
Visual search stimulus. You can find the O among the V's almost instantaneously.

The target in this display is an R.

QPQPP
PPQP
QPPPP
PRPPQ
QPPQ
PPPQ

Figure 5.45
Visual search stimulus. Finding the R among the P's and Q's is not instantaneous unless, by chance, you happen to look at the R first.

line, like the *P*, and a slanted line and a curved line, like the *Q*. When a target stimulus shares properties with other stimuli, we must focus our attention on each of the elements in the display until we find the target.

By measuring the time subjects took to detect boundaries and to find target letters in search tasks, Treisman identified the following primitives: curvature, tilt, color, line ends, and move-

ment. In addition, closed areas, contrast, and brightness have been identified as primitives (Beck, 1982; Treisman, 1986).

Remember that these primitives are extracted from the stimulus during the first (preattentive) stage of processing. By using a procedure called the **illusory conjunction technique**, Treisman showed that, before these primitives are combined in the second (focused-attention) stage, they exist independently of one another.

We can understand this procedure by describing a typical experiment: A display consisting of a red *X*, a blue *S*, and a green *T* is flashed onto a screen for one fifth of a second, followed by a random dot pattern designed to eliminate any image that may remain after the stimuli are turned off (Figure 5.46). When the subjects report

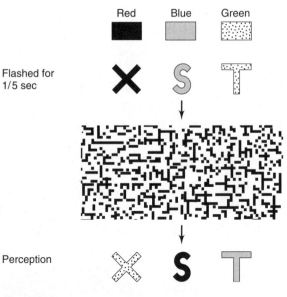

Figure 5.46
Treisman's experiment that illustrates illusory conjunctions. The X, S, and T are briefly flashed, followed by a random dot pattern flashed in the same location as the letters. On some trials observers report letters with colors different from the letter's actual color when it was presented. These changes in color are illusory conjunctions.

what they have seen, they report seeing **illusory conjunctions**, like "red *S*" or "green *X*," on about a third of the trials. This result occurs even if the stimuli differ greatly in shape and size. For example, a subject who is presented with a small blue circle and a large green square might perceive a large blue square.

What does this result mean? According to Treisman, these reports of illusory conjunctions mean that each primitive exists independently of the others during the preattentive stage. That is, primitives such as "redness," "curvature," or "tilted line" are not, at this early stage of processing, associated with a specific stimulus. They are, in Treisman's (1987) words, "free floating" and can therefore be incorrectly combined when stimuli are flashed briefly.

Although the fact that these qualities can exist independently of each other at an early stage of processing may at first seem surprising, this situation is actually what we might expect from what we know about visual physiology. Remember that properties such as color, form, and movement are processed in separate physiological streams, and that neurons that respond to different orientations and shapes are located in different columns in the cortex. Eventually all of these properties are combined to create a unified perception of an object, but before that happens, they exist independently of one another. It is possible that Treisman's psychophysical result reflects this aspect of physiological processing (Tarr, 1994).

Now that we have described some of the properties of the primitives, we can move to the second stage of FIT: combining the primitives to form objects. According to Treisman, the key to this process is focused attention.

Combining the Primitives

The process of combining units takes us from the preattentive stage, during which these units are analyzed automatically and unconsciously, to a stage that requires the observer to focus his or her attention on a particular location. Let's look at an experiment that supports the idea that attention *at a location* is important during this "combining" stage.

A display consisting of one green *X*, many red *O*'s, and many blue *X*'s is briefly flashed and is immediately followed by a random dot pattern designed to eliminate any afterimage that may remain after the stimulus is turned off (Figure 5.47a). The subject's task is to indicate whether there is a green *X* in the display and, if there is, to specify its location. Subjects find that, even though they can often detect the presence of the green *X*, they have difficulty specifying its loca-

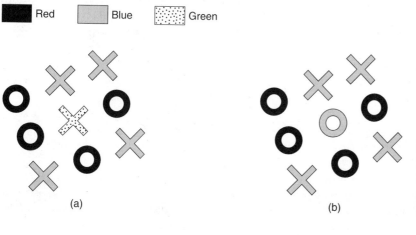

(a)

(b)

Figure 5.47
Two of Treisman's search patterns. In (a) the task is to find a green X; in (b) it is to find a blue O. See the text for details.

Perceiving Objects

tion. The reason for this difficulty, according to Treisman, is that subjects can identify the presence of the green *X* on the basis of just one primitive (color, in this case). Since only one primitive is involved, focused attention is not required, and the subject, therefore, does not pay attention to the object's location.

Consider, however, a task such as detecting a single blue *O* among many red *O*'s and blue *X*'s (Figure 5.47b). This task requires focused attention because to solve this problem the subject must locate an object that contains two properties: blueness *and* O-ness. To combine the two primitives, he or she must focus attention on a specific location. Thus, when subjects correctly identify the presence of the target in this task, they are also able to indicate its location.

We can relate this second stage of FIT to some of the things we know about the physiology of object perception from Chapter 3. Remember that there are two separate pathways: the temporal pathway, which processes information about "what" an object is, and the parietal pathway, which processes information about "where" the object is. Eventually the information from these two pathways must be combined, and according to Treisman (1993), attention is the mechanism that accomplishes this combination. Attention is the "glue" that binds together the features at a location.

After the features are combined, we perceive an object and compare this perception to a stored representation in order to identify it. Treisman didn't spell out exactly how this works, but as we get to these final stages, we are now dealing with more cognitive processes. We can distinguish between these later cognitive processes and the earlier processes by distinguishing between top-down and bottom-up processing.

Top-Down and Bottom-Up Processing

The analysis of objects into parts is called **bottom-up processing,** because processing starts with basic units and our perception is then built on the foundation laid by these units. But it is clear that object perception is influenced not only by the nature of the units that make up objects but also by the observer's knowledge of the world. We have already seen that this is so from the rat–man demonstration and Palmer's experiment from Chapter 1 (see Figures 1.24 and 1.28). These demonstrations showed that the meaning of a stimulus can affect our perception of the stimulus. Taking meaning or familiarity into account is called **top-down processing,** because processing is based on "higher-level" information, such as the meaningful context in which a stimulus is seen, or other information that causes us to expect that another stimulus will be presented.

An experiment that illustrates top-down processing was done by Irving Biederman (1981), using the stimulus in Figure 5.48. Biederman flashed this scene on a screen and asked observers to identify an object located at a particular place in the scene (they were told where to look immediately before seeing the picture). When the observers were asked to identify the fire hydrant, Biederman found that they made more errors when the hydrant was in a strange location, such as on top of the mailbox, than when it was located where it belonged, on the sidewalk. The observers'

Figure 5.48

Stimulus used in Biederman's (1981) experiment. In this picture, observers were asked to identify the fire hydrant.

knowledge of where fire hydrants belong influenced their ability to recognize the hydrant.

This effect of meaning on perception first comes into play during the focused-attention stage, in which primitives are being combined. For example, our knowledge of the world allows us to rule out certain combinations of properties, so that it is unlikely that we would see blue bananas or furry eggs. Also, our knowledge of the world must come into play when we respond to an object. Saying "That is a fire hydrant" is based on our prior knowledge of fire hydrants.

Top-down processing becomes even more important at the end of Treisman's scheme, during the process of identification. Our prior knowledge of the characteristics of objects enables us to classify what we have seen and saying "This is a fire hydrant" or "Those are bananas" depends on applying our knowledge of the world.

Julesz's textons and Treisman's feature integration theory describe object perception in terms of the combining of elementary elements. Another approach that involves elementary elements has been proposed by Irving Biederman, who focuses on our third question from the beginning of the chapter: How do we recognize three-dimensional shapes? Biederman's answer

to this question is a theory he calls *recognition by components*.

THREE-DIMENSIONAL SHAPE RECOGNITION: RECOGNITION-BY-COMPONENTS THEORY

While Treisman's FIT focuses on how different attributes, such as shape, color, texture, and size, are integrated into a single object, Irving Biederman's (1987) **recognition by components (RBC)** mechanism is concerned with how we recognize three-dimensional objects based on our perception of the components that make up these objects.

Biederman's theory is based on primitives, as is FIT, but rather than being elementary properties such as color and shape, the primitives in RBC are volumetric primitives called **geons** (for "geometric ion"). The cylinder, rectangular solid, and other volumes at the left of Figure 5.49 are

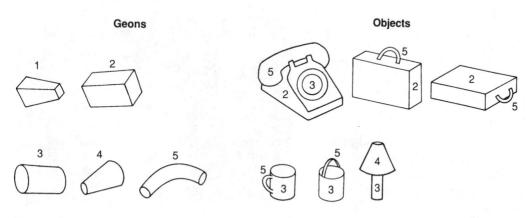

Figure 5.49

Left: Some geons. Right: Some objects created from the geons on the left. The numbers on the objects indicate which geons are present. Note that recognizable objects can be formed by combining just two or three geons. Also note that the relations between the geons matter, as illustrated by the cup and the pail. (From Biederman, 1987.)

Perceiving Objects

some of the 36 different primitives in Biederman's system. These geons are, according to Biederman, the building blocks of perception, because it is possible to construct many thousands of objects by various arrangements of these components. Some examples of objects created from these components are shown at the right of Figure 5.49.

The basic idea behind RBC is that we recognize an object by perceiving its geons. According to the **principle of componential recovery,** we can easily recognize an object if we can identify its geons. To illustrate this property, Biederman obscured parts of the geons that make up the object in Figure 5.50 but left enough of each geon so it could still be identified. We can identify this object (what is it?) even though over half of its contour is obscured because we can still identify its geons. If, however, we occlude the object's geons by obscuring their intersections (Figure 5.51), we can no longer identify them, and it becomes impossible to recognize the object.

Another way to obscure an object's geons, and therefore make it difficult to recognize, is to view the object from an unusual viewpoint. For example, when we view the blender of Figure 5.52a from the unusual perspective in Figure 5.52b we can't see its basic geons and, therefore, have difficulty identifying it.

The basic message of Biederman's theory is that, if enough information is available to enable us to identify an object's basic geons, we will be able to identify the object (also see Biederman & Cooper, 1991; Biederman et al., 1993). Biederman has also shown that it is possible to identify objects even if only a few of their geons are present. He demonstrated this by flashing line drawings like the ones in Figure 5.53 and asking subjects to name the object as rapidly as possible. The result of this experiment was that most objects could be named in less than a second based on only a few geons. For example, although the airplane consists of nine geons when complete (Figure 5.53c), it was identified correctly 80 percent of the time when only three geons were

present (Figure 5.53a) and 90 percent of the time when four geons were present (Figure 5.53b).

The ideas we have described in the last two sections—Julesz's textons, Treisman's FIT, and Biederman's RBC—all have in common the idea that our perception of objects involves a number of stages, beginning with primitives and ending with the combination of these primitives into the perception of an object. Another approach that

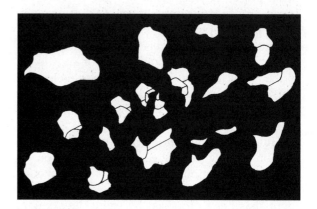

Figure 5.50

What is the object behind the mask? See the legend of Figure 5.51 for the answer. (From Biederman, 1987.)

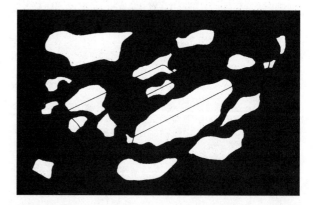

Figure 5.51

The same object as in Figure 5.50 (a flashlight) with the geons obscured. See text for details. (From Biederman, 1987.)

Figure 5.52

(a) A blender. (b) The same blender seen from a viewpoint that obscures most of its geons and therefore makes it difficult to recognize.

sees object perception as beginning with primitives and then occurring in a sequence of stages is called the **computational approach** to object perception.

THE COMPUTATIONAL APPROACH TO OBJECT PERCEPTION

The pioneer in the computational approach to object perception is David Marr, a vision researcher who, at the age of 32, discovered that he had leukemia and spent the last two years of his life writing a book titled *Vision* (1982). This book, along with a number of papers (Marr, 1976; Marr & Hildreth, 1980; Marr & Nishihara, 1978), set forth the basis of the computational approach.

Marr's (1982) approach sees object perception as occurring in a number of different stages, a familiar idea since this is exactly what the texton, FIT, and RBC theories hypothesize. What distinguishes Marr's approach from the others is that in his stages the image is mathematically processed (hence the term *computational approach*), and he is concerned more with natural scenes that contain shadows and other characteristics that make object perception more difficult.

Without getting into the complexities of this mathematical processing, we will briefly describe Marr's stages to give you a flavor for the computational approach. The stages are shown

Perceiving Objects

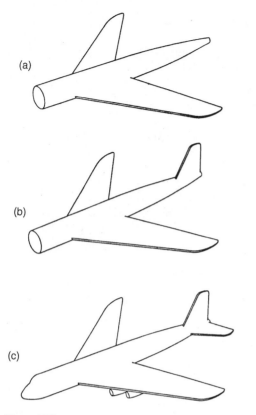

(a)

(b)

(c)

Figure 5.53
An airplane, as represented (a) by three geons, (b) by four geons, and (c) by nine geons. (From Biederman, 1987.)

Figure 5.55
Intensity changes occur both at the edges of this object and at the borders created by the shadows and highlights on the surface of the object. To identify the object's shape, the visual system must identify the object's true edges.

in Figure 5.54. The starting point for this approach is the image of the object or scene on the retina, and the end point is a three-dimensional representation: our perception of a scene or an object. The main "action" of the computational approach is in the two intermediate stages that are interposed between the image and our per-

ception of the object or scene. Let's consider these two stages.

In the first stage, which results in the raw primal sketch, the visual system's major task is identifying an object's edges. We can appreciate the difficulty of doing this by looking at Figure 5.55. In this figure, intensity changes are caused both by the edges of the object and by shadows and highlights caused by the lighting conditions. To determine the shape of an object, the visual system must ignore these shadows and highlights and locate the object's true edges.

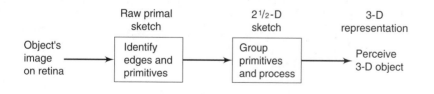

Figure 5.54
Flow diagram indicating the stages in Marr's computational approach to perception.

How does the visual system accomplish this? Marr proposed that the visual system (1) analyzes the intensity changes in the image and (2) takes into account the properties of intensity changes that occur in the world. One of the properties of real-world intensity changes is that intensity usually changes gradually at the borders of shadows and highlights but changes more abruptly at borders created by an object's edges. According to Marr, this property enables the visual system to ignore the gradual borders created by shadows and highlights and to locate the object's real edges where sharper intensity changes occur.

As the visual system analyzes the intensities of an object or scene to locate the edges, it also identifies a number of *primitives,* such as (1) blobs (closed loops), (2) segments of edges, (3) bars (open passages), and (4) terminations (the ends of edge segments). These primitives, plus the object's edges, make up the **raw primal sketch.**

The raw primal sketch is the result of the initial stage of computations, but we do not see it. Before conscious perception can occur, the visual system must process the information contained in the raw primal sketch. First, primitives that are similar in size and orientation are grouped, following Gestalt principles. These groups of primitives are then processed further, by procedures we will not describe here (see Marr, 1982, for details), to yield a representation of the object's surfaces and their layouts that Marr called the **2½-D sketch.** The information in the 2½-D sketch is then transformed into a 3-D representation that we actually see.

One way to look at Marr's system is to think of it as a computer that is programmed to take into account certain physical properties of the world (for example, the fact that shadows often have fuzzy borders). The data fed into this computer are the characteristics of the retinal image, particularly the pattern of light and dark areas in the image. The computer calculates the existence of objects in the environment based on these data and on what it knows about the properties of images in the world. Our description of the way these calculations are carried out has been vague, because of the complexity of the calculations and also because Marr did not have time to work out many of the specific details of his system.

The importance of Marr's system is that it proposes that we can perceive forms based on an analysis of the information in the retinal image. Marr's system does not rely on top-down processes that involve things like the observer's knowledge of what specific objects are used for or where certain objects are usually found (see Figure 5.48). It is therefore accurate to say that Marr's system relies primarily on bottom-up processing. This feature makes Marr's approach compatible with computer vision, since computers are well suited to bottom-up processing, which depends only on manipulation of the data fed into the computer.

The four approaches to object perception we have described—textons, feature integration theory, recognition by components, and computational—all theorize that perception occurs in a series of stages, but they differ in a number of ways. We can appreciate a few of these differences by again considering the red ball that we introduced in Chapter 3 (Figure 5.56). The texton and FIT approaches focus on extracting a number of primitives, such as roundness and redness, and then recombining them; the RBC approach sees the ball as a single spherical primitive; and the computational approach analyzes the light distributions of the ball and its surroundings to locate its edges and then determines the primitives. Each of these approaches, with their similarities and differences, emphasizes the psychophysical approach to object perception. But what about the physiological approach? In Chapter 3 we saw that neurons that respond to specialized stimuli provide a physiological mechanism for perceiving objects (see page 109). We will now consider another physiological approach that is based not on neurons that respond to specific features of a stimulus, but on neurons that respond to spatial frequencies in the stimulus.

Perceiving Objects

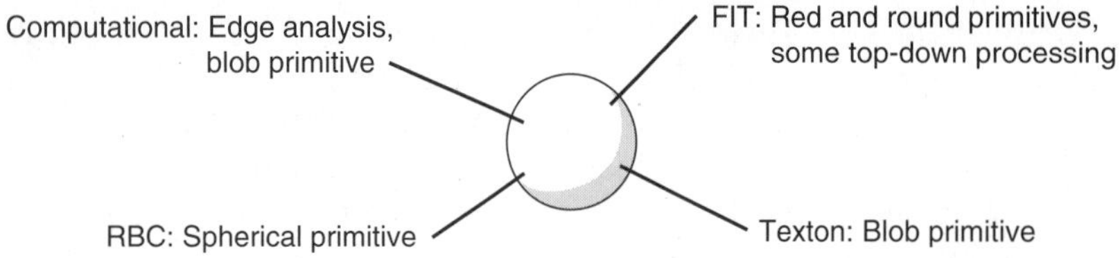

Computational: Edge analysis,
blob primitive

FIT: Red and round primitives,
some top-down processing

RBC: Spherical primitive

Texton: Blob primitive

Figure 5.56

Our red ball, showing some of the ways it would be analyzed according to four different descriptions of the process of object perception.

THE SPATIAL FREQUENCY APPROACH TO OBJECT PERCEPTION

The **spatial frequency approach** to object perception focuses on the stimulus property of spatial frequency. *Spatial frequency* refers to how "fine-grained" a stimulus is. Thus, the grating at the right in Figure 5.57 has a higher spatial frequency (more bars per unit distance) than the one at the left. In the same way we can apply the idea of spatial frequencies to natural scenes like the one in Figure 5.58. The low spatial frequencies in the scene are the overall shapes of the buildings, the medium spatial frequencies are medium-sized details such as the windows in the church in the foreground, and the high spatial frequencies are fine details such as the shingles on the church roof or the windows on the faraway buildings.

The idea behind the spatial frequency approach to perception is that, when you look at a scene such as Figure 5.58, there are neurons that

fire to the spatial frequencies in the scene. For example, some neurons fire to low spatial frequencies, so they fire to the massive shapes of the buildings; others fire to high spatial frequencies, so they fire to small details like the shingles on the roof. This spatial frequency information from many neurons that fire to different spatial frequencies is then combined to result in our perception of the scene.

The visual system must solve two problems if this approach is to work: (1) It has to have a way to detect the spatial frequencies in a scene, and (2) it has to have a way to transform that spatial frequency information into a perception of the scene. We will consider each of these problems in turn.

Detection of Spatial Frequencies by the Visual System

Much of the research designed to determine how the visual system detects spatial frequency has used grating stimuli similar to the ones in Figure 5.57. To understand this research we need to describe some of the properties of these grating stimuli.

The Grating Stimulus To specify the properties of a grating, we specify its waveform, contrast, spatial frequency, orientation, and phase. The **waveform** of a grating refers to the grating's intensity distribution—the pattern of intensities across the grating. The intensity distributions shown below each grating in Figure 5.59 indicate that the intensity of the bars of the grating in Figure 5.59a alternates abruptly between high (for each white bar) and low (for each black bar). Since the distri-

Figure 5.57

Two gratings. The one on the right has a higher spatial frequency than the one on the left.

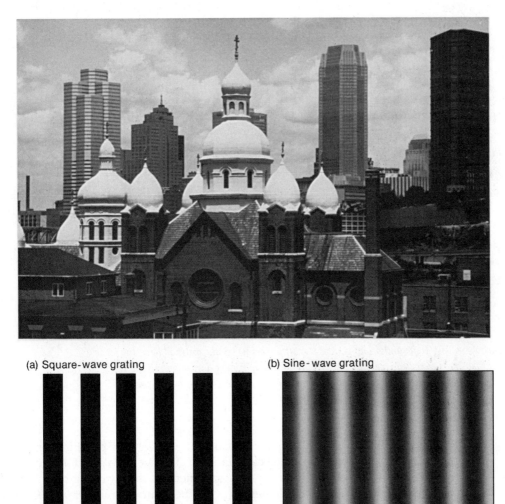

Figure 5.58
A Pittsburgh scene illustrating a wide range of spatial frequencies. See text for details.

(a) Square-wave grating

(b) Sine-wave grating

Intensity

Intensity

Figure 5.59
(a) A square-wave grating and its intensity distribution. (b) A sine-wave grating and its intensity distribution. The abrupt changes in intensity of the square-wave grating are seen as sharp contours, whereas the more gradual changes in intensity of the sine-wave grating are seen as fuzzy contours.

bution looks like a series of squares, this grating is called a **square-wave grating.** The intensity distribution for the grating in Figure 5.59b shows that this grating's intensity alternates more gradually between high and low. Since this distribution follows a mathematical function called a *sine wave*, this grating is called a **sine-wave grating.** There

are also sawtooth-wave gratings, triangle-wave gratings, and many others, all named from the shape of their intensity distributions, but most research on the perception of contrast has used square-wave and sine-wave gratings.

A grating's **contrast** is equal to its amplitude, A, divided by its mean intensity, M, which is

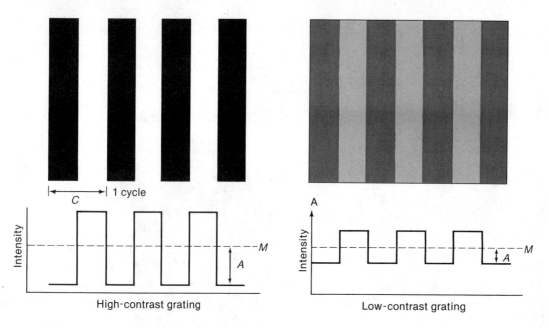

Figure 5.60

A high-contrast square-wave grating (left) and a low-contrast grating (right). Both gratings have the same mean intensity (M), indicated by the dashed line, but the grating on the left has a larger amplitude (A). The contrast of the gratings can be determined by dividing the amplitude of the grating by the mean intensity. The distance marked C on the grating on the left indicates the size of one cycle. Each of these gratings contains 3½ cycles.

indicated by the dashed line in Figure 5.60. This figure shows two gratings with different contrasts. In Figure 5.60a, the contrast is high, whereas in Figure 5.60b, the contrast is lower. A grating's **orientation** is its angle relative to vertical. Gratings may be oriented vertically, as in Figure 5.60, or may be tilted at various angles. The **phase** of a grating is the position of the grating relative to a landmark, such as the small vertical line below the lower left corner of the grating in Figure 5.60a. Thus, if we were to shift the grating horizontally relative to this line, we would be changing its phase.

The most important characteristic of a grating, for our purposes, is its **spatial frequency**—the number of cycles (one white bar plus one black bar) per unit distance across the grating. For example, the gratings in Figure 5.60 contain 3½ cycles, and since the gratings are about 2 inches wide, we could say that they have

a spatial frequency of 3½ cycles per 2 inches, or 1¾ cycles per inch. However, spatial frequency is usually not specified in this way; rather, it is specified as cycles per unit distance *on the retina*.

How can we determine the distance that a stimulus occupies on the retina? This distance is usually expressed in terms of the visual angle of the stimulus. To understand what visual angle is and how it is related to distance on the retina, look at Figure 5.61. The **visual angle** of an object is the angle between two lines that extend from the observer's eye, one to one end of the object and the other to the other end of the object. Figure 5.61a shows two determinations of the visual angle. The observer is indicated by the eye, and the "object" in this example is a person who is located near the observer (Figure 5.61a) or farther away (Figure 5.61b). We can see that the visual angle is smaller when the person is farther away, and that the size of the image on the retina

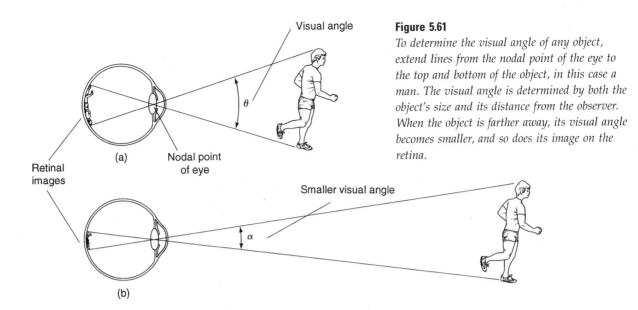

Visual angle

θ

(a)

Retinal images

Nodal point of eye

Smaller visual angle

α

(b)

Figure 5.61

To determine the visual angle of any object, extend lines from the nodal point of the eye to the top and bottom of the object, in this case a man. The visual angle is determined by both the object's size and its distance from the observer. When the object is farther away, its visual angle becomes smaller, and so does its image on the retina.

is smaller for the smaller visual angle. In fact, there is a direct relationship between the visual angle and the size of the image on the retina, smaller visual angles being associated with smaller images on the retina.

The spatial frequency of a grating stimulus is specified in cycles per degree of visual angle. When the gratings in Figure 5.60 are viewed from a distance of about 3 feet, they have a spatial frequency of about 1 cycle per degree. This means that one white and one dark bar fit within a visual angle of 1 degree. To understand this more clearly, do the following demonstration:

![icon] **D E M O N S T R A T I O N**

Determining the Spatial Frequency of a Grating

To determine a grating's spatial frequency, we need to find out how many cycles of a grating fit within a 1-degree visual angle. To do this, we will use the grating in Figure 5.60a and the following "rule of thumb": The visual angle of your thumb held at arm's length is about 2 degrees (O'Shea, 1991). Close one eye, and holding your thumb at arm's length, adjust your

distance from the book until your thumb covers two cycles of the grating (see Figure 5.62). Since the visual angle of your thumb is 2 degrees at arm's length, the spatial frequency of the grating will be 2 cycles/2 degrees = 1 cycle per degree.

What happens to the grating's spatial frequency if we view the grating from closer or farther than the distance that results in a spatial frequency of 1 cycle per degree? You can demonstrate that moving an object closer decreases its spatial frequency by moving closer to the grating so that your thumb is touching it (be sure to keep your thumb at arm's length). When you do this, your thumb will cover fewer than 2 cycles, so the cycles per degree are less than they were before, and the spatial frequency is also less. Similarly, if you were to move farther away so that your thumb covers more than 2 cycles of the grating, the grating's spatial frequency would be greater than 1 cycle per degree. ●

Now that we know how to precisely specify a grating stimulus, we will consider both psychophysical and physiological research indicating that the visual system contains mechanisms for determining the spatial frequencies in a stimulus.

The Psychophysics of Spatial Frequency Channels
Psychophysics has shown that there are spatial frequency channels in the visual system. This research has focused on measuring a curve called

Perceiving Objects

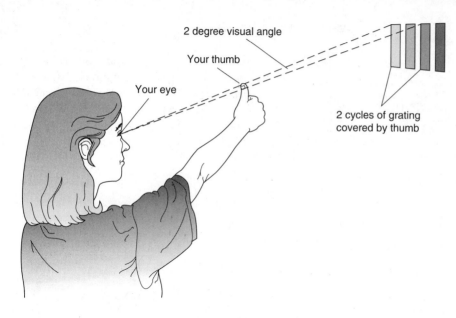

2 degree visual angle

Your thumb

Your eye

2 cycles of grating
covered by thumb

Figure 5.62
*Procedure for viewing the
grating in Figure 5.60a so its
spatial frequency is about 1
cycle/degree. Holding your
thumb at arm's length, position
the grating so your thumb
covers two pairs of black and
white bars.*

the **contrast sensitivity function (CSF),** which is a plot of the contrast needed to see a grating versus the grating's spatial frequency. To measure the CSF, we start with a sine-wave grating of very low frequency (wide bars) and with contrast so low that the grating cannot be seen; that is, it appears to be a homogeneous gray field. We then slowly increase the contrast of the grating until the observer reports that he or she can just barely see its bars. This level of contrast is the *threshold* for seeing the bars. To plot the CSF, we convert the threshold into contrast sensitivity, by the relationship contrast sensitivity = 1/threshold, just as we did when we measured the spectral sensitivity curve in Chapter 2. The result of this determination is point A in Figure 5.63.

Next, we increase the grating's spatial frequency by narrowing the bars, and we repeat the above procedure, again determining the contrast needed for the observer to just barely see the bars. If we repeat this procedure using gratings with higher and higher spatial frequencies, we get the solid curve in Figure 5.63, which is the contrast sensitivity function determined by Fergus Campbell and John Robson (1968) for a sine-wave grating. This CSF tells us that the visual system is most sensitive to sine-wave gratings

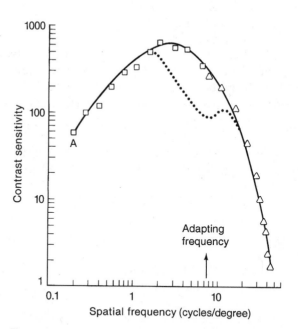

Figure 5.63
Squares and solid curve: Contrast sensitivity function for a sine-wave grating. (From Campbell & Robson, 1968.) Dotted curve: Contrast sensitivity measured after adaptation to a 7.5 cycles/degree grating.

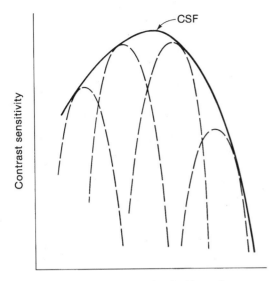

Spatial frequency (cycles/degree)

Figure 5.64

The contrast sensitivity function (solid line) and some of its underlying channels (dashed lines). These channels, each of which is sensitive to a narrow range of frequencies, add together to create the CSF.

with frequencies between about 2 and 4 cycles per degree (observers can see these gratings even if the contrast between the bars is very low) and that sensitivity drops off at lower and higher frequencies. (The contrast must be much higher in order for an observer to see these frequencies until, eventually, very low frequencies or very high frequencies can't be seen at all, even if the contrast is very high.) You can verify that spatial frequency affects your perception by viewing the two gratings in Figure 5.57 from a distance of about 2 feet; the bars of the lower-spatial-frequency grating on the left will appear sharper than the bars of the grating on the right.

Now that we know that our ability to perceive a grating depends on the grating's spatial frequency, we can ask what mechanism might be responsible for this relationship. One idea is that the contrast sensitivity function reflects the activity of a number of *detectors*, or **spatial frequency channels,** each of which is sensitive to a narrow

range of spatial frequencies. This idea is supported by the results of selective adaptation experiments in which we adapt a subject to a particular spatial frequency by having him or her view a high-contrast grating with that frequency and then by determining how adaptation to this frequency affects the contrast sensitivity function. The procedure for a typical experiment is as follows:

1. Determine a person's contrast sensitivity function.

2. Adapt the person by having him or her look at a high-contrast 7.5 cycle/degree grating for 1 or 2 minutes.

3. Redetermine the contrast sensitivity function. The resulting CSF, indicated by the dotted line in Figure 5.63, shows decreased sensitivity in the frequency range around the adapting frequency of 7.5 cycles/degree. If we repeat this experiment using an adapting stimulus with a different spatial frequency, we will get the same result, except that the CSF will be decreased in sensitivity only near the frequency of the new adapting stimulus.

The results of this selective-adaptation experiment and many others like it support the idea that the CSF is generated by the action of a number of channels like the ones in Figure 5.64, each of which is sensitive to a narrow range of spatial frequencies.

The Physiology of Spatial Frequency Channels
What is the physiological basis for the adaptation in Figure 5.63? Many researchers believe it likely that spatial-frequency channels correspond to simple cells in the visual cortex. According to this idea, the decrease in sensitivity observed in our psychophysical selective-adaptation experiment occurs when inspection of the adapting grating fatigues simple cells in the cortex that are sensitive to a narrow range of frequencies around the adapting frequency. When we redetermine the CSF, the decreased responsiveness of these neu-

Perceiving Objects

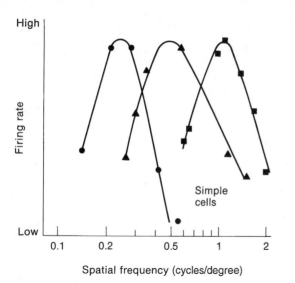

Figure 5.65

Tuning curves for three simple cortical cells to gratings moved across their receptive fields. These cells, each of which responds to gratings with a narrow range of frequencies, may correspond to the channels that underlie the broader CSF. (Adapted from Maffei & Fiorentini, 1973.)

rons decreases the sensitivity around the adapting frequency.

The hypothesis that neurons tuned to selected spatial frequencies are responsible for the CSF is supported by experiments that measure how simple cortical cells respond when gratings with different spatial frequencies are moved across their receptive fields. Figure 5.65, which shows tuning curves for three simple cells, indicates that each cell responds best to a different spatial frequency, and that each cell is tuned to respond to a narrow range of frequencies, just as are the psychophysically determined channels of Figure 5.64 (Maffei & Fiorentini, 1973; also see Robson, 1985). Perhaps these cells are the hypothesized spatial frequency channels.

Now that we have evidence that there are mechanisms in the visual system that detect spatial frequency, we can consider the second problem facing the visual system: It has to have a way of transforming this spatial frequency information

into the perception of an object or a scene. According to the spatial frequency approach, the information about spatial frequency contained in the firing of many neurons is combined to result in our perception of a scene. This idea of combining the information from neurons' firing is similar to a physiological approach to object perception that we introduced in Chapter 3: a stimulus causes firing in neurons that fire to different features of the stimulus, and these features are then somehow combined to create a perception of that stimulus. This idea of combining features to create a whole stimulus is easy to imagine, because it is like using toy blocks to construct a building, where each block represents a feature. It is not as easy, however, to imagine how combining spatial features can result in the perception of an object or a scene. How do we get from a collection of different spatial frequencies to a scene? The answer to this question involves mathematical procedures called *Fourier analysis* and *Fourier synthesis*.

Fourier Analysis and Fourier Synthesis

Fourier analysis is a mathematical procedure developed by the French mathematician Jean Baptiste Fourier (pronounced *Foor*-yay) in the 1800s. This analysis shows that any intensity pattern can be broken down into a number of sine-wave components. For example, the square-wave grating indicated by the intensity distribution in Figure 5.66a can be broken down into a sine wave with a frequency equal to that of the square wave (Figure 5.66b) plus sine waves with amplitudes equal to one third (Figure 5.66c) and one fifth (Figure 5.66d) the amplitude of the square wave, and with frequencies three and five times the frequency of the square wave, respectively.

These three sine waves are called the fundamental (Figure 5.66b), the third harmonic (Figure 5.66c), and the fifth harmonic (Figure 5.66d). When we add these sine waves together, we get the curve in Figure 5.66e, which looks something like a square wave. By adding the seventh and ninth harmonics (according to Fourier's equations a

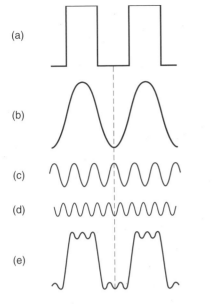

(a)

(b)

(c)

(d)

(e)

Figure 5.66

The sine-wave components for the square-wave grating at the top of the figure, determined by Fourier analysis. When Fourier analysis is applied to the square-wave grating with the intensity distribution shown in (a), the sine waves shown in (b), (c), and (d) result. The dashed line is included to emphasize that the sine waves must be lined up correctly. See text for details.

square wave consists of only odd harmonics), the result gets closer and closer to our square wave.

This demonstration illustrates Fourier's idea that a square wave consists of a number of sine-wave components. In fact, using procedures too

complex to describe here, any visual stimulus can be broken down into sine waves with different spatial frequencies, amplitudes, contrasts, and phases. The idea behind Fourier analysis in vision is, therefore, that the visual system carries out a Fourier analysis by breaking a scene down into a number of sine-wave components. This information is contained in the firing of spatial frequency detectors—neurons that fire best to specific frequencies. The visual system then uses the information from these neurons to carry out the reverse process—called **Fourier synthesis**—in which the information is combined to create the scene, just as combining the sine waves in Figure 5.66 created the square wave (see Figure 5.67).

Although it may seem radical to propose that the visual system breaks a scene down into spatial frequency components and then recombines them to create the perception of the scene, this proposal is actually similar to the idea that a visual stimulus is broken down into primitives. In this case, the spatial frequencies are analogous to the primitives we described earlier.

Although we can show mathematically that a square-wave grating or a more complex scene can be broken down into sine-wave components, is there any evidence that the visual system actually does this? Evidence supporting the idea that the visual system breaks a stimulus down into spatial frequency components was described in a paper by Fergus Campbell and John Robson (1968) entitled "Application of Fourier Analysis to the Visibility of Gratings." This experiment

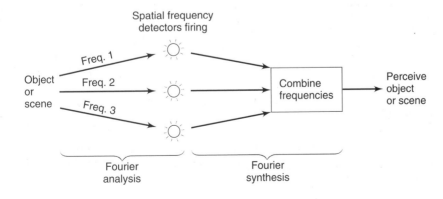

Figure 5.67

A simplified diagram showing how a scene is broken down into spatial frequency components by Fourier analysis and then reconstituted into the scene by Fourier synthesis.

Perceiving Objects

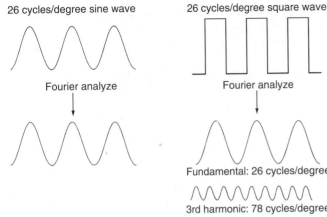

26 cycles/degree sine wave   26 cycles/degree square wave

Fourier analyze   Fourier analyze

Fundamental: 26 cycles/degree

3rd harmonic: 78 cycles/degree

5th harmonic: 130 cycles/degree

Figure 5.68

The sine-wave components of a 26 cycles/degree sine wave (left) and a 26 cycles/degree square wave (right), as determined by Fourier analysis. When we Fourier-analyze the sine wave, we get the same sine wave. However, when we Fourier-analyze the square wave, we get a number of sine waves; the fundamental (26 cycles/degree), the third harmonic (78 cycles/degree), and the fifth harmonic (130 cycles/degree) are shown here. If we were to add these harmonics together, plus the seventh and ninth harmonics, we would end up with an intensity distribution closely approximating the square wave.

involved two gratings, a square-wave grating and a sine-wave grating, each with frequencies of 26 cycles per degree. As shown in Figure 5.68, if the visual system performs a Fourier analysis on these two gratings, then the sine-wave grating will remain unchanged (since, when a sine wave is Fourier-analyzed, you end up with the same sine wave), but the square-wave grating will be broken down into sine waves with frequencies of 26 cycles per degree (the fundamental), 78 cycles per degree (the third harmonic), and 130 cycles per degree (the fifth harmonic). (There are more harmonics than this, but as you will see, they turn out to be irrelevant.)

Now, turn back to the contrast sensitivity function (CSF) of Figure 5.63 to determine how the visual system responds to each of the sine waves that make up our sine- and square-wave gratings. Since the visual system is sensitive to 26 cycles/degree gratings, it has no trouble detecting the 26 cycles/degree sine-wave grating and the 26 cycles/degree fundamental of the square-wave grating. However, as you can see from the CSF, the visual system is totally insensitive to the square wave's third and fifth harmonics (78 and 130 cycles/degree). Thus, as far as the visual system is concerned, only the 26 cycles/degree sine wave, which is the square-wave grating's fundamental,

is present. Campbell and Robson predicted, therefore, that the square-wave grating should look like the sine-wave grating, and this is what happened: The two were indistinguishable.

Our application of Fourier theory to visual gratings tells us that we should be able to tell the difference between the square-wave grating and the sine-wave grating only when some of the square wave's harmonics become visible. We can accomplish this by moving the two gratings closer to the observer. Since a grating's spatial frequency decreases as it is moved closer (because moving the grating closer makes the grating's bars larger on the retina), we can easily move the two gratings close enough to change their spatial frequencies from 26 cycles/degree to, say, 5 cycles/degree. When we do this, the fundamental of the square wave becomes 5 cycles/degree, the third harmonic becomes 15 cycles/degree, and the fifth harmonic becomes 25 cycles/degree. Since the visual system responds to frequencies of 15 and 25 cycles per degree, the square-wave grating should now look different from the sine-wave grating, and this is what Campbell and Robson found.

Since Campbell and Robson's experiments, many researchers have provided further evidence that the visual system can perform a Fou-

Table 5.1

Approaches to object perception

Approach	Proponents	Main Concern	Basic Principles
Gestalt	Max Wertheimer	Perceptual organization	• Laws of organization • Wholes and parts • Figure–ground
Constructivist	Hermann von Helmholtz Richard Gregory Julian Hochberg	Perceiving objects	• Likelihood principle • Hypothesis testing • Integration by eye movements
Textons	Bela Julesz	Texture segregation	• Preattentive processing • Textons
Feature integration theory	Ann Treisman	Texture segregation Recognizing objects	• Preattentive processing • Primitives
Recognition by components	Irving Biederman	Recognizing 3-D objects	• Geons • Principle of componential recovery
Computational	David Marr	Perceiving objects in "real-world" setting	• Primitives • Primal sketch • 2½-D sketch
Neural feature detectors (see Chapter 3)	David Hubel Torsten Wiesel Others	Physiology of object perception	• Feature detectors • Columnar organization
Spatial frequency	Fergus Campbell John Robson	Physiology of object and scene perception	• Spatial frequency detectors • Fourier analysis and synthesis

rier analysis on the stimulus. The spatial frequency approach has therefore become an influential approach to the study of object perception, and many researchers have used a scheme like the one in Figure 5.67 as their starting point for explaining how we perceive objects or scenes. It is important to note, however, that despite evidence that frequency-selective channels exist, and that the visual system does use frequency information, we still don't know how necessary spatial frequency analysis is in perceiving objects and scenes, or exactly how the visual system may use spatial frequency information. One thing that is certain, however, is that the process is more complex than the one

in Figure 5.67 (for some more recent research on the spatial frequency approach, see Beck, 1993; Graham, 1992; Graham, Beck, & Sutter, 1992).

PUTTING IT ALL TOGETHER: MULTIPLE QUESTIONS AND MULTIPLE APPROACHES

Now that you have reached the end of this chapter, you would be justified in asking why there are so many different proposals to explain object perception (Table 5.1). In considering an analogous question—"Why are many different treatments often available for some diseases?"—a physician friend of mine once answered that, if there are a lot of treatments, we still don't understand the disease well enough to be able to cure it. If, on the other hand, there are just one or two treatments, this means that we have found a cure for the disease. If we were to draw an analogy with my friend's statement about treatments for disease, we could say that the large number of proposals for explaining object perception means that we don't understand object perception well enough to settle on the one correct explanation. While there may be some truth to this idea, it is also not the whole answer. Let's consider some of the other reasons for the large number of explanations of object perception:

1. Different approaches explain different things about object perception. For example, the Gestalt approach attempts to explain perceptual organization, that is, how smaller elements become grouped together to form larger wholes. In contrast, feature integration theory is concerned with looking at more rapid preattentive processes that occur without our awareness, and recognition-by-components theory is concerned primarily with explaining how we perceive three-dimensional objects.

2. The different explanations overlap. Although they differ in important details, all of the approaches except Gestalt theory include a rapid initial stage in which the object is broken down into primitives and then one or more later stages in which the primitives are reconstructed into the whole object.

3. Different explanations explain object perception at different levels. For example, texton and FIT theory take a psychophysical approach to isolating primitives whereas the neural detector approach records from cortical neurons.

4. Object perception is extremely complex and may require a number of different types of mechanisms working simultaneously. In considering why a number of simultaneous mechanisms may be necessary for perception, V. S. Ramachandran (1990) proposes the following two reasons:

a. Multiple mechanisms may complement each other and serve as a backup if just one can't handle the job. To illustrate this point, he uses the analogy of two drunks, "neither of whom can walk unsupported but, by leaning on each other, they manage to stagger along towards their goal!" (p. 23).

b. Multiple mechanisms may create faster processing to enable object perception to work in the "noisy" environment of real-world stimuli.

Whatever the reasons that so many different approaches have been proposed to explain object perception, the existence of these approaches confirms the principle, introduced in Chapter 4, that we can explain perception at both the psychophysical and the physiological levels. Another principle central to this chapter is that perceptual processing is largely hidden from our awareness. We have seen that, while on one hand our conscious perceptual experience consists of whole objects, the *process* of perception takes place behind the scenes, as the brain takes apart objects; analyzes them into qualities such as shape, color, orientation, and spatial frequency; and then puts them back together—all of this taking place without our giving it a thought or, for that matter, even knowing what is happening.

We will see in the next chapter that our perception of depth and size is also determined by multiple mechanisms, working together at both psychophysical and physiological levels, and also involving behind-the-scenes processing of which we have little or no awareness.

CONTRAST SENSITIVITY IN CATS AND IN HUMAN INFANTS

How well do animals see forms? One way to answer this question is to measure the contrast sensitivity function (CSF), because this function indicates both how well the animal sees details (indicated by the high-frequency end of the curve) and how well it can perceive forms of different sizes at a range of intensities (indicated by the rest of the curve). As we look at the results of measurements of the CSF of the cat and also of human infants, we will see that both the cat and the human infant perceive high spatial frequencies poorly, and the infant's vision is also depressed at all frequencies. In addition, we will see that despite the differences between cat and human CSFs, they seem to use the same mechanisms for detecting spatial frequencies.

One way to determine the cat's CSF is by presenting two displays—a grating of a particular spatial frequency and a gray screen—and rewarding the cat for pushing a key next to the screen showing the grating (Figure 5.69). The cat's contrast sensitivity is determined by decreasing the grating's contrast until the cat can't tell the difference between the grating and the gray field, as indicated by chance performance on the key-pushing task. Behavioral tests such as these have yielded the cat's CSF (dashed line in Figure 5.70). Comparison with the curve for adult humans indicates that cats have a greater sensitivity to low spatial frequencies than humans but see high frequencies much more poorly (Bisti & Maffei, 1974; Blake, Cool, & Crawford, 1974). Cats can therefore see very dim large objects, like large shadows, better than humans, but they see the small details of the world more poorly than humans.

In this chapter, we introduced the idea that our perception of objects may depend on the firing of neurons sensitive to specific spatial frequencies. We know that cats have such neurons because much of the physiological research that

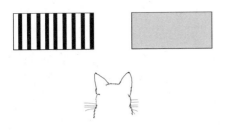

Figure 5.69
A cat viewing two screens in a behavioral test to determine its CSF. The cat is trained to push a key (not shown) next to the screen showing the grating.

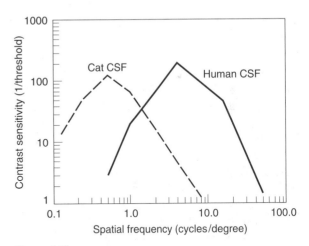

Figure 5.70
Contrast sensitivity function of cat (left) and adult human (right). The fact that the cat's CSF is shifted to the left means that cats see details more poorly than humans, but that they see large, dim forms better. (From Blake, 1988.)

219

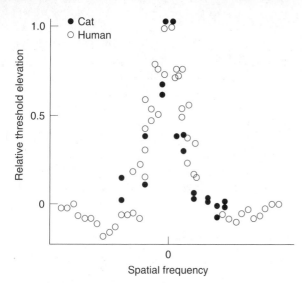

Figure 5.71

Elevation of contrast sensitivity due to selective adaptation. The similarity of the cat and the human suggests that the mechanisms determining their sensitivity to spatial frequency may be similar. (Adapted from Berkley, 1990.)

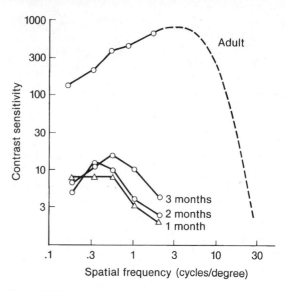
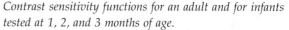

Figure 5.72

Contrast sensitivity functions for an adult and for infants tested at 1, 2, and 3 months of age.

established their existence was based on recordings from neurons in the cat's striate cortex. We also know that humans also probably have such neurons because of the results of psychophysical selective-adaptation experiments. We saw that adapting a person to a grating of a particular spatial frequency raises that person's threshold for seeing gratings of that frequency and nearby frequencies, but that it has no effect on the ability to see gratings with other frequencies.

Mark Berkley (1990) wanted to know how the cat's spatial frequency channels compared to a human's. To answer this question, he conducted psychophysical selective-adaptation experiments on cats and found that, when a cat is adapted to a grating of a particular spatial frequency, its ability to see gratings at or near this

adapting frequency decreases in exactly the same way that the human's does. Berkley found, in fact, that data obtained from humans and from cats were essentially indistinguishable (Figure 5.71). This means that cats and humans are likely to possess the same mechanisms for seeing spatial frequencies. Thus, even though cats and humans may not see the spatial frequencies in exactly the same way, their spatial frequency mechanisms appear to function according to the same plan.

The CSF has also been measured in human infants (Figure 5.72) (Banks, 1982; Banks & Salapatek, 1978, 1981; Salapatek & Banks, 1978). Comparing the infant CSF curves with the adult curve indicates that (1) the infant's contrast sensitivity is lower than the adult's by a factor of 50–100 at all frequencies; (2) the infant's sensitivity is restricted to lower frequencies; and (3) the infant can see little or nothing at frequencies above

1 month

2 months

3 months

Adult

Figure 5.73

Simulations of what 1-, 2-, and 3-month-old infants see when they look at a woman's face from a distance of about 50 cm. These pictures were obtained by using a mathematical procedure that applies infant CSFs to the photograph on the right, which depicts what an adult perceives. (From Ginsburg, 1983.)

about 2–3 cycles/degree, the frequencies to which the adult is most sensitive.

What does the young infant's depressed CSF tell us about its visual world? Clearly, infants are sensitive to only a small fraction of the pattern information available to the adult. At 1 month, infants can see no fine details and can see only relatively large objects with high contrast. The vision of infants at this age is slightly worse than adult night vision (Fiorentini & Maffei, 1973; Pirchio et al., 1978), a finding consistent with the fact that the undeveloped state of the infant's fovea forces it to see primarily with the rod-dominated peripheral retina.

We should not conclude from the young infant's poor vision, however, that it can see noth-

ing at all. At very close distances a young infant can make out some gross features, as indicated in Figure 5.73, which simulates how 1-, 2-, and 3-month old infants perceive a woman's face from a distance of about 50 cm. At 1 month the contrast is so low that it is difficult to make out facial expressions, but it is possible to see very high-contrast areas, such as the contour between the woman's hairline and forehead. By 3 months, however, the infant's contrast perception has improved so that the perception of facial expressions is possible, and behavioral tests indicate that, by 3–4 months, infants can tell the difference between a face that looks happy and faces surprised, angry, or neutral (LaBarbera, Izard, Vietze, & Parisi, 1976; Young-Browne et al., 1977).

The pictures of what young infants perceive show that infants have a very different "window on the world" from that of adults. Infants see the world as if they are looking through a frosted glass that filters out the high frequencies that would enable them to see fine details, but that leaves some ability to detect larger, low-frequency forms. The cat's CSF also indicates that the window through which it sees its world eliminates much of the high spatial frequencies visible to adult humans. However, the cat's curve is not as depressed as the infant's, so within its range of frequency discrimination the cat sees quite well, as attested to by the cats' ability to hunt rodents and play with objects dangled in front of them by humans.

TEXTONS AND INFANT PERCEPTION

According to Bela Julesz's (1981) theory of object perception, our perception of objects begins with a preattentive stage in which the objects are broken down into elementary features called *textons*. Julesz demonstrated the effects of textons on perceptual organization and visual recognition by showing that rapid texture segregation occurs if two fields are made up of elements that differ in their textons, as in Figure 5.42, and by visual "pop-out" effects like that in Figure 5.44, in which a single element that has a different texton from elements in the rest of the field immediately pops out, being perceived almost immediately.

Do textons also operate for young infants? Carolyn Rovee-Collier, E. Hankins, and R. Bhatt (1992) showed that the answer to this question may be yes for 3-month-old infants. They came to this conclusion by using an ingenious procedure in which they presented stimuli to the infants on mobiles like the one in Figure 5.74. They presented a mobile with either *L*'s, *T*'s, or +'s on the blocks and, during a training session, attached a ribbon to the infant's leg that was connected to the mobile, so that every time the infant kicked, the mobile moved. Thus, during the learning session, the infant learned that kicking in the presence of a particular stimulus caused the mobile to move.

Twenty-four hours after the learning session, the infant was tested with another mobile. The rationale behind this test was that, if the mobile appeared similar to the original mobile, then the infant's kicking rate should be high, because she or he would associate that display with kicking. If, however, the mobile appeared different, the infant's kicking rate should be low, because the infant would not associate that display with kicking.

Let's look at two experiments with 3-month-old infants. In the first experiment, infants were trained with mobiles that consisted of all *L*'s, all *T*'s, or all +'s and were then tested with mobiles that were either identical to the training mobiles or consisted of different elements from those in the training mobiles. When the training and test mobiles were identical, the kicking rate was high,

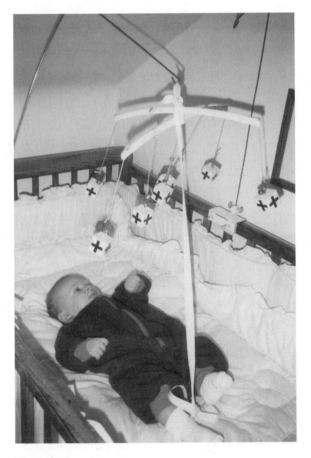

Figure 5.74

An infant viewing a mobile consisting of all +'s. Since the infant's leg is attached to the mobile, the mobile moves when the infant kicks. (Photograph courtesy of Carolyn Rovee-Collier.)

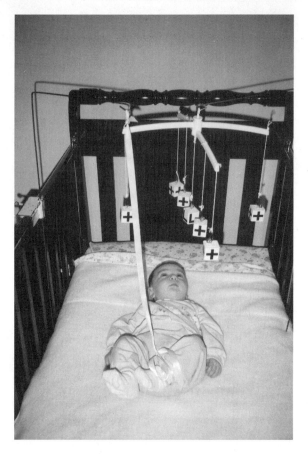

Figure 5.75
Infant viewing a mobile with one L *and the rest* +*'s that tests for visual pop-out. (Photograph courtesy of Carolyn Rovee-Collier.)*

indicating that the infants remembered the elements from the training. If the infants saw L's during training and T's during testing (or T's during training and L's during testing), the kicking rate was also high, indicating that the infants were treating L's and T's as similar, a result consistent with the results from adults, which indicate that adults find it difficult to distinguish L's and T's from each other because they have similar textons.

If, however, the infants were trained with +'s and tested with L's or T's (or trained with L's or T's and tested with +'s), the kicking rate was low, indicating that the infants perceived the + as being different from the L's or the T's. This result is also consistent with results from adults, which show that they easily distinguish a + from either an L or a T because the + has the "line-crossing" texton and the L and T do not. The finding that infants reacted to the L's and the T's as if they were similar but saw +'s as different from L's and T's is consistent with predictions made by Julesz's texton theory.

Do infants also show the "visual pop-out" effects predicted by texton theory? To answer this question, Rovee-Collier and her co-workers (1992) trained infants with a mobile consisting entirely of L's and then tested them with mobiles with either six L's and one + or with six +'s and one L (Figure 5.75).

What should happen if the infants are experiencing the visual pop-out effect? If the test array is six L's and one +, the + should pop out, causing the infant to perceive the test mobile as different from the training mobile (since no +'s were present in the all-L training mobile). The kicking rate should therefore be low in this condition, and this is what happened. If, however, the test mobile has six +'s and one L, the L should pop out and cause the infant to perceive the test mobile as similar to the training mobile (since this L corresponds to the L's from the training mobile). Kicking should therefore be high in this condition, and it was.

These results do not show that infants' perceptions are the same as adults', but they do show that infants respond to some perceptual stimuli in a way that would be predicted by texton theory. This means, according to Rovee-Collier et al., that at a very early age infant perception involves basic mechanisms of preattentive processing like those proposed by texton theory (also see Adler & Rovee-Collier, 1994; Inslicht, 1994).

REVIEW

The Problem of Object Perception

Outline

- This chapter describes a number of different explanations of object perception and illustrates that what seems to be a simple process is actually difficult to explain.

- Although object perception is usually effortless, the complexity of object perception becomes more obvious when we consider objects that are degraded or ambiguous.

Questions

1. Why do computers have such a difficult time "perceiving" objects? (176)

2. What do Figures 5.4 and 5.5 illustrate about object perception? (178)
3. What are five questions that have been posed by researchers about object perception? (178)

Perceptual Organization: The Gestalt Approach

- Perceptual organization is the grouping of parts into larger units.
- In the 1920s a group of psychologists founded an approach to psychology called Gestalt psychology, which was especially concerned with explaining perceptual organization.
- The Gestalt psychologists proposed that the whole is different from the sum of its parts.

- The Gestalt psychologists were also interested in specifying rules about how we organize parts into wholes. These rules are the laws of organization.

- Another aspect of perceptual organization is a process called figure–ground segregation, the separation of an object from its background.

4. What are some examples of perceptual organization? (180)
5. Describe the origins of Gestalt psychology, especially its relation to structuralism. What did structuralism propose? Describe Wertheimer's argument against the structuralist's proposal. (180)
6. How do Figures 5.10–5.12 illustrate the Gestalt idea that the whole is different from the sum of its parts? (181)
7. Describe the following laws of organization: *Pragnanz* (or simplicity), similarity, good continuation, nearness, common fate, and meaningfulness. (183)
8. What is a reversible figure–ground pattern? Which stimulus properties influence what areas of a display or scene will be seen as figure and which will be seen as ground? (187)

- Present-day perceptual research has been influenced by Gestalt principles; however, the Gestalt approach has been criticized on a number of grounds.

9. Describe a criticism of the Gestalt approach that is based on the law of simplicity. What do the "overlapping rectangle" and "star" stimuli show? Is it valid to judge similarity by comparing one stimulus to another? (190)

- Present-day researchers have taken a quantitative approach to studying Gestalt principles.

10. Describe the Weisstein and Wong experiment. What aspect of perception does this experiment study? (193)

Perception as a Constructive Process: The Constructivist Approach

- The constructivist approach to perception is concerned with how perceptions are constructed by the mind. This approach dates back to Helmholtz's proposal of the likelihood principle in the 19th century, but it also includes current research. Any approach to perception that is concerned with perceptual processing is included within the constructivist approach.

11. Describe the likelihood principle and Gregory's idea of hypothesis testing. What does Külpe's experiment demonstrate? What are two purposes of eye movements? How are local depth cues relevant to object perception? (195)

Perceiving Objects in Stages: Preattentive and Focused Processing

- A number of researchers have proposed that the perception of objects occurs in a sequence of stages, which begins when an object is broken down into elementary units called primitives.

12. Describe the difference between the preattentive and focused-attention stages of object perception. (198)

- Two researchers who explain object perception in terms of primitives are Julesz, who introduced the idea of textons, and Treisman, who proposed feature integration theory (FIT). Both of these approaches propose that a stimulus is broken down into primitives during the preattentive stage of processing.

13. What are textons? How does Julesz illustrate the existence of textons? What are the five stages of feature integration theory? Describe how Treisman uses pop-out boundaries and visual search to identify primitives. (198)

14. What are illusory conjunctions? What does the existence of illusory conjunctions tell us about primitives? (200)

- Feature integration theory proposes that primitives are combined in the focused-attention stage of processing.

- A process called bottom-up processing occurs when perception starts with basic units and is built on the foundation provided by those units. A process called top-down processing occurs when perception is influenced by higher-level information, such as the meaning of the stimulus or the observer's knowledge.

15. Describe Treisman's experiment in which she used different-colored stimuli with different shapes. What do her results tell us about the process of combining primitives? (201)
16. What is the relationship between FIT and the two physiological pathways for processing information about objects? (202)
17. Give examples of bottom-up and top-down processing. When does the effect of meaning come into play during the process of object perception? (202)

Three-Dimensional Shape Recognition: Recognition-by-Components Theory

- Biederman's recognition by components (RBC) theory proposes that we perceive the shapes of objects by perceiving three-dimensional primitives called geons, which make up the object.

18. What is the principle of componential recovery? What is the relationship between perceiving geons and perceiving an object? (204)

The Computational Approach to Object Perception

- According to Marr's computational approach, object perception occurs in a number of stages, just as in the texton, FIT, and RBC theories.

19. What distinguishes Marr's theory from the texton, FIT, and RBC approaches to object perception? (205)
20. Describe the stages of Marr's approach. At which stage are the primitives determined? When do we actually see an object? Does Marr's approach involve predominantly bottom-up or top-down processing? (206)

- The spatial frequency approach to object perception focuses on the stimulus property of spatial frequency. Spatial frequency is related to how "fine-grained" a stimulus is.

- Much of the research designed to determine how the visual system detects spatial frequency has used grating stimuli.

- Psychophysical research has shown that there are spatial frequency channels in the visual system.

- Many researchers believe that simple cortical neurons are the mechanism responsible for the psychophysically determined spatial-frequency channels.

- According to the spatial frequency approach, the spatial frequency information contained in the firing of many neurons is combined to result in our perception of a scene.

- Fourier analysis is a mathematical procedure which shows that any pattern can be broken down into sine-wave components. This way of analyzing a stimulus provides a clue to how the visual system determines the spatial frequencies in a stimulus.

21. What is the basic idea behind the spatial frequency approach to object perception? What two problems must the visual system solve if the spatial frequency approach is to work? (208)

22. What are the basic properties of grating stimuli? Be sure you understand how spatial frequency is specified in terms of visual angle. (208)

23. Describe how to measure the contrast sensitivity function. Describe the procedure and results of experiments in which a subject is selectively adapted to a particular spatial frequency. What do these results mean? (212)

24. What result suggests that simple cortical neurons are responsible for psychophysically determined spatial-frequency channels? (214)

25. How do simple cortical neurons respond when gratings with different spatial frequencies are moved across their receptive fields? (214)

26. What is the other physiological approach to object perception that was described in Chapter 3? (214)

27. Describe the procedure by which a square wave can be broken down into a number of sine waves. Can a similar procedure also be applied to complex scenes? (214)

- Fourier synthesis is the process by which all of the sine-wave components of a scene are added together to create the perception of the scene.

- Campbell and Robson carried out a psychophysical experiment that supported the idea that the visual system carries out a Fourier analysis of a square-wave grating. The idea of Fourier analysis has been extremely influential in research on object perception.

28. How is the proposal that the visual system carries out a Fourier analysis and synthesis of a scene similar to the idea of primitives we discussed earlier? (215)

29. Describe the procedures and conclusions of Campbell and Robson's experiment. Has it been proved that our perception of complex scenes is the result of a Fourier analysis and synthesis by the visual system? (215)

Putting It All Together: Multiple Questions and Multiple Approaches

- We have considered a number of different approaches to object perception. These approaches are similar to one another in some respects, but each has its distinctive characteristics.

30. What are some possible reasons for the large number of explanations that have been proposed to explain how we perceive objects and scenes? (218)

Contrast Sensitivity in Cats and Human Infants

- The contrast sensitivity function provides more information about an animal's vision than measuring visual acuity because it indicates not only detail vision, but also the ability to see forms of different sizes in a wide range of contrasts.

31. How does the cat's CSF compare to the human's, and what does that comparison indicate about what the cat perceives? What do the results of selective adaptation experiments on cats tell us about the mechanism responsible for their perception of spatial frequencies? (219)

32. Describe the procedures for measuring the CSF of the human infant and the results of these procedures. What can we conclude about infant vision based on their CSF? (220)

Textons and Infant Perception

- According to Julesz, our perception of forms begins when an object is broken down into primitives called textons. He demonstrated this hypothesis by testing for texture segregation and visual pop-out.

33. Describe the procedure and results of Rovee-Collier et al.'s experiments on textons and infant vision. (223)

PERCEIVING DEPTH AND SIZE

Imagine that you are standing on the hill overlooking the neighborhood of Figure 6.1. From this position, you effortlessly see the car as nearby, the ridge as far in the distance, and the space between them as having "depth." The amazing thing about your three-dimensional perception of this scene is that it is based on an image that exists in only two dimensions on the surface of your retinas. How is this two-dimensional *representation* transformed into your three-dimensional *perception?* There are a number of answers to this question, because most scenes contain many sources of information, and because different theoretical approaches have focused on different aspects of this information.

One theoretical approach, called **cue theory,** focuses on identifying information in the retinal image that is correlated with depth in the world. Most of this chapter considers this approach to depth perception and also shows how this approach has been used to explain the perception of size and the perception of visual illusions—two things that are closely related to our perception of depth.

After discussing the cue approach, we will consider a second theoretical approach, the **ecological approach** proposed by J. J. Gibson. We will see that the ecological approach focuses not on depth information in the retinal image, but on the information that exists "out there" in the environment.

THE CUE APPROACH

The cue approach to depth perception looks for connections between stimuli in the environment, the images these stimuli create on the retina, and a person's perception of depth. For example, if one object partially covers another object, as the houses in the foreground of Figure 6.1 cover the houses in the background, the object that is partially covered must be at a greater distance than the object that is covering it. This situation, which is called *overlap,* is a signal, or cue, that one object

Figure 6.1
A neighborhood in Pittsburgh that contains many depth cues.

is in front of another. According to cue theory, we learn the connection between this cue and depth through our previous experience with the environment. After this learning has occurred, the association between particular cues and depth becomes automatic, and when these **depth cues** are present, we experience the world in three dimensions.

Another way of stating the cue approach is to say that our perception of depth cues enables us to make inferences about the depth in a scene. For example, we can infer that A is in front of B by reasoning, "If A covers B, then A is in front of B." This way of describing the cue approach emphasizes its constructivist nature. Remember from Chapter 5 that the constructivist approach assigns an active role to the observer and sees perception as the outcome of processing.

Proponents of the cue approach have identified a number of different types of cues that signal depth in the scene. We can divide these cues into the following groups:

1. **Oculomotor cues** are based on our ability to sense the position of our eyes and the tension in our eye muscles.

2. **Pictorial cues** are those that can be depicted in a still picture.

3. **Movement-produced cues** are created by movement of the observer or by movement of objects in the environment.

4. **Binocular disparity** creates depth perception by comparing the slightly different images of a scene that are formed on the left and right retinas.

We will now describe each of these types of depth cues.

Oculomotor Cues

Oculomotor cues are based on feelings in the eyes that occur when the eyes move inward to point toward nearby objects, a process called **convergence,** and when the lens of the eyes change shape to focus on nearby objects, the process of **accommodation** that we described in Chapter 2. (See page 45.)

Convergence and Accommodation

You can experience the feelings in your eyes associated with convergence and accommodation by doing the following demonstration:

 D E M O N S T R A T I O N
Feelings in Your Eyes

Look at your finger as you hold it at arm's length. Then, as you slowly move your finger toward your nose, notice how you feel your eyes looking inward and become aware of the increasing tension *inside* your eyes.   ●

The feelings you experience as you move your finger closer are caused by (1) the **convergence angle** as your eye muscles cause your eyes to look inward, as in Figure 6.2a, and (2) **accommodation** as the lens bulges to focus on a near object (see Figure 2.7). If you move your finger farther away, the lens flattens, and your eyes move until they are both looking straight ahead, as in Figure 6.2b.

Convergence and accommodation serve as cues to depth because the position of the eyes and the shape of the lenses are related to the distance of the object we are observing. These cues are effective, however, only at distances closer than about 5–10 feet from the observer (see Liebowitz, Shina, & Hennessy, 1972).

PICTORIAL CUES

Pictorial cues are sources of depth information that can be depicted in a picture, such as the illustrations in this book or the picture formed on the retina. These cues are also called **monocular depth cues** because they work even if we use only one eye.

Overlap

We have already described the depth cue of **overlap.** If object A covers part of object B, then object A is seen as being in front of object B. Note that overlap does not provide information about an

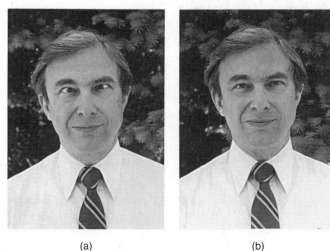

(a)   (b)

Figure 6.2
(a) Convergence of the eyes occurs when a person looks at something very close. (b) The eyes look straight ahead when the person observes something far away.

object's distance from us; instead, it indicates relative depth—we know that one object is closer than another object, but we don't know how much closer.

Paul Signac's painting *Place des Lices, St. Tropez* (1893), shown in Figure 6.3, makes extensive use of overlap. Place a piece of paper so that it covers everything below mark A, and notice how overlap helps you determine the relative positions in depth of the tree branches in the top part of the picture. Then, move your paper up that so it covers everything below mark B. Since there is little overlap within the upper left corner of the picture, it is difficult to tell which branches are in front and which are in back.

Size in the Field of View

In addition to noticing that the houses in the background in Figure 6.1 are overlapped by those in the foreground, you can also see that the houses in the background take up less of your field of view than those in the foreground. The cue of **size in the field of view,** which apparently has fooled the large person in Figure 6.4 into thinking that a small person is far away, was demonstrated by Adelbert Ames, who had observers view illuminated balloons in a darkened room. When he increased the size of one balloon by pumping more air into it, the observers reported that the expanding balloon appeared to be

— B

— A

Figure 6.3
Place des Lices, St. Tropez *by Paul Signac (1893). (Museum of Art, Carnegie Institute, Pittsburgh, Pa.)*

"Excuse me for shouting—I thought you were farther away."

Figure 6.4

Reproduced by special permission of Playboy Magazine. Copyright 1971 by Playboy.

Atmospheric Perspective

Atmospheric (or aerial) perspective causes us to see distant objects as less sharp because, to observe these distant objects, we look through air that contains small particles such as dust, water droplets, and various forms of airborne pollution. The farther away an object is, the more air and particles we have to look through, and they make far objects look less sharp than close objects. Figure 6.6 illustrates atmospheric perspective. Compare the details visible in the mountains in the distance to the sharp details visible in the rock in the foreground.

If instead of viewing these California mountains you were standing on the moon, where there is no atmosphere, and hence no atmospheric perspective, far craters would look just as clear as near ones. But on earth, there is atmo-

moving closer. Other things being equal, larger size causes an object to appear closer.

Height in the Field of View

The houses in the background of Figure 6.1 not only take up less of your field of view than those in front, but they are also higher in the scene. This is the cue of **height in the field of view.** Objects that are *higher* in your field of view, like the men in Figure 6.5, are usually seen as being more distant. This rule holds for objects that are below the horizon line, but objects like the clouds, which are above the horizon line, appear more distant when they are *lower* in your field of view.

Not only are the more distant houses of Figure 6.1 the highest in the scene, but they also appear slightly less sharp than those in the foreground. This brings us to our next pictorial cue, atmospheric perspective.

Figure 6.5

Relative height. Other things being equal, objects below the horizon that appear higher in the field of view are seen as being farther away. Objects above the horizon that appear lower in the field of view are seen as being farther away.

spheric perspective, the exact amount depending on the nature of the atmosphere.

An example of how atmospheric perspective depends on the nature of the atmosphere occurred when one of my friends took a trip from Pittsburgh to Montana. He started walking toward a mountain that appeared to be perhaps a two- or three-hour hike away but found after three hours of hiking that he was still far from the mountain. Since my friend's perceptions were "calibrated" for Pittsburgh, he found it difficult to accurately estimate distances in the clearer air of Montana, so a mountain that would have looked three hours away in Pittsburgh was over six hours away in Montana!

Familiar Size

Look at the coins in Figure 6.7. If they were real coins, which would you say is closer? If you are influenced by your knowledge of the actual size of dimes, quarters, and half-dollars, you would probably say that the dime is closer. If you did, the cue of **familiar size** is influencing your judgment of depth. An experiment by William Epstein (1965) shows that, under certain conditions, our knowledge of an object's size influences our perception of that object's distance from us. The stimuli in Epstein's experiment were equal-sized photographs of a dime, a quar-

Figure 6.7

Line drawings of the stimuli used in Epstein's (1965) familiar-size experiment. The actual stimuli were photographs that were all the same size as a real quarter.

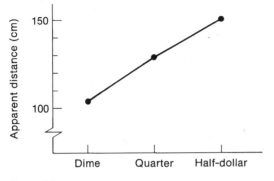

Figure 6.8

Results of Epstein's (1965) familiar-size experiment. Although the oversized dime, the actual-sized quarter, and the undersized half-dollar were actually at the same distance, they were perceived to be at different distances when viewed monocularly.

ter, and a half-dollar, which were positioned the same distance from an observer. By placing these photographs in a darkened room, illuminating them with a spot of light, and having subjects view them with one eye, Epstein created the illusion that these pictures were real coins.

When the observers judged the distance of each of the coin photographs they estimated that the dime was closest, the quarter was farther than the dime, and the half-dollar was the farthest of them all (Figure 6.8). Clearly, the observers' judgments were influenced by their knowledge of the sizes of real dimes, quarters, and half-dollars. This result did not occur, however, when the observers viewed the scene binocularly—with both eyes. When they did this, they were able to tell that all of the coins were at the same distance because, as we will see below, the use of two eyes provides important information for the perception of depth. Thus, when the observers in Epstein's experiment used two eyes, this extra information enabled them to disregard the effect of familiar size and correctly judge the distances of the coins. The cue of familiar size is therefore most effective when

other information about depth is absent (see also Coltheart, 1970; Schiffman, 1967).

Linear Perspective

How can we create a three-dimensional impression of depth on the two-dimensional surface of a canvas? This question has concerned artists since before the ancient Greeks, but it wasn't until 1435 that Leon Battista Alberti wrote *De Pictura,* the first book describing the principles of a drawing system called **linear perspective,** which made it possible to convincingly depict depth on a two-dimensional surface (see Hagen, 1979, 1986; Kubovy, 1986; White, 1968). Alberti's book describes a geometrical procedure for drawing a picture in linear perspective.

Another way of creating a perspective picture is based on the idea stated by Leonardo da Vinci that "perspective is nothing else than seeing a place behind a plane of glass, quite transparent, on the surface of which the objects behind the glass are to be drawn" (Gombrich, 1960). By using this technique, which has been called **Alberti's window,** anyone can draw in perspective. You need only obtain a transparent surface such as a piece of glass or a rigid piece of transparent plastic; then, keeping your eye fixed in one place, look at a scene through the transparent surface and trace the contours of the scene onto the surface. This procedure is being used by the artist in Figure 6.9, but instead of drawing the picture on the window, he is using a grid on the window to transfer the scene to a canvas. This procedure results in a picture drawn in linear perspective that creates an impression of depth on the canvas. Another way to create a perspective picture is to take a photograph. The optical system of a camera accomplishes essentially the same thing as Alberti's window and records the result on film.

When a picture is drawn in linear perspective, lines that are actually parallel in the scene

Perceiving Depth and Size

pear to converge as distance increases. This convergence, which provides information about depth, is referred to as the depth cue of **linear perspective.**

Texture Gradient

Another source of depth information is the **texture gradient**—elements that are equally spaced in a scene appear to be packed closer and closer as distance increases, such as the squares in the Renaissance street of Figure 6.10. We will describe this source of depth information in more detail when we discuss the ecological approach to depth perception at the end of the chapter.

MOVEMENT-PRODUCED CUES

All of the cues we have described so far work if the observer is stationary. As we stand on the hill observing the scene in Figure 6.1, these cues contribute to our perception of depth in the scene. If, however, we decide to take a walk, new cues emerge that further enhance our perception of depth. Hermann von Helmholtz (1866/1911) described the following situation in which movement enhances depth perception:

> Suppose, for instance, that a person is standing still in a thick woods, where it is impossible for him to distinguish, except vaguely and roughly, in the mass of foliage and branches all around him what belongs to one tree and what to another. . . . But the moment he begins to move forward, everything disentangles itself, and immediately he gets an apperception of the material contents of the woods and their relations to each other in space. (p. 296)

Figure 6.9

An artist drawing a picture in perspective using the method of Alberti's window.

(such as the sides of the street in Figure 6.1) converge as they get farther away (Figure 6.10). The greater the distance, the greater the convergence, until, at a distance of infinity (very far away!), these lines meet at a vanishing point. This convergence that we see in perspective pictures also occurs in the environment, as we know from the familiar observation that railway tracks ap-

Figure 6.10
A Street with Various Buildings, Colonnades, and an Arch *(c. 1500); artist unknown (school of Donate Brumante). This is an example of a picture drawn in perspective so that lines that are parallel in the actual scene will converge to a vanishing point if extended into the distance. (Museum of Art, Carnegie Institute, Pittsburgh, Pa.)*

We will describe two different **movement-produced cues:** (1) motion parallax and (2) deletion and accretion.

Motion Parallax

Elaborating further on the effect of movement on depth perception, Helmholtz (1866/1911) described how, as we walk along, nearby objects appear to glide rapidly past us, but more distant objects appear to move more slowly. This effect becomes particularly striking when you look out the side window of a moving car or train. Nearby objects appear to speed by in a blur, while objects on the horizon may appear to be moving only slightly. This difference in the speed of movement for near and far objects is called **motion parallax,** which we can use as a cue to perceive the depths of objects based on how fast they move as we move: Far objects move slowly; near objects move rapidly.

We can understand why motion parallax occurs by looking at the eye in Figure 6.11. This figure shows what happens to the images of two objects, a near object at A and a far object at B, when a single eye moves from position 1 to position 2. First, consider how the image of the near object moves across the retina as the eye moves from 1 to 2. When the eye is at position 1, the image of object A is at A_1 on the retina, and when the eye has moved to position 2, the image of object A has moved all the way across the retina to A_2. Thus, when the eye moves from position 1 to position 2, the image of object A moves from one side of the observer's field of view to the other. The image of object B, on the other hand, moves only from B_1 to B_2 on the retina and therefore moves only a short distance across the observer's field of view. Thus, as the observer moves from left to right, the near object travels a large distance across the retina and therefore moves rapidly across the observer's field of view, but the far object travels a much smaller distance

Perceiving Depth and Size

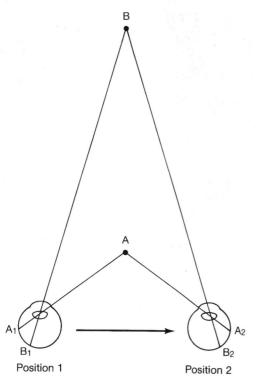

Figure 6.11

One eye, moving from left to right, showing how the images of two objects (A and B) change their position on the retina because of this movement. Notice that the image of the near object, A, moves farther on the retina than the image of the far object, B.

across the retina and therefore moves much more slowly across the observer's field of view.

Deletion and Accretion

When two surfaces are located at different distances, as in Figure 6.12a, any movement that is not perpendicular to these surfaces causes them to appear to move relative to one another. The back surface is covered up, or **deleted,** by the one in front when the observer moves in one direction (Figure 6.12b), and the back surface is uncovered, or **accreted,** when the observer moves in the other direction (Figure 6.12c). These cues, which are re-

lated both to motion parallax and overlap, since they occur when overlapping surfaces move relative to one another, are especially effective for detecting depth at an edge (Kaplan, 1969).

BINOCULAR DISPARITY AND STEREOPSIS

All the other cues we have discussed, with the exception of convergence, are monocular depth cues because they work even if we look through only one eye. We will now discuss **binocular disparity,** which is called a **binocular depth cue** because it involves both eyes. This cue is based on the fact that we see two slightly different views of the world because our eyes view the world from different positions.

Two Eyes: Two Viewpoints

The fact that we view the world from two different positions means that there are slightly different images in the two eyes. We can illustrate the existence of two images perceptually by the following demonstration:

◢◢ D E M O N S T R A T I O N
Switch Eyes and the Image Changes

Hold your two index fingers vertically in front of you, about 6 inches from your face, with about an inch between them. With your right eye closed, position your fingers so that, between them, you can see an object that is a foot or more away (Figure 6.13a). Then, close your left eye and open your right eye, and notice how your fingers seem to move to the left, so that the object is no longer visible between them (Figure

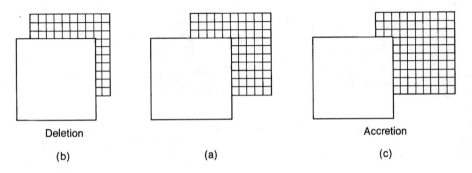

Deletion

(b)

(a)

Accretion

(c)

Figure 6.12

Deletion and accretion occur when an observer moves in a direction not perpendicular to two surfaces that are at different depths. If an observer perceives the two surfaces as in (a) and then moves to the left, deletion occurs so that the front object covers more of the back one, as in (b). If the observer starts at (a) and moves to the right, accretion occurs, so that the front object covers less of the back one, as in (c). Try this with two objects.

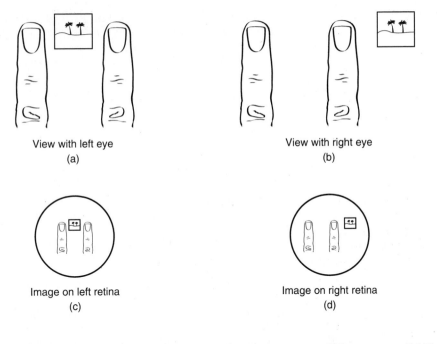

View with left eye

(a)

View with right eye

(b)

Image on left retina

(c)

Image on right retina

(d)

Figure 6.13

Observer's views (a and b) and retinal images (c and d) for the demonstration. See text for instructions.

6.13b). These two perceptions reflect the different views that are imaged on your left and right retinas (Figures 6.13c and 6.13d). ●

The fact that the two eyes see different views of the world was used by the physicist Charles Wheatstone (1802–1875) to create the **stereoscope,** a device that produces a convincing illusion of depth by using two slightly different pictures. This device, extremely popular among adults in the 1800s and called the View Master in its modern form, presents two photographs that are made with a camera with two lenses sepa-

Figure 6.14

A stereoscopic photograph from the Super Bowl Pittsburgh Steelers of the 1970s. This photograph shows Terry Bradshaw (right) of the Steelers talking to Joe Ferguson of the Buffalo Bills after a game at Three Rivers Stadium in Pittsburgh. The picture on the left is the view seen by the left eye, and the picture on the right is the view seen by the right eye. Although the two pictures may at first glance look the same, a closer look shows that the relationship between the foreground and the background is different in the two views. For example, compare the distance between Bradshaw's head and the lighted upper stands in the background, or compare the people in the stands in the space between Bradshaw and Ferguson. This slight displacement results in binocular disparity when a stereoscope presents these two views to each eye separately, and we see the scene in depth. (Stereogram by Mike Chikiris, Pittsburgh Stereogram Company, Pittsburgh, Pa., 1977.)

rated by the same distance as the eyes. The result is two slightly different views, like those shown in Figure 6.14. The stereoscope presents the left picture to the left eye and the right picture to the right eye so that they combine to result in a convincing three-dimensional perception of the scene.

 D E M O N S T R A T I O N

Binocular Depth from a Picture, without a Stereoscope

Place a 4″ × 6″ card vertically, long side up, between the stairs in Figure 6.15, and place your nose against the card so that you are seeing the left-hand drawing with just your left eye and the right-hand drawing with just your right eye. (Blink

back and forth to confirm this separation.) Then *relax* and wait for the two drawings to merge. When the drawings form a single image, you should see the stairs in depth, just as you would if you looked at them through a stereoscope. ●

The principle behind the stereoscope—presenting one image to the left eye and the other to the right eye—is also used in 3-D movies. These movies became quite popular when introduced commercially in the 1950s. I still vividly remem-

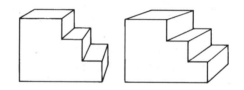

Figure 6.15

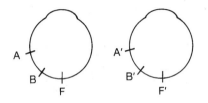

Figure 6.16

Corresponding points on the two retinas. To determine corresponding points, imagine that one eye is slid on top of the other one.

ber a scene from a film called *The Maze*, in which a terrible froglike creature plummeted from a castle window directly toward me! Luckily, I survived to write this book.

Looking into a stereoscope shows that, when our two eyes receive slightly different images of the same scene, we experience an impression of depth. Wheatstone realized this and called the impression of depth that results from two different images on the retina **stereopsis.** But what exactly is it about the differences between the images on the two retinas that creates stereopsis? To answer this question, we introduce the concept of corresponding retinal points.

Corresponding Retinal Points

For every point on one retina, there is a corresponding point on the other. **Corresponding retinal points** are the places on each retina that connect to the same places in the visual cortex. We can determine approximately where these points are by locating where points on the retinas would overlap if one retina could be slid on top of the other. In Figure 6.16, we see that the two foveas, F and F', fall on corresponding points, and that A and A' and B and B' also fall on corresponding points.

To apply our knowledge of corresponding points to depth perception, let's assume that you are sitting in the lifeguard chair of Figure 6.17. If you look directly at your friend Ralph, his image will fall on your foveas (F and F'), which are corresponding points. However, Ralph is not the only person whose image falls on corresponding points.

The images of everyone who is located on the dashed line also fall on corresponding points. This dashed line, which is called the **horopter,** is part of an imaginary circle that passes through the point of fixation (Ralph's head) and also through the heads of Harry and Susan in this example. Thus,

Figure 6.17

When the lifeguard looks at Ralph, the images of Ralph, Susan, and Harry fall on the horopter indicated by the dashed line. Thus, Ralph's, Susan's, and Harry's images fall on corresponding points on the lifeguard's retinas, and the images of all of the other swimmers fall on noncorresponding points.

Perceiving Depth and Size

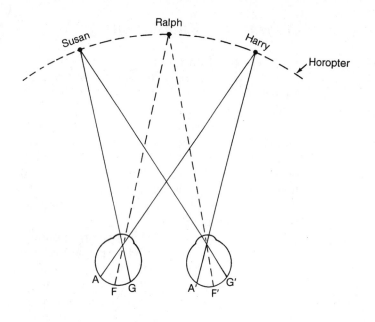

Figure 6.18
What's happening to the images of Susan, Ralph, and Harry inside the lifeguard's eyes? Susan's image falls on corresponding points G and G'; Ralph's image falls on the foveas, F and F' (which are corresponding points); and Harry's image falls on corresponding points A and A'.

Harry's and Susan's images fall on corresponding points on your retinas, as shown in Figure 6.18. (It is important to remember that the situation we are describing here holds only as long as you are looking at Ralph. If you change your point of fixation, then a new horopter is created that passes through the new point of fixation.)

What does the horopter have to do with depth perception? To answer this question, let's continue looking at Ralph and consider where Carol's and Charlie's images fall on the retinas. Since their heads are not located on the horopter, their images fall on **noncorresponding (disparate) points,** as indicated in Figure 6.19. For ex-

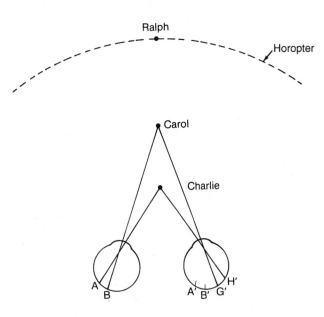

Figure 6.19
What's happening to the images of Carol and Charlie in the lifeguard's eyes? Since Carol and Charlie are not located on the horopter, their images fall on noncorresponding points.

ample, Carol's image falls on noncorresponding points B and G'. (Note that if you slid the retinas on top of each other, points B and G' would not overlap.) The corresponding point to B is, in fact, located at B', far from G'. The angle between G' and B' is called the **angle of disparity**, and the key to binocular depth perception is that *the farther the object is from the horopter, the greater is the angle of disparity.* You can understand this by noticing what happens on the retinas to the images of a closer object, such as Charlie. As Charlie moves closer (while you keep looking at Ralph), his images move farther and farther out to the sides of your retinas, and the angle of disparity increases. So Charlie's images, which fall on A and H', are more disparate than Carol's images. Thus, the amount of disparity tells you how far Charlie and Carol are from where you are looking. Since Charlie's angle of disparity is greater than Carol's, he must be located farther from the horopter and is therefore closer to you.

When objects are located in front of the horopter, as Carol and Charlie are, their images move out to the sides of the retinas, and the resulting disparity is called **crossed disparity.** If, however, objects are located beyond the horopter, as in Figure 6.20, their images move inward on the retinas, creating a condition called **uncrossed disparity.** The farther behind the horopter an object is, the more its images move inward on the retinas, and the greater is their disparity. Thus, crossed disparity indicates that an object is nearer than the horopter, and uncrossed disparity indicates that an object is farther than the horopter. (To remember which disparity is crossed and which is uncrossed, just remember that you have to cross your eyes to fixate on objects as they get nearer. Near objects create crossed disparity.)

We have seen that the disparity information contained in the images on the retinas provides information indicating an object's distance from where we are looking. Thus, when we look in a stereoscope or at a scene in the world, the different views we see with our left and right eyes create disparity, and this disparity generates stereopsis (Figure 6.21).

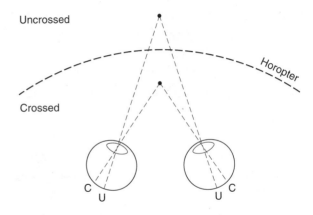

Figure 6.20
Crossed disparity occurs for objects in front of the horopter; uncrossed disparity occurs for objects behind the horopter. Notice how the retinal images move inward, toward the nose, as the object moves farther away.

Although our conclusion—that disparity creates an impression of depth—may seem reasonable, showing that we perceive depth when two different views are presented to the left and the right eyes doesn't prove that disparity is creating the perception of depth: Our scene may contain many pictorial depth cues, such as overlap, height in the field of view, and linear perspective, that could be contributing to our perception of depth. How can we tell whether depth perception is caused by disparity, by pictorial cues, or by a combination of both? Bela Julesz answered

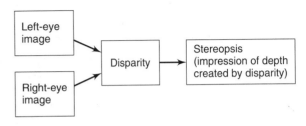

Figure 6.21
Disparity is created by the left-eye and right-eye images, and stereopsis occurs when an impression of depth is created by disparity.

 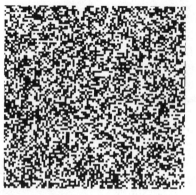

1	0	1	0	1	0	0	1	0	1
1	0	0	1	0	1	0	1	0	0
0	0	1	1	0	1	1	0	1	0
0	1	0	A	A	B	B	1	0	1
1	1	1	B	A	B	A	0	0	1
0	0	1	A	A	B	A	0	1	0
1	1	1	B	B	A	B	1	0	1
1	0	0	1	1	0	1	1	0	1
1	1	0	0	1	1	0	1	1	1
0	1	0	0	0	1	1	1	1	0

1	0	1	0	1	0	0	1	0	1
1	0	0	1	0	1	0	1	0	0
0	0	1	1	0	1	1	0	1	0
0	1	0	Y	A	A	B	B	0	1
1	1	1	X	B	A	B	A	0	1
0	0	1	X	A	A	B	A	1	0
1	1	1	Y	B	B	A	B	0	1
1	0	0	1	1	0	1	1	0	1
1	1	0	0	1	1	0	1	1	1
0	1	0	0	0	1	1	1	1	0

Figure 6.22

Top: A random-dot stereogram.
Bottom: The principle for constructing the stereogram.
See text for an explanation.

this question by creating a stimulus that contained no pictorial cues, called the *random-dot stereogram*.

Random-Dot Stereogram

By creating stereoscopic images of random-dot patterns, Julesz (1971) showed that subjects can perceive depth in displays that contain no depth information other than disparity. Two such random dot patterns, which constitute a **random-dot stereogram,** are shown in Figure 6.22. These patterns were constructed by first generating two identical random-dot patterns on a computer and then shifting a square-shaped section of the dots to the right, in the pattern on the right. This shift is too subtle to be seen in these dot patterns, but we can understand how it is accomplished by looking at the diagrams below

the dot patterns. In these diagrams, the black dots are indicated by 0's, A's, and X's and the white dots by 1's, B's, and Y's. The A's and B's indicate the square-shaped section where the shift is made in the pattern. Notice that the A's and B's are shifted one unit to the right in the right-hand pattern. The X's and Y's indicate areas uncovered by the shift that must be filled in with new black dots and white dots to complete the pattern.

The effect of shifting one section of the pattern in this way is to create disparity, which causes the perception of depth when the two patterns are presented to the left and the right eyes in a stereoscope. When these patterns are viewed in the stereoscope, we perceive a small square floating above the background. Since binocular disparity is the only depth information present in these stereograms, disparity alone causes the perception of depth.

Julesz's demonstration provides psychophysical evidence that disparity alone can create the perception of depth. But how is this disparity information on the retinas translated into depth information in the brain? A number of researchers have shown that neurons in the visual cortex of the cat and the monkey respond to specific degrees of disparity.

Disparity Information in the Brain

Horace Barlow, Colin Blakemore, and John Pettigrew (1967) found cells in the visual cortex of the cat that respond best to stimuli that fall on points separated by a specific angle of disparity on the two retinas. Records from such a cell in the visual cortex of the monkey, which David Hubel and Torsten Wiesel (1970) call a **binocular depth cell,** are shown in Figure 6.23. The record in Figure 6.23a shows that this cell does not respond when corresponding points (indicated by the overlap of the crosshairs to the left of the record) on the two eyes are simultaneously stimulated by a bar moving either from left to right or from right to left. Figures 6.23b, c, d, and e show that this cell does respond, however, when the disparity of the moving bar is increased, the maximum response occurring in Figure 6.23c, at 30 minutes

(half a degree) of disparity. Figures 6.23f and 6.23g indicate that no response occurs when each eye is *individually* stimulated by bars separated by 30 minutes of arc, even though a large response results when these same bars are presented to both eyes simultaneously, as in Figure 6.23c.

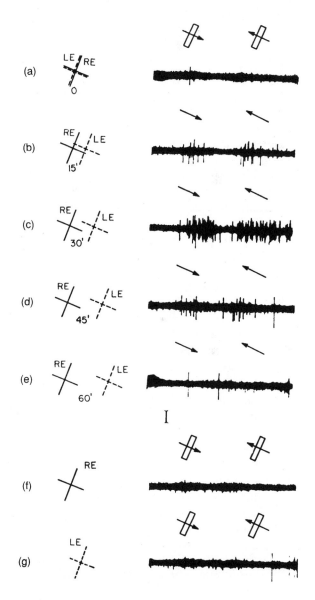

Figure 6.23

The response of a binocular depth cell in the visual cortex of the monkey. The positions of the crosshairs indicate the position of the bar in relation to the right eye (RE) and to the left eye (LE). This cell responds to movement of the bar in either direction (indicated by the arrows) and responds best when the two bars are presented simultaneously but are displaced 30 minutes in position, as shown in record (c). In records (f) and (g), bars are presented to the same positions as in record (c), but each bar is presented to the left and the right eyes separately. The cell does not respond in (f) and (g) because both eyes must be stimulated to cause a binocular depth cell to fire. (From Hubel & Wiesel, 1970.)

Perceiving Depth and Size

Do disparity-selective neurons cause stereopsis? Showing that these neurons exist does not prove that they have anything to do with perceiving depth. To show that these neurons are actually involved in depth perception, we need to do a behavioral experiment. Randolph Blake and Helmut Hirsch (1975) did such an experiment, in which they raised cats so that they experienced only monocular vision for the first six months of their lives. Their vision was alternated between the left and right eyes every other day during this period. As we saw in the Chapter 3 Developmental Dimension, "Sensitive Periods in Perceptual Development," monocular rearing eliminates binocular neurons, and this is what Blake and Hirsch found. In addition to recording from the cats' neurons, however, Blake and Hirsch also tested the cats behaviorally and found that cats without binocular neurons were not able to use binocular disparity to perceive depth. Thus, Blake and Hirsch showed that eliminating binocular neurons eliminates stereopsis and confirmed what everyone suspected all along, that disparity-selective neurons are responsible for stereopsis. Thus, if an animal's convergence is fixed (that is, if its eyes are positioned to look at a particular point in space and don't move), the cells that fire best to different disparities will be excited by stimuli lying at different distances from the animal, and the animal will perceive these stimuli as being at different distances.

Other researchers have extended the initial work on disparity-sensitive neurons. For example, Simon LeVay and Thomas Voigt (1988) surveyed 272 neurons in areas V1 and V2 of the cat's cortex to create the distribution in Figure 6.24, which shows that some neurons respond to zero or near-zero disparity and many respond to either crossed (near) or uncrossed (far) disparity. Other researchers have found disparity-selective neurons all along the parietal (or "where") pathway, in areas V1, V2, and MT (Kandel, 1991); neurons involved in depth perception are also found in the temporal (or "what") pathway (Tyler, 1990).

With the identification of disparity information on the retinas and of cortical neurons that

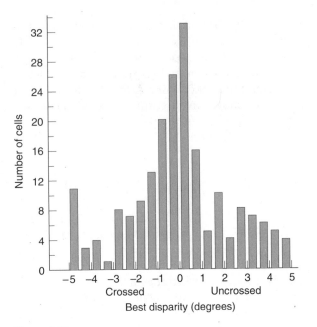

Figure 6.24

Histogram based on 272 neurons, which shows the number of cells that respond best to different angles of disparity.

respond to different degrees of disparity, it may appear that our understanding of binocular depth perception is complete. However, before we conclude our discussion of disparity, we need to consider an important step in the determination of stereopsis that we have so far ignored. To determine disparity, the visual system needs to match points on one image with similar points on the other image. This is called the **correspondence problem.**

The Correspondence Problem

To help us understand the correspondence problem, let's return to the stereoscopic images of Figure 6.14. When we view this image in a stereoscope, we see different parts of the image at different depths because of the disparity between images on the left and right retinas. Thus, Terry

Bradshaw and the man with the hose appear to be at different distances when viewed through the stereoscope, because they create different amounts of disparity. But in order for the visual system to calculate this disparity, it must compare the two images of Terry Bradshaw on the left and right retinas and the two images of the man with the hose on the left and right retinas.

How does the visual system compare the two Terry Bradshaws? The answer to this question is that the visual system may match Bradshaw's images on the left and right retinas on the basis of the specific features of the images, matching his face on the left with his face on the right, and so on. Explained in this way, the solution to the correspondence problem seems simple: Since most things in the world are quite discriminable from each other, it is easy to match an image on the left retina with the image of the same thing on the right retina. However, as we have seen many times already in this book, things are often not as simple as they seem. The correspondence problem is a perfect example because it becomes more complex when we consider Julesz's random-dot stereograms.

You can appreciate the problem involved in matching similar parts of a stereogram by trying to match up the points in the left and right images of the stereogram in Figure 6.22. Most people find this to be a difficult task, involving switching their gaze back and forth between the two pictures and comparing small areas of the pictures one after another. Clearly, matching similar features on a random-dot stereogram is much more difficult and time-consuming than matching features in the real world, yet the visual system somehow matches similar parts of the two stereogram images, calculates their disparities, and creates a perception of depth.

Although a number of proposals, all too complex to describe here, have been put forth to explain how the visual system solves the correspondence problem for random-dot stereograms, no totally satisfactory answer has yet appeared (Blake & Wilson, 1991). We do know, however,

that neurons in the striate cortex of the monkey fire when random-dot stereograms with specific degrees of disparity are presented to the left and the right eyes (Poggio et al., 1985). Somehow, these neurons receive information that enables them to match similar areas of the stereograms and to calculate their disparities.

The Autostereogram

We end our discussion of binocular disparity by describing a stereogram that results in a three-dimensional perception by creating disparity within a single image. These single-image stereograms, which are called **autostereograms,** have found wide popularity in books such as *Magic Eye* (Thomas, 1993) that have appeared on the best-seller lists. You can experience this effect for yourself by doing the following demonstration:

DEMONSTRATION
An Autostereogram

Color Plate 6.1 is an autostereogram from the book *Magic Eye* (1993). To see this image in three dimensions you need to cause your eyes to look into the distance, past the page. There are a number of ways to do this. Try them to see which one works for you.

1. Hold the book in front of you, but below your eye level so that you are looking over it. Stare at an object 1–10 yards beyond the book and then, *without changing your focus,* move the book up into your field of view and wait for the image to appear three-dimensional.

2. Position your eyes very near the book, staring blankly as if you are looking at something in the distance. Slowly move away from the book, maintaining your focus into the distance, until the image appears three dimensional.

3. Place a shiny transparent surface, such as a piece of glass, Plexiglas, Saran Wrap, or blank overhead

Perceiving Depth and Size

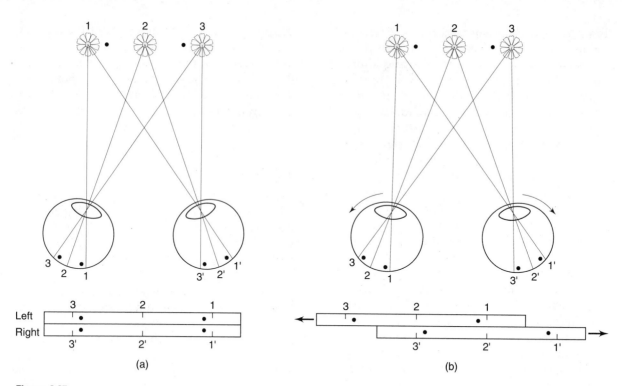

Figure 6.25

(a) When the flower and dot patterns are viewed normally, the images of the flowers and the dots fall on corresponding points on the two retinas and we see no depth. This correspondence is indicated here by the diagram below the eyes, which depicts the left and right retinas as flattened strips and shows how the flowers and dots overlap on the two retinas. (b) When the eyes diverge, as indicated by the arrows, the images on the left and right eyes shift in opposite directions, as shown on the diagrams below the eyes. Since the flowers are shifted exactly one unit, the images of flowers 2 and 3' and 1 and 2' overlap. Since these identical flowers overlap exactly there is no disparity and therefore no perception of depth. However, the images of the dots no longer line up, and so do not fall on corresponding points. The resulting disparity creates stereopsis, so the dots are perceived to be at a different depth than the flowers.

transparency, over the page. Then view the page from about a foot away, focusing on your reflection. Focusing on your reflection causes you to focus your eyes into the distance. Sometimes, it helps to move back and forth slightly to keep the reflection in view. Continue until you see the three-dimensional image.

There is a wide variation in people's ability to see these images. I find it difficult (the third method works best for me), but some people can achieve the three-dimensional perception easily. ●

The autostereogram effect is achieved by using repeating images that create disparity when the picture is viewed with the eyes diverged, as occurs when you look into the distance. We can understand how this works by considering a situation in which a person is observing a repeating pattern of identical images, such as the evenly spaced flowers in Figure 6.25a. If the person is focusing on the surface of the picture, the images of flowers 1, 2, and 3 fall on points 1, 2, and 3 on the left retina and on points 1', 2', and 3' on the right retina. Since these are corresponding points (1 corresponds to 1' and so on), there is no disparity and the flowers are seen as being on the flat surface of the picture.

If the person diverges their eyes, as you did to view Color Plate 6.1, the left and right eyes rotate in opposite directions, as shown in Figure 6.25b, and this causes the images of the flowers to shift in opposite directions on the two retinas. If the eyes are moved so that the flowers shift a distance on the retina that matches the spacing between their images, then identical flowers will still be on corresponding points on the two retinas, and there will still be no disparity for the flowers. The reason we perceive depth when we diverge our eyes is that disparity occurs for *all of the repeating images that are spaced differently than the flowers.* We can see how this works by looking at the two dots, which represent a repeating image that is spaced more widely than the flowers.

Before the eyes diverge, the images of the dots fall on corresponding points on the two retinas (Figure 6.25a). However, when the eyes diverge, so that all of the images on the retina are shifted one "flower" unit, the more widely spaced dots fall on disparate points (Figure 6.25b). You can appreciate that depth is caused by the way repeating images are spaced, by looking back at Color Plate 6.1 and noticing how the spacings between the various kinds of birds and bees differ when the eyes are diverged.

Visual scientist Christopher Tyler and computer programmer Maureen Clarke took the autostereogram effect shown in Color Plate 6.1 a step further by developing a computer program to create autostereograms using random-dot patterns. These random-dot autostereograms are particularly striking because, like Julesz's double image random-dot stereograms (Figure 6.22), they at first they appear to contain no image at all, but when depth perception is achieved, an image is revealed (Tyler, 1983; Tyler & Clarke, 1970, 1990). When Tyler and Clarke first developed these autostereograms in the early 1980s, they would show them to colleagues at work and

at dinner parties. Tyler describes their reactions as follows:

> Often, people would have difficulty seeing them at first and would wonder what was interesting about a sheet of random dots. The cries of delight from those who had seen the 3-D view would encourage them, however, until most people were able to get the effect. I was always pleased when people would say, without much enthusiasm, that they thought they were getting the effect, to which I would reply that stereopsis is like love; if you're not sure then you're not seeing it. Soon they would reach the right visual state and emit the inevitable "Oh wow" reaction when the depth image emerged from the page. There are few experiences as visually exciting as having a really clear 3-D image filling your visual field. (Tyler, 1994, p. 85)

A random-dot autostereogram created by Thimbleby, Inglis, and Witten (1994) is shown in Figure 6.26. This type of autostereogram is harder to see in three dimensions than the one in Color Plate 6.1, but follow the instructions outlined in the demonstration and be patient. When viewed correctly, this stereogram is perceived as an annulus floating above the surface (Figure 6.27).

Our discussion of depth perception has revealed a number of cues contribute to our perception of depth, including binocular disparity, the pictorial cues, movement-based cues, and oculomotor cues. No one of these depth cues is crucial to our perception of depth. For example, we can eliminate binocular disparity by closing one eye, yet because of the remaining monocular cues we still see some depth. All of the depth cues work together, and the more cues we have, the better are our chances of accurately deducing the three dimensions of the world from the two-dimensional information on our retinas. We will now see how this depth information contributes not only to our perception of depth but to our perception of size.

Figure 6.26

An autostereogram. See text for viewing instructions. (From Thimbleby, Inglis, & Witten, 1994.)

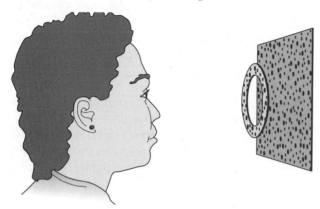

Figure 6.27

The perception of a floating annulus occurs when depth perception is created by the autostereogram in Figure 6.26.

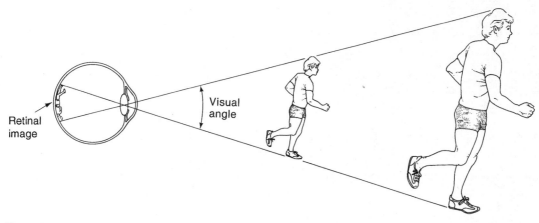

Figure 6.28
Two objects with the same visual angle have the same retinal size.

PERCEIVING SIZE

Our perception of size is greatly influenced by our perception of depth. As we discuss this idea, we will be referring to *visual angle,* a measure we introduced in Chapter 5 (see Figure 5.61). Two facts about visual angle are especially important to our study of size perception:

1. Visual angle depends on an object's size *and* its distance from the observer. Thus, two equal-sized objects at different distances can have different visual angles (see Figure 5.61), and two objects that differ in size can have the same visual angle if they are positioned at appropriate distances from the observer (Figure 6.28).

2. An object's visual angle is directly related to the size of the object's image on the retinas. Thus, since the two people in Figure 6.28 have the same visual angle, they cast the same image on the retina.

To better appreciate this idea, do the following demonstration.

⬛ DEMONSTRATION
Visual Angle and Distance from the Observer

An object's visual angle depends on both its size and its distance from the observer. Look at your fingernail from a distance of 3 inches (Figure 6.29). When you do this, your fingernail has a visual angle of about 10 degrees (assuming your fingernail measures about 1/2 inch from top to bottom). Now place about 2 feet away an object, such as a cup, with a physical height of about 3 inches, and, closing one eye, position your fingernail so that it is just to the side of the object and its height matches the object's height in your field of view. When you do this, both your fingernail and the object will have the same visual angle, and they will also be casting the same-sized images on your retinas. ⬤

A more "cosmic" example of a situation in which near and far objects with different sizes have the same visual angle is the correspondence of the visual angles of the moon and the sun. The fact that the moon and the sun have identical visual angles becomes most obvious during an eclipse of the sun. Although we can see the flaming corona of the sun surrounding the moon, as

Perceiving Depth and Size

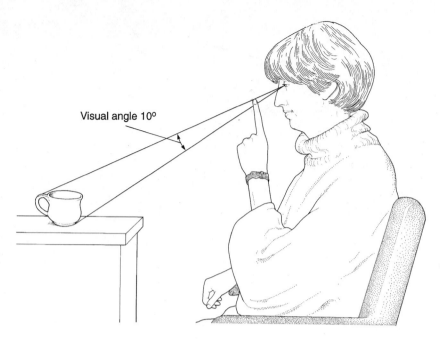

Figure 6.29

When you look at your fingernail from a distance of about 3 inches, it has a visual angle of about 10 degrees, and anything that it covers also has a visual angle of 10 degrees.

Visual angle 10°

shown in Figure 6.30, the moon's disk almost exactly covers the disk of the sun.

If we calculate the visual angles of the sun and the moon, the result is 0.5 degrees for both. As you can see in Figure 6.30, the moon is small (diameter 2,200 miles) but close (245,000 miles from earth), while the sun is large (diameter 865,400 miles) but far away (93 million miles from earth). The situation is therefore similar to the ones depicted in Figure 6.28, in which a small object that is close casts the same-sized image on the retina as a large object that is far away. (Note that you can use your fingernail to visually estimate the visual angle of the moon. If you view

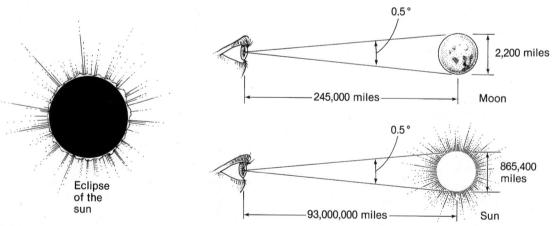

Eclipse of the sun

0.5°
2,200 miles
245,000 miles
Moon

0.5°
865,400 miles
93,000,000 miles
Sun

Figure 6.30

The moon's disk almost exactly covers the sun during an eclipse because the sun and the moon have the same visual angles.

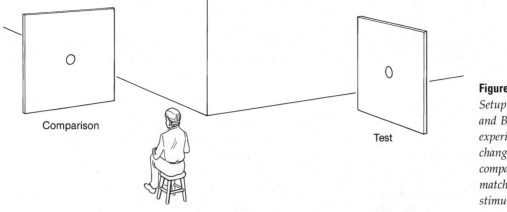

your 1/2-inch fingernail from a distance of 24 inches—about arm's length—its visual angle is 1.2 degrees. If you position your fingernail next to the moon, the moon should take up about half as much of your field of view as your fingernail. Do not try this with the sun, as it is so intense that it may burn your retinas.)

Visual angle is important in research on size perception because it can be used to specify the size of a retinal image. Since visual angle and retinal size are so closely related, we will use these terms interchangeably in the remainder of our discussion.

Perceiving Size as Visual Angle Changes

How do we perceive an object's size as its visual angle (or retinal size) changes? I introduce this question in my classes by standing about 4 feet from a person in the front row and asking them to estimate my height. They are usually pretty close, guessing around 5 feet 10 inches. I then step back and ask them how tall I appear when I am 8 feet distant. Even though I have doubled my distance and therefore have halved the size of my image on their retina (see Figure 5.61), I have never had anyone tell me that at a distance of 8 feet I look half as tall as I appeared at 4 feet (which would be 2"11' !). Most people see me as

being the same height at 8 feet away as at 4 feet away. Thus, changing the size of my image on a person's retina has little or no effect on her or his perception of my height.

In fact, the same result occurs even if we use an unfamiliar stimulus, such as a board. Moving the board away decreases its visual angle but causes little or no change in our perception of its size. Thus, our perception of an object's size remains constant as the size of the object's image on the retina changes.

The fact that we perceive an object's size as remaining constant at different distances is called **size constancy.** According to the **law of size constancy,** we correctly perceive an object's *physical size* no matter what its distance from us or what the size of its image on our retina. The phenomenon of size constancy means that our perception of size must depend on information in addition to the size of the retinal image. In a classic experiment, A. H. Holway and Edwin Boring (1941) showed that size constancy depends on our perception of depth.

Size Constancy and Depth Perception

The setup for Holway and Boring's experiment is shown in Figure 6.31. The observer sits at the intersection of two hallways and sees a luminous

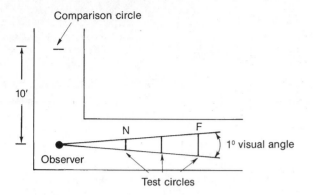

Figure 6.32

Top view of Holway and Boring's experiment. The key feature of this experiment is that the test circles all have the same visual angle and therefore cast the same image on the observer's retinas. (Adapted from Holway & Boring, 1941.)

test circle when looking down the right hallway and a luminous comparison circle when looking down the left hallway. The comparison circle is always 10 feet from the observer, but the test circles are presented at distances ranging from 10 feet to 120 feet. The observer's task on each trial is to adjust the diameter of the comparison circle to match that of the test circle. The key to this experiment is that each test circle has a visual angle of 1

degree. Thus, as shown in the top view of Holway and Boring's setup in Figure 6.32, larger and larger test circles must be used as the distance of the test circles from the observer increases, if the visual angle is to be kept constant at 1 degree. Note that, in this phase of the experiment, many depth cues are available to the observer.

The results of this experiment are indicated by line 1 in Figure 6.33. It is clear that the observers based their judgments on the physical sizes of the circles, since when they viewed a large test circle that was located far away (such as F in Figure 6.32), they made the comparison circle large. If, however, they viewed a small test circle that was located nearby (such as N in Figure 6.32), they made the comparison circle small. The fact that they always made the comparison circle match the *actual physical size* of the test circle—even though all test circles had the *same visual angle* and therefore cast identical images on the retina—supports the law of size constancy.

Holway and Boring then asked how the presence of depth information affected the observer's perception of size. To determine the role of depth in size perception, Holway and Boring systematically eliminated depth cues from the hallway by having the observer view the test circles with one eye (line 2), then by having the observer view the

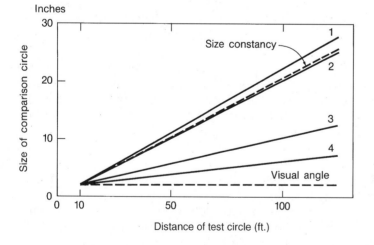

Figure 6.33

Results of Holway and Boring's experiment. The dashed line marked "size constancy" is the result that would be expected if the observers adjusted the diameter of the comparison circle to match the actual diameter of the test circle. The line marked "visual angle" is the result that would be expected if the observers adjusted the diameter of the comparison circle to match the visual angle of the test circle. (Adapted from Holway & Boring, 1941.)

test circles through a peephole (line 3), and finally by adding drapes to the hallway to eliminate reflections (line 4). The results of these experiments indicate that, as it becomes harder to determine the distance of the test circles, the observer's judgments cease to follow the law of size constancy. When the observer looks down the draped hallway through a peephole, he or she judges all of the test circles to have about the same size (lower dashed line)—the result that would be predicted by the **law of visual angle.** The law of visual angle states that our perception of an object's size is determined solely by its visual angle. In a later experiment similar to Holway and Boring's, Lichten and Lurie (1950) eliminated all depth cues by using screens that permitted the observer to see only the test circles. These conditions completely eliminated size constancy, so the observer's perceptions exactly followed the law of visual angle.

Another example of perception according to the law of visual angle is our perception of the sizes of the sun and the moon. Even though these two celestial bodies are vastly different in size, we perceive them to be the same size because they have the same visual angle, and because we are not able to perceive the distances of these faraway objects.

The results of Holway and Boring's experiment indicate the importance of depth information in perceiving size. This link between depth and size perception has led to the proposal that a *constancy-scaling mechanism* supplements the information available on the retinas by taking an object's distance into account (Gregory, 1966). We will call this constancy-scaling mechanism **size-distance scaling.** Thus, when a 6-foot-tall person is far away and casts a small image on your retinas, the size–distance scaling mechanism takes his or her distance into account, and you still perceive the person to be 6 feet tall.

Figure 6.34

retinas, the size–distance scaling mechanism takes his or her distance into account, and you still perceive the person to be 6 feet tall.

DEMONSTRATION

Size–Distance Scaling and Emmert's Law

You can demonstrate size–distance scaling to yourself by looking at the center of the circle in Figure 6.34 for about 60 seconds. Then, look at the white space to the side of the circle and blink to see the circle's afterimage. Now, repeat this procedure, but look at a wall far across the room. Blink to bring back the afterimage if it fades. You should see that the size of the afterimage depends on where you look. If you look at a distant surface such as the far wall of the room, you see a large afterimage that appears to be far away. If you look at a near surface such as the page of this book, you see a small afterimage that appears to be close. ●

Figure 6.35 illustrates the principle underlying the effect you just experienced, which was first described by Emmert in 1881. Staring at the circle in Figure 6.34 bleaches a small circular area of visual pigment on your retina. This bleached area of the retina determines the *retinal size* of the afterimage and stays constant.

The *perceived size* of the afterimage, as shown in Figure 6.35, is determined by the distance of the surface against which the afterimage is viewed. This relationship between the apparent distance of an afterimage and its perceived size is known as **Emmert's law:** The farther away an afterimage appears, the larger it will seem. Stated mathematically, this law is $S_p = K(S_r \times D_p)$, where S_p is the perceived size of the afterimage, K is a constant, S_r is the size of the retinal image, and D_p is the perceived distance of the afterimage. Thus, the size of the afterimage gets larger when you view it

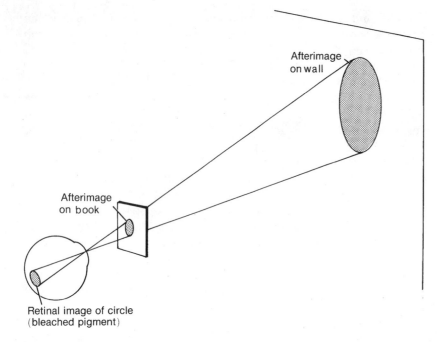

Afterimage on wall

Afterimage on book

Retinal image of circle
(bleached pigment)

Figure 6.35
The principle behind the observation that the size of an afterimage increases as the afterimage is viewed against more distant surfaces.

against a far wall because viewing it against the wall increases the perceived distance (D_p), but the size of the retinal image (S_r) stays constant.

This same equation can be applied to size constancy: the fact that your perception of a person's size remains constant as she walks away. As she walks away, the size of her image on your retina (S_r) gets smaller, but your perception of her distance (D_p) gets larger. These two changes cancel each other, and the net result is that you perceive her size (S_p) as remaining constant.

Can We Perceive an Object's Visual Angle?

You may now be thinking that while you can indeed see a 6-foot-tall person as staying 6 feet tall when he is far away, he does look different than when he is close. This occurs because the person's visual angle is smaller when he is far away, and even though the size–distance scaling mechanism causes us to see him at his correct 6-

foot size, there is still information available that tells us that his visual angle is small. Perhaps the most obvious information that tells us this is that, when the person is far away, he takes up a much smaller fraction of our field of view than when he is close. When a person stands 2 feet from you, he may cover almost your entire field of view, but when he is the length of a football field away, he is just one small object in a large field of view. In fact, experiments have shown that, when observers are asked to judge an object's visual angle, they can do so, though they tend to slightly overestimate the visual angle of distant objects, probably because they can't completely overcome the tendency to perceive in terms of size constancy when good depth information is available (Gilinsky, 1965).

Though it is possible to estimate the visual angle of an object, our everyday experience is dominated by size constancy. A faraway mountain looks huge, even though its visual angle may be smaller than that of many nearby objects, and a 6-foot-tall person appears 6 feet tall, no matter where he is. This dominance of size constancy occurs because our everyday experience usually includes abundant depth information. In some situations, however, erroneous depth information may lead us to misperceive size—a situation that creates a number of different visual illusions.

ILLUSIONS OF SIZE

Size illusions due to erroneous depth information sometimes occur in our everyday experience. I remember once looking into a room through a window that had a small decal on it. I misperceived the depth of the decal because, instead of seeing it as being attached to the window, I thought it was attached to the far wall of the room. This incorrect perception of the decal's distance made it look huge. But as soon as I realized that it was actually attached to the nearby window, my perception changed, and it became the small decal that it actually was.

Another example of a situation in which poor depth information leads to inaccurate size perception is the experience of looking down from high places, such as tall buildings or airplanes. Normal objects in the world invariably look like tinker toys, and people have the scale of ants. The reason is that the normal distance cues that operate on the ground are absent or reduced, so distance cannot be accurately estimated. Although it is unclear why the person in Figure 6.36 is having a hard time accurately perceiving the size of the boat (maybe being stranded on the island affected his depth perception!), the following real-life account of what can happen during inclement weather at an Antarctic research base shows that sometimes being unable to perceive depth accurately is no laughing matter:

> The most treacherous weather phenomenon is something known as a whiteout, in which light is reflected from a thick cloud cover and back

THE FAR SIDE   By GARY LARSON

Figure 6.36

1981 The Far Side cartoon by Gary Larson is reprinted by permission of Chronicle Features, San Francisco, CA. All rights reserved.

up from the snow, obscuring the horizon and surface definition, and surrounding one with a dazzling whiteness. Someone flying a helicopter during a whiteout can't tell up from down; pilots have been known to drop smoke grenades to determine their altitude only to find that they were a few feet above the ground. Others have flown at full power directly into the ice. What one can see is distorted—a discarded matchbox may look like a tent or a vehicle. (*New Yorker*, March 1981)

Illusions of size have also been produced in a number of different ways by psychologists. One of the most famous of these illusions is called the *Ames room.*

Figure 6.37

The Ames room. All three men are actually the same height (Wittreich, 1959). (Photograph courtesy of William Vandivert.)

The Ames Room

The **Ames room,** which was first constructed by Adelbert Ames, causes two people of equal size to appear very different in size (Ittleson, 1952). In the photograph of the observer's view of an Ames room in Figure 6.37, you can see that the man on the right looks much bigger than the one on the left. This perception occurs even though the two men are actually the same size. The reason for this erroneous perception of size lies in the construction of the room. Because of the shapes of the wall and the windows at the rear of the room, it looks like a normal rectangular room when viewed from a particular observation point; however, as shown in the diagram in Figure 6.38, the Ames room is, in fact, shaped so that the left corner of the room is almost twice as far away from the observer as the right corner.

What's happening in the Ames room? Because of the construction of the room, the man on the left has a much smaller visual angle than the man on the right. We think, however, that we are looking into a normal rectangular room, and our perception that both men are at the same distance prevents our size–distance scaling mechanism from correcting for the left man's greater depth. We therefore use the only other available information—the visual angles of the two men. Since the man on the right has a larger visual angle than the one on the left, he looks taller. Here's another way to think about this: If you perceive two people to be the same distance from you, the one who has the larger visual angle appears larger. This is really a statement of the obvious: If a tall person and a short person stand next to each other, you perceive the tall person as being taller. The Ames room causes you to think that you are seeing two men at the same distance, which makes the closer one, with the larger visual angle, appear to be taller.

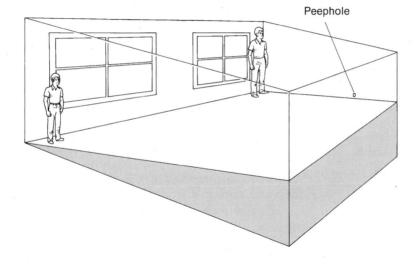

Peephole

Figure 6.38
The Ames room, showing its true shape. The man on the left is actually almost twice as far away from the observer as the man on the right; however, when the room is viewed through the peephole, this difference in distance is not seen. In order for the room to look normal when viewed through the peephole, it is necessary to enlarge the left side of the room.

The Moon Illusion

The moon illusion is another perceptual effect that may be influenced by the perception of depth. You may have noticed that, when the moon is on the horizon, it appears much larger than when it is higher in the sky. This enlargement of the horizon moon compared to the elevated moon, shown in Figure 6.39, is called the **moon illusion.** An explanation of the moon illusion that involves depth perception is called the **apparent-distance theory.** This theory is based on the idea that an object on the horizon, which is viewed across the filled space of the terrain, which contains depth information, should appear to be farther away than an object that is elevated in the sky and is therefore viewed through empty space, which contains little depth information. The key to the moon illusion, according to apparent-distance theory, is that both the horizon and the elevated moons have the same visual angle, and that, if two objects have the same visual angle and one appears farther away, the one that appears more distant will appear larger (see Figure 6.28 and the Holway

and Boring experiment). The apparent-distance theory, therefore, states that, since the horizon moon and the elevated moon have the same visual angle, the farther-appearing horizon moon should appear larger.

Figure 6.39
An artist's conception of the moon illusion showing the moon on the horizon and high in the sky simultaneously.

The Visual Angle of the Moon

Do the horizon and elevated moons really have the same visual angle? Since the moon's physical size (2,200 miles in diameter) and distance from the earth (245,000 miles) are constant throughout the night, the moon's visual angle must be constant. You can verify this in two ways: (I) Photograph the horizon and the elevated moons, and measure the resulting photograph. You will find that the diameters in the resulting two pictures are identical. (2) View the moon through a 1/4-inch-diameter hole (the size produced by most standard hole punches) held at arm's length. For most people, the moon will just fit inside this hole, and the fit will appear exactly the same wherever the moon is in the sky. ●

Evidence supporting a connection between the moon illusion and perceived distance has been provided by a series of experiments by Lloyd Kaufman and Irvin Rock (1962a, 1962b; Rock & Kaufman, 1962). For example, they showed that the enlarged perceived size of the horizon moon is strongly influenced by viewing the moon over the terrain, which causes it to appear farther away. They demonstrated this in a number of ways. They found that when the horizon moon was viewed over the terrain, it appeared 1.3 times larger than the elevated moon; however, when the terrain was masked off so that the horizon moon was viewed through a hole in a sheet of cardboard, the illusion vanished. Kaufman and Rock developed an apparatus that created artificial moons over different horizons. When they had observers view the moon over horizons that were 2 miles away and 2,000 feet away, they found that the observers saw the moon viewed over the far horizon as larger than the moon viewed over the near horizon. A number of other experiments in which Kaufman and Rock varied the apparent distance to the horizon showed that, when the distance appeared greater, the moon appeared larger.

Another piece of evidence that has been proposed to support the apparent-distance theory is based on the finding that, when people are asked to estimate the distance to the horizon and the distance to the sky directly overhead, they report that the horizon appears to be farther away. That is, the heavens appear "flattened" (Figure 6.40). If the horizon moon is seen as being on the surface of the sky, then the flattened heavens would cause the horizon moon to appear farther away, as the apparent-distance theory proposes. However, some researchers have reported that subjects see the horizon moon as floating in space in front of the sky, a result that has caused these researchers to question whether the "flattened heavens" can be used to explain the illusion (Plug & Ross, 1994).

The principle involved in the apparent-distance explanation of the moon illusion is the same one that causes an afterimage to appear

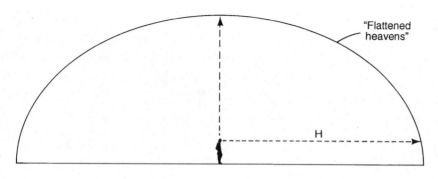

Figure 6.40
If observers are asked to consider that the sky is a surface and are asked to compare the distance to the horizon (H) and the distance to the top of the sky on a clear moonless night, they usually say that the horizon appears farther away. This results in the "flattened heavens" shown above.

larger if it is viewed against a faraway surface. Just as the near and far afterimages of Figure 6.35 have the same visual angles, so do the horizon and the elevated moons. The afterimage that appears to be on the wall across the room simulates the horizon moon; the circle appears farther away, so your size–distance scaling mechanism makes it appear larger. The afterimage that appears to be on the page of the book simulates the elevated moon; the circle appears closer, so your scaling mechanism makes it appear smaller (King & Gruber, 1962).

Another theory of the moon illusion, which is called the **angular size-contrast theory,** focuses not on the moon's apparent depth, but on the moon's visual angle compared to surrounding objects (Baird, Wagner, & Fuld, 1990). According to this idea, the moon appears smaller when it is surrounded by larger objects. Thus, when the moon is elevated, the large expanse of sky surrounding it makes it appear smaller. However, when the moon is on the horizon, less sky surrounds it, so it appears larger.

The angular size-contrast theory explains Kaufman and Rock's finding that the moon appears larger when it is seen over horizons that appear farther away by pointing out that objects on the terrain, such as buildings, trees, or the texture of the ground, take up less of the field of view if they are farther away. Thus, when the moon is seen against a far horizon, it is compared to objects with small visual angles, and therefore, the moon appears larger.

Which theory of the moon illusion is correct? In a recent book devoted entirely to various explanations of the moon illusion, the editor concluded that most researchers do not yet agree on an explanation (Hershenson, 1989). According to Cornelis Plug and Helen Ross (1994), the moon illusion is best explained by a combination of factors, which in addition to the ones we have considered here also include atmospheric perspective (looking through haze on the horizon can increase size perception), color (redness increases perceived size), and oculomotor factors (convergence of the eyes, which tends to occur when we look toward the horizon, can cause an increase in perceived size). Just as many different sources of depth information work together to create our impression of depth, many different factors may work together to create the moon illusion.

The Muller–Lyer and Ponzo Illusions

The **Muller–Lyer illusion,** shown in Figure 6.41, is analogous to the moon illusion in that the two central lines are actually equal in length and therefore have the same visual angle, but the line on the right looks longer. You can measure the size of this illusion by using the simple matching procedure described in the following demonstration.

D E M O N S T R A T I O N

Measuring the Muller–Lyer Illusion

The first step in measuring the Muller–Lyer illusion is to create some stimuli. To do this, create a "standard stimulus" by drawing a line 30 millimeters long on an index card and adding outward-going fins, as in the right figure in Figure 6.41. Then, on separate cards, create "comparison stimuli" by drawing

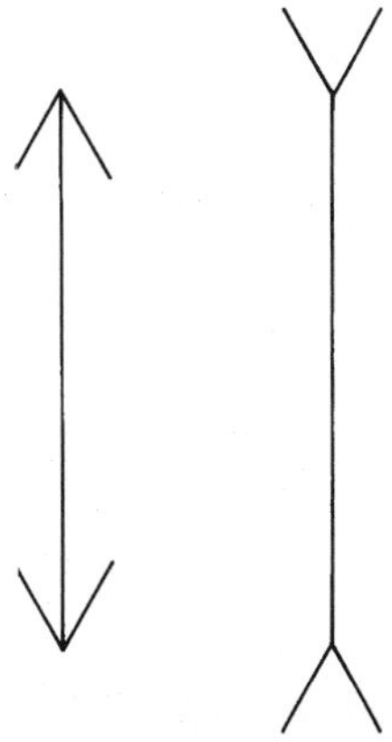

Figure 6.41
The Muller–Lyer illusion.
Both lines are actually the
same length.

lines 28, 30, 32, 34, 36, 38, and 40 millimeters long with inward-going fins, as in the left figure. Then, ask your subject to pick the comparison stimulus that most closely matches the length of the standard stimulus. The difference in length between the standard stimulus and the comparison stimulus chosen by the subject (typically between 10 percent and 30 percent) defines the size of the illusion. Try this procedure on a number of people to see how variable it is. ●

Why does this misperception of size occur? Richard Gregory (1966) explains the Muller–Lyer illusion on the basis of **misapplied size constancy scaling.** He points out that size constancy normally helps us maintain a stable perception of objects by taking distance into account. Thus, size constancy causes a 6-foot-tall person to appear 6 feet tall, no matter what her distance. Gregory proposes however, that this mechanism, which

helps us maintain stable perceptions in the three-dimensional world, sometimes creates illusions when applied to objects drawn on a two-dimensional surface. We can see how this works by comparing the left and right lines in Figure 6.41 to the left and right pictures in Figure 6.42. Gregory suggests that the fins on the right line in Figure 6.41 make this line look like part of the inside corner of a room, and that the fins on the left line make this line look like part of the outside corner of a building. Since the inside corner of a room tends to look farther away than the outside corner of a building, we see the right line as being farther away, and our size–distance scaling mechanism causes this line to appear longer.

At this point, you may say that, while the Muller–Lyer figures may remind Gregory of the inside corner of a room or the outside corner of a building, they don't look that way to you (or at least they didn't until Gregory told you to see

Figure 6.42
According to Gregory (1973), the Muller–Lyer line on the left in Figure 6.41 corresponds to the outside corner of a building, and the line on the right corresponds to the inside corner of a room.

Figure 6.43

The Ponzo (or railroad track) illusion. The two horizontal rectangles are the same length on the page (measure them), but the far one appears larger.

them that way). But according to Gregory, it is not necessary that you be consciously aware that the Muller–Lyer lines can represent three-dimensional structures; your perceptual system unconsciously takes the depth information contained in the Muller–Lyer figures into account, and your size–distance scaling mechanism causes the left line to shrink and the right line to expand. This theory of visual illusions can also be applied to other illusions that contain depth information, such as the **Ponzo** (or railroad track) **illusion,** shown in Figure 6.43. Here, both horizontal lines have the same visual angle, but the one on top appears farther away and is therefore perceived as larger.

Gregory's theory of visual illusions has not, however, gone unchallenged. For example, figures like the "dumbbell" in Figure 6.44, which contain no obvious perspective or depth, still result in an illusion. And Patricia DeLucia and Julian Hochberg (1985, 1986, 1991; Hochberg, 1987) have shown that the Muller–Lyer illusion occurs for a three-dimensional display like the one in Figure 6.45, in which it is obvious that the spaces between the two sets of fins are not at different depths. You can experience this effect for yourself by doing the following demonstration:

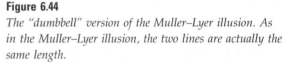

D E M O N S T R A T I O N

The Muller–Lyer Illusion with Books

Pick three books that are the same size, and arrange two of them with their corners making a 90-degree angle and standing in positions A and B, as shown in Figure 6.46. Then, without using a ruler, position the third book at position C, so that distance b appears to be equal to distance a. Check your decision, looking down at the books from the top and from other angles as well. When you are satisfied that distances a

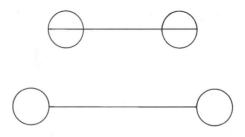

Figure 6.44

The "dumbbell" version of the Muller–Lyer illusion. As in the Muller–Lyer illusion, the two lines are actually the same length.

Perceiving Depth and Size

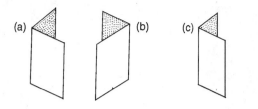

(a)   (b)   (c)

Figure 6.45

A three-dimensional Muller–Lyer illusion. The 2-foot-high wooden "fins" stand on the floor. Although the distance between edges (a) and (b) and between (b) and (c) are the same, the distance between (b) and (c) appears larger, just as in the two-dimensional Muller–Lyer illusion. Gregory's explanation of the illusion in terms of misapplied size constancy does not work in this case, since it is obvious that the spaces between the sets of fins are not at different depths.

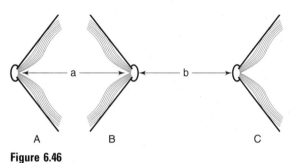

A   B   C

Figure 6.46

Creating a Muller–Lyer illusion with books (seen from the top). See text for explanation.

and b appear about equal, measure the distances with a ruler. How do they compare?   ●

If your perceptions were similar to those of the subjects in DeLucia and Hochberg's (1991) experiment, you set distance b so that it was smaller than distance a. This is exactly the result you would expect from the two-dimensional Muller–Lyer illusion, in which the distance between the outward-going finds appears enlarged compared to the distance between the

inward-going fins. You can also duplicate the illusion shown in Figure 6.41 with your books, by using your ruler to make distances a and b equal. Then, notice how the distances actually appear. The fact that we can create the Muller–Lyer illusion by using three-dimensional stimuli such as these, as well as demonstrations like the dumbbell in Figure 6.44, is difficult for Gregory's theory to explain; however, so far, no satisfactory alternative to Gregory's theory has been proposed.

All of our demonstrations of how the perception of size depends on the perception of depth have been explained within the constructivist approach that we introduced in Chapter 5, which sees perception as caused by both mental and physiological processing. Our perception of size, according to this idea, is the outcome of a calculation that takes both retinal size and perceived distance into account. But this is not the only way to explain size perception. The ecological approach, which is most closely identified with J. J. Gibson, proposes that this kind of calculation is not necessary for the perception of either depth or size. We will first consider the basic principles of the ecological approach, and we will then apply these principles to the perception of depth and size.

The Ecological Approach

The ecological approach to perception was championed by J. J. Gibson (1950, 1966, 1979) over a period spanning more than 30 years, beginning with work in the 1940s and extending to his death in 1979 (Figure 6.47). Gibson's approach to perception grew out of some experiments he did during World War II, in which he tried to determine how to improve a pilot's ability to land an airplane. From these experiments, Gibson concluded that the traditional depth cues, such as overlap, size in the field of view, and

Figure 6.47
J. J. Gibson (1904–1979), who was a professor of psychology at Cornell University for many years, published three books and many papers that have formed the basis of the ecological approach to visual perception.

height in the field of view, which all depend on objects or groups of objects that protrude into the air, could not sufficiently explain how an airplane pilot judges the distance to a runway when coming in for a landing. Gibson's conclusion that the crucial information for depth perception is located on the surface of the ground caused him to call his theory a *ground theory* of perception.

What is so special about information located on the ground? Why is it better than the traditional depth cues we have been describing? Gibson answered this question by pointing out that his ground-based information has a very important property: It remains constant even when an observer changes position or is moving through the environment. Gibson called this constant information **invariant information,** and as we will see, invariant information plays a central role in Gibson's approach to perception.

Invariant Information in the Environment

We begin our search for invariant information by looking at the structure of the ground. According to Gibson, an important feature of the ground is that it is usually textured. This texture gives rise to the texture gradients we included in our list of depth cues.

Texture Gradients A texture gradient, such as the one created by the ridges in the sand in Figure

6.48, provides information about depth because the elements of the gradient appear to be packed closer and closer together as the distance along the ground increases. Gibson distinguished texture gradients from traditional depth cues by noting that the texture gradient contains invariant information, since the depth information provided by the gradient remains constant no matter where the observer is located on the gradient.

To understand how this property sets gradients apart from traditional depth cues, consider the scene in Figure 6.49a, which shows a beach

Figure 6.48
A texture gradient made up of ridges in the sand. If we viewed it from directly above, we would see that the distance between each sand ridge is approximately equal; however, when viewed from the ground, the ridges are spaced closer and closer together as distance increases.

Perceiving Depth and Size

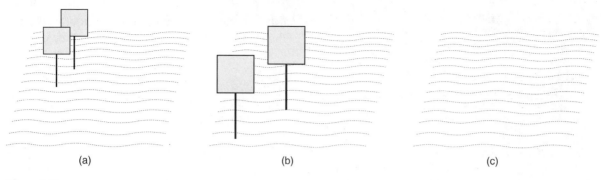

Figure 6.49

A person's views as she walks along the beach. In (a) she is walking toward two signs; in (b) she is near the signs; and in (c) she has passed them. Depth information can be obtained from the signs only from certain points of view, but it is available for the gradient as long as the person is on the beach.

scene as viewed by an observer walking along the beach. Four sources of depth information are present: the texture gradient created by the sand, the overlap of the two signs, and the relative heights and sizes of the two signs. Figure 6.49b shows the observer's view after she has walked a little way down the beach. The texture gradient information is still available, but the cue of overlap has vanished, since the two signs no longer overlap. As our observer continues to walk and leaves the two signs behind (Figure 6.49c), they no longer provide any depth information, but the gradient still does.

In addition to providing constant information about distance, texture gradients also supply information about the orientations of surfaces. For example, the rapid changes in texture of the sides of the object represented in the painting in Figure 6.50 tell us that the sides are oriented at a steep angle, whereas the smaller change of texture along the edges of the painting indicates that we are looking at that surface almost straight on.

Flow Patterns Another example of invariant information is how elements in the environment flow past a moving observer. An observer looking to the side while moving forward, like a person looking out the side window of a moving car, sees a gradient of flow: The speed of move-

ment is rapid in the foreground and becomes slower as the distance from the observer increases. This is similar to the depth cue of motion parallax, although Gibson emphasizes the flow of the whole field rather than the relative movement of just a few objects.

The deletion and accretion at edges that are at different depths (Figure 6.12) were also mentioned by Gibson as information that signals depth to the moving observer. Gibson also considered the flow that occurs as a person moves forward. In this case, the environment flows past the observer on all sides, and according to Gibson, this flow provides information that helps the person negotiate his way through the environment. We will discuss this aspect of flow patterns in more detail in the next chapter, when we discuss movement perception.

The Horizon Ratio Another source of invariant information is the **horizon ratio**—the extent of an object that extends above the horizon, divided by the extent of an object that extends below the horizon (Gibson, 1950; Sedgwick, 1973, 1983). The **horizon ratio principle** states that, if a person is standing on flat terrain, the place where the horizon intersects the object will be one eye-height above the ground. For example, if a person whose eyes are 5 feet above the ground views

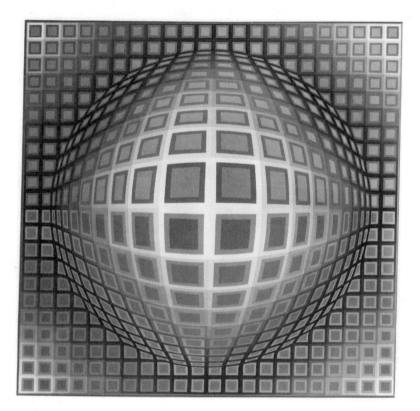

Figure 6.50
Vega-Nor *by Victor Vasarely
(1969). This painting creates
an "object" with steeply sloping
sides by using texture gradients.
(Courtesy of the Albright-Knox Art
Gallery, Buffalo, New York. Gift of
Seymour H. Knox, 1969.)*

the scene in Figure 6.51, the places where the horizon cuts across the telephone poles and the tree are all 5 feet high.

The horizon ratio principle also states that if two objects that are in contact with the ground are the same size, their horizon ratios will be the same. Thus, since all of the telephone poles in Figure 6.51 have the same horizon ratio, we know they are the same size. We also know that the tree is larger than the telephone poles because the horizon ratio of the tree is greater than the ratio of the telephone poles (i.e., a greater proportion of the tree is above the horizon line). The horizon ratio is invariant with the observer's position in the scene, so although the size of a telephone pole may become larger in the field of view as an observer approaches, the proportion of the pole that is above and below the horizon line remains constant.

Gibson's emphasis on invariant information reflects his commitment to studying perception as it occurs in the natural environment (hence the term *ecological approach to perception*). Gibson pointed out that, as people go about perceiving their environment, they are usually moving, and therefore, they need to use invariant information that doesn't change every time they observe their environment from a different point of view.

In addition to his assertion that the study of perception should be concerned with how moving observers use invariant information to perceive, Gibson made another assertion that we need to consider in order to fully appreciate his approach. Gibson argued strongly against two important components of the constructivist-based approach that we have focused on so far in this book: the retinal image and processing. Let's consider Gibson's alternatives to each of these.

The Ambient Optic Array: An Alternative to the Retinal Image

You may have noticed, as we described the various sources of invariant information in the environment, that we never mentioned the image on the retina. Our focus was *outside*, on the surfaces of the environment, rather than *inside*, on the image on the retina. Gibson felt that considering the retinal image is not productive because our perceptions often do not correspond to what is imaged on the retina. In addition, most analyses of the retinal image are based on the static image and ignore movement, which Gibson saw as providing crucial information for perception. Gibson therefore argued that perception researchers should be studying not the information in the retinal image but the information contained in what he called the **ambient optic array.**

We can illustrate what the ambient optic array is by considering the stimulation reaching the person in Figure 6.52. This person perceives the objects, surfaces, and textures in the scene because of the way the light rays reaching the person are structured by these objects, surfaces, and textures. This structure, which is extremely complex because there are rays converging on the

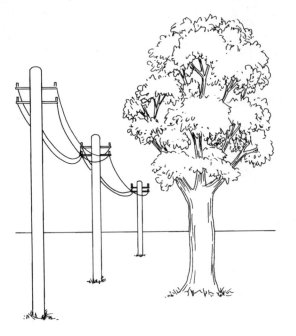

Figure 6.51

According to the horizon ratio principle, the horizon line intersects the telephone poles and the tree at a height equal to the viewer's eye level. Objects that are the same size, such as the three telephone poles, have the same horizon ratio. Since a larger proportion of the tree is above the horizon, we perceive it as being larger than the telephone poles.

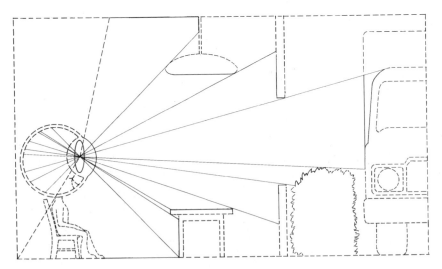

Figure 6.52

The ambient optic array is the structured pattern of light reaching our observer's eye from the environment. Environmental surfaces visible to our observer are indicated by solid lines; invisible surfaces are indicated by dashed lines. Each of the visible surfaces structures the pattern of light entering the observer's eye.

person from every part of the environment, is the ambient optic array.

The importance of the ambient optic array lies not in the structure that it defines at any point in time, but in how this structure changes as the observer moves. According to Gibson, these changes determine perception. Thus, our descriptions of texture gradients, flow fields, and the horizon ratio were descriptions of how the structure of the ambient optic array changes as the observer moves through the environment. This emphasis on the overall optic array is very different from much of the research we have discussed in this book, which focuses largely on how isolated stimuli affect perception. Remember, for example, our discussion of binocular disparity, which was concerned with comparing the stimulation at points on the two retinas, or of Holway and Boring's research on size constancy, in which a small stimulus was viewed by a stationary observer sitting in an almost empty hallway. The purpose of much of the research we have described has been to gain some understanding of how the visual system processes the incoming information. But that goal was not important to Gibson, because he thought that we can understand perception without considering processing.

Direct Perception: An Alternative to Processing

Gibson's focus on information in the ambient optic array led him to reject the idea that mental processing is necessary for perception. Instead, Gibson proposed the idea of **direct perception**—perception happens *directly* from information picked up from the optic array.

We can understand what is meant by *direct perception* by comparing how the constructivist approach and the direct approach explain size constancy. A constructivist would argue that, since the size of an object's image on our retinas depends on its distance from us, our perception of that object's size must somehow involve a "taking into account" of its distance. Thus, as the observer in Figure 6.53 moves away from the cylinder, the cylinder's image on the retina becomes smaller, so the observer makes a calculation that takes distance into account to accurately perceive the cylinder's size.

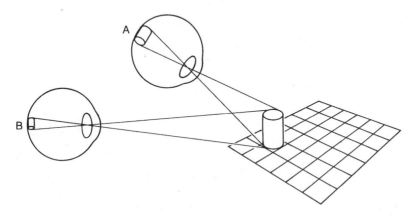

Figure 6.53
An observer, indicated by a single eyeball, looking at a cylinder on a checkerboard pattern from two different positions. The cylinder's image on the retina is larger when the observer is close (position A) than when the observer is far (position B).

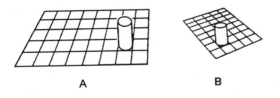

A   B

Figure 6.54

*What the observer in Figure 6.53 sees from positions A
and B. Although moving from A to B decreases the size of
the cylinder in the field of view and changes the angle of
view, the cylinder still appears to cover one unit of the
texture gradient in both situations.*

Figure 6.55

*A texture gradient with two cylinders. According to
Gibson, the fact that the bases of both cylinders cover
the same number of units on the gradient provides
direct information that the bases of the two cylinders
are the same size.*

Such a calculation is not necessary, according
to the ecological approach, because an object's
size is indicated by the number of units its base
covers on a texture gradient. This principle is
illustrated in Figure 6.54, which shows that, even
as the observer moves away, he continues to
perceive the cylinder's base as covering one unit
on the texture gradient. Another way to illustrate
how gradients help us to achieve the direct perception of size is shown in Figure 6.55, which
shows two cylinders on the texture gradient
formed by a cobblestone street. That the bases of
the front and rear cylinders both cover about half
a unit on the gradient indicates *directly* that the
bases are the same size. A calculation in which
retinal size and perceived distance are taken into
account is simply not necessary. Perception, according to Gibson, is therefore not a construction;
it happens *directly* from the information in the
optic array.

How do perception researchers feel about
Gibson's ecological approach to perception? Gibson's approach has had its supporters and de-
tractors, and there have been lively debates in the
perception literature (Cutting, 1986; Epstein,
1977; Fodor & Pylyshyn, 1981; Gibson, 1979;
Runeson, 1977; Ullman, 1980). Many researchers
appreciate Gibson's pointing out the importance
of the moving observer, his focusing on information contained on environmental surfaces, and
his identification of invariant information in the

ambient optic array (Nakayama, 1994). However,
many feel that information in addition to Gibson's invariants are involved in perception, and
that perceptual processing is far too important a
part of the perceptual process to ignore.

Many researchers also feel that, for Gibson's
approach to be truly meaningful, it is necessary
to go beyond identifying information that is *available* for perception and to determine whether that
information is actually *used* for perception. This
view is analogous to a concern we stated earlier
when we saw that there are binocular depth cells
in the cat's cortex, but pointed out that just re-

cording from neurons that respond to disparity doesn't prove that these neurons have anything to do with depth perception. A behavioral test was needed to demonstrate that cats without these neurons cannot perceive depth. One of the tasks facing the researchers who have followed Gibson's lead is to demonstrate how perceivers use the invariant information in the environment that Gibson and other researchers have identified. In the next chapter, we will consider Gibson's ideas again as we describe how we perceive movement.

THE DEPTH INFORMATION USED BY ANIMALS

It is easy to conclude, based on observing animals' behavior, that many animals have excellent depth perception. Cats leap on their prey; monkeys swing from one branch to the next; a pelican diving toward the water retracts its wings just before its beak pierces the surface; a male housefly follows a flying female, maintaining a constant distance of about 10 cm; and a tree frog accurately jumps across a chasm (Figure 6.56).

While there is no doubt that many animals are able to judge distances in their environment, we can still ask which mechanisms animals use to perceive depth. A survey of mechanisms used by different animals reveals that animals use the entire range of cues described in this chapter, some animals using many cues and others relying heavily on just one or two.

To make use of binocular disparity, an animal must have good acuity, eyes that have overlapping visual fields, and neurons that receive inputs from both eyes (Pettigrew, 1986). Animals such as cats and monkeys meet these require-ments. We know from physiological research that cats and monkeys have disparity-selective neurons and, from behavioral research, that monkeys can see depth in random-dot stereo-grams (Bough, 1970).

The pigeon is an example of an animal that only partially meets our requirements for stereopsis because its eyes are located on the sides of its head and much of the visual fields of the left and right eyes do not, therefore, overlap. Thus, while the pigeon enjoys a panoramic 340-degree field of view, the visual fields of the left and right eyes overlap only in a 35-degree area surrounding the pigeon's beak. This overlapping area, however, happens to be exactly where pieces of grain would be located when the pigeon is pecking at them. To see whether pigeons do, in fact, use binocular information in this overlapping area, Sally McFadden and J. Martin Wild (1986) trained pigeons to discriminate between two-dimensional and three-dimensional patterns and then tested their ability to make the discrimination both monocularly and

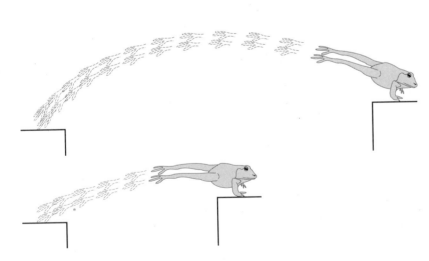

Figure 6.56
These drawings, which are based on photographs of frogs jumping, show that the frog adjusts the angle of its jump based on its perception of the distance across the chasm, with steeper take-offs being associated with greater distances. (Adapted from Collett & Harkness, 1982.)

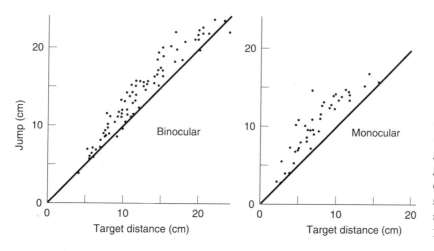

Figure 6.57

The distance a frog jumps to capture a mealworm is a function of the distance of the mealworm and is also slightly influenced by whether the frog can use one or both eyes. A jump that is exactly the same distance as the worm is indicated by the solid line. When the frog can use both eyes (left graph), its accuracy is slightly greater than when it can use just one eye (right), but accuracy is still fairly good with one-eyed vision. (From Collett & Harkness, 1982.)

binocularly. McFadden and Wild found that limiting the pigeon to monocular vision had no effect on its ability to discriminate between two two-dimensional patterns but disrupted its performance on a depth perception task that the pigeon could do when using both eyes. Based on this and other results, McFadden (1987) concluded that the pigeon has a small area of binocular depth perception in front of its beak.

Like humans, animals use more than one type of depth cue in order to obtain the most accurate depth information possible. For example, frogs and toads use stereopsis to perceive depth, but if they are able to use only one eye, they can still use accommodation to judge how far they need to jump to capture prey (Collett & Harkness, 1982). Figure 6.57 shows the relation between the distance a frog jumps and the distance of a mealworm. The frog is more accurate using binocular vision (the points fall closer to the line) but is still fairly accurate when only monocular information is available.

Many animals—especially those with small eyes—use information other than disparity to determine distances. Consider, for example, a rather strange water bug, the backswimmer *Notonecta,* which hangs upside down just below the surface of the water as it lies in wait for prey that may be approaching on the surface above it (Figure 6.58) (Collett & Harkness, 1982; Schwind, 1978). *Notonecta* initially detects its prey by sensing vibrations and then makes a distance judgment based on the position of the prey's image on its retina. The image of distant prey falls on the part of the retina nearest the surface of the water, and as the prey approaches, its image moves down on the retina.

Movement parallax is probably insects' most important method of judging distance, and they use it in a number of different ways (Collett, 1978). For example, the locust makes a "peering" response—moving its body from side to side to create movement of its head—as it observes potential prey. T. S. Collett (1978) measured the

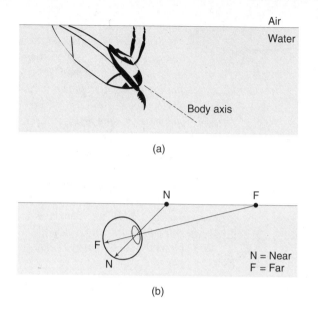

(a)

(b)

N = Near
F = Far

Figure 6.58

The backswimmer Notonecta *waits beneath the surface of the water. A faraway object located at F on the water creates an image at F on the retina, and as the object moves toward N on the water, its image moves toward N on the retina. Thus, the backswimmer can detect where its prey is on the surface of the water based on the position of its image on the retina. (From Schwind, 1978.)*

locust's "peering amplitude"—the distance of this side-to-side sway—as it observed prey at different distances and found that the locust swayed more when targets were farther away.

Since farther objects move less across the retina than nearer objects for a particular amount of observer movement (see Figure 6.11), a larger sway would be needed to cause the image of a far object to move the same distance across the retina as the image of a near object. The locust may therefore be judging distance by noting how much sway is needed to cause the image to move a particular distance across its retina. Another example of an animal that uses image movement to detect depth is the honeybee, which uses the information produced by the image movement that occurs as it flies across a field to determine the distances of nearby and faraway flowers (Lehrer et al., 1988).

From just the few examples described, we can see that animals use a number of different sources of depth information. The type of information used depends on the animal's specific needs and on its anatomy and physiological makeup. *Notonecta*, lying in wait for prey just under the waterline, needs only very rudimentary depth perception and has limited physical capabilities, so it uses a simple system to perceive its potential prey's distance. Humans, monkeys, and pigeons, which must negotiate their way through complex environments, need more precise depth perception that operates over a variety of distances. They therefore make use of a number of different depth cues that enable them to rapidly determine the locations of both nearby and faraway objects.

THE EMERGENCE OF DEPTH PERCEPTION IN INFANTS

When infants are born, they have poor visual acuity and little or no depth perception. At what age are infants able to use different kinds of depth information? The answer to this question is that different types of information become operative at different times, binocular disparity becoming effective early and the pictorial depth cues becoming effective later.

Binocular Disparity

One requirement for the operation of binocular disparity is that the eyes must be able to **binocularly fixate**—to direct their foveas to exactly the same place. Newborns have only a rudimentary ability to fixate binocularly, so their binocular fixation is imprecise, especially on objects that are changing in depth (Slater & Findlay, 1975).

To determine when precise binocular fixation develops, Richard Aslin (1977) did a simple ex-

periment. He filmed infants' eyes while moving a target between a near point, 12 cm away, and a far point, 57 cm away. If the infant directs both eyes at a target, the eyes should diverge (rotate outward) as the target moves away and should converge (rotate inward) as the target moves closer (Figure 6.59). Aslin's films indicate that while some divergence and convergence does occur in 1- and 2-month-old infants, these eye movements do not reliably direct both eyes toward the target until about 3 months of age.

Although binocular fixation may be present by 3 months of age, this does not guarantee that the infant can use the resulting disparity information to perceive depth. To determine when infants can use this information to perceive depth, Robert Fox and co-workers (Fox et al., 1980; Shea et al., 1980) presented random-dot stereograms to infants ranging in age from 2 to 6 months.

The beauty of random-dot stereograms is that the binocular disparity information in the

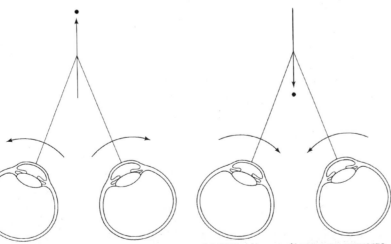

(a) Object moves away: eyes diverge   (b) Object moves closer: eyes converge

Figure 6.59

If an infant is fixating on an object that is moving, its eyes (a) diverge (rotate outward) as it follows an object that is moving away and (b) converge (rotate inward) as it follows an object that is moving closer.

Figure 6.60

The setup used by Fox et al. (1980) to test infants' ability to use binocular disparity information. If the infant can use disparity information to see depth, he or she sees a rectangle moving back and forth in front of the screen.

stereograms results in stereopsis only (1) if the stereogram is observed with a viewer that presents one picture to the left eye and the other picture to the right eye, and (2) if the observer's visual system can convert this disparity information into an impression of depth. Thus, if we present a random-dot stereogram to an infant whose visual system cannot yet use disparity information, all he or she will see is a random collection of dots.

In Fox's experiment, a child wearing special viewing glasses was seated in its mothers' lap in front of a television screen as shown in Figure 6.60. The child viewed a random-dot stereogram that appeared, to an observer sensitive to disparity information, as a rectangle-in-depth, moving either to the left or to the right. Fox's premise was that an infant sensitive to disparity will move his or her eyes to follow the moving rectangle. He found that infants younger than about 3 months of age would not follow the rectangle, but that infants between 3 and 6 months of age would follow it. He therefore concluded that the ability to use disparity information to perceive depth emerges sometime between 3½ and 6 months of age.

Richard Held and his group (Held, Birch, & Gwiazda, 1980) also showed that infants develop the ability to use disparity information by about 3½ months of age. They showed this by measuring infants' **stereoacuity,** the ability to resolve differences in disparity. The question Held asked was "What is the smallest disparity that results in an infant's perception of depth?"

Held measured the infants' stereoacuity by having them view the display shown in Figure 6.61. One stimulus in this display is a flat picture of three black bars, and the other is a stereogram that, when viewed through special glasses, appears three-dimensional to adults. This type of stereogram can create smaller differences in disparity than the random-dot stereogram and therefore provides a more sensitive measure of infants' abilities.

Held used the preferential looking technique. The infants, who sat on their mother's laps and wore special viewing glasses, saw the bar stereogram on one side of the display and the flat bar pattern on the other side. If given a choice, infants prefer a three-dimensional stimulus to a two-dimensional one (Fantz, 1965), so if they per-

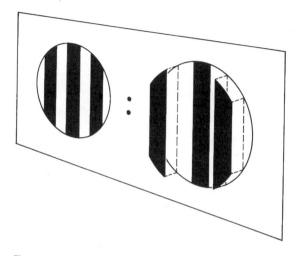

Figure 6.61

Stimuli used by Held, Birch, and Gwiazda (1980) to test stereoacuity. The pattern on the left is a two-dimensional grating. The one on the right is a stereogram that looks three-dimensional when viewed through special glasses. This three-dimensional perception occurs, however, only if the subject can perceive depth based on disparity.

ceive depth based on disparity, they look preferentially at the stereogram.

Held's results agreed with Fox's: By about 3½ months of age, infants are able to use disparity to perceive depth. By showing the infants stereograms with a number of different disparities, Held was able to trace the development of the ability to use disparity. At 3½ months, infants are able to detect disparities of about 1 degree of visual angle, and their stereoacuity increases rapidly to less than 1 minute of visual angle over the next month (1 minute of visual angle = 1/60 degree). Thus, Held showed that, once the ability to detect disparity appears, infants show a rapid increase in stereoacuity to fairly good levels by between 4 and 5 months of age.

What causes the relatively sudden development of the ability to use disparity information to

perceive depth? Held (1985, 1991, 1993) proposed that this development is caused by a change in how neurons from the lateral geniculate nucleus (LGN) synapse in the striate cortex. Remember that information from the left and the right eyes is separated in different layers of the LGN. This information enters the newborn's cortex, and the neurons from the left and the right eyes both synapse on the same neurons in layer IV of the cortex (Figure 6.62a). Layer IV neurons are not selective for disparity, so the information from

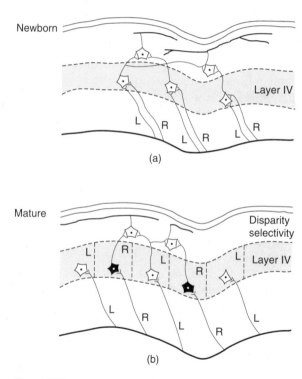

Figure 6.62

Richard Held proposes that the infant's ability to use disparity information to perceive depth depends on a change in how incoming LGN fibers synapse on neurons in layer IV of the striate cortex. See text for an explanation.

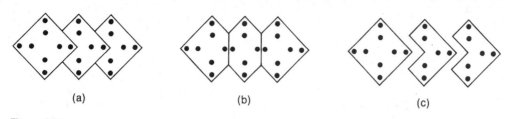

Figure 6.63

Stimuli for Granrud and Yonas's (1984) interposition experiment. See text for details.

the left and the right eyes is simply combined in these neurons, so that any possibility of comparing left-eye and right-eye information in other neurons is eliminated. However, during the first few months of life, the wiring changes, so the left- and right-eye geniculate neurons synapse on separate neurons in layer IV, and this information is then relayed to neurons in the cortex that are disparity detectors (Figure 6.62b). This change in wiring apparently occurs at about 3–4 months— the same age at which the infant begins to use binocular disparity to perceive depth. Thus, the development of the ability to use binocular information to perceive depth may depend on this change in the way geniculate neurons synapse in the cortex.

Pictorial Cues

Albert Yonas, Carl Granrud, and their colleagues have shown that infants begin to use the pictorial cues of overlap, familiar size, relative size, shading, linear perspective, and texture gradients sometime between 5 and 7 months of age (Granrud, Haake, & Yonas, 1985; Granrud & Yonas, 1984; Granrud, Yonas, & Opland, 1985; Yonas et al., 1986); (Yonas, Petterson, & Granrud, 1982). Let's look at two of their experiments, one for overlap and one for familiar size.

Carl Granrud and Albert Yonas (1984) tested infants' ability to perceive depth from overlap by showing them two-dimensional cardboard cut-outs of the displays depicted in Figure 6.63. The infants viewed the cutouts with just one eye, because binocular viewing would reveal that the displays were flat and could lower the chances that the infants would respond to the pictorially induced depth. The display in Figure 6.63a contains the depth cue of overlap, whereas the displays in Figures 6.63b and 6.63c do not. Since infants tend to reach for objects they perceive as being nearer, they should reach for (a) more than for (b) or (c) if they are sensitive to overlap. This was the result for 7-month-olds, but not for 5-month-olds. Thus, the ability to perceive depth based on overlap appears sometime between 5 and 7 months.

Granrud, Haake, and Yonas (1985) conducted a two-part experiment to test for familiar size. In the *familiarization phase*, 7-month-old infants played with a pair of wooden objects for 10 minutes. One of these objects was large and one was small (as pictured in Figures 6.64a and 6.64b). In the *test phase*, the two objects in Figure 6.64c were presented at the same distance from the infant. The prediction in this experiment was that infants sensitive to familiar size would perceive the right object in Figure 6.64c to be closer after playing with the pair in 6.64a and would perceive the left object in Figure 6.64c as closer after playing with the pair in 6.64b.

When tested monocularly, the 7-month-olds reached for the "apparently nearer" stimulus

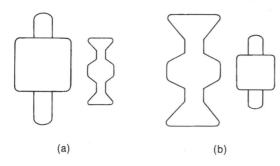 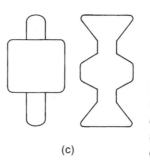

(a)   (b)   (c)

Figure 6.64

Stimuli for Granrud, Haake, and Yonas's (1985) familiar-size experiment. See text for details.

predicted by familiar size. The 5-month-olds, however, did not reach more for the "apparently nearer" object in the test phase, a result indicating that these infants were not responsive to familiar size. Thus, just as for overlap, the ability to use familiar size to perceive depth appears to develop sometime between 5 and 7 months.

This experiment is interesting not only because it indicates when the ability to use familiar size develops, but also because the infant's response in the test phase depends on a cognitive ability—the ability to remember the sizes of the objects that he or she had played with in the familiarization phase. The 7-month-old infant's depth response in this situation is therefore based both on what is perceived *and* what is remembered. The fact that familiar size and others of the pictorial depth cues depend on the development of cognitive abilities is one reason that infants' ability to use these cues does not develop until after binocular disparity, which apparently depends more on neural wiring than on cognition.

REVIEW

Questions

The Cue Approach

- The cue approach to depth perception looks for connections between specific stimuli and a person's perception of depth. This approach proposes a number of types of cues that signal depth in a scene.

1. Describe the rationale behind cue theory, using overlap as an example. (231)
2. What are the four types of depth cues? (232)

Oculomotor Cues

- Oculomotor cues are based on feelings in the eyes caused by convergence and accommodation.

3. What are convergence and accommodation, and why can they serve as cues to depth? (232)

Pictorial Cues

- Pictorial cues are sources of depth information that can be depicted in a picture. They are also called monocular depth cues because they work even if we use only one eye.

4. Describe the following cues: overlap, size in the field of view, height in the field of view, atmospheric perspective, familiar size, linear perspective, and texture gradients. (233)
5. Describe Epstein's familiar-size experiment. Why did it work only for monocular viewing? (236)
6. What is Alberti's window? What is the connection between depiction in perspective pictures and perception of the environment? (237)

Movement-Produced Cues

- Movement creates cues that enhance the perception of depth.

7. Describe motion parallax. Be sure you understand its retinal basis, diagrammed in Figure 6.11. (239)
8. When do deletion and accretion occur? What kinds of depth are they most effective in detecting? (240)

Binocular Disparity and Stereopsis

- Binocular disparity is a binocular depth cue that depends on both eyes and is based on the fact that our eyes see the world from slightly different viewpoints.

- Disparity information, which is contained in images on the retinas, indicates an object's distance from where the observer is fixating.

9. What is a stereoscope? How are pictures produced for it? Why do we see depth in these pictures? What is stereopsis? (241)

10. What are corresponding points? When do images of objects fall on corresponding points? What is the horopter, and how does an object's position relative to it relate to the perception of the object in depth? Define the angle of disparity, crossed disparity, and uncrossed disparity. (243)

- The random-dot stereogram is a stimulus that creates disparity without providing any other depth information.

11. How is a random-dot stereogram constructed? What do people see in random-dot stereograms? What does this effect prove? (246)

- Disparity information exists not only on the retina, but also in the brain in neurons called binocular depth cells.

12. Under what conditions does a binocular depth cell fire? What is the behavioral evidence that disparity-selective neurons cause stereopsis? (247)

- To determine disparity, the visual system needs to match points in one image with similar points in the other image. This is the correspondence problem.

13. How does the visual system solve the correspondence problem for naturalistic images? Why has it been difficult to solve the correspondence problem for random-dot stereograms? (248)

- Pictures called autostereograms can create depth in just a single image. A perception of depth is created when these images are viewed by a technique that creates disparity information in the two eyes.

14. What is the basic principle behind construction of an autostereogram? How must an autostereogram be viewed to achieve three-dimensional perception? Explain how disparity is created by using this technique? (249)

Perceiving Size

- Our perception of size is greatly influenced by our perception of depth.

- Although an object's visual angle and retinal size change when the object moves to different distances from an observer, we perceive the size of the object as remaining constant. This is called size constancy.

- It has been hypothesized that the link between size and depth perception is achieved through a mechanism called size–distance scaling.

- Although we can estimate the visual angles of objects, our everyday experience is dominated by size constancy.

15. What is the relationship between visual angle and an object's distance? The object's size? The size of the object's image on the retinas? (253)

16. The phenomenon of size constancy means that our perception of size must depend on what? (255)

17. Describe the procedures, results, and conclusion of Holway and Boring's experiment. What is the law of visual angle, and when does it hold? (255)

18. What is Emmert's law, and how does it relate to size–distance scaling? How can the equation developed for Emmert's law be applied to size constancy? (257)

19. How well can we judge an object's visual angle? Why is our everyday experience dominated by size constancy? (258)

Illusions of Size

- A number of size illusions are caused by erroneous depth perception.

- The moon illusion is the perception of the horizon moon as being larger than the moon that is elevated in the sky. A number of theories have been proposed to explain this illusion, but it is likely that a combination of factors contributes to creating it.

- The Muller–Lyer and Ponzo illusions are illusions that cause a misperception of the length of lines.

20. Describe some examples of situations in which erroneous depth perception leads to errors in size perception. (259)

21. Describe the Ames room. Compare the distances and visual angles of the people in the far corners of the room. Why does the Ames room illusion occur? (260)

22. What is apparent-distance theory? How do the visual angles of the horizon and the elevated moons compare? What evidence supports apparent-distance theory? What is a possible flaw in the "flattened-heavens" argument for the theory? (261)

23. What is the angular size-contrast theory of the moon illusion? (263)

24. How has Gregory used the idea of misapplied size constancy scaling to explain the Muller–Lyer and Ponzo illusions? Give examples of some results that have created problems for the theory. (264)

The Ecological Approach

- J. J. Gibson was the major developer and proponent of the ecological approach to perception.

- Gibson's theory is based partially on the idea that there is invariant information in the environment—information that remains constant even if the observer moves through a scene.

- Gibson was not concerned about the image on the retina. His focus was outside, on the surfaces of the environment, rather than inside, on the image on the retina.

- Gibson was not concerned about perceptual processing. Instead, he suggested that we perceive based on a direct perception of the information in the ambient optic array.

25. What did Gibson conclude from his wartime experiments? Why did he call his theory a ground theory? (266)

26. What do we mean when we say a texture gradient contains invariant information? Distinguish between texture gradients and traditional depth cues. (267)

27. Describe flow information. Explain the horizon ratio principle. How do these provide invariant information about depth or size? (268)

28. Why did Gibson reject the idea of studying the retinal image? What is the ambient optic array? Compare the ambient optic array with the types of stimuli used in most of the experiments described in this text. (269)

29. Contrast how the constructivist approach and Gibson's ecological approach would explain size constancy. (271)

30. How do many researchers feel about Gibson's approach to perception? (272)

The Depth Information Used by Animals

- Animals perceive depth by using many different sources of information. The exact information a particular animal uses depends on the animal's physical capabilities and its environmental situation.

31. What requirements must an animal meet to use binocular disparity? Which animals meet these requirements? Describe the pigeon's depth perception. (274)

32. Describe the depth cues used by frogs and toads, the backswimmer *Notonecta*, and insects. (275)

The Emergence of Depth Perception in Infants

- When infants are born, they have poor visual acuity and little or no depth perception. These capabilities develop over the first year of life.

33. What is a requirement for binocular disparity? How was the presence of this requirement measured in infants? How did Fox determine whether infants can use binocular disparity information to perceive depth? (277)

34. What is stereoacuity? Describe Held's experiment and his conclusions. What is Held's physiological hypothesis to explain the infant's sudden development of the ability to use disparity information? (278)

- As the infant's visual system develops, different types of information become operative at different times, binocular disparity becoming effective early and the pictorial depth cues becoming effective later.

35. Describe the experiments that showed when infants can use overlap and familiar size to perceive depth. Why is the development of the ability to judge depth by familiar size particularly significant? (280)

PERCEIVING MOVEMENT

If asked what aspect of vision means the most to them, a watchmaker may answer "acuity," a night flier "sensitivity," and an artist "color." But to animals which invented the vertebrate eye, and hold the patents on most of the features of the human model, the visual registration of movement was of the greatest importance.
—GORDON WALLS (1942, P. 342)—

Motion perception evolved early, according to the comparative physiologist Gordon Walls, because, as the act of movement is intimately associated with life, the perception of this movement is intimately associated with survival. Predators that can detect the movement of potential prey are more likely to catch that prey, and prey that can detect the movement of potential predators are more likely to survive. Thus, although some animals may have poor depth perception or rudimentary color vision, none lack the ability to perceive motion.

THE INFORMATION PROVIDED BY MOVEMENT

While modern-day humans may not need movement perception to avoid predators, we do need it to avoid cars and other moving objects in our environment, and to take advantage of the information provided by movement, including the following:

1. Movement attracts our attention. If you are in a crowd and want to attract someone's attention, one of the best things you can do is wave your arms. Movement in our peripheral vision usually triggers an eye movement that brings the moving object's image onto our foveas so we can see it clearly.

2. The movement of an object relative to an observer provides information about the

object's three-dimensional shape. We may not be sure of an unfamiliar object's shape if we see it from just one viewpoint, but if it moves relative to us or if we walk around it, its shape becomes obvious.

3. Movement provides information that helps us segregate figure from ground. A good example, which is illustrated in the demonstration below, is the camouflaged animal that remains invisible as long as it is still, but that becomes instantly visible as soon as it moves. Movement segregates figure (the animal) from ground (the rest of the environment).

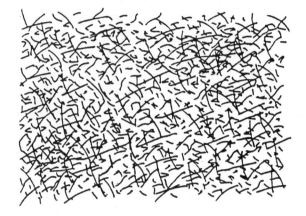

Figure 7.1
The bird becomes camouflaged if a transparency of the random lines is superimposed on a transparency of the bird. When the bird is moved relative to the lines, it becomes visible, an example of how movement enhances the perception of form. (From Regan, 1986.)

 D E M O N S T R A T I O N

Perceiving a Camouflaged Bird

For this demonstration, you will need to prepare stimuli by first Xeroxing the bird and the hatched-line pattern in Figure 7.1. Then, cut out the bird and the hatched pattern, place them on separate sheets of paper, and Xerox them onto an overhead transparency. Place the hatched pattern on top of the bird and notice how difficult it is to see the bird. Then, holding the hatched pattern in place, slide the bird so it moves relative to the pattern. When the bird moves, it becomes instantly recognizable, even though it was difficult to see when it was stationary (from Regan, 1986). ●

4. Movement provides information that enables us to actively interact with the environment. As we walk down the sidewalk or drive down the street, the movement of elements of the environment provides information that keeps us on course and helps us avoid bumping into things. Our perception of movement is also crucial for doing things like hitting or catching a baseball, playing tennis, or playing a video game. In these situations, we both perceive an object's movement and coordinate our own movement with that of the moving object. A dramatic illustration of this coordination occurs every time a fly ball is hit toward the outfield in a baseball game. Even though the ball is traveling at over 100 miles per hour, the outfielder can determine nearly instantly, based on watching just the initial flight of the ball, where the ball will land and whether there is sufficient time to reach it before it hits the ground (Todd, 1981).

But perhaps the most dramatic illustration of the importance of movement perception comes from the rare cases of motion agnosia, such as that of the woman described in Chapter 3 whose ability to perceive movement was impaired by damage to her cortex. Her difficulty in perceiving movement was not simply a minor annoyance; she had a hard time doing things we take for granted. She couldn't pour liquids because she couldn't see the liquid rising in the container (Figure 3.27); she had difficulty conversing with people because she couldn't see their mouths moving; and she was terrified to cross streets because she was often unable to see an approaching car until it was suddenly upon her (Zihl et al., 1983; 1991). This woman's severe disability because of her lack of movement perception attests to the crucial role of movement perception in our day-to-day lives.

In this chapter, we will explore the mechanisms responsible for our perception of movement. We begin by looking at some of the ways movement perception has been studied.

STUDYING MOVEMENT PERCEPTION

The problems of studying movement perception are similar to those we encountered when studying the other perceptual qualities. On one hand, we usually perceive movement effortlessly, and it seems that we can easily explain movement in terms of a stimulus, such as a spot of light, that moves across the retina stimulating one receptor after another. On the other hand, we perceive movement in many different situations in which the stimulation is far more complex than a spot of light moving across the retina. Consider, for example, the following situations in which you perceive movement:

1. A person walks across your field of view (Figure 7.2). In this case, you perceive not only the person moving across your field of view, but also the person's arms, legs, and body moving relative to each other.

2. Many people, cars, and other objects are moving in many directions at once on a busy city street (Figure 7.3).

3. A series of lights on a sign flash one after another (Figure 7.4). This is called **stroboscopic movement,** which is a type of **apparent movement,** so called because the movement is only apparent, not real.

4. You go to the movies and see movement on the movie screen even though, in reality, you are seeing a sequence of rapidly

Figure 7.2
Our environment is dominated by movement. This movement is caused by the movement of objects in the environment, as shown in this picture, or by movement of the observer. (Photograph: Detail from A Passing Umbrella *by Kenneth Antol, 1983.)*

Figure 7.3
A more complex example of movement, which involves numerous stimuli, moving relative to one another.

presented still pictures (Figure 7.5). This is another example of stroboscopic movement.

5. You look at a waterfall or a flowing stream and then look away, and the ground appears to move briefly in the direction opposite to the movement of the waterfall. This example of apparent movement is called the **waterfall illusion,** or, more generally, a **movement aftereffect** (Figure 7.6).

6. You are sitting in your car at a stoplight and perceive your car rolling backward. You jam on the brakes, only to realize that your car is actually standing still and the car next to you is moving forward. This is called **induced movement,** because the movement of one object (usually the larger one) is *inducing* the perception of movement in another object, which is usually smaller. Examples of induced movement can be found in many places. For example, you are perceiving induced movement when you think you are perceiving a pigeon's head bobbing forward and backward as it walks (it

Figure 7.4
Rapidly flashing the lights in this sign, one after another, creates stroboscopic movement, an illusion of movement.

Figure 7.5
Seven frames from Edwin S. Porter's 1903 film The Great Train Robbery. *This sequence lasts about 0.4 seconds when projected. The movement that results is an example of stroboscopic movement.*

Figure 7.6
Looking at a waterfall, such as this one, can create an aftereffect of movement called the waterfall illusion.

isn't—see Figure 7.7), or if it appears that the moon is racing through the clouds when it is the clouds that are moving and not the moon. You can demonstrate induced movement to yourself in the following way:

D E M O N S T R A T I O N
Inducing Movement in a Dot

You can demonstrate induced movement to yourself by sticking a small dot of paper to the screen of your television set, as

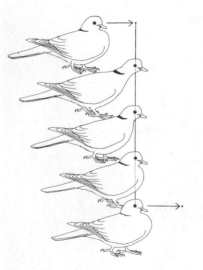

Figure 7.7

How a pigeon walks. These pictures, which were taken from a film of a pigeon walking, show that a pigeon moves its head forward and then moves its body forward while keeping its head stationary. The phenomenon of induced movement causes the pigeon's head to appear to move backward, but it never actually does. (Figure courtesy of Mark Friedman; see Friedman, 1975.)

shown in Figure 7.8, and watching a program in which the television camera moves back and forth across a scene or follows a moving person or car (football, basketball, or hockey games are particularly good). These camera movements cause the entire TV image to move across the screen, which will induce movement in your dot. ●

7. As you walk through the environment, you see the objects in the environment move across your field of view. You know, however, that it is you who are moving, and that the objects are actually stationary.

This list should convince you that, when we go beyond the movement of a single spot of light, the study of movement perception is a complex

Figure 7.8

As these basketball players race down the court, the dot stuck to the center of the TV screen races with them, an example of induced movement.

undertaking. For example, items 3–6 above represent **illusions of movement**—situations in which you perceive a stimulus as moving even though it is actually stationary. And the last item on our list describes a situation in which movement *is* occurring across your field of view, but you perceive the moving stimuli as stationary. And even explaining how we perceive something as simple as a single object moving across your field of view, as in item 1, is more difficult than we might expect at first. In this chapter, we will not attempt to explain every situation in which movement perception occurs, but we will cover most of the basic principles of movement perception.

We begin our consideration of movement perception by going back in history to Exner's 1875 discovery that, when two electrical sparks are discharged next to each other, briefly separated in time, movement appears to occur across the space between them. This perception of movement across empty space, which corresponds to the examples of apparent movement in items 3 and 4 in our list above, was put to practical use in the creation of the first motion pictures in the late 1800s.

Although by the early 1900s the motion picture industry was beginning to flourish, it wasn't until about 1912 that apparent movement began to be studied seriously by psychologists. That was the year Max Wertheimer published his paper on apparent movement, which marked the beginnings of Gestalt psychology. Remember, from Chapter 5, that Wertheimer used the existence of apparent movement in the empty space between two flashed stimuli to argue against the structuralists' idea that perceptions are created by the addition of sensations (see Figure 5.8). How, argued Wertheimer, can sensations explain a person's perception of movement through a space that is empty?

Wertheimer and later workers began studying apparent movement psychophysically and found that the nature of the movement that occurs between two flashing lights depends on both the timing between the flashes and the distance between them. Figure 7.9 shows how our perception of two flashes of light changes as the time interval between the two flashes, the **interstimulus interval (ISI),** is increased (Graham, 1965). When the ISI is less than about 30 msec, the lights appear to flash on and off simultaneously. As the interval is increased beyond 30 msec, par-

tial movement is perceived between the two lights; and at a separation of about 60 msec, the lights appear to move continuously from one to the other. Finally, at time intervals above about 200–300 msec, no movement is perceived between the two lights; they appear successively, with first one flashing on and off, and then the other.

The distance between the two lights also affects the perception of apparent movement. As the distance increases, either the time interval between the two flashes or the intensity of the flashes must be increased to maintain the same perception of movement.

D E M O N S T R A T I O N

A Demonstration of Apparent Movement

You can demonstrate some of the effects in Figure 7.9 to yourself, as follows: Place a dot on one side of a match as shown in (a) and, slightly farther down, place a dot on the other side, as in (b). Then, with the match between your thumb

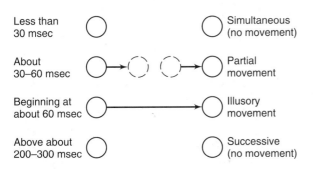

Figure 7.9

The perception of apparent movement depends on the time interval between the flashing of two lights. As the time interval is increased, the observer's perception goes through the stages shown in the figure.

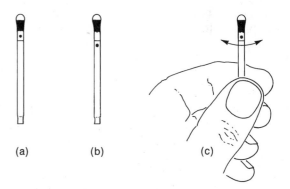

(a) (b) (c)

Figure 7.10

You can create apparent movement by drawing a dot on each side of a match as shown in (a) and (b), and by flipping the match back and forth, as shown in (c).

and forefinger, as shown in (c), slowly begin to roll the match back and forth. Notice that at slow speeds (long ISIs) you see the dots one after another. Then, as you increase the speed, notice when movement occurs. At very high speeds (short ISIs), you will see both dots simultaneously, with no movement between them. ●

While some of the early movement researchers were studying the nature of apparent movement, others were focusing on the real movement, like the examples in items 1 and 2 of our list, that occurs as an object actually moves through space. Early researchers showed that the threshold for perceiving movement in a homogeneous field is a velocity of about ⅙ to ⅓ of a degree of visual angle per second (Aubert, 1886). This means that you would just barely perceive the movement of the spot in Figure 7.11 if, when you view it from a distance of 1 foot, it takes about 14 seconds to travel from A to B. If, however, we add vertical lines to the space between A and B, you would be able to perceive the spot's movement even at velocities as low as ¹⁄₆₀ of a degree of visual angle per second (which translates into a travel time of 280 seconds from A to B). These results show that our perception of movement depends both on the moving stimulus and on its surroundings.

For many years, researchers continued to treat the apparent movement created by flashing lights and the real movement created by actual movement through space as if they were separate phenomena, governed by different mechanisms. However, today's researchers study both types of movement together and concentrate on discovering general mechanisms that apply to both real and apparent movement. In this chapter, we will follow this approach as we look for general mechanisms of movement perception. We begin with a fairly simple situation—a single spot or bar moving across the retina—and then introduce complexities like the ones we noted in our list at the beginning of the chapter. We start by showing how neural movement detectors like the ones we described in Chapter 3 signal the direction of movement of a moving spot or bar stimulus.

MOVEMENT DETECTORS

In Chapter 3 we described complex and end-stopped cortical cells in the striate cortex (area V1) and area V2 that respond best to bars moving in a specific direction. We also described cells in the medial temporal (MT) cortex that respond to specific directions of movement.

Directionally Selective Neurons in the Striate Cortex

We already know, from the experiments of Hubel and Wiesel (1959, 1965a), that there are neurons in the striate cortex (V1) and area V2 that respond to particular directions of movement. We now ask two questions about these neurons:

1. Do these neurons play a role in determining our perception of movement?

2. What mechanism causes these neurons to respond to a specific direction of movement?

The Role of Directionally Selective Neurons in the Perception of the Direction of Movement Do directionally selective neurons actually play a role in perception? We can answer this question in much the same way that we answered a similar question in the previous chapter about binocular depth cells. To determine whether binocular depth cells play a role in depth perception, we

Figure 7.11

looked at the results of monocular rearing experiments in which kittens were allowed to see out of just one eye at a time. Since this monocular rearing eliminated the kittens' binocular depth cells *and* also eliminated their ability to use binocular disparity to see depth, we concluded that these neurons are, in fact, needed to create the perception of depth from disparity.

Tatiana Pasternak (1990) used a similar tactic to determine whether directionally selective neurons are responsible for the cat's ability to perceive the direction of movement. To eliminate directionally selective neurons from a cat's cortex, she reared kittens in illumination that constantly flickered eight times per second so that their vision consisted entirely of a series of still "snapshots" of their environment. Rearing in this illumination had two effects: (1) it eliminated over 90 percent of directionally selective neurons in the striate cortex, and (2) it almost totally eliminated the cats' ability to detect the *direction* of a moving stimulus, even though they were still able to detect the *presence* of the moving stimulus. Thus, directionally selective neurons in the striate cortex appear to be necessary for the perception of the direction of movement.

A Neural Mechanism for Directional Selectivity
When an image moves across the retina, it stimulates a series of receptors, one after the other. Werner Reichardt (1961) proposed the simple circuit in Figure 7.12 that results in a neuron that

responds to movement in only one direction. To understand how this circuit works, let's look at what happens as we stimulate each receptor in turn, beginning with receptor A and moving toward the right. Receptor A synapses with G, so stimulation of A excites G, which then sends an inhibitory signal to H. (The *X* across H in Figure 7.13a indicates that H is being inhibited.) While this is occurring, the stimulus moves to receptor B and causes it to respond and to send an excitatory signal to H (Figure 7.13b). But since H has been inhibited by G, it does not fire. Thus, the signals from receptors A and B do not get past H and therefore never reach M, the neuron at the end of the circuit. This process is repeated as the

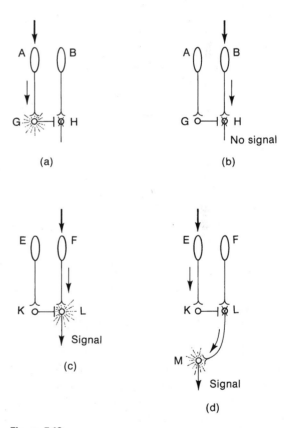

Figure 7.13
What happens as a light moves across the receptors of Figure 7.12. See text for details.

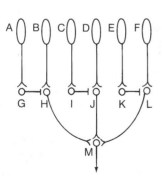

Figure 7.12
*A neural circuit in which a neuron (**M**) responds to the movement of a stimulus across the receptors from right to left. The neuron does not, however, respond to movement from left to right.*

Perceiving Movement

stimulus moves across the remaining receptors, the net result being no response in M.

The outcome is different, however, if we begin at receptor F and move the stimulus to the left. Receptor F sends a signal to L, which causes it to fire, as shown in Figure 7.13c. The stimulus then moves to receptor E, which causes K to send inhibition to L. This inhibition, however, arrives too late. L has already fired and has stimulated M (Figure 7.13d). This process is repeated as the stimulus moves across the remaining receptors, the net result being that M fires. Thus, neuron M fires to movement from right to left but does not fire to movement from left to right.

Figure 7.14 shows how a complex cell in the cat's cortex responds to different directions of movement. The cell is tuned to respond best to a moving bar oriented at about +20 degrees and responds less well on either side of this orientation, eventually dropping to the cell's spontaneous firing level. Based on this tuning curve, we might be tempted to propose that the firing of this neuron provides all the information we need to perceive movement at + 20 degrees. But if we remember the discussion of sensory coding in Chapter 4, we know that we can't determine the direction in which a stimulus is moving by simply monitoring the firing rate of this cell. The reason is that the cell's firing rate is affected not only by the direction in which the stimulus is moving but also by the velocity and intensity of the stimulus. For example, the cell in Figure 7.14 might fire equally well in response to a low-intensity bar oriented at +20 degrees and to a high-intensity bar oriented at +30 degrees (see Figure 4.8). Thus, a particular firing rate would not tell us the direction of the bar's movement.

One way the brain deals with this problem is by analyzing the overall *pattern* of responses from many cells. Thus, as our +20-degree bar moves across the retina, it causes large bursts of firing in cells that prefer this orientation and smaller bursts in cells that prefer other orientations. The resulting *pattern* of response, which holds over a wide range of intensities, signals the

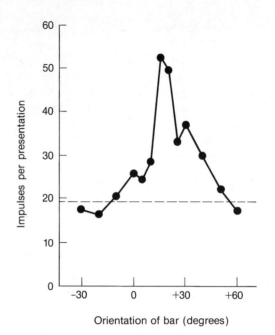

Figure 7.14

A "directional tuning curve" showing the relationship between the orientation of a moving bar and the response of a complex cell in the cat's cortex. The cell responds best when the bar is oriented at about 15–20 degrees. The dashed line indicates the rate of spontaneous firing (Blakemore & Tobin, 1972).

bar's direction of movement, as described by the across-fiber-pattern theory of sensory coding we introduced in Chapter 4. As we will see below, when we describe how cells in area MT of the extrastriate cortex fire to movement, the firing of neurons at higher stations in the visual system may code the direction of movement more according to specificity theory, so that the firing of single neurons or small numbers of neurons signals specific directions of movement.

Directionally selective neurons not only provide information regarding the direction of movement across the retina but also provide a physiological explanation of the illusion of movement called the *waterfall illusion* (number 5 on our list), which occurs after viewing a moving field such as a waterfall or a stream.

***Movement Detectors and the Movement After-
effect*** If you stare for 30–60 seconds at a waterfall or a rapidly flowing stream that fills only part
of your field of view and then look away at some
other part of the scene, the scene will appear to
move in a direction opposite to the original direction of flow. This illusion is a type of movement
aftereffect, so called because the perception of
movement is an aftereffect of viewing an inducing stimulus such as the waterfall.

Stuart Anstis and Richard Gregory (1964)
showed that the waterfall illusion depends on
movement of the inducing stimulus across the retina. Instead of having observers view a waterfall,
they had them view a belt of horizontally moving,
vertical black and white stripes, similar to the belt
pictured in Figure 7.15. The observers viewed these
moving stripes either with their eyes stationary, so
the pattern moved across the retina, or with their
eyes tracking the moving stripes, so the pattern
remained stationary on the retina. In both the
"eyes-stationary" and "eyes-tracking" conditions,
the observers perceived the movement of the
stripes, but an aftereffect of movement occurred
only after the eyes-stationary condition. Thus, the
important factor in determining this aftereffect is
not the perception of the stripes' movement but the
movement of the stripes across the retina.

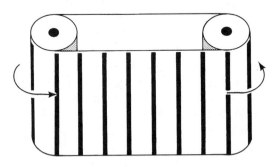

Figure 7.15
*Stimulus for creating a movement aftereffect. After
viewing the moving belt, an observer experiences an
illusion of movement in the direction opposite to the belt's
movement.*

That the waterfall illusion occurs only if the
inducing stimulus moves across the retina supports the idea that movement detectors that respond only to movement across the retina, may
help create this illusion. In fact, by recording
from directionally selective cells in the rabbit's
retina, Horace Barlow and Robert Hill (1963)
found electrophysiological evidence that movement detectors are involved in the waterfall illusion. Figure 7.16 shows Barlow and Hill's results.
When the stimulus was moved across the cell's
receptive field, the firing rate increased to above
the cell's spontaneous level, and when the stimulus was turned off, the firing rate fell to below the
cell's spontaneous level.

Barlow and Hill hypothesized that this cell
(which we will call A) is paired with another cell
(B) that is directionally selective in the opposite
direction. After stimulation of A is stopped, its
firing rate drops to below its spontaneous level;
therefore, A is firing at a lower rate than B, which
is still firing at its spontaneous level. We perceive
movement in the preferred direction of B because
it is firing at a greater rate than A. Thus, according to Barlow and Hill, aftereffects of movement
result from temporary imbalances of the discharges of cells that respond in opposite directions (for psychophysical evidence linking the
movement aftereffect to the activity of cortical
neurons, also see Barlow & Brindley, 1963; Cam-
eron, Baker, & Boulton, 1992; Mitchell & Ware,
1974; Sekuler & Ganz, 1963; for a description of
another approach to explaining this illusion
based on directionally selective neurons, see
Hiris & Blake, 1992).

Directionally Selective Neurons in the MT Cortex

While early work on movement detectors focused on the directionally selective neurons in
the striate cortex, more recent research has
looked at neurons in extrastriate areas, especially
the medial temporal area (MT), because of a
number of lines of evidence indicating that area

Perceiving Movement

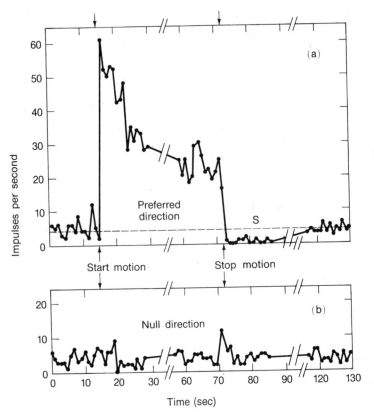

Figure 7.16
Response of a directionally selective cell in the rabbit's retina to a stimulus moving in its preferred direction. In (a) we see that, during 60 seconds of continuous stimulation, the rate of nerve firing stayed above the spontaneous level, S. After the stimulation was stopped, firing decreased to below the spontaneous level for about 30 seconds. (b) The same stimulus conditions as in (a), but in the cell's "null direction" (opposite to the preferred direction), showing that stimulation in the null direction had no effect on the response of this cell (Barlow & Hill, 1963).

MT is important in movement perception. In Chapter 3 we described the following evidence linking area MT and movement perception:

1. Ninety percent of neurons in area MT are directionally selective.

2. Lesioning area MT impairs the ability to detect the direction of movement, measured behaviorally.

3. Electrically stimulating a small number of neurons in area MT influences the monkey's ability to detect movement in a particular direction. (Salzman et al., 1992; Salzman, Britten, & Newsome, 1990)

We now consider further evidence of a link between MT neurons and movement perception by describing a study in which William New-some, Kenneth Britten, and Anthony Movshon (1989) demonstrated a connection between the firing of MT neurons and a monkey's ability to judge the direction of movement. While recording from an MT neuron, these authors presented to the monkey moving-dot displays like the ones in Figure 7.17, positioning them so they covered the receptive field of the MT neurons.

These displays are like the ones described in Chapter 3 in which the correlation between the dots' directions of movement can be varied from completely random (as in Figure 7.17a) to 100 percent correlated (as in Figure 7.17c). While the monkey was judging the direction in which the dots were moving, Newsome and his co-workers monitored the firing of an MT neuron stimulated by the moving-dot pattern. They found that, as the dots' correlation increased, two things happened: (1) the monkey judged the direction of movement

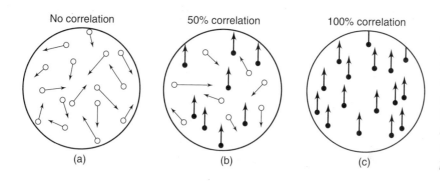

Figure 7.17

Moving-dot displays used by Newsome, Britten, and Movshon. These pictures represent moving-dot displays that were created by a computer. Each dot survives for a brief interval (20–30 microseconds), after which it disappears and is replaced by another randomly placed dot.

more accurately, *and* (2) the MT neurons fired more rapidly. In fact, the monkey's behavior and the firing of the MT neurons were so closely related that Newsome et al. could predict one from the other. For example, when the dots' correlation was 0.8 percent, the MT neuron response did not differ appreciably from the baseline firing rate on each trial, and the monkey judged the direction of movement with only chance accuracy. But at a correlation of 12.8 percent, the MT neurons always fired faster than their baseline rates, and the monkey judged the direction of movement correctly on virtually every trial.

This result and the results of the experiments we described in Chapter 3 support the idea that MT neurons are responsible for the perception of movement. However, perhaps the most significant thing about these results is that the connection between neural firing and the monkey's behavior was so close that it was possible to predict the monkey's ability to judge the direction of movement by monitoring the firing of only a few MT neurons. Since the firing of only a few neurons contains enough information to accurately signal the direction of movement, perhaps the code for movement perception follows specificity theory at this level of the visual system (Britten et al., 1993; Movshon & Newsome, 1992).

So far, the brain's detection of movement seems fairly straightforward: Movement detectors in the striate and extrastriate cortex that are sensitive to different directions of movement fire as the stimulus moves across the retina. However, movement detectors cannot explain (1) your perception of movement when there is *no* movement on the retina, as when you follow a moving object with your eyes so that your eye movements keep the object's image stationary on your fovea (Figure 7.18a), and (2) the absence of movement perception when there is movement on the retina, as when you move your eyes to look at different parts of a scene or as you walk through a scene. Though the image of the scene moves across your retina, you do not perceive the scene as moving (Figure 7.18b).

To deal with these two situations, we need a mechanism that can tell whether retinal stimulation results from movement of the stimulus, movement of the eyes, or both. We will now con-

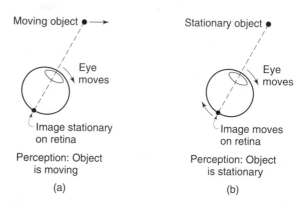

Figure 7.18

Two situations that are difficult to explain based on movement detectors. In (a), a person follows a moving object with her eyes. In (b), a person moves his eye but the object remains stationary.

sider a proposal called *corollary discharge theory* that provides a physiological mechanism that takes the observer's eye movements into account.

TAKING EYE MOVEMENTS INTO ACCOUNT

According to **corollary discharge theory**, information about the observer's eye movements is provided by signals generated when the observer moves, or tries to move, her eyes (Gyr, 1972; Teuber, 1960; von Holst, 1954). Let's consider how this theory works, by following what happens in the circuit shown in Figure 7.19 when an observer decides to move her eyes to the left.

When the observer decides to move her eyes to the left, a motor signal (M) travels from the motor area of the brain to the eye muscles to cause the eyes to move to the left. This eye move-

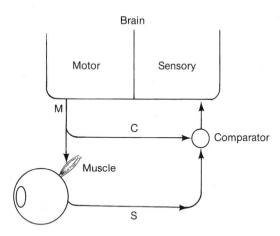

Figure 7.19

Diagram of the corollary discharge model. The brain is divided into two areas: the motor area, which sends motor signals to muscles, and the sensory area, which receives sensory signals from the sense organs. The exact location of the comparator is not specified. (From Teuber, 1960.)

ment causes the image of whatever is in the observer's view to move across the retina, and this movement of the image across the retina results in a **sensory movement signal** (S) in the optic nerve.

If the sensory movement signal reaches the cortex, it will cause the observer to perceive movement. But in this example, the scene isn't moving. Only the eyes have moved. It is here that the corollary discharge comes into play. The **corollary discharge** (C) is a copy of the motor signal that is transmitted to the **comparator**—a hypothetical structure that receives both the corollary discharge and the sensory movement signal— and informs it that the eye has received a signal to move left. When the corollary discharge reaches the comparator, it cancels the sensory movement signal and prevents it from reaching the cortex, so we see no movement in the scene.

According to this model, we will see movement when (1) just the sensory movement signal is sent to the comparator or (2) just the corollary discharge is sent to the comparator, but if both reach the comparator together, they cancel each other, and we see no movement. This model has been tested by determining whether movement perception does, in fact, occur when only the corollary discharge reaches the comparator. This has been accomplished in the following four ways, three of which you can experience for yourself:

1. By observing an afterimage as you move your eyes in a dark room (Figure 7.20a).

DEMONSTRATION

Using an Afterimage to Eliminate the Sensory Movement Signal

Illuminate the circle in Figure 6.34 with your desk lamp and look at it for about 60 seconds. Then, go into your closet (or a

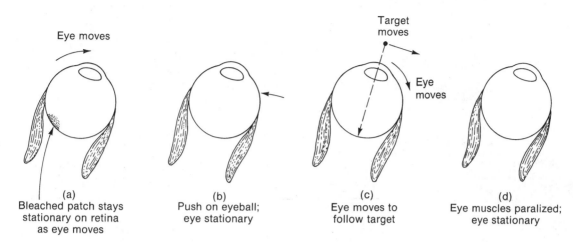

Figure 7.20

Voluntary movement of our eyes usually generates both a corollary discharge (because we send a signal to our eye muscles) and a sensory movement signal (because movement of the eyes usually causes movement of an image across the retina). There are, however, ways to create a corollary discharge without generating a sensory movement signal. In all four examples shown in the figure, a signal is sent to the eye muscles, and a corollary discharge is generated. No sensory movement signal is generated, because (a) staring at a spot for about 30 seconds bleaches a patch of retina, generating an afterimage, and the bleached spot stays at the same place on the retina as the eye moves; (b) when we push on the eyeball, we can send signals to the muscles to hold the eye steady; (c) the eye moves to track a moving object, so the object's image remains stationary on the retina; and (d) the eye is paralyzed so that the signal sent to the muscle cannot cause the eye to move.

completely dark room) and observe what happens to the circle's afterimage (blink to make it come back if it fades) as you look around. Notice that the afterimage moves in synchrony with your eye movements. ●

Why does the afterimage appear to move when you move your eyes? The answer cannot be that an image is moving across your retina, because the circle's image always remains at the same place on the retina. Without movement of the stimulus across the retina, there is no sensory movement signal. However, a corollary discharge is generated by the signals sent from your brain to your eye muscles, and since the corollary discharge is not canceled by a sensory movement signal, you see the afterimage move as your eyes move.

2. By pushing on your eyeball while keeping your eye steady (Figure 7.20b).

DEMONSTRATION
Pushing on Your Eyeball

While looking steadily at one point, *gently* push back and forth on the side of your eyelid, as shown in Figure 7.21. As you do this you will see the scene move. ●

Why do you see movement when you push on your eyeball? According to Lawrence Stark and Bruce Bridgeman (1983), when you push on

Perceiving Movement

Figure 7.21

Why is this man smiling? Because every time he pushes on his eyeball he sees the world jiggle.

your eyeball while keeping your eye fixated on a particular point, your eyes remain stationary because your eye muscles are pushing against the force of the finger so you can maintain steady fixation on the point. The signal sent to the eye muscles to hold the eye in place creates a corollary discharge, and since there is no sensory movement signal to cancel it, we see movement (also see Bridgeman & Stark, 1991; Ilg, Bridgeman, & Hoffmann, 1989).

3. By following a moving object with your eyes (Figure 7.20c).

Let's now consider how corollary discharge theory explains the perception of movement in the more normal situation in which an observer follows a moving car with her eyes as it drives past. Since the eyes move to follow the car, the car's image remains stationary on the observer's retinas and no sensory movement signal occurs. But since the eyes are moving, a corollary discharge reaches the comparator. This signal is not canceled by a sensory movement signal, so the observer perceives the car to be moving. As to the rest of the scene, its image sweeps across the observer's retinas as she follows the car with her eyes. This moving image generates a sensory movement signal, which is canceled by the corollary discharge generated by the observer's eye movements, so she perceives the rest of the scene as stationary.

4. By paralyzing an observer's eye muscles and having the observer try to move his eyes.

In this situation, when the observer tries to move his eyes, the motor signal sent to the eye muscles results in a corollary discharge, but since the paralyzed eye remains stationary, there is no sensory movement signal. In such an experiment, John Stevens (Stevens et al., 1976) was temporarily immobilized by a paralytic drug injected into his circulation. When Stevens tried to move his eyes, the scene in front of him appeared to jump to a new position, just as predicted by the corollary discharge model. (Also see Matin et al., 1982, for another paralysis experiment.)

Corollary discharge theory explains many of the facts of movement perception and has also been supported by some physiological evidence. Cells have been found in the monkey's superior colliculus (see Figure 2.5) that increase their firing rate when the eye is stationary and a bar is swept across the cell's receptive field (Figure 7.22a), but that decrease their firing rate when the eye moves so that the receptive field moves across a stationary bar (Figure 7.22b) (Robinson & Wurtz, 1976). Note that, in both cases, the bar traverses the receptive field, but that, when the eye is stationary, the cell fires, and when the eye is moving, the cell does not fire.

This result can be explained by corollary discharge theory as follows: When the eye is stationary, the bar moves across the cell's receptive field, and since the resulting movement signal is not canceled by a corollary discharge, the cell fires. However, when the eye moves, the sensory

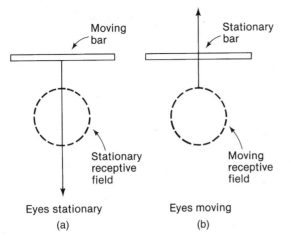

Moving bar

Stationary bar

Stationary receptive field

Moving receptive field

Eyes stationary
(a)

Eyes moving
(b)

Figure 7.22

The two conditions in the experiment in which Robinson and Wurtz (1976) recorded from single cells in the monkey's superior colliculus. In the first condition (a), the monkey's eyes remained stationary and a bar was moved across the cell's receptive field. In the second condition (b), the bar remained stationary and the monkey moved its eyes so that the cell's receptive field moved across the bar.

movement signal generated when the bar sweeps across the receptive field is canceled by the corollary discharge generated by the eye movement, and the cell doesn't fire.

In more recent research, Jean René Duhamel, Carol Colby, and Michael Goldberg (1992) found neurons in the monkey's parietal cortex that fire just before the monkey makes an eye movement. Perhaps neurons such as these provide the information about eye movements required by the corollary discharge theory.

Corollary discharge theory describes a possible physiological mechanism to explain how the visual system might take eye movements into account to determine whether an object that creates an image on the retina is stationary or moving. At the end of the chapter, we will describe a nonphysiological solution to this problem proposed by J. J. Gibson, whose ecological approach

to perception we introduced in Chapter 6. For now, however, we are going to consider some further complications of movement perception that occur when the eyes are stationary.

THE APERTURE PROBLEM

Let's return to the situation where a stationary eye views a stimulus, as in Figure 7.22a, in which bar A moves across the receptive field of neuron B, which fires to the bar's direction of movement. If no eye movements occur, this seems like a fairly straightforward situation, in which the direction of movement would be indicated by the firing of the movement detector. As it turns out, however, the situation is not quite as straightforward as it first seems, because the moving bar provides ambiguous information about the direction of movement.

The Ambiguity of Movement behind an Aperture

The best way to understand the idea that the moving bar provides ambiguous information about the direction of movement is to notice how the bar appears to move behind an aperture, as in the following demonstration.

D E M O N S T R A T I O N

Movement of a Bar across an Aperture

Make a small circle about 1-inch in diameter with the fingers of your left hand, as shown in Figure 7.23, and with the index finger of your right hand oriented straight up and down, move it horizontally, from right to left, behind the circle, as in Figure 7.23a. As you do this, focus your attention on your finger and

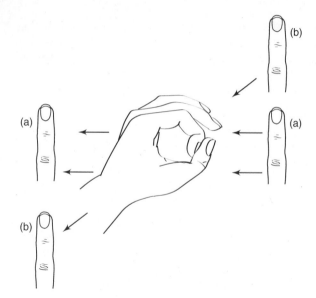

Figure 7.23

Moving a finger behind an aperture. See text for instructions.

notice that it appears to move from right to left behind the aperture—just as you would expect, since your finger is, in fact, moving from right to left. Now, again holding your right index finger straight up and down, move it behind the circle starting in the upper right and moving toward the lower left, as in Figure 7.23b. As you do this, focus on the direction your finger appears to be moving *inside the aperture*. Notice that the direction of movement, *as seen through the aperture,* appears the same as it did when you moved your finger horizontally. In both cases, your finger appears to be moving perpendicular to the direction in which it is oriented. ●

Our demonstration shows that the direction of movement of a single contour (your finger, in this example) viewed through an aperture is ambiguous. This effect is also illustrated in Figure 7.24 for the edge of a square moving behind a circular aperture.

This ambiguity of the direction of motion is called the **aperture problem,** and if we now

imagine that the aperture represents a neural movement detector, we can appreciate that a single detector cannot tell us in what direction movement is occurring.

Determining the Direction of Movement from Ambiguous Information

The fact that the movement of a single contour across a detector is ambiguous creates an interesting paradox when we consider shapes that have more than one contour. Consider, for example, the square in Figure 7.25, which is moving upward and to the right. Side A, which is viewed through aperture a, appears to be moving to the right, and side B, which is viewed through aperture b, appears to be moving upward. Edward Adelson and Anthony Movshon (1982) showed that information from both of these apertures can be combined to determine the true direction of movement of the square.

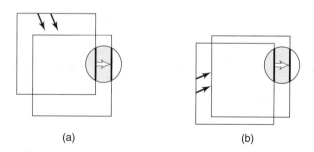

(a)   (b)

Figure 7.24

Moving a square behind a circular aperture creates an ambiguous perception of movement. In (a), a square moves down and to the right as indicated by the pair of solid arrows. The part of the square visible through the aperture, indicated by the shading, appears to move horizontally to the right, across the aperture, as indicated by the single arrow. (The rest of the square is actually hidden from view.) In (b), a square moves up and to the right. In this case, the side of the square again appears to be moving horizontally to the right across the aperture.

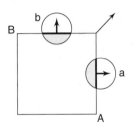

Figure 7.25

This square is moving up and to the right, but side A, viewed through aperture a, appears to be moving to the right, and side B, viewed through aperture b, appears to be moving up. (Based on Movshon et al., 1985.)

Adelson and Movshon's solution is based on the fact that a person's perception of a contour's movement across an aperture can be caused by a family of possible movements of the contour. This family can be determined as shown in Figure 7.26a. The possible movements of side A that could result in the movement observed across the aperture in Figure 7.25 are indicated by the arrows that extend to what Adelson and Movshon called the *constraint line*—a line that is oriented perpendicular to the direction in which the contour is moving across the aperture. The arrows indicate that the movement across the aperture could be caused by movement of the contour directly to the right, indicated by the solid arrow, or by other directions of movement, indicated by

the dashed arrows. The lengths of these arrows indicate the velocity of movement that would be necessary to create the movement corresponding to the solid arrow. Thus, if the square is actually moving upward at an angle, it has to be moving faster than if it were moving straight across to the right, if both movements are to be perceived as the same movement across the aperture.

To determine the actual direction of movement of the square, all we need to do is determine where the constraint lines of the two sides of the square will intersect (Figure 7.26b). This intersection, which is the only direction and velocity of movement that both sides have in common, indicates that, although side A moved horizontally across the detector and side B moved vertically, the combined information from both of these sides indicates that the square is actually moving upward and to the right. (For a further discussion of how the visual system uses information from detectors to determine movement, see Shiffrar, 1994.)

To explain how the information from the two contours may be combined, Anthony Movshon and his co-workers (1985) proposed that some neurons detect the *components* of movement in a particular direction, and other neurons respond to the overall direction of movement created by a

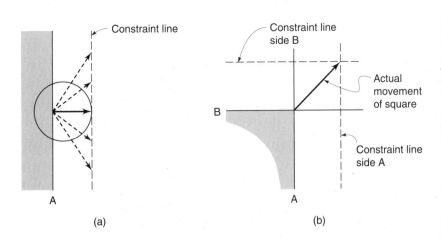

(a) (b)

Figure 7.26

(a) The constraint line for a moving contour is oriented perpendicular to the direction in which the contour appears to be moving across the aperture. The family of arrows drawn from one point on the contour to the constraint line indicates the family of movements that could create the movement that is perceived as being perpendicular to the constraint line. (b) The actual direction of movement of an object with two contours is indicated by the point where the constraint lines of two contours intersect. (Based on Movshon et al., 1985.)

Perceiving Movement

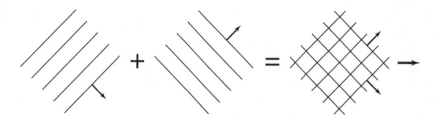

Figure 7.27
When two gratings that are moving in different directions are superimposed, the resulting plaid pattern appears to be moving as a whole and in a direction different from the movement of each grating when seen alone.

number of components moving in different directions, as in the square in Figure 7.26.

Neural Responding to Components and Patterns of Movement

To show that there are some neurons that respond to components of movement and others that respond to the overall pattern of movement, Movshon and his co-workers (1985) used moving grating stimuli that could be superimposed to create a plaid pattern (Figure 7.27). When two gratings with similar contrast and velocities are superimposed and moved in different directions, subjects perceive **coherent motion**—motion of the entire plaid pattern in one direction (Figure 7.27). The direction in which the plaid pattern appears to be moving is determined by the intersection of the constraint lines for each grating, just as in the case of the square in Figure 7.26.

When Movshon and his co-workers presented single moving gratings and two superimposed gratings that look like a moving plaid to the receptive fields of neurons in areas V1 and MT of the cortex of cats and monkeys, they discovered the following two kinds of neurons:

1. **Component cells.** These cells respond to the direction of movement of single gratings. These neurons, which are found in both V1 and MT, respond to plaids by responding to the single gratings that make up the plaid.

2. **Pattern cells.** These cells, in area MT, respond to the overall direction of

movement of a plaid pattern rather than to the direction of the movement of the pattern's components.

Figure 7.28 indicates how a component cell and a pattern cell respond to different movements of a plaid pattern made up of two superimposed gratings. The component cell responds best to a contour moving horizontally to the right, and the pattern cell responds best when the

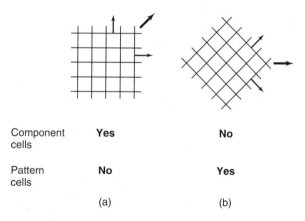

Component cells	**Yes**	**No**
Pattern cells	**No**	**Yes**
	(a)	(b)

Figure 7.28
How component cells and pattern cells respond to a plaid pattern that consists of two superimposed gratings. The component and pattern cells both respond to movement to the right, but the component cell responds to the movement of contours (small arrows) and the pattern cell responds to the movement of the overall pattern (large arrows). In (a), the component cell fires to the horizontal movement of one of the gratings, and the pattern cell does not fire. In (b), the component cell does not fire, but the pattern cell fires to the movement of the pattern to the right. (Adapted from Hildreth, 1990.)

pattern moves to the right. In (a), the individual gratings move vertically and horizontally and the overall pattern appears to move up at a 45-degree angle. In this case, the component cell fires to the grating that is moving horizontally, but the pattern cell does not fire. In (b), the individual gratings move either 45 degrees up or 45 degrees down, and the overall pattern appears to move horizontally to the right. Now, the pattern cell fires to the horizontal movement of the pattern, but the component cell does not fire. We can explain these results by assuming that a pattern cell receives inputs from a number of component cells. For example, the pattern cell in Figure 7.29, which responds best to downward movement, would receive inputs from component cells that respond to various directions of downward movement (Hildreth, 1990). The processing of movement appears, therefore, to occur in two or more stages, in which information about rela-

tively simple movement is processed early in the visual system and information about more complex stimuli and overall pattern movements is processed at higher levels of the visual system.

Continuing our discussion of complex movement, we will now describe a type of movement that is extremely common in our environment, **biological motion**—the motion produced by the movement of organisms. As we describe this type of movement, we will see that even though most of the data are psychophysical, we can still draw some physiological conclusions.

PERCEIVING BIOLOGICAL MOTION

So far, our discussion of motion perception has focused on stimuli such as moving dots, lines, gratings, or superimposed gratings. While research with these types of stimuli has greatly increased our understanding of the basic mechanisms of motion perception, these stimuli are much simpler than the stimuli we typically see in our environment. One very common kind of motion we see every day is biological motion. Biological motions created by humans walking, running, or standing up are complex, involving the movement of many components relative to one another. One way biological motion has been studied is to have people view "point-light walkers" created by outfitting a person with 10–12 small lights, as shown in Figure 7.30, and filming them as they move in the dark.

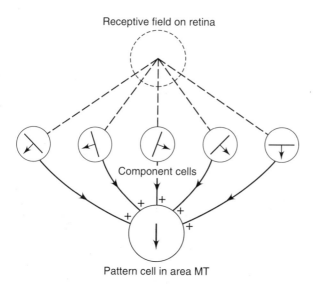

Receptive field on retina

Component cells

Pattern cell in area MT

Figure 7.29

A pattern cell that responds to the downward movement of a pattern may receive inputs from a number of component cells that respond to movement consistent with this downward movement. (Adapted from Hildreth, 1990.)

Perceiving People Walking

To create stimuli for his experiments, Gunnar Johansson (1975) filmed "point-light walkers" in a dark room where only the lights could be seen, and he created a film that begins with the person

Perceiving Movement

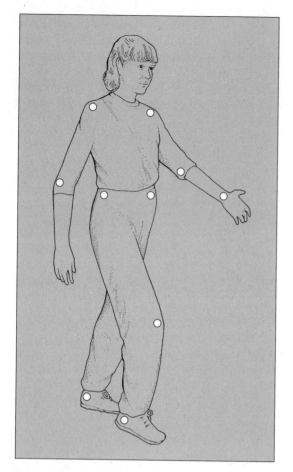

Figure 7.30

A person wearing lights for a biological motion experiment. In the actual experiment, the room is totally dark, and only the lights can be seen.

standing still and then shows her walking and engaging in various other movements. When the configuration of lights attached to the person is stationary, subjects report seeing a meaningless pattern of lights. However, as soon as the person gets up and starts walking, subjects are instantly able to identify the movement as being produced by a walking person. Thus, movement creates a structure (a person walking) out of what was initially perceived as a random arrangement of dots. This perception of structure is particularly impressive because the movement of an individual light is not seen as the movement of a person (Figure 7.31). Observers viewing the point-light walker displays do not perceive the individual bouncing movements of each light; instead, they perceive the entire configuration as a walking person.

Following Johansson's lead, Lynn Kozlowski and James Cutting (1977) found that observers could go beyond simply identifying the moving lights as walking people. Observers could label the moving lights as belonging to male or female walkers with 60–70 percent accuracy. And Sverker Runeson and Gunilla Frykholm (1981) found that observers could accurately estimate the amount of weight a person was lifting based on the movement of lights attached to the person.

These experiments show that the visual system sees more than moving "lights." It extracts information from patterns of movement that enables observers to perceive three-dimensional moving objects that become perceptions such as "I see a woman walking" or "I see a person lifting a heavy weight."

This research on point-light walkers has demonstrated the visual system's amazing ability to integrate information from individual elements into coherent forms. As we will see in the Developmental Dimension, "Infants' Perception of Movement," at the end of this chapter, this ability may depend partially on the knowledge a person gains by observing people walking. Other research has also demonstrated how knowledge affects movement perception. We will now describe research showing how knowledge affects our perception of apparent movement of the human body.

Apparent Movement of the Human Body

When simple stimuli such as two separated dots are alternated rapidly, the dots usually appear to move back and forth along the shortest possible

Figure 7.31

The path traced by one of the lights attached to the walking person's ankle. When viewing all of the lights moving together, the observer is unaware of these individual movements and perceives the entire configuration as a walking person.

path, even though a large number of paths are possible (Figure 7.32). This result led researchers to propose the **shortest-path constraint,** which states that apparent movement tends to occur along the shortest path between two stimuli.

Maggie Shiffrar and Jennifer Freyd (1990; 1993) decided to see whether the shortest-path constraint held when observers were shown meaningful stimuli that would normally violate the constraint. One of their stimuli, shown in Figure 7.33, was two pictures of the same person with her right hand in different positions. Shiffrar and Freyd asked the following question: When these pictures are rapidly alternated will observers perceive the woman's hand as moving through her left arm (apparent movement that

follows the shortest-path constraint) or around her arm (apparent movement that violates the shortest-path constraint).

The answer to this question depended on the length of time between the onset of the first and second pictures, called *stimulus onset asynchrony* (SOA). At SOAs below about 200 msec the subjects' perceptions followed the shortest-path constraint. However, at SOAs longer than 200 msec, the subjects perceived movement along the longer path around the woman's arm, which violated the shortest-path constraint. Interestingly enough, in Johansson's point-light walker studies, subjects got the impression of a walking person only if they saw the moving lights for at least 200 msecs. The visual system apparently needs some time to process information to perceive the movement of complex meaningful stimuli (although 200 msec may seem like a short period of time, it is a long processing time by the nervous system's standards). Shiffrar and Freyd concluded that the visual system needs some time to construct paths of apparent movement that are consistent with the movement limitations of the human body.

Although Shiffrar and Freyd's results were based on psychophysical experiments, they may reflect the visual system's separation into the temporal (or "what") pathway and the parietal (or "where") pathway that we described in Chapter 3. In order for subjects to perceive the

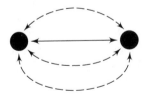

Figure 7.32

According to the shortest-path constraint, the apparent movement between the two rapidly alternating dots should occur along the shortest pathway (solid arrows) even though many other pathways are possible (dashed arrows).

Perceiving Movement

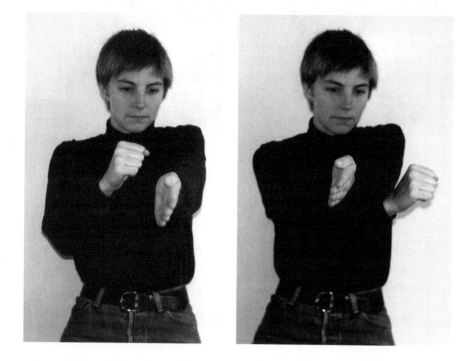

Figure 7.33
Photographs used to create the stimulus in the Shiffrar and Freyd experiment. When these pictures are alternated rapidly, the hand making a fist appears to move from one position to the other. The hand appears to go through the arm at short SOAs and around the arm at long SOAs. (Photographs courtesy of Maggie Shiffrar.)

biologically valid movement of the person's hand around (rather than through) her arm, they need to perceive both *what* the stimulus is and *where* it is located. This need to combine both what and where information, plus the long times involved, led Shiffrar (1994) to suggest that the perception of biological movement observed in her experiments occurs somewhere in the nervous system where information from the temporal and parietal streams meets. A possible candidate is a part of the cortex called the *superior temporal sulcus* (STS), which receives inputs from both visual streams and also contains neurons that respond to images of human bodies moving in a specific direction (Perrett et al., 1990) (Figure 7.34).

The results of Shiffrar's psychophysical experiments lend themselves to a physiological interpretation. In the next section, we will consider a problem that is central to understanding motion perception, but for which we

have so far been unable to propose physiological mechanisms.

THE CORRESPONDENCE PROBLEM

Consider the following problem that the brain faces in creating apparent motion. One example of apparent motion—film—presents a series of pictures that differ slightly from one another, and we perceive movement (Figure 7.5). But for this to occur, the brain must match equivalent parts in each picture. To understand how this works, look at the two images of the person in Figure 7.35. These images represent two successive views of a man walking that might be projected on a movie screen. In the initial image, the man's hand is at

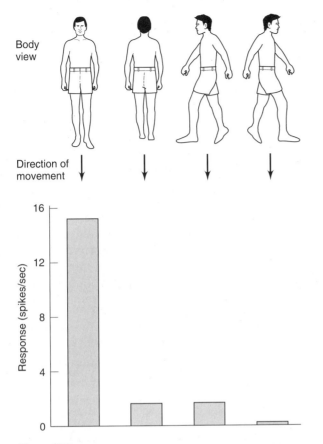

Body view

Direction of movement

Figure 7.34

The response of a neuron in the macaque monkey's superior temporal sulcus that responded best to a frontal view of a person moving downward. Other views of the body generated little response even though they were moving in the same direction. (Adapted from Perrett et al., 1990.)

parts of the man as the movement proceeds from frame 1 to frame 2.

The need to match elements of an apparent movement stimulus in one frame with similar elements in succeeding frames is called the **correspondence problem.** (You may remember that we faced a similar problem when considering depth perception in Chapter 6. In that case, the visual system needed to match similar areas of two images in each eye in order to determine their angle of disparity.) How does the visual system solve the correspondence problem for the perception of apparent motion? One idea is that the brain compares all the points in a scene.

Correspondence by Point-by-Point Comparison

Solving the correspondence problem by comparing all the points in a scene works in simple situations, such as one dot moving to another position (Figure 7.36a), but the solution starts to become more complex if we add more dots, as in Figure 7.36b. Things really become complex if we use a stimulus called a *random-dot kinematogram.*

The **random-dot kinematogram** is based on the random-dot stereogram, a stimulus we described in Chapter 6. The random-dot stereogram in Figure 6.22 was constructed by starting with two identical displays of random dots, and then by

position A, and in the next image, the man's hand is at position B and the man's knee is at position C. Although it is conceivable that the man's hand could appear to move to position C rather than position B, this does not happen. The hand in frame 1 moves to B, the position of the hand in frame 2, and the knee moves from its position in frame 1 to its new position in frame 2. The visual system correctly matches the equivalent

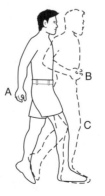

Figure 7.35

Images of a man from two film frames. The visual system matches similar elements in the two frames so that the hand at A in frame 1 moves to the hand's new position at B in frame 2 and not somewhere else.

Perceiving Movement

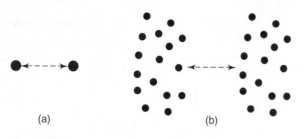

(a) (b)

Figure 7.36

(a) Creating apparent motion from a single dot moving back and forth does not pose a complex correspondence problem for the visual system to solve. However, adding dots, as in (b), poses a more complex problem for the visual system because of the added complexity of the stimulus.

shifting a square area in the middle of the right display slightly to the right. When one display is presented to the left eye and one to the right, the shifted area in the center creates binocular disparity and the viewer sees a small square in depth.

When the left component of a stereogram is presented briefly to one eye and, after a short delay, the right component is presented briefly to the same eye, the stereogram becomes a random-dot kinematogram. When the time between presentations is short, observers see a small square in the middle of the display that appears to move from left to right (Figure 7.37).

Why do we perceive this moving square? After all, when we look at the left and right halves of the kinematogram, all we see are random dots (see Figure 6.22). Neither random-dot pattern, when considered alone, contains a small square. The small moving square exists only when the two patterns are presented one after the

other. Thus, we are not flashing a square in two different positions. We are flashing two arrays of random dots: Most of the dots are in the same positions in the two arrays, but the dots in an area in the center are shifted slightly to the right in one array relative to the other.

The visual system creates movement by somehow matching the shifted dots in the two patterns. Does it achieve this match by comparing every point in each pattern? Since such a complex undertaking would involve a huge number of comparisons, most researchers have rejected the idea that the brain solves the correspondence problem by comparing all of the points in a scene. But if point-by-point comparisons aren't the answer, what is? Vilayanur Ramachandran and Stuart Anstis (1986) proposed that the human brain uses *movement heuristics*—"rules of thumb" about how movement occurs in the world.

Correspondence by Applying Heuristics

Ramachandran and Anstis's heuristics are based on the fact that objects move in characteristic and predictable ways in the real world. When a person's arm moves, the person's hand usually moves, too; when a football is thrown through the air in a spiral, the whole football spirals, not just parts of it. Ramachandran and Anstis proposed a number of heuristics that take regularities such as these into account. By using these heuristics, the visual system limits matches between frames to those that would lead to motion in the real world. Let's consider a few examples of these heuristics.

Inertia The **inertia heuristic** states that objects in motion tend to continue along the same path. Rapidly presenting the two crosses in Figure 7.38a one after the other creates an ambiguous stimulus, so that the cross rotates either clockwise or counterclockwise. If, however, an initial cross is added to the series, as in Figure 7.38b, the inertia heuristic causes the movement to be perceived as being clockwise—once movement

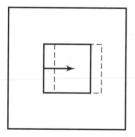

Figure 7.37

Flashing the two stimuli of the random-dot kinematogram one after the other creates the perception of a moving square.

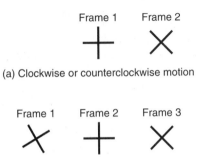

Frame 1   Frame 2

(a) Clockwise or counterclockwise motion

Frame 1   Frame 2   Frame 3

(b) Only clockwise motion

Figure 7.38
(a) Alternating an upright cross and a tilted one creates an ambiguous stimulus in which the rotation can be perceived as either clockwise or counterclockwise. (b) Adding the tilted cross on the left starts a clockwise movement, so that when the third cross is flashed, the movement follows the inertia heuristic and is perceived as continuing in that direction. Note that the two stimuli in (a) and the final two in (b) are identical.

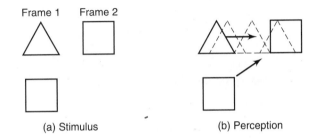

Frame 1   Frame 2

(a) Stimulus   (b) Perception

Figure 7.39
(a) The apparent motion stimulus: The triangle and the square on the left are flashed together, followed by the square on the right. (b) The resulting perception: The lower square moves up to the position of the upper square, and the triangle moves to the right and slides under the square.

starts in one direction, it continues in that direction (Ramachandran & Anstis, 1986). Notice that the inertia heuristic is similar to the Gestalt law of good continuation described in Chapter 5 for static stimuli.

Covering and Uncovering The **covering and uncovering heuristic** states that a moving object progressively covers and uncovers parts of the background. For example, if we flash the triangle and the square in frame 1 of Figure 7.39a, followed by the square in frame 2, the observer perceives a square moving diagonally from one position to another but perceives the triangle as moving to the right and moving behind the square (Figure 7.39b). The visual system solves the problem posed by the triangle by having the moving square cover it up.

Rigidity The **rigidity heuristic** states that parts of objects are rigid and are linked together, so that they move in synchrony. Thus, when a leopard jumps, we see the whole shape move, and we expect the leopard's spots to follow along. You

can demonstrate this principle with the aid of a paper clip and your TV set.

D E M O N S T R A T I O N

Visual Capture on Your TV Screen

Make a circular loop with a paper clip and, with your TV set turned to a channel where there is no station so you see "snow" on the screen, move the wire loop around in front of the screen. If you are moving the loop at the right speed (too fast doesn't work), the dots within the loop appear to move along with the loop. ●

The TV demonstration was originally proposed by Donald MacKay (1961) to illustrate an effect called *visual capture*, but it also demonstrates the rigidity heuristic, since the parts within the border follow along when the border moves.

If we were to follow in the tradition of the other motion phenomena we have discussed, we would now propose a physiological mechanism to explain the correspondence problem.

But at present we have no explanation. We have a psychophysically based result—the visual system determines features of objects and applies heuristics to create correspondence—that indicates some of the things that a physiological mechanism must explain. However, the neural mechanisms responsible for establishing the correspondence between the parts of a moving stimulus remain to be determined.

So far, our discussion has been concerned with answering the question: How do we perceive the movement of objects? But studying motion perception also involves another question: What does motion tell us about the world? We end this chapter by considering some answers to this question.

MOVEMENT AS A SOURCE OF INFORMATION

What information does movement provide about the world? At the beginning of the chapter, we discussed the importance of movement in attracting attention, providing information about an object's three-dimensional shape, helping us segregate figure from ground, and providing in-formation that helps us interact actively with the environment. We will now describe research that looks at some of these functions of movement perception in more detail. We will consider (1) how motion can create three-dimensional structure; (2) what the connection is between vision and balance; and (3) how the information from motion helps us move through the environment.

Creating Structure from Motion

We can understand why movement is important in determining our perception of an object's structure by returning to a point we made at the beginning of Chapter 5—that a given two-dimensional representation can be caused by many different three-dimensional objects. Thus, the rocks in Figure 5.3 appear to be arranged in a circle when viewed from a particular angle, even though they are not. An analogous situation is shown in Figure 7.40. In Figure 7.40a, we see what looks like two rectangles, one in front of the other. But moving to another position reveals the view in Figure 7.40b, and we see that the rectangle we thought was in front is actually in back, and that the rectangle we thought was in back isn't a rectangle at all. Thus, although what we see in Figure 7.40a looks reasonable, it is actually an ambiguous image that misleads us into the wrong conclusion about the shapes of the ob-

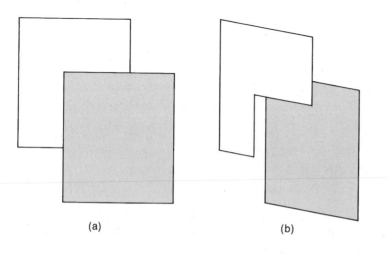

(a)   (b)

Figure 7.40

(a) At first this stimulus appears to be two rectangles, (b) but moving to another viewpoint reveals that the white shape is not a rectangle.

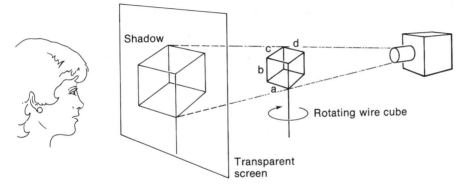

Figure 7.41
Setup similar to the one used by Wallach and O'Connell (1953) to demonstrate the kinetic depth effect.

jects in the display. By moving, we eliminate this ambiguity—an example of how movement can reveal the correct structure of a stimulus.

Another example of how movement can help us determine the structure of a stimulus is a phenomenon called the **kinetic depth effect,** in which the three-dimensional structure of a stimulus can be perceived from a moving two-dimensional image. Hans Wallach and D. N. O'Connell (1953) demonstrated this effect by casting a shadow of a cube on a transparent screen, as shown in Figure 7.41. When the shadow is stationary it looks flat, but when the cube is rotated, as indicated by the arrow, the shadow takes on a three-dimensional appearance, even though it is seen on a two-

dimensional surface. Movement, therefore, can create the perception of three-dimensional structure on a two-dimensional surface.

DEMONSTRATION

The Kinetic Depth Effect with Pipe Cleaners

You can demonstrate the kinetic depth effect to yourself by bending a pipe cleaner so that it reproduces sides a, b, c, and d of the shape in Figure 7.41. Then, cast a shadow of the pipe cleaner on a piece of paper, as shown in Figure 7.42, and

Figure 7.42
Shadow-casting by a bent pipe cleaner. To achieve a sharp shadow, position the pipe cleaner about 2 feet from your desk lamp. (If it is too close to the lamp, the shadow will be fuzzy.) To perceive the kinetic depth effect, rotate the pipe cleaner between your fingers while observing the shadow from the other side of the paper.

Perceiving Movement

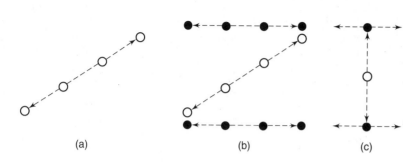

Figure 7.43

(a) The white dot moves back and forth on a diagonal path. (b) Two black dots are added and move horizontally to follow the white dot's movement. (c) The resulting perception: The black dots appear to be moving back and forth with the white dot bouncing up and down between them. Adding the black dots eliminates our perception of the white dot's diagonal motion.

(a) (b) (c)

while viewing the shadow from the other side of the paper, rotate the pipe cleaner. The result should be a more three-dimensional perception than when the shadow was stationary. ●

This creation of three-dimensional structure by means of motion is also demonstrated by the point-light walkers we described earlier. When the dots are stationary, they appear to be a geometric pattern of dots, but within 200 msec after movement begins, they are perceived as a three-dimensional walking human (also see Todd & Norman, 1991, for another example of how movement creates a three-dimensional perception in an array of dots).

Objects moving relative to one another can create a structure that doesn't exist for either object alone. For example, Figure 7.43a shows a sequence of views of a white dot moving back and forth along a diagonal path. A person's perception of this diagonal movement is changed, however, when two black dots move horizontally along with the white dot, as shown in Figure 7.43b. When the black dots are added, the white dot appears to bounce back and forth between the black dots, as the whole display moves back and forth (Figure 7.43c). As the Gestalt psychologists point out, sometimes the perception of an overall pattern is different from the sum of its parts. In this case, the presence of the black dots causes us to ignore the white dot's diagonal

movement and to restructure our perception so that we see it as moving relative to the black dots.

Figure 7.44 provides another example of an effect of relative movement. A light placed on the rim of a wheel is perceived as shown in Figure 7.44a when the wheel is rolled in a dark room. However, if we add a light to the center of the wheel, our perception changes so that we see the light on the rim as rotating around the central light (Duncker, 1929; Proffitt, Cutting, & Stier, 1979). The fact that a point on the rim of a wheel actually moves along two paths—one relative to

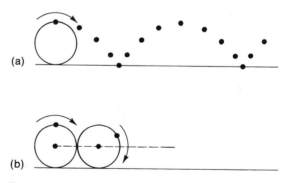

(a)

(b)

Figure 7.44

The dots in (a) show the path traced by a light on the rim of a rotating wheel. We perceive this path when the light on the rim is the only one present. However, when another light is added to the center of the wheel, the light on the rim appears to be rotating around the center light, as in (b).

the floor, as in Figure 7.44a, and another relative to the center of the wheel, as in Figure 7.44b—may not be obvious, but you can prove it to yourself by placing a dot on the edge of the bottom of a glass or a soft-drink container and rolling it along the floor. If you carefully observe the dot, you will notice that, after it hits the floor, it simultaneously moves forward relative to the floor and backward relative to the center of the container.

Vision and Balance

One of the most important functions of movement perception is its role in helping us to interact with our environment. David Lee and his co-workers (1983) had this function in mind when they said that "the visual and motor systems evolved together to support life's activities" (p. 333). Only recently, however, have researchers looked closely at the link between vision and our active interaction with the environment. We will begin our description of this research by considering the role of vision in a basic function—keeping our balance. J. J. Gibson (1966) suggested that vision is one of the proprioceptive senses—that is, one of the senses responsible for sensing the location, orientation, and movement of the body. This was seen as an unconventional suggestion when it was made because the senses usually identified as proprioceptive are the vestibular system of the inner ear, which is generally considered the major mechanism of balance, and the receptors in our muscles and joints, which help us sense the positions of our limbs. Gibson's assertion is, however, correct, as we can illustrate by a simple demonstration.

DEMONSTRATION
Keeping Your Balance

Keeping your balance is something you probably take for granted. Even when standing on one foot, most people can keep their balance with little effort. Try it. Then, as you are balancing on one foot, close your eyes. You may be surprised by how difficult balance becomes when you can't see. Vision provides a frame of reference that helps your muscles constantly make adjustments to help you maintain your balance. ●

The importance of vision in maintaining balance was demonstrated in another way by David Lee and Eric Aronson (1974). Lee and Aronson placed 13- to 16-month-old toddlers in the "swinging room" in Figure 7.45. In this room, the floor is stationary, but the walls and ceiling of the room can swing forward and backward. The idea behind the swinging room was to duplicate the visual stimulation that normally occurs as our bodies sway forward and backward. When we

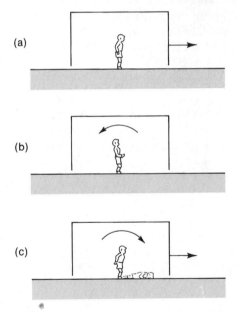

Figure 7.45
Lee and Aronson's swinging room. (a) Moving the room forward creates the same optic flow pattern (as in Figure 7.46b) that occurs when a person sways backward, as in (b). In compensating for this apparent sway, subjects sway forward, as in (c), and often lose their balance and fall down (Based on Lee & Aronson, 1974).

sway forward and backward, we create visual **optic flow patterns** as we see elements of the environment move relative to us. Swaying forward creates an expanding optic flow pattern (Figure 7.46a), and swaying backward creates a contracting optic flow pattern (Figure 7.46b).

These flow patterns provide information about our body sway, and without realizing it, we are constantly using this information to make corrections for this sway so we can stand upright. Lee and Aronson reasoned that, if they created a flow pattern that made people think they were leaning forward or backward, they could cause them to lean in the opposite direction to compensate. They accomplished this by moving the room either toward or away from the standing children, and the children responded as predicted. When the room moved toward them (creating the flow pattern for swaying forward), they leaned back, and when it moved away (creating the flow pattern for swaying backward), they leaned forward. In fact, many of the children did more than just lean: 26 percent swayed, 23 percent staggered, and 33 percent fell down!

Adults were also affected by the swinging room. If they braced themselves, "oscillating the experimental room through as little as 6 mm caused adult subjects to sway approximately in phase with this movement. The subjects were like

puppets visually hooked to their surroundings and were unaware of the real cause of their disturbance" (Lee, 1980, p. 173). Adults who didn't brace themselves could, like the infants, be knocked over by their perception of the moving room. Thus, vision is such a powerful determinant of balance that it can override the traditional sources of balance information provided by the inner ear and the receptors in the muscles and joints (also see Fox, 1990).

Moving through the Environment

As we move through the environment, we usually avoid bumping into things on our way to various destinations. Our ability to identify objects in the environment and to perceive their locations helps us, but according to J. J. Gibson, to understand how we reach destinations in our environment, we also need to consider the information that is created by our movement through the environment.

In the chapter on depth perception, we saw that Gibson identified information in the optic array—the patterns generated by surfaces in the environment—that we use to perceive depth and size. Gibson also identified information in the optic array that we use to perceive movement. We will consider here how Gibson would explain the following three situations in which movement occurs:

1. An observer is looking straight ahead as a person walks by (Figure 7.47). This is the case most easily handled by movement detectors, since the image of the walking person moves across the retina. However, Gibson was not interested in explaining perception based on information *within* the person, such as neural discharges or images on the retina. Instead, he focused his attention *outside* the person, on the information provided by the optic array. Gibson therefore explained movement perception by looking at the relationship

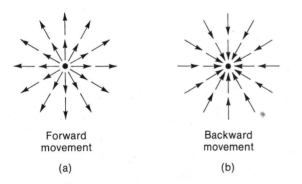

Forward
movement

(a)

Backward
movement

(b)

Figure 7.46

Flow patterns that occur (a) when we move forward and (b) when we move backward.

Figure 7.47

A person moving from left to right past a stationary observer who is looking at a spot straight ahead. In this situation, the person moves across the observer's field of view, as indicated by the arrows, but the background remains stationary.

Figure 7.48

A person moves from left to right, as in Figure 7.47, but the observer follows the person with her eyes. The image of the moving person remains stationary on the observer's retina, while the background flows across the retina from right to left, as indicated by the arrows.

between objects in the environment and their background. When we apply this approach to the situation in Figure 7.47, we find that information indicating that the person is moving is provided by the fact that the walking person covers and then uncovers part of the background as he walks by.

2. The observer moves her eyes to follow the person as he walks by (Figure 7.48). The image of the moving person remains stationary on the observer's retina, but the image of the background moves across the retina in the direction opposite to the direction of the person's movement. The observer perceives the walking person as moving even though his image does not move on her retina, because the walking person moves relative to the background. According to Gibson, in both this situation and the one above, the walking person's movement relative to the background provides the information we need to perceive that the person is moving.

3. The observer walks past the person, who is stationary (Figure 7.49). Both the stationary person and the background sweep across the observer's retina. In this case, the crucial information that the person and the background do not move relative to one another indicates that the observer is moving, and not the stationary person or the background.

Gibson's explanations work in an environment in which the background is visible, but they can't explain how we perceive movement when the background is not visible, as occurs when a spot of light is seen in a dark room or when an object is seen against a completely textureless background. However, Gibson maintained that it was not necessary to explain artificial situations such as isolated spots of light moving in dark perception laboratories. His main concern was with the kind of stimulation described above,

Perceiving Movement

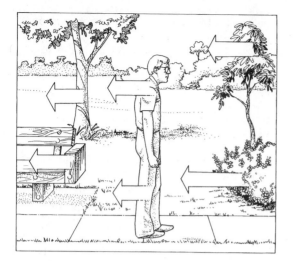

Figure 7.49

The observer moves from left to right past a stationary person, and the images of the stationary person and the background move together from right to left across the observer's field of view, as indicated by the arrows.

which is more typical of what we encounter in the environment.

Gibson's approach is important because it broadened the scope of perceptual analysis past simple stimuli, such as the dots and lines used in laboratories, to include more real-world stimuli.

Another of Gibson's contributions was his insight that we need to look to the whole environment to identify the information important for perception. This insight led him to identify the following sources of information that we use when we move through the environment.

The Optic Flow Pattern   Gibson proposed that a major source of information for the moving observer is the optic flow pattern. Optic flow is created by the movement of elements in the optic array that occurs as an observer moves through the environment. For example, when we are looking out the front window of a moving car, or when we are walking down the street, elements flow past us on all sides, as illustrated in Figure 7.50. The size of the arrows in this figure indicates the rate of flow. We can see that at greater distances the rate becomes less, until it reaches the **focus of expansion** (f.o.e.), the point in the distance where there is no movement. Gibson proposed that the f.o.e. always remains centered on the observer's destination and therefore provides invariant information indicating where the observer is heading. Thus, to reach a particular place, it is simply necessary to keep that place centered on the f.o.e. of the optic flow pattern.

Figure 7.50

The flow of the environment as seen from a car speeding across a bridge toward point A. The flow, shown by the arrows, is more rapid closer to the car (as indicated by the increased blur) but occurs everywhere except at A, the focus of expansion, toward which the car is moving.

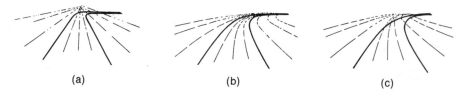

Figure 7.51

Optic flow lines for (a) movement along a straight stretch of road; (b) the correct negotiation of a curved stretch of road; and (c) the incorrect negotiation of a curved stretch of road. In (c) the car will go off the road unless a steering correction is made (Lee, 1980).

One problem with this idea, however, is that observers won't notice the f.o.e. if they aren't looking directly at where they are going. This appears to be true of automobile drivers, who tend to look at the center lines and the road's edge as they are driving (Schiff, 1980). To deal with this situation, David Lee (1974, 1980) proposes that drivers use optic flow information other than the focus of expansion to help them stay on course. Consider Figure 7.51a, which shows a straight stretch of road and a bend. If the driver is on course on the straight stretch, the optic flow line that passes from view directly below the driver, which Lee calls the **locomotor flow line,** is centered on the road. This line, which is generated by the movement of the road relative to the car, indicates the course that the car will follow if no changes are made in steering. In addition, when the driver is on course, the optic flow lines and the edges of the road coincide, as in Figure 7.51a for the straight stretch of road, and as in Figure 7.51b for the curved stretch. In Figure 7.51c, the optic flow lines and the road do not match, a situation to be avoided if you want to stay on the road.

Not only do optic flow lines provide information that drivers are likely to pay attention to, but they are also useful when drivers negotiate curved roads, where the f.o.e. would be useless since the "destination point" is constantly changing throughout a curve. (See Warren, Morris, & Kalish, 1988; Warren et al., 1991, for additional information on optic flow.)

Angular Expansion Information about flow in the optic array not only helps a driver stay on course but also informs the driver of the possibility of colliding with another vehicle. Consider what occurs if you are following another car. If you stay at the same distance from this car, its visual angle remains constant. If, however, you are gaining on the other car, its visual angle expands until, eventually (if you don't brake or change lanes to pass), you will collide with the other car. David Lee (1976) showed that the rate of **angular expansion** provides information that enables drivers to estimate when they will collide if they maintain the same speed and course.

The idea that the rate of angular expansion provides this information is supported by experiments in which an observer views a film of an object that is expanding as if it were on a collision course with the observer (Figure 7.52). The film is stopped before the "collision," and the observer is asked to estimate how long it would be before a collision occurred. Although observers tend to

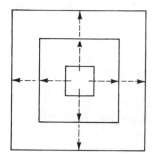

Figure 7.52

Three "snapshots" of a square as it moves directly toward an observer. The dashed arrows indicate that the square appears to be expanding outward as it moves closer.

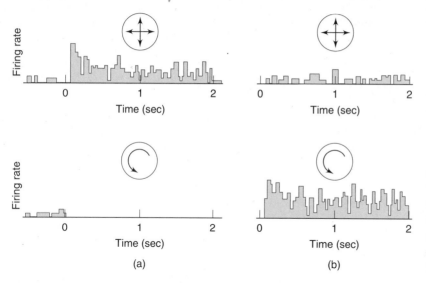

Figure 7.53

*(a) Response of a neuron in the monkey's **MST** that responds with a high rate of firing to an expanding stimulus (top record), but that hardly fires to a stimulus that moves with a spiral motion (bottom record) or with other types of motion (not shown). (b) Another neuron that responds best to spiral movement but does not respond well to an expanding pattern or other types of movement. (From Graziano, Andersen, & Snowden, 1994.)*

underestimate the time to collision, they are able to use the angular expansion information, as indicated by the finding that, when the time to collision was longer, observers' estimates were longer (McLeod & Ross, 1983; Schiff & Detwiler, 1979). It appears, therefore, that the rate of angular expansion provides information that can be used to avoid colliding with other objects in the environment.

As we saw in Chapter 6 and again here, the Gibsonian approach illustrates how we can explain perception in terms of the external stimulation available to the observer. Gibson's ideas were not widely appreciated when they were first proposed, but researchers have recently begun to appreciate his observations about the importance of movement and environmental stimuli (Blake, 1994; Nakayama, 1994). In addition to modern psychophysical research on the role of environmentally based stimulation in perception, physiological research has also begun to focus on more complex movement stimuli like those found in the environment.

An example of physiological research using these more complex stimuli is a study by Michael Graziano, Richard Andersen, and Robert Snowden (1994). They found neurons in an extrastriate

area called the *medial superior temporal area* (MST) that respond best to patterns of dots that are expanding outward, like the flow pattern in Figure 7.53a, and also neurons that respond best to circular motions and spiral motions (Figure 7.53b). Neurons such as these, which respond to complex movements, may provide the physiological mechanism that underlies our perception of environmental stimuli such as optic flow patterns (also see Duffy & Wurtz, 1991; Orban et al., 1992; Regan & Cynader, 1979).

It is fitting that we end this chapter with this example of the coming together of psychophysical and physiological research. As we have seen throughout the first seven chapters, progress in our understanding of perception depends on considering perception at both the psychophysical and the physiological levels. We have also seen that cognition plays a role in perception. In the chapters that follow, we will begin considering senses other than vision, beginning with three chapters on hearing. In these chapters, we will continue our practice of looking at perception from both the psychophysical and the physiological standpoint, as well as considering the role that cognition plays in determining our perceptions.

THE CAT'S PERCEPTION OF BIOLOGICAL MOTION

Researchers who have searched for answers to the questions "What do animals perceive?" and "What do infants perceive?" are faced with a difficult challenge: Their subjects can't describe what they are perceiving. Therefore, most perceptual research on nonverbal organisms is based on measuring their ability to *discriminate* between two stimuli. If an animal or an infant responds differently to two stimuli, by looking at one more than another or by picking one in preference to the other, we have learned something about their perception—we know that they can tell the difference between the two stimuli. But what does showing that an organism can discriminate between two stimuli tell us about what it is actually perceiving? We begin our consideration of this question by describing some research that investigates how cats respond to biological motion.

A cat observing another cat as it walks by would undoubtedly recognize it as a walking cat. But would it come to the same conclusion if it could see only the movement information provided by 10–12 lights attached to the body and limbs of the other cat? To answer this question, Randolph Blake (1993) created an animated "point-light walking cat," a stimulus based on a film of an actual cat outfitted with lights like the one shown in Figure 7.54. He presented this stimulus to cats to determine whether they could discriminate between sequences that corresponded to a cat's movements and "foil" movement sequences that did not correspond to a cat's movements.

Blake used a number of different types of foil sequences, including the following: (1) stationary—the dots remained stationary; (2) random movement—the dots moved randomly; (3) Brownian motion—the dots moved in random directions, as they did in "random movement," but the distances the dots moved matched the point-light walker's distances; (4) positionally scrambled movement—the dots were scrambled, so their starting positions were different from those of the walking cat, but they underwent the same movements as the walking cat; and (5) phase scrambled movement—the dots were in the same positions as on the walking cat and underwent the same motions, but the motions of the dots occurred at different times, relative to one another, from the motions of the walking cat.

Cats were trained to pick the biological motion sequence by pressing their noses against a key corresponding to the monitor on which the biological movement was displayed. By rewarding correct choices with a small amount of food, Blake was able to quickly train cats to respond to the biological motion when it was paired with a stationary foil. Once the cats could make this easy discrimination, Blake successfully trained them to make the more difficult discriminations

Figure 7.54

The point-light walking cat used by Blake (1993) was created from films of cats outfitted with small lights. The resulting stimuli were lights moving against a dark background.

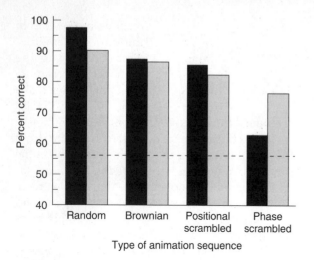

Figure 7.55

Percentage of trials on which two cats discriminated biological movement from other types of movement (see text). Performance above the horizontal line (56 percent) indicates better-than-chance discrimination. (From Blake, 1993.)

between the biological motion stimulus and the other moving foils (Figure 7.55).

Blake concluded from these results that cats can perceive biological motion. But is this conclusion justified? After all, couldn't the cats simply have learned to identify the particular biological motion sequence, which was repeated on every trial? Blake answers this objection by noting the following findings:

1. The cats quickly picked the biological motion sequence when the direction of movement was reversed to right to left, the direction opposite the direction originally shown.

2. One cat could discriminate a different biological motion sequence, a running-

point-light cat, that looks different from the foils.

3. The cats were not able to tell the difference between the foils and biological motion when the displays were presented upside down. Thus, there was something special about right-side-up biological motion that enabled the cats to discriminate it from the foils.

4. The cats were not able to tell the difference between the foils and a stimulus created by increasing the speed of the walking cat to three times its normal speed. This speeded-up movement, which looks different from that of a running cat, does not actually happen in the environment, and therefore appears unnatural.

All of these results taken together support the idea that there is something special about biological motion that enables cats to distinguish it from other types of point-light motion. Blake interprets his results as providing some insight into the possible mechanism of biological motion perception in humans. He suggests that cats' ability to perceive biological motion means that humans' perception of biological motion may not depend on higher-level cognitive processes that cats are incapable of.

But can we conclude, based on the data, that cats perceive the point-light-walker displays in the same way humans do? Even if cats do see biological motion as "special," we still don't know what they are actually perceiving. If cats perceive biological motion in the same way that humans perceive it, they are perceiving the point-light displays as representing three-dimensional walking cats. However, as we pointed out earlier, all we can conclude from discrimination experiments is that an organism can *discriminate* between two stimuli. We have no way of knowing exactly how the cats perceive the point-light walker or on what basis they discriminate the point-light stimulus from the foils. Thus, while it appears that cats are capable of grouping the complex pattern of moving dots created by point-light walkers into a perceptual "whole," we still don't know exactly what they are perceiving and whether their perception corresponds to a humans' perception. We will consider this problem further when we discuss how human infants perceive biological motion in the Developmental Dimension that follows.

INFANTS' PERCEPTION OF MOVEMENT

Human infants come into the world specially adapted to perceive motion, and this ability is apparent shortly after birth (Nelson & Horowitz, 1987). Thus, one of the best ways to attract a young infant's attention is to move something across his or her visual field. Newborns move their eyes toward moving stimuli and follow them with a combination of head and eye movements (Haith, 1983; Kremenitzer et al., 1979). If presented with a choice between a moving stimulus and a complex three-dimensional form, the infant prefers the moving stimulus (Fantz & Nevis, 1967), and if presented with two stimuli that are identical in all respects, except that one is moving and the other is stationary, infants as young as 2 weeks old will look at the moving stimulus (Nelson & Horowitz, 1987).

It isn't surprising that infants begin perceiving movement at an early age. After all, movement is everywhere in an infant's environment, and it provides the infant with rich information about various characteristics of its world. But although infants perceive movement at an early age, this doesn't mean that they perceive movement in the same way as adults. For example, although infants can follow moving objects with their eyes, their eyes move in a series of short, jerky movements, called *saccades*, up to about 6–8 weeks of age. It isn't until about 10–12 weeks that infants can make smooth eye movements to follow a moving stimulus (Aslin, 1981).

As infants get older, they become able to use movement to gain information about properties of their environment. For example, when you look at a scene like the one in Figure 7.56, you probably perceive a person who is partially hidden by a fence. But does a young infant perceive the "parts" of the person as separate objects or as belonging to a single object? Philip Kellman and Elizabeth Spelke (1983) used a habituation procedure to show that movement helps infants perceive objects as continuing behind an occluding object. They habituated 4-month-old infants to a rod moving back and forth behind a block (Figure 7.57a). After presenting the display until the infants' looking time had decreased to a low level, they presented the test stimuli shown in Figures 7.57b and 7.57c.

Figure 7.56

An occluded person. Do young infants perceive this person as a single "unit" or as separated parts?

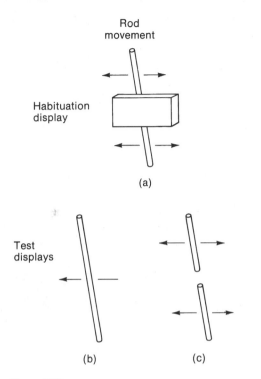

Rod
movement

Habituation
display

(a)

Test
displays

(b)

(c)

Figure 7.57
*Stimuli for the Kellman and Spelke (1983) experiment
described in the text.*

If the infant had perceived the display in Figure 7.57a as a long rod moving behind the block, we would expect him or her to look longer at the two rods in Figure 7.57c. (Remember that the basis of the habituation procedure is that infants usually look longer at a *novel* stimulus than at a familiar one. Thus, if the infant saw the rod as continuing behind the block, the two short rods would be the novel stimulus.) This is, in fact, what happened, and Kellman and Spelke therefore concluded that 4-month-old infants perceive the partly occluded rod as continuing behind the block. This result does not, however, occur if the rod is stationary. Thus, movement provides information that can be used by a 4-month-old infant to indicate that one object extends behind another.

Four-month-old infants can also distinguish the biological motion created by a walking person. We have seen that people can easily identify as a person the patterns of movement created by 12 lights attached to a person walking in a dark room. Robert Fox and Cynthia McDaniel (1982) used the preferential looking technique to determine whether infants are also capable of recognizing this biological motion. One videotape of the lights attached to a running person was shown on one screen, and another videotape of randomly moving lights was shown on the other screen. When placed in front of the two screens, 2-month-old infants showed no preference, looking at both screens equally. But 4- and 6-month-old infants looked at the biological motion tape about 70 percent of the time. Thus, by age 4 months, infants can tell the difference between these two types of motion and prefer the biological motion.

This demonstration of infants' discrimination between biological motion and other types of motion brings up the question we considered in our description of cats' perception of biological motion. What does this result tell us about how infants actually *perceive* biological motion? Bennett Bertenthal and his co-workers have done a series of experiments that give us some insight into this question. Their goal was to determine what qualities of the biological motion stimulus help infants discriminate biological from nonbiological motion. In one experiment, Bertenthal, Dennis Proffitt, and Steven Kramer (1987) showed that 5-month-old infants could discriminate between a display of a normal point-light walker and a display in which the distances between the lights changed during the movement. Adults can also make this discrimination and can tell us that the normal display looks like a walking person and the other one looks like a person with elastic joints.

Does the fact that both infants and adults can discriminate between these two types of displays mean that they perceive the normal walker in the same way? The results of another experiment by Bertenthal and co-workers (1985) suggest that the answer to this question may be no. In this experiment, Bertenthal et al. tested infants to see if they were sensitive to a property of point-light walkers that is obvious to adults—as the walker moves, certain lights are occluded from view by movement of the limbs relative to other parts of the body. For example, notice in Figure 7.30 that the light on the walker's left knee is blocked from view by her right leg. As she walks, this light will become visible, then it will become occluded again, and so on.

The occlusion of some of the lights during the walker's movement is one of the properties that helps make moving point-light-walker stimuli appear three-dimensional to adults. They easily recognize displays with occlusion as a walking person, but they rarely perceive a walking person when they are shown displays in which occlusion has been eliminated so that all of the lights are always visible. When Bertenthal et al. presented occluded and nonoccluded displays to infants, they found that 8-month-old infants were able to discriminate the occluded from the nonoccluded displays, but 5-month-old infants were not.

The results of this occlusion experiment suggest that although 5-month-olds can *discriminate* between the biological motion of point-light walkers and other types of point-light movement, they may not *perceive* the biological motion as a three-dimensional walking person, as adults do. Before they can achieve this perception they need to become sensitive to occlusion, which occurs at about 8 months of age. Of course, we don't really know what 8-month-old infants perceive. All we can safely say is that their perception of point-light walkers is probably more adultlike than the 5-month-olds' perception. From this example, as well as our discussion of research on the cat's perception of biological motion, it is clear that determining what nonverbal organisms perceive is far more complex than determining the perceptions of adults, who can follow verbal instructions and can describe what they are perceiving.

REVIEW

The Information Provided by Movement

Outline

- Motion perception evolved early because of the close link between the perception of movement and survival.

Questions

1. What are four functions of movement perception? (289)

Studying Movement Perception

- We perceive movement in many cases in which the stimulus is far more complex than a spot of light moving across the retina.

- An early event in the study of movement perception was Exner's 1875 observation that discharging two spatially separated electrical sparks one after the other creates a perception of movement in the space between them.

- Research on movement perception has focused on determining conditions that affect movement perception and on uncovering mechanisms underlying movement perception in both simple and complex displays.

2. What is stroboscopic movement? Apparent movement? Induced movement? What kind of movement occurs in the movies? What is an illusion of movement? (289)

3. What was Wertheimer's discovery about apparent movement? How does apparent movement change as the ISI changes? (293)

4. How is the perception of an object's real movement affected by its surroundings? (294)

5. Do modern researchers assume that real and apparent movement have the same or different mechanisms? (294)

Movement Detectors

- There are neurons in areas V1 and V2 of the cortex that respond to particular directions of movement.

- Neurons are directionally selective because of the way they are connected to other neurons.

6. Describe Pasternak's experiment that showed that directionally selective neurons are responsible for a cat's ability to perceive the direction of movement. (295)

7. Describe Reichardt's neural circuit. Be sure you understand how inhibition operates to cause a neuron to respond to only one direction of movement. (295)

- A directional tuning curve indicates a neuron's firing rate as a function of stimulus orientation.

- The waterfall illusion occurs after a person stares for 30–60 seconds at movement that fills only part of the field of view.

- Recent research shows that there are directionally selective neurons in area MT of the extrastriate cortex.

8. Why can't we determine the direction in which a stimulus is moving from the firing of just one directionally selective neuron? How does the brain probably use information from these directionally selective neurons to determine the direction in which a stimulus is moving? (296)

9. What experiment showed that the waterfall illusion occurs only if a stimulus moves across the retina? (297)

10. Describe Barlow and Hill's evidence that motion detectors are involved in the waterfall illusion. (298)

11. What evidence did we present in Chapter 3 that linked area MT and movement perception? Describe Newsome et al.'s experiment. What is the most significant thing about their results? (298)

Taking Eye Movements into Account

- Movement detectors can't explain movement perception in cases where movement perception occurs without movement across the retina, or where no movement perception occurs even though there is movement across the retina. One mechanism that has been proposed to explain situations such as these is corollary discharge theory.

- Corollary discharge theory is a physiological theory based primarily on psychophysical evidence. However, neurons have been discovered that may be involved in a mechanism like the one proposed by the theory.

12. Describe the mechanism proposed by corollary discharge theory to provide information about an observer's eye movements. According to this theory, when do we perceive movement? (300)

13. Describe how corollary discharge theory explains movement perception under the following conditions: (1) observing an afterimage; (2) pushing on the eyeball; (3) following a moving stimulus with the eyes; and (4) paralyzing an observer's eye muscles. (300)

14. Describe the neuron in the monkey's superior colliculus that responds as corollary discharge theory predicts. (302)

The Aperture Problem

- The movement of a contour across a receptive field provides ambiguous information about the direction of the contour's movement. This ambiguity is called the aperture problem.

- Movshon and his co-workers found that some neurons detect the components of movement in a particular direction and that other neurons respond to the overall direction of movement created by a pattern made up of a number of components.

15. Be able to show why contours moving in a number of different directions can cause the same perception of movement when the contours are viewed through an aperture. Describe Adelson and Movshon's solution to the aperture problem. (303)

16. Under what conditions do observers perceive coherent motion when two moving gratings are superimposed? (306)

17. Describe how component cells and pattern cells respond to the movement of superimposed gratings. (306)

Perceiving Biological Motion

- Motion created by the movement of organisms is called biological motion. Biological motion stimuli have been created by placing small lights on people and having the people move in a dark room.

- Apparent movement stimuli have been created by alternating photographs of people whose arms are in different positions, so that movement is created between one position and the other.

18. What do observers perceive when they see the movement of point-light walkers? What does this result mean? (307)

19. What is the shortest-path constraint? According to the results of Shiffrar and Freyd's experiment, when does movement perception follow and when does it violate the shortest-path constraint? What physiological mechanism did Shiffrar propose to explain the results of her experiments? (309)

The Correspondence Problem

- The visual system needs to match similar elements of two stroboscopic movement stimuli in order for movement perception to occur. This need to match similar stimuli is called the correspondence problem.

20. What is a random-dot kinematogram? Why does this stimulus pose particular problems for the visual system? (311)

21. What is a movement heuristic? What principle is Ramachandran and Anstis's heuristics based on? Describe three of their heuristics. (312)

Movement as a Source of Information

- Movement provides a number of kinds of information about the world, helping us to create structure from motion, keep our balance, and find our way through the environment.

- Movement perception plays an important role in helping us to interact with the environment.

- According to J. J. Gibson's ecological approach, movement perception can be explained by the relationships between objects in the environment and their background.

- Gibson also proposed that we perceive movement based on our perception of the flow pattern created by the movement of elements in the optic array that occurs as an observer moves through the environment.

22. How can movement help reveal the correct structure of a stimulus? What is the kinetic depth effect? What are some examples of how objects moving relative to one another create a structure that doesn't exist for either object alone. (314)

23. Explain the link between movement perception and balance, as demonstrated by the swinging-room experiments. (317)

24. Describe how Gibson would explain motion perception in the following situations: (1) A stimulus moves past a person looking straight ahead; (2) a stimulus moves by a person who is following the stimulus with his or her eyes; and (3) the person moves past a stationary stimulus. (318)

25. What is the optic flow pattern? The focus of expansion (f.o.e.)? How did Gibson propose we use the f.o.e. to tell us where we are heading? What is a problem with this explanation, and what other movement information may we use to determine the direction in which we are moving? What is angular expansion, and what does it tell us? Describe a physiological mechanism that may help us detect angular expansion. (320)

The Cat's Perception of Biological Motion

- Most perceptual research on nonverbal organisms measures their ability to discriminate between two stimuli.

26. Describe Blake's experiments on cats' perception of biological motion. If we find that a cat can discriminate biological motion, what can we say about exactly what the cat perceives? (323)

• Infants begin perceiving movement at an early age. However, it is likely that they do not perceive movement in the same way as adults.

27. What evidence indicates that infants perceive movement differently from adults? Describe Kellman and Spelke's experiment. Describe experiments on infants' perception of biological motion. What evidence indicates that 5-month-old infants can discriminate biological motion, but may not perceive it in the same way as adults? (326)

8

AUDITION I: AUDITORY PHYSIOLOGY

The Functions of Hearing

The Stimulus for Hearing

Structure and Functioning of the Auditory System

The Code for Frequency

The Physiology of Sound Localization

Comparing the Senses: Audition and Vision

Wherever you are sitting, look around and notice what your visual sense tells you about your environment. Whether you are at a desk, or in a library, or outside, looking around provides information about the sizes, shapes, colors, locations, and identities of objects and people who are within your field of vision. Now try the same thing for hearing. Close your eyes for a minute, listen carefully, and notice what your sense of hearing tells you about your environment.

My experience from carrying out these instructions was that, as I looked around my office, I saw my desk, a phone, some papers, a can of Pepsi, pictures on the wall, and my computer, stereo, and CD collection, among other things. However, when I closed my eyes and listened, my perceptual world changed drastically. Based on sound alone, I perceived a person in the street below my window, a dog nearby, and a car driving down the street in front of my house. My perceptions soared to great heights, as I detected an airplane flying overhead, and entered dark places, as I became aware that my stomach was digesting my lunch. I know these things because of what I heard—a person talking loudly, a dog

barking, the sound of a car's wheels rolling down the pavement, the faint drone of an airplane overhead, and a gurgling sound from my stomach. In informing us of events that are happening in our environment, many of which we would not be aware of if we had to rely on vision alone, hearing serves a number of very important functions (Figure 8.1).

THE FUNCTIONS OF HEARING

Our ability to hear events that we can't see serves an important signaling function for both animals and humans. An animal living in the forest is alert to the rustle of leaves or the snap of a twig, since these sounds may signal the approach of a predator. Or consider the many signaling functions that hearing serves for humans, among them the warning sound of a smoke alarm or an ambulance siren, the particularly

Figure 8.1
The auditory world of the people sitting on the bench includes a large number of stimuli that are hidden from the visual system but that can be sensed through hearing.

high-pitched cry of babies who are distressed, or tell-tale noises that signal problems in a car engine that is not running smoothly.

But hearing also has functions in addition to signaling. On the first day of my sensation and perception class, I ask my students which sense they would choose to keep if they had to pick between hearing and vision. There are arguments in favor of both senses, but two of the strongest arguments for keeping hearing instead of vision are music and speech. Many of my students hesitate to consider giving up hearing because of the pleasure they derive from listening to music. But speech is also extremely important because it creates communication between people.

Helen Keller, who was both deaf and blind, stated that she felt being deaf was worse than being blind, because blindness cuts you off from things, but deafness cuts you off from other people. It not only creates an isolation that keeps people from forming relationships with others but also sometimes makes it difficult even to know what is going on. A poignant example of deaf people's difficulty in determining what is going on is provided by the following description, by a deaf person, of what it was like to watch TV before closed captioning became available:

> When I was little, before captioning came in, we used to watch TV as a family. It was great. We would compare notes on what we saw and propose our own versions of the plot. Later if we saw other Deaf friends who had seen the same show, we would all discuss what we thought had happened. We would construct personalities and events from our guesswork and imaginations; it was practice for the guesswork and humor we needed to interpret the world. We laughed so much, and it brought us so close together. (Solomon, 1994, p. 45)

This quote captures both how difficult it can be to determine what is happening without hearing and also the fact that deaf people have created a culture that helps many deal with their isolation from the hearing world (Cohen, 1994; Solomon, 1994). This isolation is perhaps most keenly felt by people who have experienced hearing and have then lost it. Hannah Merker (1994), who lost her hearing over a period of time following a skiing accident, described her realization that her hearing was slowly slipping away, as follows:

> I noticed the world was getting quieter . . . a silence, a soundlessness was softening the edges of my sometimes strident life. The noticing did not appear in a single startling revelation. No, it was with a slow astonishing surprise that I sensed the increasing hush around me, with no glimmer yet of the stunning reality: only *my* world was growing quieter. I was becoming deaf.

Given the difficulties experienced by deaf people and the many functions that hearing serves for those able to hear, it makes sense that a way to detect the stimuli for hearing—pressure changes in the air (or water, for species that live there)—would have evolved in humans and most other species of animals. The goal of this chapter is to describe how pressure changes in the air result in electrical signals in the ear and, then, how these electrical signals are transmitted to higher auditory centers and are eventually transformed into experiences such as the perception of pitch and the location of sounds. We will first describe the nature of the pressure changes that we call sound. We then describe the anatomy

of the auditory system and how the structures in this system respond to various properties of the sound stimulus. Our primary goal will be to understand the physiological mechanisms for pitch perception and for our ability to localize sounds in space (Figure 8.2). In the next chapter, we will consider these two qualities from a psychophysical point of view and will describe the psychophysics and physiology of loudness perception.

THE STIMULUS FOR HEARING

Our perception of sound depends on the vibrations of objects. We don't, however, perceive an object's vibrations directly. We hear the object's effect on the air, water, or any elastic medium that surrounds it. To understand how this works, consider your radio or stereo system's loudspeaker, which is really a device for producing vibrations to be transmitted to the surrounding air. People have been known to turn their stereos up loud enough so that these vibrations can be felt through a neighbor's wall, but even at softer levels, these vibrations are there. (Turn on your

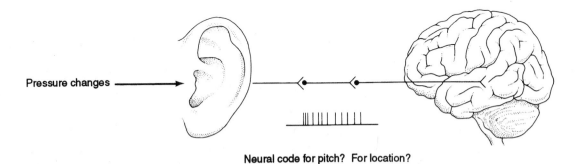

Neural code for pitch? For location?

Figure 8.2
Pressure changes entering the ear are transduced into electrical signals that are eventually transformed into our perceptions of various auditory qualities. Our major concern in this chapter is identifying the codes for pitch and location.

Audition I: Auditory Physiology

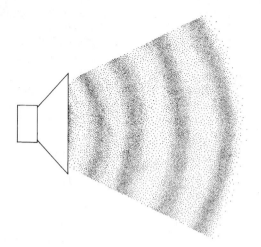

Figure 8.3

The effect of a vibrating speaker diaphragm on the surrounding air. Dark areas represent regions of high air pressure, and light areas represent areas of low air pressure.

radio or stereo and feel the vibrations by placing your hand on the speaker. This technique is sometimes used by deaf people to "listen" to music.)

The vibrations you feel when you place your hand on the speaker affect the surrounding air, as shown in Figure 8.3. When the diaphragm of the speaker moves out, it pushes the surrounding air molecules together and increases the density of molecules near the diaphragm. This increased density increases the air pressure. When the speaker diaphragm moves back in, it decreases the density of molecules near the diaphragm and so decreases the air pressure. By repeating this process many hundreds or even thousands of times a second, the speaker creates a pattern of alternating high- and low-pressure regions in the air that is repeated as neighboring air molecules affect each other. This pattern of air pressure changes, which travels through air from its source at 340 meters per second (and through water at 1,500 meters per second), is called a **sound wave.** The nature of the sounds we hear,

particularly a sound's pitch and loudness, is related to properties of this sound wave.

Pure Tones

We first consider a simple kind of sound wave, called a **pure tone,** in which pressure changes occur in a pattern described by a mathematical function called a sine wave, as shown in Figure 8.4. Tones with this pattern of pressure changes are found occasionally in the environment. A person whistling or the high-pitched notes produced by a flute are examples of natural sounds that are close to pure tones. Pure tones are used extensively in laboratory studies of hearing and are produced in the laboratory by an electronic device called an *oscillator*. An oscillator causes a

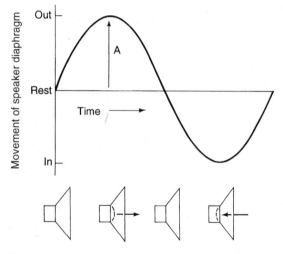

Figure 8.4

In response to a sine-wave stimulus from an oscillator, a speaker diaphragm moves out and then back in, as shown in the pictures in the figure. The time course of this motion is indicated by the sine-wave curve, which indicates the amount that the diaphragm has moved as a function of time. The amplitude (A) represents the maximum deflection of the speaker diaphragm from its rest position.

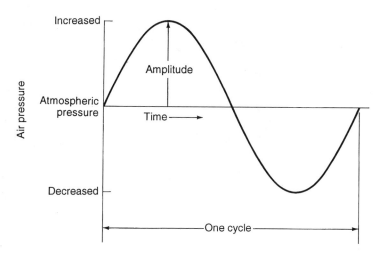

Figure 8.5

The sinusoidal vibration of the speaker diaphragm results in a sinusoidal change in the air pressure, as shown in the figure.

speaker diaphragm to vibrate in and out with a sine-wave motion (Figure 8.4). We can adjust the oscillator so that it causes the diaphragm to vibrate with a certain **amplitude**—the distance the diaphragm moves from its rest position, labeled A in Figure 8.4. We can also adjust the oscillator so that it causes the speaker to vibrate with a certain **frequency**—the number of times per second that the speaker diaphragm goes through the cycle of moving out, back in, and then out again.

The sine-wave vibration of the diaphragm causes a sine-wave pattern of pressure changes in the surrounding air that creates a pure tone (Figure 8.5). We can describe these pressure changes in terms of *frequency* (the rate at which the pressure changes occur) and *amplitude* (the size of the pressure changes). A tone's frequency is indicated in units called **Hertz** (Hz), where one Hertz is one cycle per second. Thus, a 1,000-Hz tone is a pure tone that goes through 1,000 cycles per second. As we will see in Chapter 9, humans can hear frequencies between about 20 and 20,000 Hz.

One way to specify a tone's amplitude would be to indicate the difference in pressure between the high and low peaks of the sound wave. However, this method of specifying amplitude would run into difficulty because of the wide range of

pressure changes humans can hear. If we set the pressure change caused by a near-threshold sound, such as a barely audible whisper, equal to 1, then the amplitude of a loud rock band would be about 10 million.

To deal with this 10-million-to-1 range of amplitudes, auditory researchers have developed the decibel (dB) scale, which converts the large range of amplitudes into a much smaller range of decibels. **Decibels** are defined by the following equation:

$$dB = 20 \log(p/p_o)$$

where p is the amplitude (or pressure) of the sound wave, and p_o is a reference pressure set by the experimenter. Most researchers set the reference pressure at 0.0002 dynes/cm², a pressure close to the threshold for hearing in the ear's most sensitive frequency range. To indicate that this is the chosen reference pressure, we use the term **sound pressure level (SPL).** Thus, saying that a tone is 50 dB SPL means that this value was calculated based on a reference pressure of 0.0002 dynes/cm².

To appreciate how decibels relate to sounds in the environment, look at Table 8.1, which shows sound pressure levels in decibels for

Audition I: Auditory Physiology

Table 8.1

Some common sound pressure levels (in decibels)

Sound	SPL (dB)
Barely audible sound (threshold)	0
Leaves rustling	20
Quiet residential community	40
Average speaking voice	60
Loud music from radio/heavy traffic	80
Express subway train	100
Propeller plane at takeoff	120
Jet engine at takeoff (pain threshold)	140
Spacecraft launch at close range	180

sounds ranging from threshold to the level that causes pain and damage. The nice thing about the decibel scale is that it converts the 10-million-to-1 sound pressure range into the much more manageable 0-to-140-dB range.

Perceptual Dimensions of Sound

The physical characteristics of sound, such as frequency and amplitude, are associated with a number of different perceptual experiences. This chapter and Chapter 9 are concerned with the following perceptual dimensions:

Loudness Though **loudness** is difficult to define, we all know what it means to say that a jet plane taking off is loud, while a whisper is quiet. We know that loudness is related to a tone's amplitude because, if we hold a tone's frequency constant and increase its amplitude, the tone's loudness increases.

Pitch The **pitch** of a tone refers to how high or low it sounds. The pitch of a pure tone is related to its frequency: lower frequencies cause low pitches and high frequencies cause high pitches. In Chapter 9, we will see that the pitch of com-

plex tones is also related to frequency, but that these tones contain a number of frequencies.

Localization Most sounds are related to events, and events have specific locations—in front of us, behind us, up, down, or off to the left or right. **Localization** refers to our ability to determine where in space a sound originates. Localization is largely determined by differences in the sounds received by the left and the right ears.

Timbre When two tones with the same loudness and pitch are presented in the same way but sound different, this difference is a difference in **timbre** (pronounced tim'-ber or tam'-bre). For example, consider the sounds of two different musical instruments that are playing the same pitch. A trumpet and an oboe playing the same note sound very different. We might describe the sound of the trumpet as "bright" or "brassy" and the sound of the oboe as "nasal" or "reedy." These differences occur because most tones involve more complex patterns of pressure changes than the simple pure tones we have described so far. We will see in Chapter 9 that two tones with the same pitch can consist of different patterns of pressure changes. It is these differences that result in the different timbres of different musical instruments.

Complex Sounds and Fourier Analysis

The simplicity of pure tones makes them the starting place for much auditory research. Most of our auditory experience, however, is not with pure tones, but with more complex sounds such as music, speech, and the various sounds produced by nature and machines. We begin our description of complex tones with the piano keyboard in Figure 8.6. As we move from left to right on the keyboard, the frequency of the notes increases from 27.5 Hz for the lowest note on the keyboard to 4,186 Hz for the highest note. Although each note on the keyboard is associated with a single frequency, each tone produced by

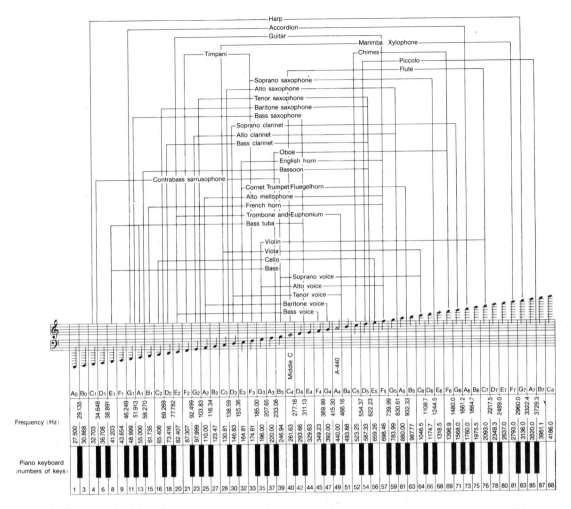

Figure 8.6

The piano keyboard, showing the frequencies associated with each note and the ranges of various other instruments. (From Conn, Ltd.)

the piano and other musical instruments actually contains a large number of frequencies and is therefore much more complex than the pure single-frequency tones produced by our oscillator.

As we strike a key on the piano we set one of the piano's strings into vibration, and this vibration produces pressure changes like the one shown in Figure 8.7. Although these pressure changes are more complex than the sine-wave

pressure change of a pure tone, they have something in common with our pure tone. Both our pure tone and the note on the piano create periodic pressure changes—changes that repeat in a regular pattern. This property of regular repetition of the pressure changes, which is called **periodicity**, enables us to use the technique of Fourier analysis that we introduced in Chapter 5. You may remember from that description that Fourier

Audition I: Auditory Physiology

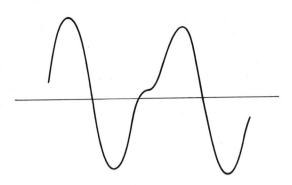

Figure 8.7

Pressure changes as a function of time for a musical tone. This waveform is more complex than the sine wave associated with pure tones like the one in Figures 8.4 and 8.5.

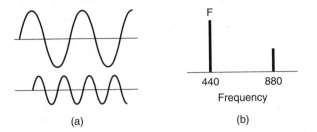

(a)   (b)

Figure 8.8

(a) The musical tone in Figure 8.7 can be broken down into these two sine waves. This breakdown can be accomplished for any periodic waveform by the use of a procedure called Fourier analysis. (b) The Fourier frequency spectrum for the tone in Figure 8.7. The spectrum indicates that the tone is made up of one component with a frequency of 440 Hz and another component with a frequency of 880 Hz. The fact that the line for the 440-Hz component is higher means that there is more energy at that frequency.

analysis is a mathematical procedure that can be used to analyze a visual grating stimulus (or a more complex scene) into its sine-wave components. We can apply Fourier analysis to auditory stimuli in the same way by using it to analyze a complex sound into its sine-wave components.

Although the mathematics of Fourier analysis is too complex to describe in this book, we can show the outcome of applying this mathematical procedure. When we apply Fourier analysis to the musical tone in Figure 8.7 we find that it consists of two sine-wave components with different amplitudes and frequencies (Figure 8.8a). The sine wave with the lowest frequency is called the **fundamental frequency** (or the first harmonic) of the tone, and any other sine waves are called **harmonics.**

Another way of describing the components of the complex tone is shown in Figure 8.8b. This is called a **Fourier frequency spectrum,** and it indicates each harmonic's frequency by a line positioned on the horizontal axis; the harmonic's amplitude is indicated by the height of the line. The line marked F is the fundamental frequency of the tone in Figure 8.7 and corresponds to the frequency marked on the piano keyboard (in this case, the 440 Hz of A above middle C). The harmonics are all multiples of the fundamental

frequency, so the second harmonic of the tone in Figure 8.7 has a frequency of $440 \times 2 = 880$ Hz. As we will see in Chapter 9, the tones produced by most musical instruments have many harmonics, and it is these harmonics that create the distinctive timbres of different instruments. For now, the important point is that this complex musical tone can be broken down into a series of simple sine-wave components.

Why is it important to be able to analyze complex periodic sounds into sine-wave components? The answer to this question is contained in **Ohm's acoustic law.** This law, which was proposed by the 19th-century German physicist G. S. Ohm (who also formulated the more famous Ohm's law of electricity), states that the ear analyzes tones into their simple components. In other words, not only can a complex sound be analyzed into sine-wave components by means of a mathematical procedure, as Fourier demonstrated, but the ear does this analysis as well.

How does the ear carry out this analysis of complex tones into simpler components? As we will see below, the ear can accomplish this feat because of the way structures inside the ear vibrate in response to different frequencies and because individual neurons are tuned to respond to a narrow range of frequencies. This analysis takes place early in the auditory system, and then, at higher levels in the system, neural information about these frequency components is combined to create our perception of sound. The first step toward appreciating how this process occurs is to describe the structure of the auditory system.

STRUCTURE AND FUNCTIONING OF THE AUDITORY SYSTEM

The first task in describing the structure of any sensory system is to describe how energy from the environment reaches the receptors. This was easy to explain for vision—light enters the eye through the pupil and reaches the rods and cones that line the back of the eyeball. The story for audition, however, is much more complicated. The stimulus for hearing—pressure changes in the air—follows a complex path between the time it enters the ear and the time it reaches receptors called **hair cells** (Figure 8.9).

A key component of the hair cells is tiny structures called *cilia*, which are the "hairs" that give the hair cells their name. When these cilia are bent, they initiate a sequence of events that begins with the generation of electrical signals in the receptors and culminates with these signals reaching the auditory receiving area in the temporal lobe of the brain. Our major goal in describing the structure of the auditory system is to show that sound vibrations entering the ear cause these cilia to vibrate. To do this, we will begin with sound waves entering the outer ear and follow the effect of these sound waves as they travel through the various structures of the ear.

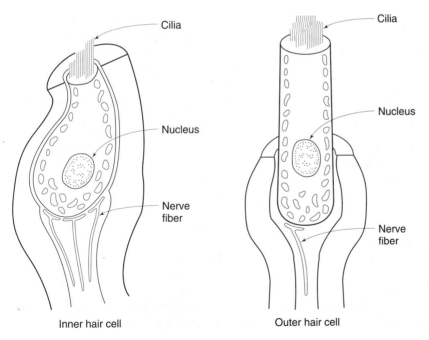

Inner hair cell   Outer hair cell

Figure 8.9
The inner and outer hair cells. Vibration of the cilia, or hairs, generates an electrical signal that causes the release of a chemical transmitter, which generates a response in nerve fibers, which then conduct signals that travel toward the brain in the auditory nerve. (Adapted from Gulick, 1971, and Gulick, Gescheider, & Frisina, 1989.)

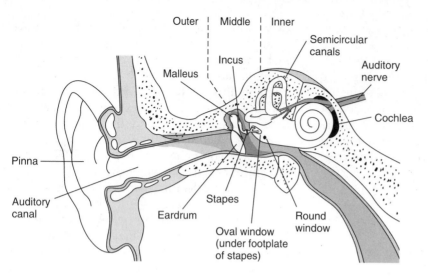

Outer | Middle | Inner

Semicircular canals

Auditory nerve

Incus

Malleus

Cochlea

Pinna

Auditory canal

Stapes

Eardrum

Oval window (under footplate of stapes)

Round window

Figure 8.10

The ear, showing its three subdivisions—outer, middle, and inner.

The Outer Ear

When we talk about the "ears" in everyday conversation, we are usually referring to the pinnae, the funny-looking structures that stick out from the sides of the head. While this most obvious part of the ear is of some importance in helping us locate sounds and is of great importance for those of us who wear eyeglasses or earrings, it is the part of the ear we could most easily do without. The major workings of the ear are found inside the head, hidden from view.

Sound waves first pass through the **outer ear,** which consists of the **pinna** and the **auditory canal** (Figure 8.10). The auditory canal is a tubelike structure about 3 cm long that protects the delicate structures of the middle ear from the hazards of the outside world. The auditory canal's 3-cm recess, along with its wax, which has an apparently unpleasant effect on curious insects (Schubert, 1980), protects the delicate **tympanic membrane,** or **eardrum,** at the end of the canal and helps keep this membrane and the structures in the middle ear at a relatively constant temperature.

In addition to its protective function, the outer ear has another role: to enhance the intensities of some sounds by means of the physiological principle of **resonance.** Resonance occurs when sound waves near the **resonant frequency** of the auditory canal are reflected from the closed end of the canal and, on their way back out, reinforce the incoming sound waves of the same frequency. The resonant frequency of the auditory canal, which is determined by the length of the canal, is about 3,400 Hz, and measurements of the sound pressures inside the ear indicate that the auditory canal has a slight amplifying effect on frequencies between about 2,000 and 5,000 Hz.

The Middle Ear

When airborne sound waves reach the tympanic membrane at the end of the auditory canal, they set it into vibration, and this vibration is transmitted to structures in the middle ear, on the other side of the tympanic membrane. The **mid-**

dle ear is a small cavity, about 2 cm² in volume, which separates the outer and inner ears (Figure 8.11). This cavity contains the **ossicles,** the three smallest bones in the body, which are suspended by four ligaments. The first of these bones, the **malleus,** is set into vibration by the tympanic membrane, to which it is attached, and transmits its vibrations to the **incus,** which, in turn, transmits its vibrations to the **stapes.** The stapes then transmits its vibrations to the inner ear by pushing on the membrane covering the **oval window.**

Why are the ossicles necessary? We can answer this question by noting that both the outer ear and middle ear are filled with air, but the inner ear contains a watery liquid called *cochlear fluid,* which is much denser than the air (Figure 8.12). The mismatch between the low density of the air and the high density of the cochlear fluid creates a problem: Pressure changes in the air are transmitted poorly to the much denser cochlear

Air	Air	Liquid
Outer	Middle	Inner

Figure 8.12
Environments inside the outer, middle, and inner ears. The fact that liquid fills the inner ear poses a problem for the transmission of sound vibrations from the air of the middle ear.

fluid, so if these vibrations had to pass directly from the air to the fluid, only about 3 percent of the vibrations would be transmitted (Durrant & Lovrinic, 1977). The ossicles help solve this problem in two ways:

1. The ossicles concentrate the vibration of the large tympanic membrane onto the smaller stapes. The tympanic membrane has an area of about 0.6 cm², whereas the stapes footplate has an area of about 0.032 cm²—a ratio of about 17 to 1. Concentrating the vibration of the large tympanic membrane onto the smaller stapes, as shown in Figure 8.13, increases the pressure per unit area in the same way that a 110-lb woman wearing shoes with 1-cm spiked heels can generate a pressure of 110,000 pounds per

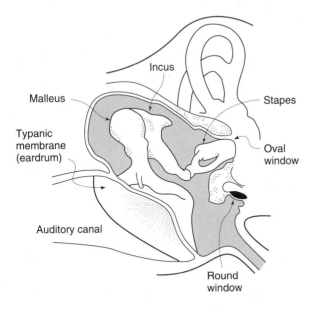

Malleus

Incus

Typanic membrane (eardrum)

Stapes

Oval window

Auditory canal

Round window

Figure 8.11
The middle ear. The three bones of the middle ear transmit the vibrations of the tympanic membrane to the inner ear.

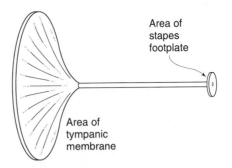

Area of stapes footplate

Area of tympanic membrane

Figure 8.13
A diagrammatic representation of the tympanic membrane and the stapes, showing the difference in size between the two. (From Schubert, 1980.)

Audition I: Auditory Physiology

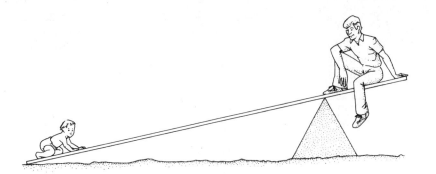

Figure 8.14
The lever principle. The baby on the long end of the board can overcome the weight of the man on the short end. (The baby will, however, be in for a surprise if it crawls very far toward the man.)

square foot by concentrating all of her weight on one heel.

2. The ossicles act according to the lever principle. Figure 8.14 illustrates this principle. If a board is balanced on a fulcrum, a small weight on the long end of the board can overcome a larger weight on the short end of the board. Though it is not obvious from looking at the ossicles, they are hinged so that they increase the vibration by a factor of about 1.3 by means of this lever principle.

These two mechanisms increase the strength of the vibrations by a factor of at least 22 ($1.3 \times 17 = 22.1$); (Durant & Lovrinic, 1977), with some calculations setting this value as high as a factor of 100 (Schubert, 1980). In any case, without the middle ear, it would be much more difficult for us to hear. In fact, the effect of losing the ossicles has been measured in patients whose ossicles have been damaged beyond surgical repair. In such cases, an operation is sometimes performed so that sound is transmitted directly to the inner ear through the air. When the ossicles are absent, the sound pressure must be increased by a factor of 10–50 for the person to achieve the same hearing ability as when the ossicles were present.

The middle ear also contains the **middle ear muscles,** the smallest skeletal muscles in the body. These muscles are attached to the ossicles, and at very high sound intensities, they contract to dampen the vibration of the ossicles, thereby protecting the structures of the inner ear against potentially painful and damaging stimuli.

The Inner Ear

The main structure of the **inner ear** is the liquid-filled **cochlea.** The liquid inside the cochlea is set in vibration by the vibration of the stapes against the oval window. The cochlea, which is a bony snail-like structure, is difficult to visualize because it is rolled into 2¾ turns. But we can see the structure inside more clearly by imagining how the cochlea would appear if uncoiled to form a long straight tube (Figure 8.15a and b). The most obvious feature of the uncoiled cochlea is that the upper and lower halves are separated by a structure called the **cochlear partition,** which extends almost the entire length of the cochlea. Note that this diagram is not drawn to scale and so doesn't show the cochlea's true shape. In reality, the uncoiled cochlea would be a cylinder 2 mm in diameter and 35 mm long.

We can best see the structures within the cochlear partition by looking at the cochlea end-on and in cross section, as in Figure 8.16. When we look at the cochlea in this way, we see that it is divided into three compartments, the *scala vestibuli,* the *scala tympani,* and the *scala media,* and that the cochlear partition contains a large structure called the **organ of Corti.** Details of the organ of Corti are shown in a side view in Figure 8.17 and in perspective in Figure 8.18. Its three structures of primary importance are the **basilar membrane,** the **tectorial membrane,** and the hair cells.

The hair cells are shown in Figure 8.9. There are two types of hair cells, the inner hair cells and

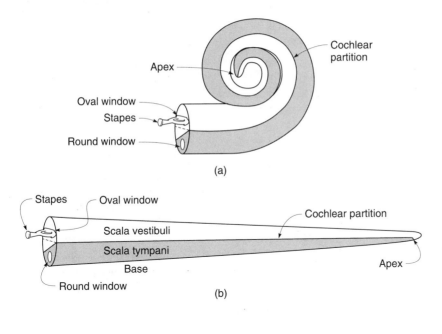

(a)

(b)

Figure 8.15
*(a) A partially uncoiled cochlea.
(b) A fully uncoiled cochlea.
The cochlear partition, which is
indicated here by a line, actually
contains the basilar membrane
and the organ of Corti, which
are shown in Figures 8.16, 8.17,
and 8.18.*

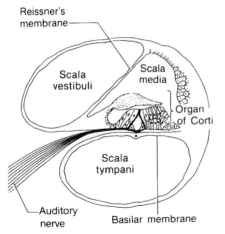

Figure 8.16
A cross section of the cochlea.

the outer hair cells (Figures 8.17 and 8.18). Although there are fewer inner hair cells than outer hair cells (3,500 inner hair cells vs. 12,000 outer hair cells), 95% of the auditory nerve fibers receive their signals from the inner hair cells. The reason is that each inner hair cell connects to about 8–30 auditory nerve fibers, whereas a number of outer hair cells connect to branches of the same auditory nerve fiber. Another way to put this is to say that the signals from a single inner hair cell *diverge* onto a number of fibers, whereas the signals from many outer hair cells *converge* onto one fiber.

The cilia (or hairs) of the inner and outer hair cells are the target of the vibrations we have been following through the ear, because when they bend, they cause the release of a chemical transmitter onto a nerve fiber, which then transmits the resulting electrical signal toward the brain.

What causes the hair cells to bend? To answer this question, let's return to the oval window, where the stapes is vibrating. When the stapes pushes in on the oval window, it transmits pressure to the liquid inside the cochlea. From Figure 8.15b, we might think that this pressure would be transmitted down the scala vestibuli, around the opening at the end of the cochlear partition, and down the scala tympani to the **round window.** However, this is not what happens. Very little pressure is transmitted around the end of the cochlear partition; the opening joining the scala tympani and the scala vestibuli acts almost as if it were closed. Rather than transmit pressure through the

Audition I: Auditory Physiology

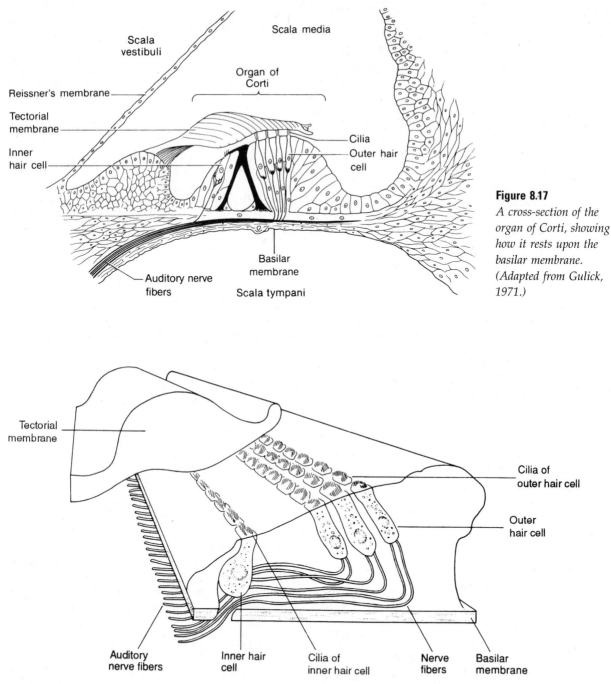

Figure 8.17
A cross-section of the organ of Corti, showing how it rests upon the basilar membrane. (Adapted from Gulick, 1971.)

Figure 8.18
A perspective view of the organ of Corti. The tectorial membrane is actually closer to the hair cells than is shown here (see Figure 8.17). (Adapted from Kiang, 1986.)

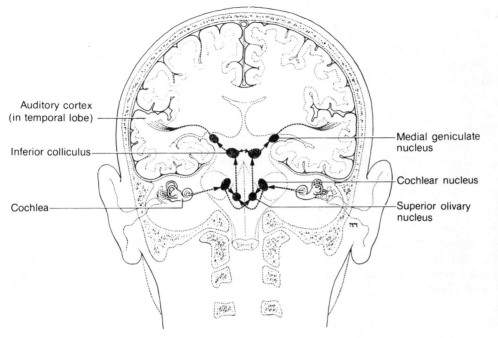

Auditory cortex
(in temporal lobe)

Inferior colliculus

Cochlea

Medial geniculate
nucleus

Cochlear nucleus

Superior olivary
nucleus

Figure 8.19
Diagram of the audi-
tory pathways. This
diagram is greatly sim-
plified, as numerous
connections between
the structures are not
shown. (Adapted from
Wever, 1949.)

opening, the liquid in the scala vestibuli pushes on the cochlear partition. This push, which causes the elastic cochlear partition to move downward, is followed by a pull, which occurs when the stapes pulls back from the oval window, decreasing the pressure inside the scala vestibuli and causing the cochlear partition to move upward. This pushing and pulling sets the cochlear partition into an up-and-down motion, so that it vibrates at exactly the same frequency as the stapes.

The vibration of the cochlear partition sets the organ of Corti into an up-and-down motion and causes the cilia of the hair cells to bend, since they are either embedded in the tectorial membrane or bent by pressure waves in the surrounding liquid. When the hair cells bend in one direction, they depolarize (their charge decreases as does that of the nerve fiber in Figure 1.6), and when they bend in the other direction, they hyperpolarize (their charge increases). This alternation between increases and decreases in charge causes the hair cells to release a burst of neuro-

transmitter every time the cochlear partition vibrates, and this transmitter causes bursts of firing in fibers in the auditory nerve (Kelly, 1991). The amount of bending needed to cause this release of transmitter is extremely small. At threshold, movements as small as 100 trillionths of a meter (100 picometers) can generate a response in the hair cell (Hudspeth, 1983).

The Auditory Pathways

When signals are generated in the fibers of the auditory nerve, they begin their journey toward the auditory receiving area in the cortex. Figure 8.19 shows the pathway they follow from the cochlea to the auditory cortex. The route is quite complex, and we do not yet know many of its details. Figure 8.19 does, however, identify the most important structures through which signals pass on their way to the cortex. Nerve fibers from the cochlea first synapse in the **cochlear nucleus,** then in the superior olivary nucleus, and then in the inferior colliculus of the midbrain, before reaching the medial geniculate nucleus of the thalamus. From the medial geniculate nucleus, fibers go to the primary **auditory receiving area,** which is located in the temporal lobe of the cortex.

The complexity of the auditory system becomes apparent from the fact that, in addition to the pathway from the cochlea to the cortex, there are also connections between nuclei on the opposite sides of the brain. For example, the cochlear nucleus of the right ear sends axons to the superior olivary nucleus and the inferior colliculus of the left ear, and the left and right inferior colliculi communicate with each other. In addition to these fibers, which send signals from the cochlea toward the brain, other fibers send signals from the brain back to the cochlea.

THE CODE FOR FREQUENCY

Now that we have looked at the structure of the auditory system and have seen how pressure changes entering the outer ear become transformed into bursts of firing in the auditory nerve, we will ask one of the central questions of auditory research: How does the firing of these neurons signal different pitches? This question is analogous to one we considered in the chapter on color vision, when we asked: How does the firing of neurons signal different colors? We saw that the first step in answering this question about color vision was to identify wavelength as the stimulus property most closely associated with our perception of color. Once we determined this relationship, our question became: How does the firing of neurons signal *wavelength?*

Our task for audition is the same as it was for vision: to identify the stimulus property that is most closely associated with the perceptual quality we want to explain—in this case, pitch. We know that the frequency of sound is associated with pitch, high frequencies being associated with high pitches and low frequencies being associated with low pitches. We can therefore ask the question about pitch perception as follows: How does the firing of neurons signal *frequency?* The following two answers to this question have been proposed:

1. There is a **place code for frequency.** Different frequencies are signaled by activity in neurons that are located at different *places* in the auditory system. According to this idea, neurons connected to receptors in different places in the cochlea signal different frequencies, as shown in Figure 8.20.

2. There is a **timing code for frequency.** Different frequencies are signaled by the *timing* of nerve impulses in nerve fibers or groups of nerve fibers. For example, low frequencies are signaled by low firing rates, and higher frequencies are signaled by higher firing rates, as illustrated in Figure 8.21.

We will describe research on the code for frequency by first showing how both place and timing codes for frequency work in the cochlea and in

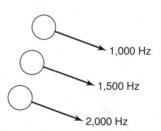

1,000 Hz

1,500 Hz

2,000 Hz

Figure 8.20
The idea behind a place code for frequency is that different frequencies are signaled by neurons located in different places in the auditory system. This drawing, which doesn't represent any particular structure in the auditory system, shows three different neurons located in different places that fire best to different frequencies.

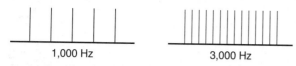

Figure 8.21

The idea behind the timing code for frequency is that different frequencies are signaled by the rate or pattern of nerve firing. Here, the rate of firing to a 3,000-Hz tone is higher than the rate of firing to a 1,000-Hz tone.

the firing of auditory nerve fibers. We will then describe how more central structures in the auditory system respond to the place and timing information provided by the auditory nerve fibers.

The Place Code

The basic idea behind the place code for frequency is that frequency is signaled by hair cells that fire to specific frequencies. The research that led to this conclusion started with a series of studies begun in 1928 by Georg von Békésy, which culminated in his being awarded the Nobel Prize in physiology and medicine in 1961. Békésy focused his attention on the basilar membrane—the structure that stretches from one end of the cochlea to the other and that supports the structures of the organ of Corti. Békésy's major concern was determining how the basilar membrane vibrated in response to different frequencies. He determined this in two ways: (1) by actually observing the vibration of the basilar membrane, and (2) by building a model of the cochlea that took into account the physical properties of the basilar membrane.

Békésy observed the vibration of the basilar membrane by boring a hole in the ear of a human cadaver and observing the membrane's vibration with a microscope (Békésy, 1960). He found that the vibrating motion of the basilar membrane is similar to the motion that occurs when two people hold the ends of a rope and one "snaps" the rope, sending a wave traveling down the rope. This **traveling wave** motion of the basilar membrane is shown in Figure 8.22.

Békésy also determined how the basilar membrane vibrates by analyzing its structure, taking note of two important facts: (1) The **base of the basilar membrane** (the end located nearest the oval window and the stapes) is three or four times narrower than that of the **apex of the basilar membrane** (the end of the membrane located at the far end of the cochlea; Figure 8.23), and (2)

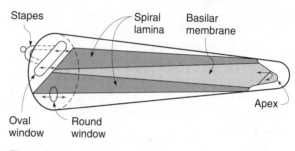

Figure 8.23

A perspective view of an uncoiled cochlea, showing how the basilar membrane gets wider at the apex end of the cochlea. The spiral lamina is a supporting structure that makes up for the basilar membrane's difference in width at the stapes and the apex ends of the cochlea. (From Schubert, 1980.)

Figure 8.22

A perspective view showing the traveling wave motion of the basilar membrane. This picture shows what the membrane looks like when the vibration is "frozen" with the wave about ⅔ of the way down the membrane. (From Tonndorf, 1960.)

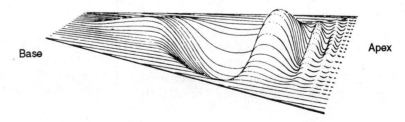

the basilar membrane is about 100 times stiffer at its base than at its apex. Using this information, Békésy constructed models of the cochlea which revealed that the basilar membrane vibrates in a traveling wave in response to the pressure waves caused by vibration of the cochlear fluid.

Figure 8.24 shows what a traveling wave looks like at three successive instants in time. The solid horizontal line represents the basilar membrane at rest. Curve 1 shows the position of the basilar membrane at one instant during its vibration, and curves 2 and 3 show the positions of the membrane at two later instants. Since the shape of the traveling wave changes with each instant, it is difficult to visualize its overall effect on the basilar membrane. We can, however, visualize its overall effect more easily by determining the maximum displacement that the wave causes at each point along the membrane. This maximum displacement, which is indicated by the dashed line, is called the **envelope of the traveling wave.** The envelope helps us to determine the effect of the basilar membrane's vibration on the hair cells, because the degree to which the hair cells are bent—and the resultant rate of firing in the fibers of those hair cells—depends on the amount that the basilar membrane is displaced, with greater displacement resulting in greater firing rates.

Békésy's (1960) observations of the basilar membrane's vibrations led him to conclude that the envelope of the traveling wave of the basilar membrane has two important properties:

1. The envelope is peaked at one point on the basilar membrane. The envelope of Figure 8.24 indicates that point P on the basilar membrane is displaced the most by the traveling wave. Thus, the hair cells near point P will send out stronger signals than those near other parts of the membrane.

2. The position of this peak on the basilar membrane is a function of the frequency of the sound.

We can see in Figure 8.25, which shows the envelopes of vibration for stimuli ranging from 25 to 1,600 Hz, that low frequencies cause maximum vibration near the apex, while high frequencies cause maximum vibration near the base. (One way to remember this relationship is that A for "apex" is a lower note on the musical scale than B, for "base.")

Békésy's linking of place on the cochlea with frequency has been confirmed in studies such as one in which electrodes were placed on different places on the cochlea, and the electrical response to different frequencies was measured (Culler et al., 1943). The result is a **tonotopic map**—an orderly map of frequencies along the length of the cochlea—that confirms the idea that the apex of the cochlea is stimulated best by low frequencies and the base by high frequencies (Figure 8.26).

Békésy's place theory explains the signaling of frequency by the firing of specific hair cells. A particular frequency causes hair cells at a specific place along the basilar membrane to fire more than others, and this firing signals that frequency. However, a problem with this idea is that Békésy's measurements indicate that a large por-

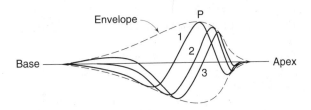

Figure 8.24

Vibration of the basilar membrane, showing the position of the membrane at three instants in time, indicated by the solid lines, and the envelope of the vibration, indicated by the dashed lines. P indicates the peak of the basilar membrane vibration. Hair cells located at this position on the membrane are maximally stimulated by the membrane's vibration. (Adapted from Békésy, 1960.)

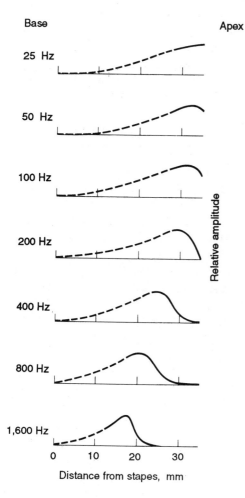

Base   Apex

25 Hz

50 Hz

100 Hz

200 Hz

400 Hz

800 Hz

1,600 Hz

Relative amplitude

0   10   20   30

Distance from stapes, mm

Figure 8.25

The envelope of the basilar membrane's vibration at frequencies ranging from 25 to 1,600 Hz, as measured by Békésy (1960).

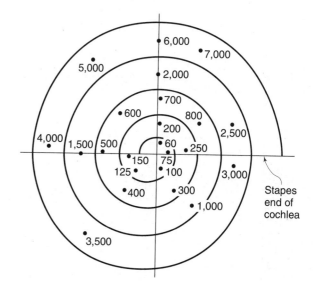

Stapes end of cochlea

Figure 8.26

Tonotopic map of the cochlea. Numbers indicate the location of the maximum electrical response for each frequency. Low frequencies cause the largest response near the apex end of the spiral, and high frequencies cause the largest response at the base, at the stapes end of the cochlea. (From Culler et al., 1943.)

tion of the basilar membrane vibrates, even when it is stimulated by a single frequency. For example, Figure 8.25 shows that, for frequencies below 200 Hz, the entire basilar membrane vibrates. Thus, not only do hair cells at a particular place fire in response to one frequency, but many other hair cells fire as well.

How does the ear achieve its impressive ability to discriminate between similar frequencies if

a particular frequency causes a large portion of the basilar membrane to vibrate? The answer to this question is that the basilar membrane does not vibrate as broadly as Békésy's measurements seemed to indicate. The reason Békésy observed such widespread vibration is that, with the methods he had available, he had to use very high sound intensities in order to detect the membrane's vibration. However, a newer method, called the **Mössbauer technique,** has enabled researchers to measure how the basilar membrane vibrates in response to lower sound intensities. The technique involves placing a small radioactive source, which emits gamma radiation, on the membrane. When the membrane vibrates, the wavelength of this radiation shifts, and the amount of the shift is related to the distance that the membrane is being displaced.

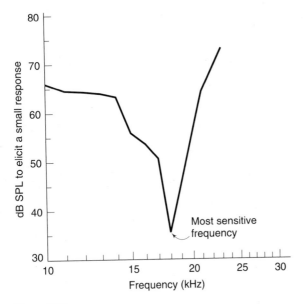

Figure 8.27

The tuning curve of a single inner hair cell in the guinea pig cochlea. This hair cell is most sensitive at 18,000 Hz and responds well only to a narrow range of frequencies above and below this frequency. (Data from Russell & Sellick, 1977.)

Using this technique, Johnstone and Boyle (1967) were able to measure displacements of the basilar membrane in the guinea pig cochlea as small as a few hundred millionths of a centimeter. They found that the membrane's vibration is more sharply tuned than Békésy had reported, so that a particular frequency causes a narrower region of the membrane to vibrate.

The narrower vibration of the basilar membrane measured by the Mössbauer technique makes it more reasonable to think of frequency as being signaled by the firing of specific hair cells. However, the strongest evidence supporting this idea is the finding, shown in Figure 8.27, that individual hair cells are tuned to respond to a narrow range of frequencies (Russell & Sellick, 1977). This figure shows the **frequency tuning curve** of a single inner hair cell in the guinea pig

cochlea—a plot of the intensity necessary to elicit a small response from the hair cell as a function of frequency. This hair cell is most sensitive at about 18,000 Hz, and its sensitivity drops off rapidly above and below this frequency. This finding that individual hair cells are tuned to specific frequencies, combined with the way the basilar membrane vibrates to different frequencies, means that hair cells at the apex of the basilar membrane signal low frequencies both because low frequencies cause more vibration at the apex and also because hair cells located there are tuned to respond best to low frequencies (Kelly, 1991). Another way to illustrate this tuning is by determining the tuning curve of the cochlear nerve fibers that receive their signals directly from the hair cells. Tuning curves for three auditory nerve fibers, which indicate the intensity necessary to elicit a threshold response at frequencies covering the audible range, are shown in Figure 8.28. The frequency at which each neuron has the lowest threshold, indicated by the arrows, is called the *best frequency*, or **characteristic frequency,** of the neuron.

The Timing Code

The major mechanism for coding frequency is the firing of specific hair cells described above, but the timing or rate of nerve firing also provides information about frequency. An early proposal linking the rate of nerve firing and the frequency of the stimulus was Rutherford's (1886) proposal that the frequency of the stimulus is signaled by the frequency of nerve firing. According to this idea, a 3,000-Hz tone would be signaled by an auditory nerve fiber firing 3,000 impulses per second. This proposal cannot work, however, because of the refractory period, which limits the nerve fibers' maximum rate of firing to about 500 impulses per second (see Chapter 1). Thus, a single nerve fiber cannot fire at 3,000 impulses per second. To deal with this problem, E. Glen Wever (1949) proposed the **volley principle,**

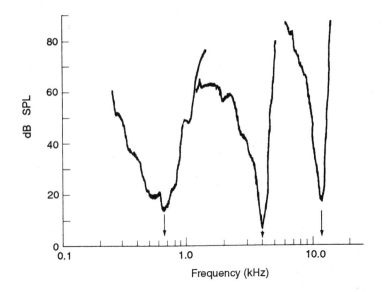

Figure 8.28

The tuning curves of three auditory nerve fibers in one animal. The characteristic frequency of each fiber is indicated by the arrows along the frequency axis. (From Kiang, 1975.)

which states that high rates of nerve firing can be accomplished if nerve fibers work in the manner illustrated in Figure 8.29. In this illustration, five fibers work together, each fiber firing every fifth period of the sound wave. Fiber a fires to the first period and then becomes refractory. While a is refractory, fibers b, c, d, and e fire to the second, third, fourth, and fifth periods, respectively, and then a, which has now recovered from its refractory period, fires to the sixth period, and so on. Thus, although the rate of firing of each individual fiber is limited by its refractory period,

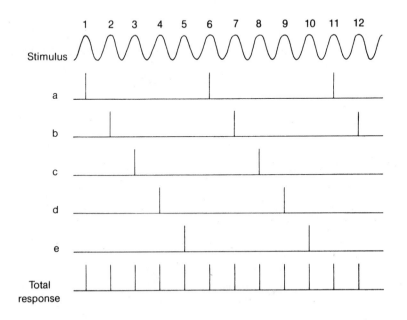

Figure 8.29

How a number of nerve fibers work together, according to Wever's volley principle. (See text for details.)

Audition I: Auditory Physiology

groups of fibers can work together to signal high frequencies of stimulation, as indicated by the bottom record of Figure 8.29.

Wever's proposal that stimulus frequency is signaled by groups of nerve fibers is supported by the results of experiments published almost 20 years after his original proposal. This research describes a phenomenon called **phase locking** — the firing of neurons in synchrony with the phase of a stimulus (Rose et al., 1967). This synchronous firing is illustrated in Figure 8.30, which shows the relationship between a pure tone stimulus and the firing of three auditory nerve fibers. We can see that fiber a fires irregularly, but that when it does fire, it fires at the peak of the sine-wave stimulus. Similar results for two more fibers are also shown in this figure. Note that, although the rates and patterns of firing are different for each fiber, the firing of all three is phase-locked to the stimulus.

When large groups of fibers are phase-locked to a stimulus, they create a firing pattern like the one shown in Figure 8.31. This figure shows that, when a large number of fibers fire in response to a tone of a particular frequency, the fibers fire in bursts separated by silent intervals, and that the timing of these bursts depends on the frequency of the stimulus. Thus, the timing of firing in the auditory nerve can indicate the frequency of the

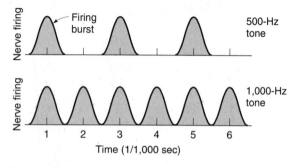

Figure 8.31

Phase locking causes large numbers of nerve fibers to fire in bursts separated by silent intervals.

stimulus. We will see, however, in the next section, when we consider how neurons at higher centers in the auditory system respond, that this timing mechanism is probably effective only for signaling very low frequencies.

Place and Timing Information in the Central Auditory System

What happens to the place and timing information contained in the firing of the auditory nerve fibers as these signals travel from the cochlea to the auditory cortex? Place information is maintained, as indicated by tonotopic maps like the one in Figure 8.32, which shows that neurons with the same characteristic frequencies are arranged in an orderly way in the cat's auditory cortex, neurons that respond best to high frequencies are located to the left, and neurons that respond best to lower frequencies are located to the right. In addition to the surface map shown in Figure 8.32, there is also a **columnar arrangement** similar to that observed in the visual system. Thus, neurons recorded along an electrode track that is perpendicular to the surface of the cortex all have the same characteristic frequency (Abeles & Goldstein, 1970). This type of tonotopic map, which has been found in all of the nuclei along the pathway from the cochlea to the

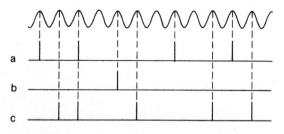

Figure 8.30

The response of three nerve fibers (a, b, and c) that are phase-locked to the stimulus. Notice that the fibers don't fire on every cycle of the stimulus, but when they do fire, they fire only when the stimulus is at its peak.

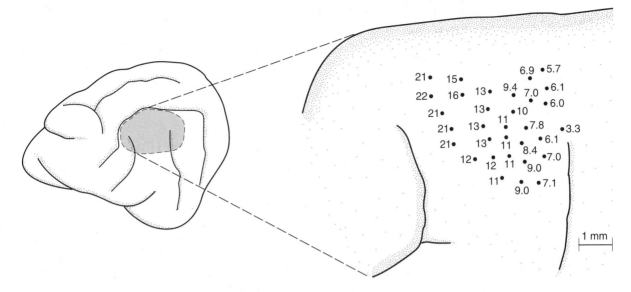

Figure 8.32
Left: The cat's brain, showing the location of the auditory receiving area (shaded). Right: A close-up of the auditory receiving area, showing the tonotopic map on the cortical surface. Each large dot represents a single neuron, and the number beside each dot represents the characteristic frequency of that neuron in thousands of Hz. (From Abeles & Goldstein, 1970, and Gulick, Gescheider, & Frisina, 1989.)

cortex, supports the idea that the frequency of a tone can be indicated by the place where activity is occurring.

Is the timing information carried by auditory nerve fibers that phase-lock to stimulus frequency represented in nuclei along the auditory pathway? As we travel higher in the system, phase locking does not occur in all neurons, and in the neurons in which it does occur, phase locking is limited to frequencies below about 1,000 Hz. Since the higher auditory centers contain timing information only for low-frequency stimuli, it appears that information about sound frequency is determined primarily by the place mechanism, which signals the frequency to which neurons are firing, the timing mechanism's main contribution being to signal frequencies at the low end of the range of hearing.

This combination of place and timing mechanisms provides a reasonable explanation of the

neural code for perceiving pitch, but some questions still remain. According to place theory, a tone's frequency is signaled when one group of neurons, which respond best to that frequency, fire vigorously while other neurons, which do not respond well to that frequency, are silent or fire only a little. According to this idea, a 1,000-Hz tone is signaled by a high firing rate in neurons with a characteristic frequency of 1,000 Hz combined with lower rates in neurons with characteristic frequencies above and below 1,000 Hz. But this description of auditory coding ignores an important fact: As we increase the stimulus intensity to high levels, the pattern of vibration of the basilar membrane becomes broader, so that, at higher intensities, neurons all along the membrane begin to fire to the 1,000-Hz tone.

We can see how this works by looking at Figure 8.33. We see that increasing intensity increases the rate of firing of a 1,000-Hz fiber up to

Audition I: Auditory Physiology

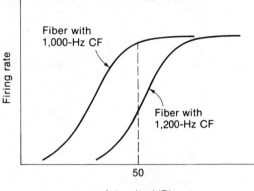

Stimulus = 1,000-Hz tone

Fiber with
1,000-Hz CF

Fiber with
1,200-Hz CF

Firing rate

Intensity (dB)

50

Figure 8.33

The relationship between the intensity of a 1,000-Hz tone and the response of two nerve fibers, one with a characteristic frequency (CF) of 1,000 Hz and another with a CF of 1,200 Hz. This graph shows that, at 50 dB, the 1,000-Hz fiber fires better than the 1,200-Hz fiber to the 1,000-Hz tone. However, at higher intensities, both fibers fire at the same rate to this tone.

50 dB, at which point the fiber **saturates**—it reaches its maximum response so that further increases in intensity cause no further increase in response. But as we increase the intensity above 50 dB, other fibers, farther down the basilar membrane, like the one marked "1,200 Hz CF," increase their firing rate and also eventually saturate. Thus, at very high intensity levels, both the 1,000- and 1,200-Hz fibers fire equally rapidly. Yet, we still perceive the tone as having a pitch corresponding to 1,000 Hz. How can place theory explain this result? One possibility is that the place mechanism is aided at very high intensities by some form of timing code, although the exact nature of this code remains to be determined.

Such complexities mean that we can only partially explain the mechanism for pitch perception in terms of simple place or timing mechanisms. In the next chapter, we will see that we need to consider additional complexities as well before we totally understand the physiology of pitch perception. We can say, however, that, to a

first approximation, place and timing theory working together account for our perception of pitch, but that some of the details remain to be worked out.

The Physiology of Sound Localization

How do we know where sounds are coming from? One hint at an answer to this question comes from the observation that people or animals with only one functioning ear have difficulty accurately locating sounds. Just as two eyes are better than one for seeing depth, two ears are better than one for detecting a sound's location in space.

Why Two Ears Are Better Than One: Binaural Cues

We can understand why localizing a sound is easier with two ears than with one by considering two basic cues for sound localization; interaural time difference and interaural intensity difference, both of which depend on the fact that when sounds are located to the left or the right, each ear receives different sound stimulation.

Interaural Time Difference The basis for the idea that the two ears receive different sounds is illustrated in Figure 8.34. We can see from this figure that, when a sound originates from directly in front of the listener, at A, the distance to each ear is the same, but if a sound originates from the side, as in B, the sound must travel farther and therefore takes longer to get to the left ear than to the right ear. This difference in the time it takes for the sound to get to the left and the right ears is called the **interaural time difference**.

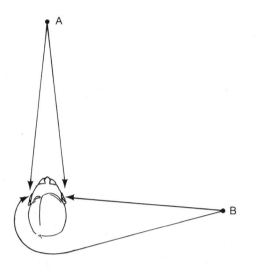

Figure 8.34

The principle behind interaural time difference. The tone directly in front of the listener, at A, reaches the left and the right ears at the same time. However, if the tone is off to the side, at B, it reaches the listener's right ear before it reaches the left ear.

Interaural Intensity Difference In addition to a difference in the time when the sound arrives at the two ears, there is also a difference in the intensity of the sound reaching the two ears. This **interaural intensity difference** occurs because the head casts a "shadow," which decreases the intensity of the sound reaching the far ear. This shadow, however, occurs mainly for high-frequency tones, because high-frequency tones have short wavelengths compared to the size of the head, and so they bounce off the head. In contrast, low-frequency tones have long wavelengths compared to the size of the head, so they are unaffected by the presence of the head (Figure 8.35). This cue for localization therefore works only for high-frequency tones.

Neurons That Respond to Interaural Time Difference

There are neurons in the rhesus monkey's cortex that respond best to specific interaural time dif-

ferences. Such a cell fires best when there is a specific delay between the presentation of a sound to the left ear and to the right ear. For example, one of these cells fires best when a sound reaches the left ear 800 microseconds before it reaches the right ear (Brugge & Merzenich, 1973). This cell, which can be called an **interaural time difference detector,** is similar to the binocular depth cells, described in Chapter 6, that respond best to specific angles of disparity between the two eyes. These interaural time difference cells have been recorded not only from the auditory cortex but also from nuclei as early in the

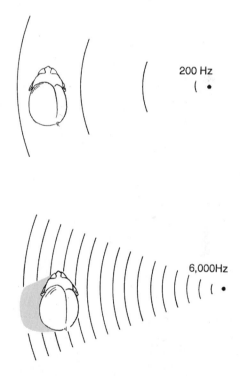

Figure 8.35

The principle behind interaural intensity difference. Low-frequency tones are not affected by the listener's head, so the intensity of the 200-Hz tone is the same at both ears. High-frequency tones are affected by the presence of the listener's head, and the result is a sound "shadow" that decreases the intensity of the tone reaching the listener's far ear.

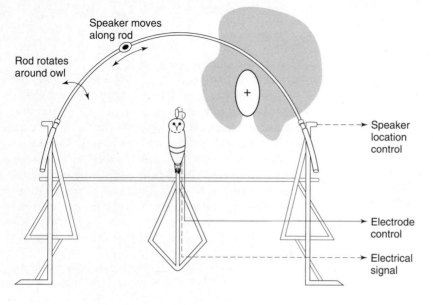

Figure 8.36

The apparatus used by Knudsen and Konishi (1978a, b) to map auditory receptive fields in space. The sound was moved to different positions in space by sliding the speaker along the curved rod, and by moving the rod around the owl. The elliptical area marked with a "+" is the excitatory area of a typical receptive field, and the shaded area is the inhibitory area.

auditory system as the superior olivary nucleus, the first nucleus in the system to receive inputs from both ears (Hall, 1965).

The existence of cells like the interaural time difference detectors shows that the auditory system has a way of detecting specific cues for location in auditory space. But detecting a cue is not the same thing as detecting a particular location in space. Are there neurons that respond to sounds that originate from a particular location?

Neurons That Respond to Particular Locations in Space

Recent research has discovered cells that respond only when a sound source is located in a particular area of space relative to an animal's head. One of the earliest reports of these neurons came from recordings from cells located in the barn owl's **mesencephalicus lateralus dorsalis (MLD),** a nucleus roughly equivalent to the inferior colliculus of mammals. Eric Knudsen and Masakazu Konishi studied these cells (1978a, 1978b) by using the apparatus shown in Figure 8.36. By recording

from cells while stimulating them from different positions in space, Knudsen and Konishi found cells that respond only when the sound originates from a small elliptical area in space, the receptive field of the cell. Furthermore, they found that some of these receptive fields have excitatory centers and inhibitory surrounds, so that an excitatory response that was elicited by a sound in the center of the receptive field could be inhibited by another sound presented to the side of or above or below the center. This property of the MLD cells means that center–surround receptive fields exist not only on the retina (Figure 2.35), but also in space!

Knudsen and Konishi not only found cells with receptive fields at particular locations in space but also discovered that these cells are arranged so that there is a map of auditory space on the MLD. That is, each cell on the MLD responds to a specific area in space (relative to the position of the head), and adjacent cells respond to adjacent areas of space (Figure 8.37). We can compare this mapping of space on the MLD to other maps in the nervous system: Each point on the cochlea is represented by a small area on the auditory cortex (Figure 8.32), and each point on the retina is represented by a small area on the visual cortex. (We will see in Chapter 11 that a similar situation also exists for points on the skin.) Thus, this point-by-point mapping of space that occurs in the owl's MLD is similar to the point-by-point mapping that occurs in the auditory and visual cortices.

Although we can see parallels between the point-by-point mapping of space in the owl's MLD and the mapping in the auditory and visual cortices, there is an important difference between them. Consider, for example, the principle behind the map of the retina on the visual cortex. This map occurs because sequences of neurons connect points on the retina to areas on the visual cortex (Figure 8.38a). But where is the connection between points in space and the owl's MLD? Clearly, no connections exist (Figure 8.38b). The map of space in the MLD is created not by anatomical connections formed by neurons, but by calculations made by groups of neurons that receive inputs from both left and right ears.

The fact that the owl's receptive fields in space depend on inputs from both ears is supported by a simple experiment: Plugging one of the owl's ears eliminates the receptive fields in space. And partially plugging one ear, so that it receives less sound than it ordinarily would, shifts the location of the receptive field, so that the sound source must be moved to a new location to excite the neuron (Konishi, 1984).

Although the receptive fields of owl MLD neurons provide a beautiful example of a neural mechanism for sound localization, we don't know whether this type of mechanism is responsible for localization in humans. Neurons have been discovered in the cat's superior colliculus, a center important for determining visual orientation toward sounds, that respond best to sounds coming from specific locations (Middlebrooks, 1988), but it has been difficult to find neurons in the cat's auditory cortex that respond to sounds coming from precise locations in space. Middlebrooks and Pettigrew (1981) did find neurons in the cat's auditory cortex that responded to sound location, but their receptive fields were large and were not organized into an orderly map of space like the one in the owl. However, recently, Middlebrooks and his co-workers (1994) discovered neurons in another area of the cat's auditory

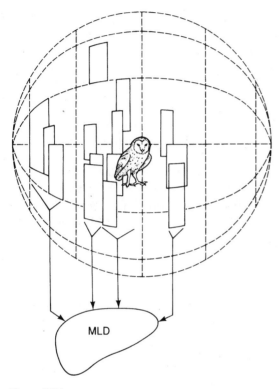

Figure 8.37

The top of this figure shows the owl surrounded by the locations of a number of receptive fields. The receptive fields are indicated by rectangles, although in reality they are shaped more like the one in Figure 8.36. The arrows point to the MLD location from which the bracketed receptive fields were recorded. The three receptive fields to the left of the figure were recorded from the left side of the MLD, whereas the group of receptive fields to the right were recorded from the lower right of the MLD. Thus, there is a map on the MLD that corresponds to the positions of its neurons' receptive fields in space. (Adapted from Knudsen & Konishi, 1978.)

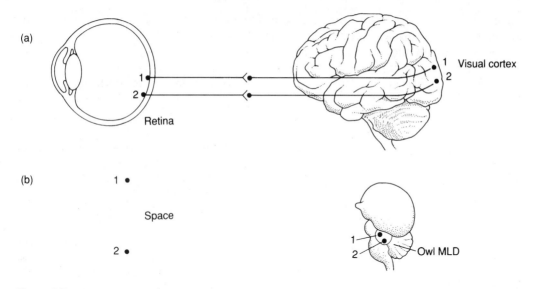

Figure 8.38

The map of retinal locations in the visual cortex (a) and the map of locations in space in the owl's MLD (b) are constructed according to different principles. The retinal map on the visual cortex occurs because there are neural connections linking points on the retina with neurons in the cortex. There is, however, no such anatomical connection between neurons in the owl's MLD and its receptive fields in space. The map in the MLD is constructed from information received by the left and right ears rather than from anatomical connections.

cortex that appear to signal location by the timing of their neural discharges.

The way location is signaled by these neurons is illustrated in Figure 8.39, which shows the pattern of firing of one cortical neuron to sounds coming from a number of directions. Notice that the neuron fires to sounds coming from all directions, but that the pattern of impulses is different for different directions. These results indicate that each neuron in this area of the cat's cortex is panoramic—it fires to sounds originating in any direction and indicates each location by its pattern of firing. Since a large number of neurons fire to a particular tone, these neurons could potentially achieve precise localization of sound by pooling their information (Barinaga, 1994). Whether neurons such as these "panoramic" neurons, or some other neural mechanism, are responsible for sound localization in humans remains to be determined.

COMPARING THE SENSES: AUDITION AND VISION

All sensory systems are different, since they are adapted to dealing with different forms of environmental energy. Thus, the auditory system has a complex mechanism that has evolved to convert pressure changes in the air into electrical signals, and the visual system has evolved a very different mechanism to convert electromagnetic energy into electrical signals. Although these differences exist, there are many similarities between the two senses.

Similarities between Audition and Vision

As we have surveyed the physiological mechanisms for pitch perception and localization, you

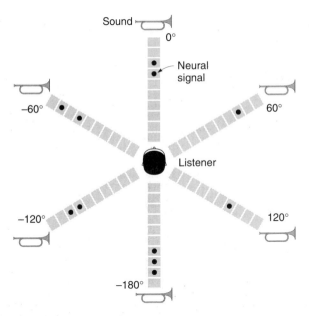

Figure 8.39

How one neuron can indicate the location of a sound based on its pattern of firing. When the sound is directly in front of the listener, at 0 degrees, the nerve fires two impulses in quick succession, as indicated by the dots on the line. However, when the sound is at −60 degrees, there is a slight pause between the two impulses. Other directions cause other patterns of firing. Thus, this neuron has a different timing code for each direction. (Based on data from Middlebrooks et al., 1994.)

may have noticed some things that are similar to what happens in the visual system. To end this chapter, we will briefly summarize some of the similarities in the ways the auditory and visual systems operate. First, we will describe a specific mechanism, and then, we will point out parallels in the two senses.

Fourier Analysis   When we discussed visual object perception, we saw that Fourier analysis can be used to analyze a scene into its spatial frequency components, and we also saw that there is evidence for spatial frequency channels in the visual system. In our discussion of audition, we saw that Fourier analysis can be used to analyze a periodic auditory stimulus into its sine-wave components, and that neurons in the auditory system also analyze a sound stimulus into frequency components by firing only to narrow ranges of frequencies. In the next chapter, we will present psychophysical evidence for these neural frequency analyzers.

Response Selectivity   Response selectivity occurs when neurons respond to selected aspects of the environment. Examples in the visual system are directionally selective neurons that respond best to specific directions of movement, as well as the three kinds of cone receptors that respond best to specific parts of the visible spectrum. Response selectivity in the auditory system occurs in the hair cells of the cochlea, which are tuned to respond to a specific, fairly narrow range of frequencies. This specificity is then transmitted to the auditory nerve fibers and other neurons in the auditory system that continue to respond best to a narrow range of frequencies.

Convergence   Convergence occurs when one neuron receives inputs from many other neurons. In the visual system, many rod receptors converge on a single bipolar cell. This convergence allows the signal from many rods to add together and creates the high sensitivity of the dark adapted visual system. In the auditory system, many outer hair cells send their inputs onto single auditory nerve fibers, and these cells may therefore be responsible for the detection of low-intensity sounds. This conclusion is supported by the finding that destroying the outer hair cells increases the threshold for hearing by 40–60 dB (Prosen et al., 1981; Stebbins et al., 1979). The inner hair cells, in contrast, each send their signals to a number of auditory nerve fibers and are most heavily involved in pitch perception (Aitkin, 1986).

Center–Surround Receptive Fields   Center–surround receptive fields occur when a neuron responds with excitation or inhibition to the stimulation of one area and in the opposite way to the stimulation of a surrounding area. For example, Figure 2.35 shows an excitatory-center–inhibitory-surround receptive field of a neuron in the retina. In the auditory system, neurons in the owl MLD have center–surround receptive fields in space. As discussed in the text, there are important differences between visual and auditory center–surround receptive fields, but it is noteworthy that they are both organized in the same way.

Mapping   Mapping occurs when a stimulus characteristic is mapped in an orderly way on a structure's surface. Retinotopic mapping occurs in the visual system as points on the surface of the retina are mapped in an orderly fashion on the lateral geniculate nucleus and on the visual cortex. Tonotopic mapping occurs in the auditory system since hair cells are arranged according to their best frequency in the cochlea and there is a map of a neuron's best frequency on each of the nuclei in the auditory system. We also saw that there is a map of space on the owl MLD, neurons that respond to specific areas in space being arranged in an orderly way on the surface of this structure.

Columnar Organization   Columnar organization occurs when neurons responsive to similar properties are arranged in columns. In the visual cortex, there are location columns, ocular dominance columns, orientation columns, and columns of neurons with the same color coding. In the auditory system, neurons with the same best frequencies are organized in columns in both the auditory cortex and other structures.

Neurons That Respond to Specialized Stimuli
In the discussion of neurons in the visual system, we saw that neurons in each succeeding structure in the visual pathway respond to increasingly complex stimuli. This specialization also occurs

in the auditory system, although so far nothing as dramatic as the visual neurons that respond to faces has been discovered. There are, however, neurons in the auditory cortex that respond to complex tones. For example, cells have been found that respond neither to pure tones nor to combinations of tones but that do respond to noises like keys jingling or paper tearing. I. C. Whitfield and E. F. Evans (1965) found cortical cells in the cat that responded only to smooth changes in the frequency of a tone: Some cells responded only when the tone was swept from low to high frequencies, and others responded only when the tonal frequency was swept from high to low. These cells are called **frequency sweep detectors,** because they respond well to changes in frequency but poorly or not at all to steady tones of a single frequency. Thus, the auditory cortex, like the visual cortex, contains neurons that respond to specialized stimuli.

From the above summary, we can appreciate that even though there are vast differences in the structure and functioning of the visual and auditory systems, they have many mechanisms in common. Since vision and hearing share the same nervous system, it isn't very surprising that they share many of the same basic mechanisms. In the chapters on the somatic senses (touch, temperature, and pain) and the chemical senses (olfaction and taste), we will see that these senses all have mechanisms in common with hearing and vision.

In the next chapter, we will explore the functioning of the auditory system by using psychophysics to measure how sensitive the ear is to different frequencies, how the frequency composition of a tone affects how it sounds, and how well humans are able to localize sounds presented at different positions in space. As we consider these capabilities, we will encounter some psychophysical results that confirm some of the physiological results presented here, as well as other results that raise some interesting questions for future physiological research.